LAW FOR LEGAL EXECUTIVES

Part I, Year I

(Second Edition)

English Legal System
The Law Relating to Land
Criminal Law
Law of Tort

Timothy Blakemore, LLB, LLM, Cert Ed, Solicitor
&
Brendan Greene, LLB, MA

BLACKSTONE
PRESS LIMITED

First published in Great Britain 1991 by Blackstone Press Limited,
9–15 Aldine Street, London W12 8AW. Telephone 081-740 1173

© T. Blakemore and B. Greene, 1991

First edition 1991
Reprinted 1992
Reprinted 1993
Second edition 1994

ISBN: 1 85431 332 0

British Library Cataloguing in Publication Data
A CIP catalogue record for this book is available from the British Library

Typeset by Style Photosetting Ltd, Mayfield, East Sussex
Printed by Ashford Colour Press, Gosport, Hampshire

CONTENTS

2   THE LAW RELATING TO LAND

Introduction

3   CRIMINAL LAW

Introduction

Nuisance   325
1 Introduction 2 Private nuisance 3 Public nuisance 4 Differences between public and private nuisance

Rylands v *Fletcher*   335
1 Introduction 2 The basic principle 3 Requirements 4 Type of damage 5 Defences

Vicarious liability   339
1 Introduction 2 Vicarious liability of employers

Limitation of actions   347
1 Introduction 2 Limitation of actions 3 Latent damage 4 Other relevant matters

Remedies   350
1 Introduction 2 Damages 3 Injunctions 4 Non-judicial remedies

Questions   356

Index   358

PREFACE

Not only have there been changes in the law since the first edition of this book in 1991, but also in the requirements for the Institute of Legal Executives examinations. The examination paper for Part I, Year I now comprises two parts, and the format and layout of the questions at the end of each section of this book reflect that change. There have also been numerous changes in the law, as any law student must expect and accept with resignation. We have tried to strike a balance by incorporating not only essential developments in the law, but also a few more up-to-date references, while at the same time avoiding change for changes sake. The relationship between the law and the Practice Syllabus has also been borne in mind, so that we have taken into account changes in procedure wherever relevant. This has necessitated some minor alterations to the land law chapter in particular.

Nevertheless, the law being such a dynamic subject, there were some important developments even while we were checking the final proofs for publication. In the area of criminal law, the Court of Appeal decision in *R v Kingston* (1993) has now been reversed by the House of Lords (*The Times*, 22 July 1994), perhaps as expected. In *R v Adomako* (*The Independent*, 1 July 1994), on the other hand, the House of Lords has approved, and perhaps even strengthened, the Court of Appeal ruling on involuntary manslaughter by gross negligence (reported *sub. nom. R v Sulman* 1993). The implications of these two judgments will need to be considered when they are reported fully.

Finally, we must once again record our thanks to our partners Anneliese and Michele for their patience and assistance during the sometimes traumatic moments as we strove (and usually failed) to meet our deadlines. Our publishers have similarly shown extraordinary understanding! We have also benefited from the continued support and enthusiasm of Graham Rowley, the Consultant Editor for the first edition, and a driving force behind the project to produce textbooks suitable for the Institute of Legal Executive law examinations. We hope this second edition meets the criterion of suitability for Year I, as any errors or omissions are solely our responsibility.

Timothy Blakemore
Brendan Greene

ACKNOWLEDGMENTS

The authors and publishers would like to thank the following for their kind permission to reproduce the following:

Butterworths & Co. (Publishers) Ltd for *R* v *Formosa* and *R* v *Upton*.

TABLE OF CASES

Please note that for ease of reference, the majority of citations in this Table are for the All England Reports, whereas the years cited in the text may refer to rulings in the House of Lords, Court of Appeal, Divisional Court or Privy Council.

ONE

ENGLISH LEGAL SYSTEM

INTRODUCTION

The 'bashing' to which the legal system has been subjected in recent years, seems to continue unabated. Although the 'Birmingham Six' have had their convictions formally quashed by the Court of Appeal (*R* v *McIlkenny* (1992)), the list of miscarriages of justice lengthens almost daily. One of the most worrying was the conviction for murder in 1976 of Stefan Kiszko, after sperm was found on the victim's clothes. In 1992 his conviction was quashed when it was discovered he was infertile and could not have produced sperm, evidence which was available at the time of the trial. According to *The Sunday Times* (20 March 1994) the Home Office has secretly earmarked £7 million to pay compensation to the victims of miscarriages of justice. In civil law the efforts of those injured or bereaved in disasters, such as the sinking of the ferry *Herald of Free Enterprise* and the bombing of the Pan Am plane at Lockerbie, are directed towards establishing negligence. In *Alcock* v *Chief Constable of South Yorkshire Police* (1991) the House of Lords rejected the claims for nervous shock brought by relatives of the victims of the Hillsborough football stadium disaster. Such events raise the question of whether the legal system is able to deal, in a just and effective manner, with the problems which arise.

In order to try to answer this question, we need to examine the present structure of the system. However, 'English Legal System' should not be seen as a separate 'compartment' of any study of law, to be learnt in a block, but should permeate the study of the substantive branches of law, like criminal law and the law of contract, to help in the understanding of how the rules work in practice and how litigants can enforce their rights.

The syllabus for English Legal System, covers the main sources of law, the classification of law, legal personality, the system of courts and other methods used for settling disputes. The system has existed in one form or another for nearly 1,000 years. Perhaps it has only done so because it has adapted to changes in society. The present time is no exception. Under the driving force of the Lord Chancellor, Lord Mackay, great changes have been made in the legal system and more will be made. They include directing more cases through the county courts, suggestions for 'fast track' justice in the county courts, reducing the numbers eligible for legal aid, allowing 'conditional fee' arrangements in certain cases enabling the winning side to charge double fees, giving solicitors in private practice rights of advocacy in the higher courts and allowing banks and building societies to carry out conveyancing. Following the Report of the Royal Commission on Criminal Justice in July 1993, legislation will implement many of its 352 recommendations for reform, including the setting up of an independent review authority to investigate suspected miscarriages of justice. It remains to be seen whether such changes will alleviate the legendary complaints about access to the law, the enormous cost, the long delays and whether they can restore public confidence in the system as a whole.

SOURCES OF ENGLISH LAW

1 Introduction

The term 'sources of law' can mean different things. It may mean historical sources – where the law has come from, like common law and equity. It may also mean the rules which are used in deciding what the law is today, such as statutes, precedents, European Community law, customs and textbooks. That is the meaning used here.

2 Statutes

Statutes (or legislation) are laws passed by Parliament. It is an important source of law, and is wide-ranging in nature and vast in quantity. In any one year Parliament passes between 70 and 100 statutes, some of which run to many pages, e.g., the Education Act 1993 which has 308 sections and is 290 pages in length. In 1992 61 public Acts of Parliament were passed.

2.1 Parliament

This consists of three separate parts:

  (a) House of Commons, comprising 651 elected members (MPs);
  (b) House of Lords, comprising hereditary and life peers and 26 C of E bishops (1,200 in total);
  (c) Her Majesty the Queen.

The 'Government' is the political party with a majority in the House of Commons.

Parliament is said to have 'legislative supremacy', which means that its laws must be followed by the courts. Since 1 January 1973 this principle has been qualified to the extent that European Community law now applies to the United Kingdom.

2.2   What pressures lead to statutes being passed?

2.2.1   Pressure groups.
A pressure group is any group of people with a common aim or interest. A distinction is made between two types of pressure groups (but these are not completely exclusive):

(a)   Sectional groups – which act on behalf of their members; e.g., a trade union; the British Medical Association.

(b)   Cause groups which have a particular aim and act to promote that aim; e.g., RSPCA; Greenpeace.

Pressure groups are useful in helping to identify important issues for legislation. They can lobby MPs and some MPs are involved in pressure groups; e.g., some MPs are sponsored by trade unions.

2.2.2   The Government.
Before an election the party which eventually forms the Government will have set out its policies in a document called a 'manifesto'. Many people believe that most statutes result from such manifestos, but a study has shown that in the Conservative Government of 1970–74 only 8 per cent of bills came from the manifesto; in the Labour Government of 1974–79 the figure was 13 per cent (Rose, R., *Do Parties Make a Difference?*, 2nd edn, 1984).

Sometimes the Government will issue *Green* or *White papers. Green papers* set out proposals for discussion.

Example

In December 1993 the Lord Chancellor, Lord Mackay, issued a consultation paper on the reform of divorce laws: 'Looking to the Future: Mediation and the Ground for Divorce' (Cm 2424).

White papers set out firm Government policy on a particular matter.

Example

'Children Come First' (Cm 1264) was published in October 1990 and proposed to make absent fathers pay maintenance for their children. This was followed by the Child Support Act 1991 and the setting up of the Child Support Agency.

However, this distinction between Green and White papers is not always maintained. 'One believes that one knows the difference between White Papers, Green Papers and their kin, but under close examination they often tend to merge to a uniform grey' (Gordon, G., 'Grey Papers', *Political Quarterly*, 1977, vol. 48).

Some matters have to be dealt with every year, like the Finance Act which is passed to raise taxation. Sometimes events lead to legislation, like the outbreak of 'joyriding' in the summer of 1991, which led to the passing of the Aggravated Vehicle Taking Act 1992.

2.2.3   Commissions and Committees.   These may be appointed to investigate a particular matter. A Royal Commission is appointed by the Queen (on the advice of the appropriate Secretary of State). A Departmental Committee is appointed by the Minister concerned. They may be asked to investigate a particular matter and make recommendations. Critics have said that they are used to avoid doing anything.

Example

The Royal Commission on Civil Liability and Compensation for Personal Injury 1974, under the chairmanship of Lord Pearson. It reported in 1978 but none of its proposals has been implemented.

The Law Commissions are constantly examining the law and proposing amendments in the form of draft Bills.

2.2.4   The Civil Service.   These are the permanent officials who advise Government Ministers. They are politically neutral but nonetheless are a very powerful influence. Much legislation arises from matters which have been carefully researched by civil servants and which are already 'in stock'. This can be persuasively presented to Government Ministers. In recent years as Ministers have changed jobs rapidly and have had less control over the civil servants working for them, simply because they have needed time to get to know the system, the opportunity for civil servants to present this pre-researched matter to Ministers has increased.

2.3   The functions of legislation

   (a)   Reform. Parliament does not normally initiate reforms but relies on reports from Commissions.
   (b)   Social legislation. This is legislation which introduces completely new principles. For example, the Leasehold Reform, Housing and Urban Development Act 1993 which, amongst other things, gives the owners of long leases of flats the right to buy the freehold collectively or the right to a new lease individually. In a democratic society it is better that such major changes are made through legislation rather than through the courts, as Parliament is the elected body.
   (c)   Consolidation. A consolidating statute is one which brings together all existing statutory provisions on a particular topic in one statute. For example, the Social Security Contributions and Benefits Act 1992 which brings together all the rules on contributions, on which benefits are based. It is part of a wider scheme of consolidation which includes the Social Security Administration Act 1992 and the Social Security (Consequential Provisions) Act 1992.
   (d)   Codification. This is a statute which brings together both common law and statutory rules; for example, the Sale of Goods Act 1893 (now 1979).

2.4   Bills

The proposed legislation will be introduced in the House of Commons in the form of a 'Bill', which is a draft of the intended Act. Most Bills are introduced by the Government. Government Bills are drafted by Parliamentary Counsel to the Treasury, who are civil servants. The office of Parliamentary Counsel to the Treasury was established in 1869. Its members may be barristers or solicitors. They normally work in pairs and collaborate with civil servants from other Government departments. There are approximately 30 draftsmen at the present time. Other Bills must be drafted privately and this will be done by barristers specialising in Parliamentary matters.

An example of a Bill may be seen below. It proposes to make it a criminal offence for restaurants to add service charges to their prices, which may seem a popular measure but as a private members' bill it is unlikely to succeed. See if you can find out its fate.

A

B I L L

TO

Prohibit the levying of service charges in restaurants; and for connected purposes. A.D. 1994.

BE IT ENACTED by the Queen's most Excellent Majesty, by and with the advice and consent of the Lords Spiritual and Temporal, and Commons, in this present Parliament assembled, and by the authority of the same, as follows:—

5   **1.** After section 21 of the Consumer Protection Act 1987 there is inserted the following section— Service charges.

"Service charges.   21A. For the purpose of section 20 above, an indication given to any consumers that food or drink is or may be for sale by retail for consumption on any restaurant premises is misleading as to a price if what is conveyed by the indication, or what those consumers might reasonably be expected to infer from the indication or any ommission from it, is not fully inclusive of all charges, including charges for the service of food or drink."

10

15

     2.—(1) This Act may be cited as the Abolition of Service Charges in Restaurants Act 1994. Short title and commencement.

     (2) This Act shall come into force at the end of the period of three months beginning on the day on which this Act is passed.

2.5   *Constraints on the preparation of Bills*

(a)   Because Bills are legal documents, the draftsman must ensure that what he writes will mean what he intends, even after detailed scrutiny. It must also fit in with the language of existing laws.

(b)   Once a Bill has been introduced, it is difficult to alter its structure to meet any changes that may arise.

(c)   There is always a shortage of time. A Parliament only lasts five years and this is divided into five sessions of 12 months. A Bill which does not complete the whole process in one session will lapse and have to be re-introduced in the next session. The House only sits for 160 days in a session and only about 60 days are for Government Bills, in which time it must get through its entire legislative programme.

Many criticisms have been made about the quality of drafting. Often the words used are obscure, the phrases long winded and the structure of Bills is illogical. Sometimes Acts dealing with the same subject-matter do not relate to each other, which makes it difficult to determine exactly what the law is on a particular matter.

2.6   The process of legislation

In order to become law, a Bill must be passed by 'The Queen in Parliament'. This means it must go through certain stages in the House of Commons, the House of Lords and receive the Royal Assent. This must all be done in one session. A session normally starts in October with the opening of Parliament and the Queen's Speech, and lasts for approximately 12 months. If a General Election is called, a session may be shorter than this.

A Bill may start out in either House, the exceptions being 'money' Bills and those dealing with voting rights, both of which must start in the House of Commons. (The former are based on the principle 'no taxation without representation'.) Non-controversial Bills are often introduced in the House of Lords.

2.6.1   House of Commons.   The first reading is purely formal. The title of the Bill is read out and an order made that it be printed.

The second reading is important and involves a debate on the general principles behind the Bill and whether it is necessary. At the end of the second reading a vote is taken.

The next stage is the committee stage when the Bill goes to one of the standing committees. These committees, which meet in the mornings, consist of between 16–50 members, who are appointed by the Committee of Selection which must take into account the qualifications of members and the composition of the House. Thus the composition of standing committees will reflect the political balance in the House and the Government will have a majority in these committees. The job of the committees is to examine Bills clause by clause and they can make amendments. The committees are newly formed for each public Bill. If a Bill is very important, it may be considered by a Committee of the Whole House.

Next is the report stage, when the chairman of the committee reports to the House. Further amendments may then be made.

The third reading normally takes place immediately after the report stage and a vote is taken. After this the Bill is taken to the House of Lords.

2.6.2 House of Lords. The Bill must go through the same stages again, although the House of Lords takes a much more informal approach and is not so party orientated as the House of Commons. The main differences are that: (i) there are no standing committees, they are made up *ad hoc* as the occasion demands; (ii) debates cannot be ended quickly as they can in the Commons by use of the 'guillotine' (a procedure for fixing a time limit for a Bill and if it is not passed within that time, it is thrown out); and (iii) amendments may be made at the third reading.

If the House of Lords amends a Bill introduced in the House of Commons, the Bill must go back to the House of Commons to be approved or changed. The same is true of a Bill introduced in the House of Lords and amended by the House of Commons.

2.7 The Royal Assent

When a Bill has passed all stages in both Houses, it goes for the Royal Assent. It is a constitutional convention that the Sovereign does not refuse to grant the assent, the last time this happened being in 1707. The Royal Assent has not been given personally by the Sovereign since 1854. It may be given by Commissioners on behalf of the Sovereign but is usually given under the Royal Assent Act 1967 by notification to each House by the Speaker (Commons) and the Lord Chancellor (Lords) respectively. Once this has been done, the Bill becomes an Act of Parliament. An example can be seen below, i.e. the Sexual Offences Act 1993.

HOW A BILL BECOMES AN ACT OF PARLIAMENT

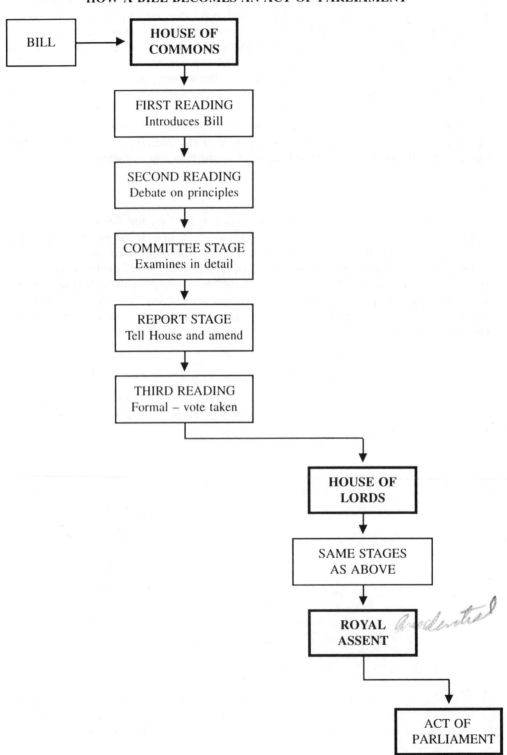

Sexual Offences Act 1993

1993 CHAPTER 30

An Act to abolish the presumption of criminal law that a boy under the age of fourteen is incapable of sexual intercourse.

[20th July 1993]

BE IT ENACTED by the Queen's most Excellent Majesty, by and with the advice and consent of the Lords Spiritual and Temporal, and Commons, in this present Parliament assembled, and by the authority of the same, as follows:—

1. The presumption of criminal law that a boy under the age of fourteen is incapable of sexual intercourse (whether natural or unnatural) is hereby abolished.

Abolition of presumption of sexual incapacity.

2.—(1) This Act may be cited as the Sexual Offences Act 1993.

Short title, commencement and extent.

(2) This Act shall come into force at the end of the period of two months beginning with the day on which it is passed.

(3) This Act does not apply to acts done before its comencement.

(4) This Act extends to England and Wales only.

The Act comes into force on the day it receives the Royal Assent, or some later date stated in the Act, or at a date to be fixed. Major Bills may take up to six months to pass through all these stages, but in an emergency a Bill may be passed very quickly, e.g. the Official Secrets Act 1911 which was passed in one day.

2.8 Types of Bill

2.8.1 Public Bill. This is a measure which alters the general law and affects the whole country or a certain class of person.

Example

The Theft Bill which became the Theft Act 1968.

There are two categories of public Bill:

Government Bills which are introduced by a Government Minister;
Private members' Bills which are introduced by an individual Member of Parliament.

There are three ways for a private MP to introduce a Bill:

(a) Ballot. At the start of each session a ballot is held and 20 names are drawn in order.
(b) Standing Order 58. After the 20 balloted Bills have been presented, any MP can present a Bill by giving one day's notice. However, even if one MP objects that ends the life of such a Bill.

(c)   The '10 Minute Rule'. Standing Order 19 allows any MP to make a speech of up to 10 minutes in support of a Bill. Two of these speeches are allowed each week. These opportunities are usually used to make political points.

The time allowed for private members' bills is only 12 Fridays in a session, from 9.30 a.m. to 2.30 p.m. If opponents are still speaking at 2.30 p.m. the sponsor moves 'that the question be now put'. The Bill will then be 'talked out' unless there are at least 100 MPs present to vote in its favour.

Usually about half of the 20 private members' Bills will be successful but in the 1992–93 session, only six of the 20 balloted bills became law. Probably the most important factor is whether or not they get the support of the Government. There are no party constraints on attending or voting during private members' time. Such Bills may be the brainchild of a particular MP or a group, like the Law Commission or they may be Bills which the Government cannot fit into its normal programme of legislation. Some important measures have been passed in this way.

Example

The Bail (Amendment) Act 1993 introduced by Michael Stephen MP after public concern was expressed about offences committed by those on bail. The Act gives the prosecution a right of appeal against decisions to grant bail for offences under the Theft Act 1968 or those carrying a sentence of five years or more.

2.8.2   *Private Bill.*   A private Bill is a measure which only affects a particular section of the community, like certain individuals or an organisation or a particular place.

Example

At one time divorce could only be obtained by Act of Parliament. The modern use of private Bills, however, is by local authorities and large companies, to give them extra powers. There are some differences from the procedure for public Bills: (i) at the committee stage the committee acts like a court and hears evidence from both sides; (ii) in the House of Lords the Bill misses the report stage; (iii) they do not have to pass all stages in one session.

2.9   *Criticisms of the legislative process*

2.9.1   *What influence does Parliament have over legislation?*   If amendments are taken as one measure of the influence over legislation passing through Parliament, the table below shows that apart from Government Ministers, MPs have little effect on legislation. Indeed, the amendments by Government MPs and the Opposition, were mainly of a technical or minor nature.

Proposed amendments	Percentage carried
20 per cent by Ministers	100
10 per cent by Government MPs	9
70 per cent by Opposition MPs	4

Figures taken from Griffith, JAG, *Parliamentary Scrutiny of Government Bills*, (1974) pp. 15–16.

2.9.2 Does the process serve any useful purpose, apart from 'rubber stamping' the Government's legislation? The real value must be the opportunity it gives for public debate on important principles and issues. With the televising of Parliament this is not simply an academic point as people can now see their own MP in action and they should therefore feel part of the democratic process. It also allows changes to be made if defects are pointed out in proposed legislation. One important weapon in fuelling this debate is the *parliamentary question*. In 1992–93 there were approximately 65,000 such questions, the vast majority being written ones (House of Commons, Sessional Information Digest, HMSO, 1992/93).

2.10 The Role of the House of Lords

Briefly, the membership of the House includes hereditary peers, who have inherited their titles; life peers appointed under the Life Peerages Act 1958; the Lords of Appeal in Ordinary (Law Lords); and 26 bishops of the Church of England.

Originally, the House of Lords had a power of 'veto' over any Bills sent up by the House of Commons, which meant that they could reject them. In 1911 the Liberal Government had a number of their Bills rejected by the House of Lords, so they decided to introduce a Bill to restrict the powers of the House of Lords to merely delaying Bills for two years. This Bill became the Parliament Act 1911 (further amended by the Parliament Act 1949). The present powers of the House of Lords are as follows.

2.10.1 Money Bills. A 'money Bill' is one raising taxation and it must be certified as such by the Speaker of the House of Commons. If passed by the House of Commons it must be passed by the House of Lords within one month or it goes to the Sovereign for the Royal Assent, without being passed by the House of Lords. The reason for this rule is that if the Government cannot raise taxes it is powerless to govern.

2.10.2 Public Bills. Any public Bill which is passed by the House of Commons in two successive sessions, but rejected by the House of Lords, will go for the Royal Assent. A Bill is regarded as rejected if it is not passed without amendment. These provisions do not apply to:

(a)   Bills to extend the life of Parliament;
(b)   Private Bills;
(c)   Bills introduced in the House of Lords.

2.11 Reform of the House of Lords

Calls have been made to abolish or reform the House of Lords throughout this century. The preamble to the Parliament Act 1911 actually provided for the replacement of the House of Lords by an elected chamber. The criticisms have been mainly based on:

(a)   Composition. The presence of hereditary peers means that many members are from a narrow social class. The introduction of life peers enabled people from all walks of life to become members.
(b)   The fact that members are not democratically elected. A non-elected body should not be allowed to check or impede the work of an elected body.

(c)   Conservative bias. The Conservative Party has a majority of over 400 in the House of Lords. This is modified by the life peerage system and the fact that working members do not reflect this bias. Nonetheless, 'backwoodsmen' (those who attend infrequently) may be called on if needed for an important measure.

That the House of Lords has still got some life in it and cannot be taken for granted was seen in April 1991 when it rejected the War Crimes Bill. This forced the Government to use its powers under the Parliament Acts for the first time in over 40 years, in order to pass the War Crimes Act 1991. Many people who have seen the televised debates from the House of Lords are of the opinion that they are of a much higher standard than the debates in the House of Commons and the House of Lords still serves a useful purpose in providing a second opinion.

STATUTORY INTERPRETATION

1   Introduction

Why should statutes have to be interpreted in the first place? After all, they are written in English. The problem is essentially one of communication.

Example

Judge:	'Why are you late?'
Witness:	'I was held up on the train.'
Judge:	'Oh! How awful. Are you alright? Have you told the police?'
Witness:	'I mean, I was delayed.'

All conduct has to be interpreted but words pose particular problems, if only because, as in the above example, they have different meanings. Thus the words used in statutes and all legal documents have to be constantly interpreted. This is something which happens daily, in Government departments, local councils, businesses and lawyers' offices, as people make decisions about what words mean.

The importance of courts making such decisions is that they are binding on others and must be followed. Legislation attempts, amongst other things, the impossible task of providing for future events. It cannot be too particular and cover every situation and eventuality or it would be too long. The draftsman has to use general words and this leaves them open to wider interpretation. There inevitably will be mistakes and omissions in drafting, which also cause problems. The links between interpretation and drafting can be seen from what has been said above. The draftsman will take into account how his work is likely to be interpreted and will draft Acts accordingly.

The law distinguishes between rules and principles. A rule must be followed; a principle need not be. Some of the 'rules' of statutory interpretation are contradictory and they cannot all be followed. It is better, therefore, to regard them as principles.

The student must endeavour to see these various principles not as being blindly picked out of a hat and used at random (even though this may sometimes be the impression given by the courts), but as having a place in an overall scheme, in which there are two basic approaches. These are the literal approach in which words are given their ordinary meaning, and the purposive approach in which some account is taken of the purpose of the statute.

The importance of interpretation lies not only in the effect it has but its significance in the work of the higher courts. Over half the cases going to the Court of Appeal and three quarters of cases going to the House of Lords involve matters of interpretation.

2   What is the role of the judge in interpretation?

The doctrine of 'separation of powers' says that the three functions of the state, i.e., legislative, executive and judicial should be carried out by separate bodies. Hence it is Parliament which makes the law, the Government which enforces it and the judges who interpret it.

The judge has two main tasks:

(a)   interpreting the meaning of words which are unclear;
(b)   even if words are clear, defining the extent of their application.

Many judges see their task as interpreting what Parliament has actually said in the words of the statute. This is giving words a literal interpretation.

Other judges see their task as discovering the 'intention' of Parliament in passing the Act. This would take into account the purpose of passing the Act. There are two difficulties with this approach. First, how can anyone find the intention of a disparate group of people? The intention cannot mean that everyone in Parliament has the same intent in passing the Act, in fact many of them will not even be there. It can be assumed, though, that there is a 'consensus' if the Act has been passed. Secondly, can the purpose behind an Act of Parliament be found? It would be unusual for an Act to have one purpose, although this has not stopped the courts discovering one purpose when interpreting a statute. But even if these difficulties are overcome, the objection remains that by giving words a wider meaning, the judges are in effect making laws.

3   Principles of interpretation

3.1   Literal

The judge will look at the words used and give them their ordinary and literal meaning. No account is taken of the result of applying this principle.

Whiteley v Chappell (1868)
A statute made it an offence '. . . to personate any person entitled to vote'. The defendant had impersonated a dead person and voted. He was charged under this provision. The court held that the words, 'person entitled to vote' must mean a person entitled to vote at the time of the impersonation. As a dead person has no right to vote the defendant was not guilty.

Here the court had interpreted the words literally, without enquiring about the purpose of the legislation.

The literal approach was emphasised in the House of Lords, in *Magor and St Mellons* v *Newport Corporation* (1951), by Lord Simonds who delivered a rebuke to Lord Denning in the Court of Appeal, for suggesting that the task of the court was to find out the intention of Parliament.

> The duty of the court is to interpret the words that the legislature has used. Those words may be ambiguous, but even if they are, the power and duty of the court to travel outside them on a voyage of discovery are strictly limited.

By ignoring the consequences of a literal interpretation, the courts have reached some pretty odd decisions.

R v *Governor of Brixton Prison ex p Kahan* (1989)

The Fugitive Offenders Act 1967 applied to any 'designated Commonwealth country'. Fiji had been made such a country by an Order in Council but left the Commonwealth in 1986. In 1988 Kahan, a Fijian citizen, was arrested under the 1967 Act. The Order in Council had not been changed. Kahan now claimed that Fiji was not a 'designated Commonwealth country' and his arrest was therefore invalid. The court held, in applying a literal meaning to the Order in Council, that Fiji was a Commonwealth country. Therefore Kahan's application that he should be released was dismissed.

The literal approach often tries to give words a meaning 'as they stand'. This ignores the fact that all words are used in a particular context and that a word may have many meanings, so it is impossible to give it one meaning. In favour of this approach is the fact that by using it judges are keeping to interpreting the law rather than making it.

3.2   Golden

This is really a qualification on the literal principle. If a literal interpretation leads to an 'absurd' result, then the court will give the words a different meaning.

> . . . in construing wills and indeed statutes, and all written instruments, the grammatical and ordinary sense of the words is to be adhered to, unless that would lead to some absurdity, or some repugnance or inconsistency with the rest of the instrument, in which case the grammatical and ordinary sense of the words may be modified, so as to avoid that absurdity and inconsistency, but no farther.

(*Grey* v *Pearson* (1857) 6 HL Cas 61 at p. 106, per Lord Wensleydale.)

An example of this is to be seen in the following case.

R v *Allen* (1872)

Under the Offences Against the Person Act 1861 bigamy was defined as '. . . whoever being married, shall marry another'. It is a legal requirement that anyone getting married must not already be married. If this definition was interpreted literally, it would mean that no one could commit an offence because if a person were already married he or she could not legally get married again. The court held that Parliament could not have intended this meaning because it did not make sense. The court therefore gave the words 'shall marry' an extended meaning of 'goes through a ceremony of marriage' and the defendant was convicted.

The main problem with the golden principle is deciding when a particular meaning is absurd. This is left to individual judges with the predictable result that there are many individual and contradictory ideas as to when the principle can apply.

3.3 Mischief

This principle was first set out in *Heydon's Case* (1584). Under this the court must consider four things:

(a) what was the common law before the Act?
(b) what was the mischief which the common law did not cover?
(c) what remedy has Parliament decided on?
(d) what was the true reason for that remedy?

Then the court has to give the words a construction which would suppress the mischief and advance the remedy.

The classic example of this approach is seen in the following case.

Smith v Hughes (1960)
The Street Offences Act 1959, s. 1, provided: 'It shall be an offence for a common prostitute to loiter or solicit in a street or public place for the purposes of prostitution'. In this case prostitutes were calling from balconies or tapping on windows. Could this be regarded as being 'in a street'?

If interpreted literally, the prostitutes were obviously not 'in a street'. The court, however, looked at the mischief which the legislation was designed to remedy, and also at what remedy Parliament had decided on. The mischief comprised people being pestered in the street by prostitutes and the remedy was to stop this happening. In the light of this, the court held that the defendants were guilty. It did not matter that the prostitutes were not physically in the street as they were affecting people in the street.

A more recent example of this approach is to be found in the following case.

Bodden v Commissioner of Police (1989)
The plaintiff was claiming false imprisonment after being arrested for using a loud-hailer while protesting outside a magistrates' court. The question arose about the meaning of the Contempt of Court Act 1981, s. 12(1)(b): '... wilfully interrupts the proceedings of the court or otherwise misbehaves in court'. It was held at first instance, that the words 'in court' limited the behaviour to things done inside the court and so the arrest was unlawful. The Court of Appeal, however, said that the mischief was the interruption of magistrates' courts and held that the words 'in court' only referred to 'otherwise misbehaves'. Thus interrupting

the proceedings could be done from inside or outside the court and the appeal was allowed. Otherwise people could interrupt the proceedings from outside the court with impunity.

3.4   Purposive

The purposive approach means that the court, in interpreting a statute, will take into account the purpose of the Act and construe it in the light of that purpose. This is really a wider version of the mischief principle, which only regards statutes as preventing mischiefs whereas in fact many statutes attempt to impose positive rules. A clear example of this approach can be seen in the following case.

Royal College of Nursing v *DHSS* (1981)

The Abortion Act 1967 provided that an abortion was lawful if carried out 'by a registered medical practitioner' (a doctor). At that time abortions were mainly done by a surgical process and had to be carried out by doctors. Later a method was developed (induction) which simply involved administering drugs through a drip and which could be given by nurses. The question was whether such action by nurses fell within the prescribed action which could only be carried out by a 'registered medical practitioner'. The House of Lords looked at the purpose of the Act which was to allow women to have abortions and to ensure they were carried out with proper skill. In view of this they held, by a majority of three to two, that the words could be interpreted to mean 'under the supervision of a doctor'. This meant that nurses could legally carry out such procedures.

The chief argument against the purposive approach is that by taking into account the purpose, courts can widen the meaning given to words and thus make law. At its extreme, the court can ignore the words of a statute and concentrate on the purpose. In *RCN* v *DHSS* (1981) the minority in the House of Lords argued against a purposive construction, saying that it was up to Parliament to make such an important change in the law. As was mentioned above, there are also problems in determining what the 'purpose' of a statute is, although sometimes the statute may state its purpose or one of its purposes.

Example

The Courts and Legal Services Act 1990, s. 17, sets out the general objective of Part II as the development of legal services.

4   Other principles

Apart from the main principles there are many others which are subsidiary, in the sense that they are of narrower application and will be used in more limited circumstances, although they are of equal legal validity. Some of these principles are explained below, a number of them taking the form of a Latin maxim.

4.1   Eiusdem generis

If particular words are followed by general words in a statute, the general words must be limited to things 'of the same kind' (*eiusdem generis*) as the particular words.

Powell v Kempton Park Racecourse Co. (1899)

The Betting Act 1853 prohibited the keeping of a 'house, office, room or other place' for the purposes of betting. The question arose whether 'Tattersalls Ring' (bookmakers' pitches outside) was within the general words 'other place'. It was held that the particular words 'house, office, room' showed some form of building was intended, so the general words were limited to things 'of the same kind' and did not cover bookmakers outside.

Problems can arise in deciding if the specific words belong to a class.

Derrick v Commissioners of Customs and Excise (1972)

The Customs Consolidation Act 1876 prohibited the import of 'indecent or obscene prints, paintings, photographs, books, cards, lithographic and other engravings, or any other indecent or obscene articles'. The question arose whether 35mm pornographic film was within the meaning of the general words 'any other . . . articles'. The appellant argued that the general words should be read *eiusdem generis* and thus cover articles which could be seen to be indecent by visual inspection. This would not include the film which was too small to see on inspection. It was held that the items in the list were not a 'class' because a quick look at a book would not disclose if it was obscene. Therefore the film was within the general words and could be confiscated.

4.2 Expressio unius est exclusio alterius

This means 'the expression of one thing excludes the others'. An example of this can be seen in the following case.

R v Sedgeley Inhabitants (1831)

The word 'lands' would normally include houses and mines. But if used in the phrase 'lands, houses and coalmines', however, the word 'lands' would not include houses and mines. Thus other types of mines, apart from coalmines were not within the word 'lands'.

4.3 Noscitur a sociis

This is sometimes translated as 'a word is known by the company it keeps', meaning that the words in a particular section must be read in their context.

Muir v Keay (1875)

The Refreshment Houses Act 1860 provided that all houses kept open at night for 'public refreshment, resort and entertainment' had to be licensed. The defendant's café was found serving at night without a licence. The defendant argued that he did not need a licence because he did not provide entertainment. The court held that the word 'entertainment' did not mean musical entertainment, but the reception and accommodation of people, so the defendant was guilty.

4.4 No change in the law

A statute does not change the common law unless this is clear from its words.

4.5   Strict interpretation of criminal statutes

Statutes imposing criminal liability must be interpreted strictly in favour of the accused, the object being to protect the liberty of the individual. If there is any ambiguity then the accused must not be prejudiced by this.

4.6   Criminal offences need mens rea

If a statute creates a criminal offence, then that offence requires *mens rea* (a guilty mind).

Sweet v *Parsley* (1969)
A teacher rented a house to students. The house was used for smoking cannabis but the teacher did not know this. The teacher was charged with 'being concerned in the management of premises used for the smoking of cannabis'. It was held that where no state of mind was expressed in the statute, a conviction could only be obtained if it was proved that a person intended or knew that the premises would be used for such a purpose. As the teacher neither intended nor knew that the house was used for smoking cannabis, the verdict was not guilty.

4.7   No retrospective effect

Statutes do not have retrospective effect. This means that they cannot affect acts carried out before the statute was passed. There are exceptions to this, but only if the statute makes it clear that it has such an effect.

4.8   Statutes do not bind the Crown

This presumption may be changed by express words or necessary implication.

5   Aids to construction

The general principle to be followed by a court in interpreting a statute is that it must be read 'as a whole'. There are a number of other 'aids' to help the court in reaching a decision about the meaning of the statute.

5.1   Internal aids

These are items contained within the Act being interpreted. Those internal aids which are allowed will normally only be used if the meaning of words is not clear.

5.1.1   Long title.   This is found under the title and it explains the aims of the Act. An example can be seen in *Sources of English Law*, 2.7, i.e., 'An Act to abolish the presumption of criminal law that etc.'. The long title may be used as a guide to interpretation.

5.1.2   Short title.   This is really a 'nickname' for the Act and because it is not as accurate as the long title it will not be used.

5.1.3   Preamble.   This is a longer version of the long title, not used in modern statutes.

5.1.4   Interpretation sections.   Most Acts will contain a section defining terms used in the Act. The Criminal Justice and Public Order Bill 1994, for example, defines a 'rave'.

5.1.5   Headings.   These are used to divide the Act into more manageable portions. They are not part of the Act and are not normally used.

5.1.6   Marginal notes.   These are found at the side of the Act. They are part of the Act but are only a brief guide to the content of sections and could therefore be inaccurate. They cannot change the meaning of the clear words of a statute.

5.1.7   Punctuation.   Although not found in Acts before about 1850, it is used in modern Acts. It may be used to give effect to the purpose of the statute.

5.1.8   Schedules.   These are normally found at the back of statutes and are used for illustrations, lists etc. An example is Schedule 2 to the Unfair Contract Terms Act 1977, which sets out guidelines for the courts when deciding whether an exclusion clause in a contract is 'reasonable'.

5.2   External aids

These are to be found outside the actual Act.

5.2.1   Earlier statutes.   If statutes are '*in pari materia*' (about the same subject-matter), then a word may be given the same meaning as in an earlier statute.

British Amusement Catering Trades Association v Westminster City Council (1988)
The question arose whether a video game was within the phrase 'exhibition of moving pictures' in the Cinematograph Act 1982. It was held, after examining the phrase in such Acts dating back to 1909, that it meant showing moving pictures to an audience and did not cover moving pictures on a video screen.

5.2.2   Interpretation Act 1978.   This sets out some words commonly used and provides for example, that the singular includes the plural.

5.2.3   Dictionaries.   These may be used if a word has not previously been defined by a court but the problem is that dictionaries usually give a word several meanings.

5.2.4   Government publications.   These include reports of Royal Commissions, the Law Commissions and other 'official' reports. They cannot be used to enable a court to interpret words in a statute but they may be used to help the court to identify the mischief which the statute is trying to stop. Unofficial guides produced by civil servants in Government departments to help in understanding a Bill may not be used in interpretation.

5.2.5   Parliamentary debates.   Previously, it was an established rule that the courts could not refer to Hansard (the report of debates in Parliament) as an aid to interpreting statutes. Lord Denning had criticised this rule, as groping 'about in the dark for the meaning of an Act without switching on the light'. In support of the rule, it was argued that what was said in Parliament was not necessarily the same as the contents of the Act. This rule has now been changed.

Pepper v *Hart* (1993)

Teachers at Malvern College paid only 20 per cent of the normal fees for their children to attend the College. A question arose over the basis on which this benefit should be taxed, which depended on the meaning of the Finance Act 1976, s. 63. Could Hansard be used in interpreting the section? It was held by the House of Lords that reference could be made to Hansard if: (a) legislation was ambiguous or obscure or if a literal meaning led to an absurdity; (b) the statement in Hansard was clear; (c) the material disclosed the mischief or the legislative intention behind the words. The House of Lords said it was unlikely a statement would meet these criteria, unless it was made by a Minister or other promoter of the Bill. The House of Lords allowed reference to what the Minister said in Parliament about s. 63, that such benefits should be taxed on the basis of the additional costs to the employer, e.g. food, and should not take account of fixed costs.

This has been followed by a *Practice Direction* from the House of Lords, in February 1993, which states, 'Supporting documents, including extracts from Hansard, will only be accepted in exceptional circumstances'. However, exactly which statements can be referred to and in what circumstances will be determined by how *Pepper* v *Hart* is applied in a later case. There have already been a number of these, for example, in *Warwickshire County Council* v *Johnson* (1993) the House of Lords referred to Hansard, even though the above requirements were not met.

5.2.6 International conventions.   The approach of the courts in using international conventions as an aid to interpretation can be seen in the following case.

Fothergill v *Monarch Airlines* (1980)

The question arose whether the phrase 'damage to baggage' included the loss of baggage. This phrase had been used in an international convention and in domestic law and if interpreted literally, it would not have included loss. The House of Lords, however, looked at the purpose of the convention in protecting travellers and held that 'damage' did include loss. In reaching this decision they took into account that all countries where the convention applied should take the same approach.

6 European legislation

The 'European' approach to the interpretation of legislation is not the narrow literal approach but a wider view of the purpose of the legislation. European courts are willing to examine *travaux préparatoires* (literally, preparatory works, i.e., the reports and materials collected prior to legislation). There is some evidence that English courts will follow this practice when they are interpreting European legislation. The House of Lords allowed the use of *travaux préparatoires* in *Fothergill* v *Monarch Airlines* (1980) to show a clear legislative intention and in *Pickstone* v *Freemans* (1988) they allowed Hansard to be consulted.

Litster v *Forth Dry Dock* (1989)

Regulations provided that on the sale of a business, workers employed 'immediately before the transfer' were to continue as employees. In this case all employees were dismissed one hour before the sale of the business. If interpreted literally, they were not employed 'immediately before the transfer' and were not entitled to compensation for unfair dismissal. The House of Lords looked at the purpose of the Regulations which were made in accordance with a European Council Directive the aim of which was to protect employees if a business changed hands. They held that the phrase did cover workers who would have been employed immediately before the transfer if they had not been dismissed.

The courts appear to be taking a more liberal approach to interpretation in such cases, but this goes against the training of many judges. However, following *Pepper* v *Hart*, this approach may gather momentum.

7 Observations

A number of initiatives have been taken to improve the approach to interpretation. The Law Commissions produced a report on 'Interpretation of Statutes' in 1969 in which they said that there was a tendency to emphasise the literal meaning. The Commissions thought that the mischief rule was a better principle of interpretation but that it had been established when the courts, rather than Parliament, made the law. Amongst other recommendations the Law Commissions suggested that an explanatory memorandum be attached to Acts to help courts put statutes in their context.

Lord Scarman made two unsuccessful attempts in the early 1980s to bring in an Interpretation Bill, which would have implemented many of the proposals of the Law Commissions. It provided that in interpreting statutes, a construction 'which would promote the general legislative purpose . . . is to be preferred to a construction which would not'. That reform in this area has a low priority amongst legislators may be gleaned from the fact that the Law Commissions have done no further work on interpretation since 1978.

An informed insight on interpretation is given by Francis Bennion, a former parliamentary draftsman, in *Bennion on Statute Law,* 3rd edn, Longman, 1990:

> . . . the court does not 'select' one of the guides and then apply it to the exclusion of the others. The court takes (or should take) an overall view, weighs all the relevant factors and arrives at a balanced conclusion.

He argues that there is only one rule of statutory interpretation, i.e., that an Act will be construed in accordance with the guides laid down by law. If there is any conflict between these guides then the court must resolve it by a balancing exercise. He maintains it is too simplistic to think in terms of just the three 'rules', i.e., literal, golden and mischief.

Draftsmen no doubt will maintain the stalemate by heeding the words of Stephen J in *Re Castioni* (1891), who said that it was not enough for the drafting of Acts of Parliament to reach a degree of precision which a person reading them in good faith can understand, 'but it is necessary to attain, if possible, to a degree of precision which a person reading in bad faith cannot misunderstand'.

DELEGATED LEGISLATION

1 Introduction

What is delegated legislation? The term 'delegated legislation' or subordinate legislation, means laws made by anyone outside Parliament. One of the important features of the British system of government is the *sovereignty of Parliament* (or supremacy of Parliament). This means that Parliament controls the making of laws and can pass any laws it wishes. The courts cannot challenge the validity of an Act of Parliament. However, Parliament may 'delegate' to others the power to make laws and these powers are given to both public and private bodies to enable them to pass laws on a wide range of subjects.

Example

The Channel Tunnel (Emergency Medical Services) Order 1991, made under the Channel Tunnel Act 1987, provided that the tunnel is to be treated as part of England as regards the provision of emergency services.

Giving others the right to pass laws appears to take away some of Parliament's powers, but the power to make delegated legislation is given and controlled by Parliament and can also be taken away by Parliament. An important point to remember about all these delegated rules is that they are equally as binding as Acts of Parliament.

Delegated legislation is not new and there are examples of it from Tudor times. It was not until the nineteenth and twentieth centuries, however, that there was a significant growth in the use of such legislation, as Government took greater control over the regulation of people's lives and society became more complex.

2   Types of delegated legislation

2.1   Orders in Council

These are made by the Queen in Council (Privy Council), under powers given by Act of Parliament.

Example

The Emergency Powers Act 1920 gives the Government powers to act in emergencies, whether in wartime or peacetime, through Orders in Council.

Governments have been criticised for using Orders in Council to pass laws deliberately so as to avoid going through Parliament.

2.2   Ministerial orders

All Government Ministers are given rights to make delegated legislation within their own sphere which may often be called different names, e.g., rules, orders or regulations.

Example

The Foreign Satellite Service Proscription Order 1993 made by the Secretary of State for National Heritage under the Broadcasting Act 1990 (see below).

1993 No. 1024

BROADCASTING

The Foreign Satellite Service Proscription Order 1993

Made – – – –	*6th April 1993*
Laid before Parliament	*7th April 1993*
Coming into force	*1st May 1993*

Whereas the Secretary of State has received notification from the Independent Television Commission in accordance with section 177(2) of the Broadcasting Act 1990(**a**) that the quality of the foreign satellite service known as Red Hot Television is unacceptable and should be subject to an order under section 177 of that Act:

And whereas the Secretary of State, having received such notification, is satisfied that the making of such an order is in the public interest and compatible with any international obligations of the United Kingdom:

Now, therefore, the Secretary of State, in exercise of the powers conferred on him by section 177 of the Broadcasting Act 1990, hereby makes the following Order:

1. This Order may be cited as the Foreign Satellite Service Proscription Order 1993 and shall come into force on 1st May 1993.

2. The foreign satellite service which at the date of the making of this Order is known as Red Hot Television and which was formerly known as Red Hot Dutch is hereby proscribed for the purposes of section 178 of the Broadcasting Act 1990.

6th April 1993

Peter Brooke
Secretary of State for National Heritage

2.3 By-laws

These are rules made by local authorities under powers given by Act of Parliament. They will usually only apply within the geographical area of that local authority.

Example

The Local Government Act 1972, s. 235, gives local authorities power to make by-laws 'for the good rule and government of the whole or any part of the district'.

2.4   Rules made by other statutory authorities

Public corporations and nationalised industries have powers given to them under their constituent Acts to make rules for their own purposes.

Example

The British Railways Board can make rules governing railway property.

2.5   Other bodies

A wide range of other bodies have power to make rules which has been given to them by Act of Parliament.

Example

The British Medical Association; the Law Society; the General Synod of the Church of England.

The Statutory Instruments Act 1946 provided that Orders in Council and Ministerial rules were to be known as 'statutory instruments'. The Act set out certain requirements which have to be followed in such cases, e.g., they must be published.

3   The reasons for delegated legislation

3.1   Time

By delegating power, Parliament can use its limited time to discuss the principles of legislation. The minor details can then be filled in by the Minister by the passing of a statutory instrument.

3.2   Speed

Passing an Act of Parliament is usually a slow process. By contrast, delegated rules can be made quickly, being drafted within a Government department and signed by the Minister. Speed is essential if there is an emergency, and there is also the fact that Parliament might not be in session when some form of legislation was required.

3.3   Unforeseen circumstances

By leaving others to make the detailed rules, Parliament does not have to worry about trying to cover all eventualities in the original Act. Rules can be made as the occasion demands.

3.4 Technical matters

Many laws need to be very detailed and cover highly complex subjects. Not only would this be time consuming for Parliament, it might also be beyond the comprehension of many MPs.

Example

The Cosmetic Products (Safety) (Amendment) Regulations 1991 which prohibit the use of certain substances in cosmetics. By leaving such technical details as this to the Minister of Trade, it was possible to consult outside experts.

3.5 Flexibility

In many areas it is important to be able to experiment with new rules, and if they are not effective they will need to be changed. This is best done through the use of delegated powers. An example of this is provided by the Road Traffic Acts which, by providing for delegated legislation, enable various experiments, e.g., mini-roundabouts, to be carried out.

3.6 Act becoming legally effective

Acts of Parliament usually come into force when they receive the Royal Assent. However, with the increasing detail and complexity of Acts of Parliament many are brought into force in stages or at a later date. The Minister can be given power to do this when everybody is prepared. An example of this is provided by the Education Act 1993 which is being brought into force in stages.

4 Controls over delegated legislation

4.1 Parliament

4.1.1 The Bill. When the Bill setting out the powers is before Parliament, MPs can examine it to see the type and extent of delegated powers. When the Bill is passed, it becomes the enabling or parent Act.

4.1.2 Laying before Parliament. There are various possibilities here, depending on the enabling Act:

(a) Provision that the instrument is laid before Parliament after it has been made. It takes effect as soon as this is done. A copy is simply delivered to the Houses of Parliament. Although questions can be asked about it, there is no opportunity to change it.

(b) Provision that the instrument is approved by Parliament (affirmative resolution). This approval must be given within 40 days of the instrument being laid on the table of the House. The instrument may either not take effect until approved, or take effect immediately but stop being effective if not approved. As this type of procedure requires action by the Houses of Parliament, it is not often used.

(c) Provision that the instrument has to be voted against (negative resolution). This vote must be taken within 40 days of the instrument being laid on the table of the House. The two possibilities are that the rules have immediate effect and must be voted against within 40 days; or only take effect if not voted against within 40 days. This process of voting against is known as annulment. A motion for annulment is called a 'prayer'. These prayers are used more to score political points in the House than to examine delegated legislation.

One difficulty with delegated legislation is that it cannot be amended by the Houses of Parliament. It must be accepted or rejected as changing it would be regarded as interfering with the delegated powers. Also there is no requirement that all statutory instruments must be laid before the Houses of Parliament. It depends entirely on the enabling Act.

4.1.3 *Parliamentary committees.*

(a)   The Standing Committee on Statutory Instruments is a permanent committee in the House of Commons which can examine the merits of any instruments referred to it by the House. It usually consists of 17 members. It allows discussion to take place off the floor of the House and the instrument may then be voted on in the House.

(b)   The Joint Committee on Statutory Instruments was set up in 1973 by amalgamating two separate committees from the Commons and Lords. It consists of seven members from each House. It may examine all instruments which have to be laid before the House plus any other statutory instruments it chooses. Its task is to draw the attention of the House to an instrument on any of the following grounds:

(i)   it imposes a tax on the public;
(ii)   it is made under an Act excluding the instrument from challenge in the courts;
(iii)   it attempts to have retrospective effect and there is no express authority for this in the enabling Act (note that retrospective effect means that it dates back in time and affects things before it was passed, rather than just affecting the future);
(iv)   there has been a delay in publishing it or laying it before Parliament;
(v)   it takes effect before being laid and there has been a delay in notifying the Houses of Parliament;
(vi)   there is doubt about whether it is within the powers of the parent Act or it makes an unusual use of powers, e.g., regulations which put the burden of proof on the accused in a criminal case;
(vii)   its form or effect requires explanation;
(viii) its drafting is defective.

The work of this Committee is quite different from that of the Standing Committee. The Joint Select Committee is really looking at technicalities rather than the policies behind instruments. Each year these committees examine between them approximately 1,000 instruments.

(c)   In 1974 a Select Committee on European secondary legislation was set up in the House of Commons and a Select Committee on the European Community in the House of Lords. Their task was to examine legislative proposals of the European Council and Commission before reporting to the Houses of Parliament.

4.1.4 *Other Parliamentary controls.*   These include questions to the Minister responsible for a statutory instrument which is on the table of the House; a motion of censure on the

Minister responsible (which is unlikely to succeed because of the Government's majority); and a debate on Supply, when money is voted to the Crown.

4.1.5 Publication.   The 1929 Donoughmore Committee on Ministers' Powers recommended that all delegated legislation should be published so that the public knew what the law was, but this requirement has only been partially met. Under the Statutory Instruments Act 1946 all statutory instruments must be published. So far as other types of delegated legislation are concerned, the requirement to publish depends on the enabling Act. By-laws require publication, but other forms of delegated legislation may not need to be published. The Statutory Instruments Act 1946 provides that statutory instruments must be numbered, printed and sold by Her Majesty's Stationery Office (HMSO). Some instruments, however, are exempted from publication:

(a)   local instruments (domestic or local matters);
(b)   instruments made available to those affected;
(c)   temporary instruments;
(d)   bulky instruments;
(e)   those instruments whose publication would be contrary to the public interest (the Minister must provide a certificate to say this).

The Statutory Instruments Act 1946, s. 3(2), provides a defence for anyone prosecuted for breach of a statutory instrument, if it should have been published but had not been at the date of the offence. Even in this case, however, there will be no defence if reasonable steps had been taken to bring it to the attention of those affected, i.e., apart from publishing it.

4.1.6 Consultation.   This means that before anyone makes delegated rules they must tell those who will be affected by them and ask their opinions although there is no general legal duty to consult in this way. The requirement for consultation depends on the enabling Act, but it is standard practice for Government departments to consult those whom they think are interested parties. By asking people who will be affected before making the rules, this allows them to take part in the decision making process.

Example

Before choosing a site for a new town, the Minister will consult all those affected like local residents, farmers, businesses, environmental groups etc.

However, the value of such consultations will depend on two factors. First, whether those asked are allowed to express more than a brief opinion; secondly, whether any notice is taken of their opinion.

4.2 The courts

When dealing with statutory instruments the usual principles of interpretation apply. The instruments must be read in the light of the parent Act. The courts cannot say that an Act of Parliament is invalid, but they can challenge delegated legislation on the grounds it is *'ultra vires'* (i.e., outside the powers).

4.2.1 Substantive ultra vires.   In this case, the Minister has done something outside the powers which he was given in the enabling Act.

Attorney General v Fulham Corporation (1921)

The defendants had power under the Baths and Washhouses Act to provide baths and washhouses for people to use. The defendants began operating a system under which they washed people's clothes for money. The court held that this was effectively operating a laundry, which was outside the powers they had been given of simply providing the facilities. The defendants could be stopped from continuing this service.

4.2.2 Procedural ultra vires.   The parent statute may set out certain procedures to be followed before the exercise of delegated powers. This may involve holding an inquiry, consulting or serving a notice on those affected. If such procedures are not followed the outcome depends on whether the procedures are mandatory or directory. A mandatory procedure must be followed and if it is not, then any rules made are invalid. A directory procedure is merely a suggestion and does not have to be followed.

Agricultural, Horticultural and Forestry Industry Training Board v Aylesbury Mushrooms (1972)

The Minister had power to set up training boards under the Industrial Training Act 1964, but before doing this, the Minister was to consult employers with large numbers of employees. The defendants represented 85 per cent of mushroom growers and the Minister intended to consult the defendants but his letter was lost in the post. It was held that although the Minister had a discretion about whom he consulted, he had decided to consult the defendants. Therefore he could not enforce the order he had made against them because he had not consulted them.

4.2.3 Henry VIII clauses.   Sometimes an Act of Parliament will give the Minister or the Privy Council very wide powers, so it is difficult for the courts to say that they have acted ultra vires. These are known as Henry VIII clauses after the way Henry VIII used to legislate by proclamation. They are also known as 'ouster' clauses, as they effectively prevent review by the courts.

5   Criticisms of the present system

5.1   Parliament's control over legislation is reduced

By giving others power to make laws, Parliament loses control over the amount and content of those laws. Parliament should provide in the enabling Act for checks to be made and those checks must be carried out effectively.

5.2   Too many delegated laws which are also too complicated

In 1993 the number of statutory instruments was 3,359, which is a marked increase on the average of 2,000 a year in the 1970s. About half of these statutory instruments are 'local', which means that they deal with local or personal matters. Local instruments are not published in the annual editions of statutory instruments. Some statutory instruments run to hundreds of pages.

5.3   The danger of sub-delegation

The Minister may pass on the power to make the rules to a civil servant working in that department who may himself delegate the work. This is getting further away from what Parliament intended to happen.

5.4   The use of directions and codes

The last twenty years has seen the increasing use of various types of 'instructions' from Ministers, e.g., directions, codes of practice or circulars. These are sometimes referred to as 'quasi legislation'. Although they do not have to be obeyed in all cases, effectively such types of instructions are making rules without any control by Parliament. For example, under Part VIII of the Social Security Contributions and Benefits Act 1992, the Secretary of State for Social Services can issue directions and make regulations about the operation of the Social Fund. This deals with such things as cold weather payments and crisis loans.

5.5   The changing nature of statutory instruments

In Bennett, Andrew, 'Uses and Abuses of Delegated Power', *Statute Law Review*, Summer 1990, vol. 11, no. 1, the author (an MP) explains that Ministers may now be given the right under their delegated powers to change policy matters. He gives as an example the fact that the decision not to privatise nuclear reactors was made by statutory instrument. He says:

> I believe that some statutory instruments have stopped being about the nuts and bolts, the detailed design of a car, and have reached the stage of deciding whether it is to be more like a pedal bike, an armoured tank or a space shuttle, instead of a car. Their very nature has changed.

PRECEDENT

1   Judges

Before examining the doctrine of precedent it may be worth looking briefly at the people who actually operate this doctrine, i.e., the judges. On 1 January 1993, there were approximately 2,600 professional judges, some part-time, not including lay magistrates.

1.1   The judicial hierarchy

The most important office in the judicial hierarchy is that of Lord Chancellor (Lord Mackay). After that comes the office of Lord Chief Justice (Lord Taylor), head of the Criminal Division of the Court of Appeal, and that of Master of the Rolls (Sir Thomas Bingham), head of the Civil Division of the Court of Appeal. This title comes from the original duties as Keeper of the Royal Records or Rolls.

The next tier consists of Law Lords (or Lords of Appeal in Ordinary) who sit in the House of Lords when it acts as a court (the highest court in England). There are currently 11 Law

Lords, including the Lord Chancellor. They are appointed by the Queen on the advice of the Prime Minister and usually five Law Lords sit to hear a case. The next tier is made up of the Lords Justices of Appeal, who sit in the Court of Appeal. There are 29 of them and normally three will hear an appeal. After this come High Court judges, who automatically receive a knighthood on appointment, and who sit singly to hear a case.

The next level consists of circuit judges, who sit in the Crown Court and in the county courts. Part-time circuit judges are called Recorders and they usually sit for 20 days a year. District judges are officials of the county courts and deal with pre-trial matters and small claims.

Existing High Court judges and above retire at 75 years of age and circuit judges at 72 years. The Judicial Pensions and Retirement Act 1993 provides a lower retirement age of 70 years for all judges appointed after the Act comes into force. The Lord Chancellor can allow judges to continue after 70, one year at a time, to a maximum age of 75 years.

1.2   The role of the judge

'Judges do not have an easy job. They repeatedly do what the rest of us seek to avoid: make decisions. They carry out this function in public.' So begins David Pannick's book, *Judges,* Oxford University Press, 1988. When criticising judges it is pertinent to remember these two points, for how many people, doing any job, could cope with making decisions in public and justifying them to the public and the media? The judge has to act as the referee during the course of the case and then has to decide on the facts and the law, which party is to win. In criminal cases, the judge also has to sum up and, if necessary, pass sentence.

1.3   Are judges suited to this task?

The typical judge, if there can be such a person, is thought of as being white, male, middle-class, and educated at public school and Oxbridge, although this is something of a caricature. It is often argued that those from such privileged backgrounds are out of touch with ordinary people and that this affects a judge's ability to sit in judgment on them.

Professor Griffith, in his book, *The Politics of the Judiciary*, 4th ed., Fontana, 1991, argues that judges are part of the machinery of authority within the state, and as such, cannot avoid the making of political decisions.

1.4   Appointment

The appointment of High Court judges and those above them is shrouded in secrecy. Lord Scarman has said:

   It is just not good enough to rely on what the Lord Chancellor, the Lord Chief Justice or
   the Master of the Rolls tells someone privately . . . it is all too haphazard, an old boy
   network when we have grown out of school.

1.5   Training

The idea of 'training' judges is still frowned upon by many in legal circles. It has long been assumed that a barrister who has been 'raised to the bench' (i.e., been made a judge) will miraculously acquire the variety of skills needed overnight. Suggestions have been made for a system of career judges, following the Continental model, in which, after completing their legal studies, prospective judges would attend a full-time training course, just like any other profession. So far the nearest that the English legal system has got to this is the establishment by the Lord Chancellor's Department in 1979 of the Judicial Studies Board. This Board provides short courses for newly appointed and existing judges, normally over a period of three days. Therefore it is hardly surprising that judges sometimes find themselves in the public spotlight as the result of an inappropriate remark.

Example

A 15-year-old boy who raped a 13-year-old school mate was given three years supervision and ordered to pay the girl £500 compensation 'so that she could have a good holiday to forget the ordeal' (*New Law Journal*, 12 February 1993).

1.6 The future

It is important that judges retain their independence from the legislature and executive. This independence is reflected in the fact that High Court judges and above can only be removed by the Crown on an address by both Houses of Parliament, although circuit judges can be removed by the Lord Chancellor. Public expectations of judges are increasing, however, and judges must become more accountable. A suggestion has been made by the publication *Justice* for a Judicial Commission to control judges. Women and the ethnic minorities are still under represented amongst the judiciary. In January 1994 the first academic lawyer was appointed as a High Court judge (Professor Brenda Hoggett) and as solicitors are now more likely to be appointed in the light of their increasing rights of advocacy, it is hoped that the gradual widening of the spectrum will lead to a greater cross section of society on the bench and a higher quality of justice being dispensed.

2   Judicial precedent (or case law)

Most of the law in England is precedent or case law, i.e., cases decided by judges. Even though Parliament is now the main source of law-making, precedents are still important. The idea of the doctrine of precedent is that once a *principle of law* has been decided, it must be followed in later, similar cases, and this will be fully explained, with examples, later in this section. It is important to realise at the outset, however, that the doctrine of precedent has no connection with sentences passed by courts.

Example

If Adam gets fined £200 for being drunk and disorderly in public, the doctrine of precedent does *not* mean that if Bill is convicted of the same offence a week later he will be given a £200 fine.

The unique feature of precedents is that they must be followed. This distinguishes legal systems based on the common law, like England, from systems in which precedents are treated only as a guide and do not have to be followed. The latter are known as civil law systems. To understand how the system of precedent works, a brief examination of the structure of the court system needs to be made. As a general rule the decisions of a higher court bind all lower courts.

3   The court hierarchy

3.1   House of Lords

This is the highest court in the land unless a matter of Community law is involved. A decision of the House of Lords binds all lower courts. In *London Tramways* v *London County Council* (1898), the House decided that it *was* bound by its own previous decisions. The main reason for this was to bring certainty to the law. People would then know that if a decision had been made on a particular point it would be followed in similar circumstances.

However, in 1966 Lord Gardiner made a statement that in future the House of Lords would be free to depart from its own previous decisions:

> . . . too rigid adherence to precedent may lead to injustice in a particular case and also unduly restrict the proper development of the law. They propose therefore to modify their present practice and while treating former decisions of this House as normally binding, to depart from a previous decision when it appears right to do so.

This power to depart from earlier decisions has been used sparingly. In *R* v *Shivpuri* (1987) the House of Lords overruled *Anderton* v *Ryan* (1985), and said that a person could be convicted of attempting to commit a crime which it was impossible to commit. Shivpuri was convicted of attempting to import a prohibited drug, when all he had in his case was a harmless vegetable matter. In *Murphy* v *Brentwood DC* (1990) the House of Lords overruled their earlier decision in *Anns* v *Merton LBC* (1978), and said that local authorities are not liable for repairing premises which they have negligently inspected. If the courts are faced with two conflicting decisions of the House of Lords, they are bound to follow the *later* decision.

Moodie v IRC (1993)

This concerned a tax avoidance scheme which would have been valid under a 1979 House of Lords decision but not under a 1981 decision. It was held by the House of Lords that the Court of Appeal was wrong to follow the 1979 decision and the Crown's appeal was allowed.

3.2   Court of Appeal (Civil Division)

The Court of Appeal must follow earlier decisions of the House of Lords. Even if the House of Lords decision has been made *per incuriam* (see definition below), it must be followed by the lower courts. The reason is to give the law certainty. The Court of Appeal must follow earlier Court of Appeal decisions. The exceptions to this were set out in *Young* v *Bristol Aeroplane Company Ltd* (1944) by Lord Greene MR:

(a)   If there are two earlier Court of Appeal decisions which conflict, the Court of Appeal can choose which to follow. The other decision is then treated as overruled.

(b)   It is not bound by a Court of Appeal decision which has been overruled by the House of Lords.

(c)   It is not bound to follow its own earlier decision if made *per incuriam.*

(*Per incuriam* means that a court made a decision without taking note of a precedent or statute. It is, however, limited to situations where the ignorance of a particular matter led to faulty reasoning.)

3.3   Court of Appeal (Criminal Division)

The general rule is the same as for the Civil Division, so it must follow House of Lords decisions and its own decisions. The Criminal Division, however, is more flexible about the doctrine of precedent if the liberty of the individual is at stake, see *R* v *Spencer* (1985).

3.4   Divisional Courts

The High Court can sometimes act as an appeal court and is then known as a Divisional Court. When it acts as such a court two or three judges will sit. A Divisional Court is bound by the House of Lords and the Court of Appeal and is also bound by its own previous decisions.

3.5   Trial courts

Decisions of trial courts are not binding on courts of that status. This applies to the High Court, the Crown Court and county and magistrates' courts. County courts and magistrates' courts must, however, follow decisions of the High Court.

3.6   European Court of Justice

This decides all matters of Community law which are then binding on English courts. The ECJ's decisions are not binding on itself.

3.7   Judicial Committee of the Privy Council

This acts as a final court of appeal from Commonwealth countries and Dependent Territories. Its decisions are not binding on English courts but may have persuasive value.

4   The doctrine of precedent in practice

The doctrine of precedent depends on three things in order to work successfully:

(a)   having reliable reports of earlier cases;
(b)   a definitive court hierarchy;
(c)   an ability to discover the legal principle on which the earlier decision was based.

4.1   Reports

Before 1865 there was no systematic approach to law reporting and anyone could make reports of cases. In 1865 the Incorporated Council of Law Reporting was established and began producing 'The Law Reports'. A number of other reports followed such as the Times Law Reports, the All England Reports and the Weekly Law Reports. All law reports have to be made by a barrister who must be present in court when the judgment is given. The reports are then read and approved by the judge. It is up to the editors of the various series of reports to choose which cases go in the law reports. Recent years have seen the growth of a plethora of reports from bodies like tribunals and on wide ranging subjects from road traffic law to financial matters. Added to this has been the growth of computer systems with law reports, such as LEXIS. Such systems include many cases which do not appear in the standard reports but the courts have not looked favourably on the use of computer reports, especially if there is an existing 'conventional' report on the same point. The Master of the Rolls has said the general rule is that in the Court of Appeal, as in the House of Lords, the Law Reports published by the Incorporated Council of Law Reporting should be cited. These contain arguments of counsel and are more readily available (*Practice Note (CA) (1991)*).

4.2   Court hierarchy

The Judicature Acts 1873-75 amalgamated the common law courts and the courts of equity to form the Supreme Court of Judicature. This now consists of the Court of Appeal, the High Court and the Crown Court. The Acts also provided that if there was any conflict between earlier cases from the common law courts and the courts of equity, equity was to prevail. These Acts solved the problem of two different courts contradicting each other.

4.3   Legal principles

When a judge decides a case he *must* do two things:

   (a)   make a decision in favour of one of the parties;
   (b)   give the reasons for his decision. The reasons are known as the *ratio decidendi*, and they constitute the principle of law which is based on the material facts of the case. It is this part of the judgment which is binding.

The judge *may* also make some general comments about that particular area of law or discuss a hypothetical case. This part of the judgment is called the *obiter dicta* (things said by the way), and is not binding in future cases.

A difficulty arises in that, although the judge will give reasons for his decision, he will not always say what the *ratio decidendi* is, and it is then up to a later judge to 'elicit' the ratio of the case. There may, however, be disagreement over what the ratio is and there may be more than one ratio.

Example

Read *R* v *Formosa* below. See what you think the *ratio* is and compare it with the notes which follow in the text.

a
R v Formosa
R v Upton

COURT OF APPEAL, CRIMINAL DIVISION
LLOYD LJ, McCULLOUGH AND PHILLIPS JJ
17 JULY 1990
b

Firearms – Possession – Prohibited weapons – Weapon designed or adapted for discharge of noxious liquid etc – Designed or adapted – Washing-up liquid bottle filled with hydrochloric acid – Whether 'designed or adapted' for discharge of noxious liquid – Whether prohibited weapon – Firearms Act 1968, s. 5(1)(b).

c
The appellants were arrested in possession of a washing–up liquid bottle filled with 400 ml of hydrochloric acid. They were charged with and convicted of possessing a prohibited weapon, contrary to s. 5(1)(b) of the Firearms Act 1968. They appealed against their conviction on the ground that the washing-up liquid bottle had not been 'designed or adapted' for the discharge of a noxious liquid and therefore was not a prohibited weapon within s. 5 of the 1968 Act. The Crown contended that the term 'designed' meant 'intended' and that the washing-up liquid bottle had been intended to be used by the appellants to discharge the acid and had been 'adapted' for that purpose when it was filled with the acid.

d

e
Held – The term 'adapted' in s. 5 of the 1968 Act took its colour and meaning from the context in which it was used, and in conjunction with the term 'designed' it imported some physical alteration to the object in question to make it fit for the use in question. Since the washing-up liquid bottle had not been altered when it was filled with the acid it had not been 'designed or adapted' for the discharge of a noxious liquid within s. 5 of the 1968 Act and was not a prohibited weapon. The appeal would accordingly be allowed.

f

French v Champkin [1920] 1 KB 76 applied.
R v Titus [1971] Crim LR 279 approved.

Notes
g
For prohibited weapons and ammunition, see II(I) *Halsbury's Laws* (4th edn reissue) para 221.
For the Firearms Act 1968, s 5 see 12 *Halsbury's Statutes* (4th edn) (1989 reissue) 431.

h
Cases referred to in judgment
Backer v Secretary of State for the Environment [1983] 2 All ER 1021, [1983] 1 WLR 1485.
French v Champkin [1920] 1 KB 76, DC.
Maddox v Storer [1962] 1 All ER 831, [1963] 1 QB 451, [1962] 2 WLR 958, DC.
R v Titus [1971] Crim LR 279, CCC.
Taylor v Mead [1961] 1 All ER 626, [1961] 1 WLR 435, DC.
j

The question for the court to decide was whether a washing-up liquid bottle filled with hydrochloric acid, had been 'designed or adapted' to discharge a noxious liquid. The prosecution argued that 'designed' simply meant that it was intended for such use in which case the conviction would stand. The court said that the word 'designed' must be interpreted in context with the word 'adapted'. It must mean that the object had been altered in some way to fit a particular use and a bottle filled with acid has not been so altered.

The Court of Appeal followed *R* v *Titus* (1971) which held that a water pistol filled with ammonia had not been designed or adapted for discharge of a noxious liquid. *R* v *Titus* was only a persuasive precedent as it was a decision of the Crown Court, but as it was the only case on the point it was followed.

Thus the *ratio* of *R* v *Formosa* is that the use of an article without physically altering it, meant that it had not been 'designed or adapted' for the discharge of a noxious liquid. If the two defendants had pierced extra holes in the container, that would have been adapting it. The Court of Appeal therefore *reversed* the Crown Court decision in *R* v *Formosa*.

4.3.1 Persuasive precedents.   These are cases which do not have to be followed, but which may have persuasive value. A case may not be binding for a number of reasons:

(a)   if it is a decision of a lower court. This was the situation with *R* v *Titus* in *R* v *Formosa* above;
(b)   if the High Court is considering another High Court case;
(c)   if it is a decision of the Judicial Committee of the Privy Council;
(d)   if it is a decision of a foreign court;
(e)   if it is an *obiter dictum* from a higher court.

4.3.2 How important is a particular precedent?   The importance of a precedent depends on a number of factors including: which court decided the case, as the higher the court, the more weight its decisions carry; whether it is an old or recent case as it could be claimed that an old case was out of touch and therefore irrelevant; how the decision has been treated in later cases, i.e., whether it has been followed or avoided.

5 Avoiding precedents

5.1 Distinguishing

A court dealing with a case need not follow an earlier precedent if it can distinguish it from the present case. A case can be distinguished on its material facts, i.e. those which are relevant to the decision.

Example

In *R* v *Formosa* above, the fact that the washing-up liquid bottle was filled with some form of noxious liquid (acid) is a material fact. The fact it was, e.g., a 'Fairy Liquid' bottle would not be material.

The ability of courts to distinguish cases means that the doctrine of precedent is flexible.

Example

Rylands v *Fletcher* imposed liability for the escape of water from a person's land. This principle of the escape of a dangerous thing could equally be applied to an escaped tiger.

5.2 Overruling

A higher court can overrule a decision made in an earlier case by a lower court, e.g., the Court of Appeal can overrule an earlier High Court decision. Overruling has a retrospective effect which means that it dates back to the time of the earlier case. Cases may also be overruled by statute, but the statute normally only operates from when it is passed.

Example

In *Hedley Byrne* v *Heller* (1963) the House of Lords overruled *Candler* v *Crane, Christmas & Co.* (1951) a decision of the Court of Appeal, and said that there could be liability in tort for a negligent statement.

5.3 Reversing

When the case goes to appeal a higher court can reverse the decision made in the same case by a lower court.

Example

In *R* v *Formosa* (1990) above, the Court of Appeal reversed the Crown Court decision.

5.4 Per incuriam

An earlier decision made *per incuriam* does not have to be followed. Note the limitations on this, however, in 3.2 above.

6   The judges' role in precedent

The *ratio decidendi* is the part of the case which has to be followed. However, in deciding what the ratio is, the principle of law can be narrowly stated or widely stated. The wider the terms in which this principle is stated, the more flexible it is.

The old view of the judges' role was that they were merely 'declaring' the existing law (the 'declaratory theory'). Lord Esher stated in *Willis* v *Baddeley* (1892):

> There is . . . no such thing as judge-made law, for the judges do not make the law, though they frequently have to apply existing law to circumstances as to which it has not previously been authoritatively laid down that such law is applicable.

The modern view is that judges do make law. Lord Radcliffe said: '. . . there was never a more sterile controversy than that upon the question whether a judge makes law. Of course he does. How can he help it?' (Radcliffe, *Not in Feather Beds*, 1968, p. 215). The reality is that judges are continually applying the existing rules to new fact situations and thus creating new laws. The classic example is *Donoghue* v *Stevenson* (1932) where Lord Atkin developed the principle of the duty of care. The constitutional position of the judges in relation to Parliament is that Parliament comprises the elected representatives of the people (i.e., the House of Commons) and those representatives have supreme law-making power. It is not for judges, who are appointed, to make law.

Difficulties arise when decisions involve controversial *policy* issues as the view of the judge may be different from the view of Parliament. This was seen in *Bromley LBC* v *GLC* (1982) when the House of Lords ruled that the London transport system had to pay for itself and could not be subsidised from the rates. With sensitive issues it is better for judges to leave changes to be made by legislation. Professor John Griffith has argued in *The Politics of the Judiciary* that judges have a biased approach not because of their social background, but because, by virtue of their job, they are part of the establishment. This view has been countered by Lord Devlin who said that judges are no different from other professionals in the same age group.

Another problem faced by judges in making decisions is the limited resources and information available to them. If Parliament wishes to change the law a thorough investigation, often with unlimited resources, can be made on its behalf. It must be noted that English courts are not receptive to the so-called 'Brandeis brief'. This is a technique adopted by an American lawyer, Louis Brandeis, in the early twentieth century, to give evidence to the court of the effects which the court's decision might have, which might then affect the way the court decided.

7   Advantages and disadvantages of the doctrine of precedent

7.1   Advantages

(a)   Certainty. By looking at existing precedents it is possible to forecast what a decision will be and plan accordingly.

(b)   Uniformity. Similar cases will be treated in the same way. This is important to give the system a sense of justice and to make the system acceptable to the public.

(c)   Flexibility. There are a number of ways to avoid precedents and this enables the system to change and adapt to new situations.

(d)   Practical nature. It is based on real facts, unlike legislation.

(e)   Detail. There is a wealth of cases to which to refer.

7.2   Disadvantages

(a)   Ratio. Difficulties can arise in deciding what the *ratio decidendi* is, particularly if there are a number of reasons.

(b)   Waiting. There may be a considerable wait for a case to come to court for a point to be decided.

(c)   Distinguishing. Cases can easily be distinguished on their facts to avoid following a precedent.

(d)   Excess of case law. There is far too much case law and it is too complex.

8   Review of precedent

The doctrine of binding precedent has been an important characteristic of the legal system for a little over 100 years. It has brought continuity and justice to decisions and people can see that the basic principle of treating similar cases in the same way is intrinsically sound. As the volume of law has increased, however, so have the problems. The demand for codification is growing in many areas of the law, although whether this would be an improvement on the system of precedent is debatable. If precedent is to survive it must be used in a flexible manner to meet the demands of an ever changing society and the increasing influence of the European approach. Perhaps it is time for more judges to take Lord Denning's view of the doctrine of precedent, as espoused in his book *The Discipline of Law*, Butterworths, 1979:

> I would treat it as you would a path through the woods. You must follow it certainly so as to reach your end. But you must not let the path become too overgrown. You must cut out the dead wood and trim off the side branches, else you will find yourself lost in thickets and brambles. My plea is simply to keep the path to justice clear of obstructions which would impede it.

LAW REFORMS

1   Introduction

> Heart-breaking delays and ruinous costs were the lot of suitors. Justice was dilatory, expensive, uncertain, and remote. To the rich it was a costly lottery: to the poor a denial of right or certain ruin. The class who profited most by its dark mysteries were the lawyers themselves.

Although this could be a fair comment on the legal system in the 1990s, these words were written by Sir Thomas Erskine May in 1861 (*Constitutional History of England*, Longman).

The social reformer Jeremy Bentham (1748–1832), argued for constant radical legislation to achieve the greatest happiness of the greatest number. From this time efforts were made to demystify law and to see it as a set of practical rules. From the Reform Act 1832 onwards, a series of reform measures was passed. The Judicature Acts 1873–75 were followed by a series of Acts codifying substantive branches of law, like the Sale of Goods Act 1893 and the Partnership Act 1890. This continued with a series of reform Acts on land law, e.g., the law of property legislation of 1925. These various measures, however, were *ad hoc* responses to particular problems. There was no overall plan or consistency of effort and this was to remain the situation until the 1960s.

The need for continual reform arises for a number of reasons. Statutes remain in force until repealed and some statutes get overlooked, like the Innkeepers Act 1424. The vast amount of law and the increasing rate at which it is being made has become overwhelming; an example of this is that, according to the Home Office, the number of criminal offences is over 70,000. In a rapidly changing society new laws have to be made to meet new needs, e.g., the Criminal Justice and Public Order Bill 1993 which proposes to make it an offence to make, distribute, advertise or possess child pornography which is simulated by computer graphics. Responsibility for the law is somewhat diverse as the Home Secretary is responsible for the criminal law, while the Lord Chancellor is responsible for the courts and both civil and criminal procedure. There is no single body or person who can accept responsibility for reform.

2   Why not leave law reform to the courts?

The courts, through their use of the doctrine of precedent, could bring about changes in the law. Some academics favour judge-made law, because it is based on real cases rather than legislation which is made in an artificial way. However, judges changing the law conflicts with their constitutional position, as it is up to Parliament to do this. Other arguments *against* judges reforming the law have been put forward by Norman Marsh, a former Law Commissioner:

(a)   a judge cannot make assumptions about people's values, this is better left to Parliament;
(b)   reform depends on a case coming before the courts;
(c)   a reforming decision may be hard on the losing party;
(d)   the system of precedent is slower than legislation;
(e)   the courts are not well informed on the background to problems as they cannot consult experts or interested bodies.

3   Establishment of the law reform agencies

In 1921 an American lawyer, Benjamin Cardozo, in 'A Ministry of Justice' *Harvard Law Review*, 1921, suggested a permanent body:

The courts are not helped as they could and ought to be in the adaptation of law to justice. The main reason they are not helped is because there is no one whose business it is to give warning that help is needed . . .

In 1934 the Lord Chancellor set up the Law Revision Committee which became the Law Reform Committee in 1952. It is a part time body of practitioners and academics whose task is to examine and report on any matters of civil law referred to it by the Lord Chancellor.

In 1959 the Home Secretary set up the Criminal Law Revision Committee, a part time body, to carry out a similar role as regards criminal law, and it examines matters referred to it by the Home Secretary.

In 1965 a White Paper proposed setting up a full time body:

One of the hallmarks of an advanced society is that its laws should not only be just but also that they be kept up to date and be readily accessible to all who are affected by them. (Proposals for English and Scottish Law Commissions 1965 (Cmnd 2573).)

This was quickly followed by the Law Commissions Act 1965, which set up two Commissions, one for England and Wales (jointly) and one for Scotland. Section 3 of the Act provides:

> It shall be the duty of . . . the Commissions . . . to keep under review all the law . . . with a view to its systematic development and reform, including in particular the codification of such law, the elimination of anomalies, the repeal of obsolete and unnecessary enactments, the reduction of the number of separate enactments and generally the simplification and modernisation of the law . . .

The section went on to provide that the Commissions should:

(a)   consider proposals for reform made to them;
(b)   prepare and give to the Minister programmes for the reform of different branches of the law;
(c)   prepare draft bills for matters approved;
(d)   prepare the consolidation of statutes on request by the Minister;
(e)   give advice on reform to Government departments and others;
(f)   obtain information about other legal systems which might help in the task of reform.

4   Who contributes to reform of the law?

4.1   The judges

As we have seen above the judges play a part in reform of the law by adapting old decisions to new situations. The example is often given from the law of tort how the principle in *Donoghue* v *Stevenson*, i.e., that you must not injure your neighbour, has been used to impose liability in a wide range of situations.

4.2   The Law Reform Committee

This committee has produced a range of reports which have often been followed by legislation. The Occupiers' Liability Act 1957 and the Latent Damage Act 1986 are examples of this (see Chapter 4, Law of Tort).

4.3   The Criminal Law Revision Committee

This committee also produces reports from time to time, and the Theft Act 1968 was the product of one report. However, its report on criminal procedure entitled 'Evidence General' which was made in 1972 after eight years of investigation, was never implemented. This was partly because of the recommendations which it made, which included the abolition of the right of silence when a suspect is arrested.

The problems faced by the above two committees are that they are part time, have limited resources, cannot initiate reports but have to wait for the Minister to tell them what to examine, and often take a long time to produce a report. The consequence is that their reforms have been piecemeal.

The Law Commissions are dealt with separately below.

4.4   Parliament

Parliament has numerous committees which investigate various aspects of law reform from time to time. In July 1988, e.g., a Select Committee of the House of Lords was appointed to review the law and procedure relating to murder and life imprisonment. It recommended that the sentence for murder be changed from a fixed sentence of life imprisonment to a maximum of life imprisonment, i.e. the court would have power to give a lesser term.

4.5   Government departments

These constantly keep under review the law within their particular ambit. They may appoint a committee from within the department to review a topic or may help in directing the work of an independent advisory committee. An example of the latter is the Civil Justice Review which was set up in 1985 by Lord Hailsham, then Lord Chancellor. The committee of 10 members was under the chairmanship of Sir Maurice Hodgson, formerly chairman of ICI and was helped by staff from the Lord Chancellor's Department. Its terms of reference were: 'To improve the machinery of civil justice in England and Wales by means of reforms in jurisdiction, procedure and court administration and in particular to reduce delay, cost and complexity'. Its report was published in June 1988 and many of its recommendations were contained in the Courts and Legal Services Act 1990.

One example of a committee within a Government department comes from the Office of Fair Trading. Following numerous complaints about timeshare selling, a departmental report was made calling for legislation. The Timeshare Act 1992 now gives a consumer a right to cancel within 14 days, if a timeshare agreement is made with a business.

4.6   Royal Commissions

These bodies also produce ideas for reform, e.g., the Royal Commission on Civil Liability and Compensation for Personal Injury reported in 1978 (Pearson Report). One of its recommendations was a 'no fault' compensation scheme for the victims of road accidents, funded by a tax on petrol, but this was not implemented. It has been said that such commissions are merely a way of postponing dealing with a problem for at least two years. This criticism cannot be made about the report of the Royal Commission on Criminal Justice in July 1993, swiftly followed by the Criminal Justice and Public Order Bill in December 1993, which will implement many of its recommendations.

4.7   Universities and colleges

Some academics in certain universities and colleges are constantly carrying out research in various areas of law. One example of such an institution is the Centre for Socio-Legal Studies at Oxford University.

4.8   Pressure groups

Pressure groups with widely differing aims also contribute to law reform; e.g., the National Consumer Council which promotes consumers' interests; the Howard League for Penal Reform which campaigns for prisoners; the Justice organisation which upholds the principles of justice and the right to a fair trial and the Legal Action Group which campaigns to improve legal services for disadvantaged members of society.

4.9 Media pressure

The influence of the media must not be forgotten, especially with such pioneering programmes as 'Rough Justice'.

5 The Law Commission

Although reference will be made to the Law Commission, it must be remembered that there is also a Commission for Scotland. The two Commissions co-operate on matters which affect both Scotland and also England and Wales.

There are five members, namely the chairman (in March 1994 Brooke J) and four others who must be barristers, solicitors or university teachers. They are appointed initially for five years but may be asked to stay for longer. They work part time for the Commission. There is currently a staff of 20 lawyers including four draftsmen from the Office of Parliamentary Counsel. There are also 15 research assistants, normally appointed for one year, an administrative staff and consultants who are used on an ad hoc basis. The Commission is financed by the Lord Chancellor's Department and in 1992 the cost was over £3 million. There is a separate 'Conveyancing Standing Committee' which deals with matters concerning land.

6 How does the Law Commission carry out its work?

The Commission publishes a *consultation paper* (formerly called a working paper) on a particular matter, explaining the problems and making provisional recommendations. These are circulated to lawyers, academics, Government departments and other interested bodies, asking for comments. After a suitable period to allow for comments to be collated and discussed, a draft report is prepared, usually with a draft bill attached and this report is presented to the Lord Chancellor. The Commission has so far produced approximately 130 consultation papers and 200 reports and published its 27th annual report in March 1993. The main interests of the Commission are family law, criminal law, the law of property, common law and statute law revision.

7 Examples of the Commission's work

7.1 Programmes for reform

One of the tasks of the Commission under the Law Commissions Act 1965 was to prepare programmes for reform and to submit these to the Minister. Five such programmes have been produced as shown below, the last in June 1991:

   (a)   first programme (1965) contained 17 items, including the codification of the entire law of contract;
   (b)   second programme (1968) included the codification of criminal and family law;
   (c)   third programme (1973) dealt with private international law;
   (d)   fourth programme (1989) covered nine items on such diverse matters as the modernisation of conveyancing, and the law relating to mentally incapacitated adults;

(e)   fifth programme (1991) dealt with two items, i.e., judicial review and the use of damages in personal injury litigation.

7.2   Reports

Listed below is a very small selection from the 200 or so reports.

(a)   Family Law: Review of Child Law Guardianship and Custody (Law Commission No. 172): the Children Act 1989 was partly based on this.

(b)   Statute Law Revision: 13th Report (Law Commission No 179). This included a draft bill which was presented to Parliament in May 1989 and passed as the Statute Law (Repeals) Act 1989 in November 1989. It repealed a number of disused statutes, including the Innkeepers Act 1424. More recently, the Statute Law Repeals Act 1993 contains 64 pages of statutes and parts of statutes which have been repealed, from the Ordinances of Corporations Act 1503 to the present time.

(c)   Criminal Law: Computer Misuse (Law Commission No 186) was presented to Parliament in October 1989 and became the Computer Misuse Act 1990 in June 1990.

(d)   Family Law : The Ground for Divorce (Law Commission No 192). This was produced in October 1990 and included a draft bill. It suggests that the aim of divorce laws should be to dissolve the marriage with the minimum of distress, to encourage the amicable resolution of practical issues about the home, money and children, and to minimise the harm to children.

(e)   Distress for Rent (Law Commission No 194) was issued in April 1991. It examines the existing system, under which a landlord who is owed rent can enter the property and take the tenant's goods, to sell them in order to pay the rent owed. It describes this right as being *wrong in principle*.

7.3   Consultation papers

One example of the many consultation papers issued is Consultation Paper No 132: Aggravated, Exemplary and Restitutionary Damages (August 1993). As part of the fifth programme of law reform, the Law Commission is examining the effectiveness of damages and it has also criticised high awards in defamation cases.

7.4   Codification

The Commission's work on the codification of contract law was eventually abandoned, one reason being the difficulty of what to do when faced with conflicting case law. The Commission currently hopes to codify the criminal law. Report No 218 Criminal Law: Legislating the Criminal Code: Offences Against the Person and General Principles (November 1993). The Commission points out that this area of non-fatal offences against the person is in urgent need of reform and cites the archaic language of the Offences Against the Person Act 1861.

7.5   Consolidation

The Commission is constantly looking at areas which would benefit from consolidation measures. The Extradition Act 1989, for example, brought together all enactments on extradition from the Extradition Act 1870 to the Criminal Justice Act 1988.

7.6 Local legislation

The Commission has been working for some time on a programme of rationalisation of local legislation. The Statute Law (Reform) Act 1989, for example, included the rationalisation of approximately 2,900 local and private acts for South Yorkshire which had been passed between 1850 and 1864. The Law Commission is also in the final stages of preparing a chronological table of local legislation covering over 37,000 Acts of Parliament.

8 Codification

The Law Commissions Act 1965 sets out codification as one of the duties of the Commission. The idea of a code is quite simple as the rules from one branch of law would be put together in to one book or 'code'. This has its attractions, e.g., the opportunity could be taken to simplify the law, to use clearer language and all the law on a particular matter could be found in one place. However, there are difficulties associated with codification apart from the practical implications of codifying vast areas of the common law. For example: all earlier cases would not be good law; the code itself would need to be interpreted and until this was done, the law would be uncertain; if the code did not cover a particular matter, the courts would have to create a precedent; the code would eventually become outdated and have to be replaced.

There are also problems concerned with the type of code to be chosen. Would it, e.g., be a very detailed one like the German Civil Code with 2,385 sections, or like the French 'Code Civil' which sets out basic principles, leaving the courts to fill in the details? A detailed code is more certain but less flexible. The idea of a code is alien to the common law system, although in parts it has been codified, e.g., the Sale of Goods Act.

9 A Bill of rights

9.1 Points in favour of a Bill of rights

Many people have argued that Parliament has too much power and can pass whatever laws it likes and so the idea of a Bill of rights which would be a document setting out certain legal rights, has been canvassed from time to time over the last twenty years. If Parliament then passed legislation which contradicted the Bill, that legislation could be declared invalid by the courts and this would be a way of controlling the power of Parliament. The two possibilities for such a Bill would be either to make one up specially or to adopt the European Convention on Human Rights. This latter was drawn up in 1950 and the United Kingdom was the first country to ratify it in 1951. The rights contained in the Convention include the right to life, the right not to be subjected to torture or other inhuman or degrading punishment, the right to liberty and security of the person, the right to a fair trial, the right to respect for private or family life, the right to freedom of religion and of expression and the right to marry. It should be noted that many of these rights are qualified in some way.

Although the United Kingdom has agreed to abide by the Convention, i.e., by ratifying it, it has not been incorporated as a part of English law, so it does not have to be followed. The United Kingdom has a dismal record in cases brought against it in the European Court of Human Rights in Strasbourg, having lost approximately one third of them.

Such a Bill could be repealed by Parliament which would not need to feel that its powers were being permanently altered. The Bill could give people more rights, like the right to privacy, which does not exist in English law and rights under the Bill could be enforced in English courts without going to the European Court of Human Rights in Strasbourg, as happens at present.

9.2   Points against a Bill of rights

Arguments *against* the Bill include the following:

   (a)   That the existing law is adequate.
   (b)   That interpreting the Bill would give judges too much power, as all the rights are broadly set out. Judges would also be asked to make decisions on what are essentially 'policy' matters, which should be left to Parliament.
   (c)   That the Bill would have to be entrenched; i.e., to stop it being changed easily by a later Act of Parliament, provision would have to be made that it could only be repealed by a two-thirds majority. This could be regarded as undemocratic.

10   A Minister of Justice

The Haldane Committee in 1918 suggested a Minister of Justice in charge of the legal system. The present system divides responsibility between the Home Secretary and the Lord Chancellor and other Government departments, e.g., the Department of Trade is in control of consumer protection. It is said that such a Ministry would have a better control over law reform.

11   Evaluation of present position on law reform

The Law Commission has made progress in some areas e.g., it has achieved the repeal of outdated laws and it has made innovations like the preparation of draft bills containing reform measures, to save Parliament time. In its 27th Annual Report (1993), the Commission points out the declining success rate for implementation of its reports. Between 1966 and 1973, of 30 law reform reports submitted to Parliament, 28 were implemented. The Commission says that, 'in sharp contrast', of the 44 reports submitted between 1984 and 1992, only 17 have been implemented. This highlights the position of the Commission, that it is only an advisory body and that Parliament takes the decision on whether or not to change the law.

No Law Commission Bills were in the Government's legislative programme in 1991 or 1992, although it was successful with the Access to Neighbouring Land Act 1992, which was passed as a private members' bill. The system of programmes for reform (see 7.1 above) has not been consistent, with a 16-year gap between the third and fourth programmes. Problems have arisen with the schemes for the codification of certain areas of law. Enthusiasm for a Bill of rights fluctuates and the level of support for a Ministry of Justice is about what it was in 1918.

As the law increases in amount and complexity, the role and influence of the Commission in the system needs to be radically re-assessed. It has the same staff and resources as a medium-sized firm of solicitors, with which it is supposed to keep all law under review. The Commission needs more resources, the authority to co-ordinate the work of all law reform organisations, a heightened public profile with more public involvement and, above all, more commitment from Parliament to implement or at least adapt its proposals. Perhaps then it will be able to build on the work that has been done and make significant progress towards fulfilling its duties under the 1965 Act.

CLASSIFICATION OF LAW

1 Introduction

This section examines some of the ways in which law has been classified. This is an artificial exercise in many respects because law is a 'living thing' which is constantly changing to meet new situations and demands and so does not lend itself to being 'compartmentalised'. Nonetheless, the exercise serves a useful purpose by making it easier for students and textbook writers to follow and understand the law. It must always be remembered, however, that the categories into which such an exercise divides the law are often fluid.

2 Common law and equity

2.1 Historical introduction

It may seem strange to begin in 1066, but some awareness of the history and development of English law is useful in understanding the modern legal system and how it continues to adapt and change. This is an important characteristic of the English legal system, and indeed of any legal system, that the laws can be adapted to meet changing social conditions and needs. Another characteristic is the centralised nature of the system, originally instituted by the Normans through the Curia Regis and developed by Henry II (1154–1189) and later monarchs. A third feature is that all land was deemed to be owned by the Crown through conquest. Everyone else was merely a tenant and owned an 'estate' in land.

Before 1066 all laws were local and enforced in the manorial, shire and hundred courts. Under the Normans, Royal Courts began to emerge from the Curia Regis. These did not take over the jurisdiction of the local courts immediately, but over a long period of time the local courts lost jurisdiction over cases and thus lost income. A practice was started of sending judges around the country to hold assizes (or sittings) to hear cases locally. This enabled the judges, over a period of roughly 200 years, to take the best local laws and apply them throughout the land, thus creating law which was 'common' to the whole country i.e., common law.

Originally the King's Council (*Curia Regis*) carried out the three functions of state, namely legislative, executive and judicial. It dealt with all cases in which the King had a direct interest, like breaches of the peace. Eventually the courts split off from the Council and formed the main common law courts. The Court of Exchequer, which dealt with the collection of revenues, was the first to separate, in the reign of Henry I (1100–1135). The Court of Common Pleas stayed in Westminster Hall to deal with disputes between individuals, while the King's Council travelled round the country.

The Court of King's Bench separated sometime after 1230. It had jurisdiction to issue the prerogative writs of mandamus, prohibition and certiorari, which were used to control lower courts. It was also responsible for the Writ of Habeas Corpus.

Justices of the Peace (or magistrates) originated from a Royal Proclamation of 1195 creating 'Knights of the Peace' to assist the Sheriff in enforcing the law. They were later given judicial functions and dealt with minor crimes. The magistrates' courts were an exception to the system of centralised courts.

2.2   Common law procedures

As the work of the common law courts grew, the judges began to use previous decisions as a guide for later cases. This was the beginning of the doctrine of precedent.

The judges also developed the writ system. A writ is simply a document setting out the details of a claim. Writs were issued to create new rights not recognised by the local courts and this helped to attract business. Another reason for the popularity of the Royal Courts was that in claims over freehold land, they allowed trial by jury instead of trial by battle. Over a period of time the writ system became extremely formal and beset with technicalities and claims would only be allowed if they could fit into an existing writ. The rule was 'no writ, no remedy'.

Example

Certain writs of trespass would only be issued for those acts done with force and arms (*vi et armis*) against the King's Peace. If the two requirements were not met, a person had no claim.

Even if a writ was obtained, the judges would often spend more time examining the validity of the writ than the merits of the claim. Writs were issued by the clerks in the Chancellor's Office and they began to issue new writs to overcome these difficulties, in effect creating new legal rights.

In 1258 the Provisions of Oxford forbade the issue of writs without the permission of the King in Council. As a result the common law became rigid and the rules operated unjustly. One way of avoiding strict rules was the use of legal fictions (a legal fiction is something which is untrue but which is treated by the law as if it were true). An example of this is what was termed 'benefit of clergy', by which clergy could be exempt from trial in the Royal Courts. Instead they could be tried in the Ecclesiastical Courts which were less severe. This exemption was extended to clerks and the test of whether someone was a clerk was whether they could read Psalm 51, verse 1.

In 1285 the Statute of Westminster II authorised the clerks to issue new writs but only if claims were in 'like case' to those before 1258. This was restrictive and made further development of the common law very technical. There were also other faults with the common law courts, e.g., they only had one remedy, damages, which was not always suitable; and further, they did not recognise the trust.

2.3   The development of equity

The word 'equity' means fair or just in its wider sense, but its legal meaning is rather narrower than this, i.e., the rules developed to mitigate the severity of the common law. In making these rules, the courts took into account ideas of justice. The common law was concerned with formalities and its remedies were inadequate. The use of fictions could alleviate these difficulties in some cases, but could not solve them.

Litigants began to petition the King as the 'Fountain of Justice'. For a time the King in Council determined these petitions himself, but as the work increased he passed them to the Chancellor as the 'Keeper of the King's Conscience'. In 1474 the Chancellor issued the first decree in his own name, which began the independence of the Court of Chancery from the King's Council. Chancellors were mainly priests and considered petitions on the basis of what was morally right.

Common law had developed a complete system of rules, whereas equity consisted of principles to meet particular difficulties. One of its purposes was to fill the gaps in the common law system and equity was described as 'a gloss on the common law' by Sir Henry Maitland (1850–1906).

Equity was not bound by the writ system and cases were heard in English instead of Latin. It developed new procedures like ordering a party to disclose documents, and the use of the *subpoena* to compel witnesses to attend. Equity created new rights by recognising trusts and giving beneficiaries rights against trustees. (A trust arises if one party gives property to trustees to hold for the use of beneficiaries.) The common law did not recognise such a device and regarded the trustees as owners.

Equity also developed the equity of redemption. At common law, under a mortgage, if the mortgagor had not repaid the loan once the legal redemption date had passed, he would lose the property but remain liable to repay the loan. Equity allowed him to keep the property if he repaid the loan with interest. This right to redeem the property is known as the equity of redemption. (A mortgage arises if one person, the mortgagor, borrows money and gives the lender (mortgagee) a claim over the property as security for the loan.)

Equity created new remedies.

(a)   Specific performance, which is an order telling a party to perform their part of a contract. This was useful where damages were not adequate, e.g., in the sale of land. Thus if the seller refused to sell after signing a contract, the buyer could obtain an order of specific performance making the seller sell the house.

(b)   Rectification, which allowed a written document to be changed if it did not represent the actual agreement made by the parties.

(c)   Rescission, which allowed parties to a contract to be put back in their original position in the case of a contract induced by a misrepresentation.

(d)   Injunctions, usually an order to stop a person doing a particular act, like acting in breach of contract (a prohibitory injunction).

2.4   Equity and the common law

The Court of Equity (or Chancery) became very popular because of its flexibility; its superior procedures (as it was not tied to the writ system a case was started by issuing a petition which did not have to be in any particular form); and its more appropriate remedies. It took business away from the common law courts and would sometimes contradict common law verdicts. Consequently, a certain rivalry developed between the two courts and this came to a head in the *Earl of Oxford's Case* (1616) in which the common law court gave a verdict in favour of one party and the Court of Equity then issued an injunction to prevent that party enforcing the judgment. The dispute was referred to the King who asked the Attorney General to make a ruling. It was decided that in cases of conflict between common law and equity, equity was to prevail.

As equity was developing, it had no fixed rules of its own and each Chancellor gave judgment according to his own conscience. This led to criticism about the outcome of cases and John Selden, an eminent seventeenth century jurist, declared, 'Equity varies with the length of the Chancellor's foot'. To combat this criticism Lord Nottingham (Lord Chancellor 1673–82) started to introduce a more systematic approach to cases and by the nineteenth century, equity had become as rigid as the common law. Thus, delays were caused by patronage, inept officials and an inadequate number of judges.

The Judicature Acts 1873–75 rationalised the position. They created one system of courts by amalgamating the common law courts and the courts of equity to form the Supreme Court of Judicature. This court consists of the High Court, the Court of Appeal and, since the Supreme Court Act 1981, the Crown Court. The Acts provided that the principles of common law and equity should be applied in all courts and if there was any conflict between these principles, then equity was to prevail. However, this did *not* fuse the principles of common law and equity, which still remain as separate bodies of rules. 'The two streams have met and still run in the same channel, but their waters do not mix' (Maitland).

2.5   Modern application of equitable principles

This section will examine some equitable maxims and remedies.

2.5.1   Maxims.   The courts of equity developed certain 'maxims'. A maxim is not a strict rule, but a guideline, which the court takes into account in making a decision. Although many of these evolved in the early days of equity, they still permeate the decisions of the courts. Some examples of these will be explained to show their effect.

(a)   'He who comes to equity, must come with clean hands'
The courts will take into account the conduct of both parties, so that if one party has not acted in a straightforward manner in respect to the other party, he cannot expect to be helped by the court.
(b)   'Delay defeats the equities'
If a person delays for an unreasonable time, then the courts cannot grant equitable remedies because this would be unjust on the other party.

Leaf v *International Galleries* (1950)
The plaintiff bought a painting described by the sellers as a Constable. Five years later the plaintiff discovered it was a copy and claimed rescission for innocent misrepresentation. It was held that the truth could reasonably have been found out in a shorter period of time, so rescission of the contract was refused.

(c) 'Equality is equity'
The courts in awarding equitable remedies will treat all parties equally. As the decree of specific performance cannot be obtained against a minor (anyone under 18 years of age), then it cannot be obtained by a minor against someone else.

2.5.2 Remedies. In recent times the courts have used their equitable jurisdiction to develop new remedies.

(a) Mareva injunctions
In 1975 the Court of Appeal recognised the Mareva injunction for the first time. This is a court order freezing the assets of a party to an action or stopping that party moving the assets out of the country.

Mareva v *International Bulkcarriers* (1975)
A shipowner let the 'Mareva' to a foreign charterer, with payment half monthly in advance. The charterer defaulted on a payment. The shipowner found out that the charterers had money in an English bank and sought an injunction freezing the account. It was held that an order would be granted to stop the charterers from moving the money abroad before the case was heard.

Normally the application will be *ex parte*, which means that one party applies without giving notice to the other side for if the other party did have notice, they could move the assets. Lord Denning laid down guidelines in 1982 for the granting of a Mareva injunction:

(i)   the plaintiff must show he has an arguable case and give particulars of his claim and the defendant's case;
(ii)   the plaintiff must give grounds for believing the defendant has assets within the jurisdiction or assets situated abroad (in this latter case, the order would have to be recognised by a foreign court to be enforceable);
(iii)   the plaintiff must give grounds for believing the assets will be removed;
(iv)   the plaintiff must give an undertaking in damages, if his action proves to be unjustified.

However, courts should be wary about imposing a Mareva injunction which would effectively stop a business running or prevent someone paying their normal bills.

In *The Due Process of Law* (Butterworths, 1980) Lord Denning described the Mareva injunction as 'The greatest piece of judicial law reform in my time'.

(b) Anton Piller orders
In 1974 the High Court started to grant what later became known as Anton Piller orders. This is an order to a defendant to allow the plaintiff on to the defendant's premises to

inspect, copy or remove documents or other objects relating to the plaintiff's property. The aim is to stop the defendant removing or destroying vital evidence. The defendant may refuse entry, but such action would be regarded as contempt of court, for which the defendant could be sent to prison. Once again it is an *ex parte* application. The use of such orders was confirmed in the following case.

Anton Piller v *Manufacturing Processes Ltd* (1976)
The plaintiffs made electrical equipment and employed the defendant as their agent in the United Kingdom. They suspected that he was selling their technical drawings to competitors and so applied for an order. The court held that an *ex parte* mandatory injunction would be granted, to the effect that the plaintiff could enter the defendant's premises and inspect relevant documents.

Certain requirements were laid down which must be met before an order will be granted:

    (i)   the plaintiff must have a strong prima facie case;
    (ii)   the plaintiff must show actual or potential serious damage;
    (iii) there must be clear evidence that the defendant has got documents etc. in his possession;
    (iv) there must be a real possibility that those items will be removed or damaged;
    (v)   the order must not be a 'fishing expedition' (trying to find out what the other person has got).

These orders have been used for breach of copyright, passing off and matrimonial disputes.

The two remedies described above are now governed by the Supreme Court Act 1981. Section 37 allows Mareva injunctions to be granted and s. 72 allows the granting of Anton Piller orders. The Mareva injunction and the Anton Piller order have been described as the law's 'nuclear weapons' by Lord Donaldson, because they can have a devastating effect on a business or on an individual and have sometimes been granted too readily and misused by the parties.

Universal Thermosensors Ltd v *Hibben* (1992)
The plaintiff, a business competitor of the defendant, obtained an Anton Piller order against the defendant and executed it at 7.15 a.m. before the defendant could obtain legal advice. The defendant was awarded £20,000 damages. The court suggested that execution of such an order should be by an independent, experienced solicitor, who should prepare a written report, to be presented to the court a few days afterwards.

The courts have acknowledged the problems and are trying to restrict the use of such orders.

2.6   Summary

The courts are still run on a largely centralised system, with the superior courts based in London. Although the Assize system was abolished in 1971, there is still an element of it in the practice of High Court judges sitting at regional centres and also hearing important cases in the Crown Court. The courts have shown that they can still use equitable principles to meet new situations, as they did in the early period of development. The problems facing the present Lord Chancellor are much the same as those faced by some of his predecessors. The Courts and Legal Services Act 1990 provides for flexibility and change in the court system and it is to be hoped that it will meet some of the criticisms made.

3 Criminal and civil law

3.1 Introduction

All societies have rules to govern the relationships between the members and as those societies develop economically and socially the rules increase in both volume and complexity. It then becomes a problem as to how to classify those rules. One method is to do it by subject-matter, for example, land law, family law and tort but although this is useful for the purposes of study, it must be remembered that a real life problem is unlikely to fit neatly into one of these 'compartments'. One established distinction is between criminal law and civil law.

3.2 Distinctions between criminal law and civil law

A number of differences can be seen between them.

3.2.1 Type of act. A crude distinction is that a criminal wrong is an act against society, whereas a civil wrong is an act against an individual. In early times, there was no clear distinction between criminal and civil acts. During the Anglo-Saxon period, in cases of murder and theft, proceedings were taken by those affected and the main aim seemed to be compensation or restitution. This contrasts sharply with today's approach.

Civil law is the larger area and it has at least sixty different branches, e.g., contract, tort, land, family, constitutional, employment, and succession to name only a few.

(a) The law of contract regulates agreements made between people.
(b) The law of tort comprises a group of civil wrongs including negligence, nuisance, defamation and trespass.
(c) Land law covers all matters relevant to the ownership and transfer of property.
(d) Family law deals with marriage, divorce and children.
(e) Constitutional law deals with the powers of the state and its relationship with the individual.
(f) Employment law covers rights and duties of employers and employees.
(g) The law of succession makes provision for the passing of property with or without a will.

Criminal law is aimed at protecting the community from violence, theft, and public disorder etc.

The distinction mentioned above between a criminal wrong and a civil wrong, that the former is an act against society, is not wholly valid. It is little consolation for a person hit on the head with a cosh to be told that this is an act against society. Obviously criminal acts affect individuals too. By the same token civil matters are not just confined to private parties, as public bodies like Government departments and local authorities can, for example, sue for breach of a contract. Also as the state has intervened more in people's lives, civil disputes have arisen over, e.g., planning permission, family credit and other benefits, which are under the control of the state.

3.2.2 Language. The language used is very different. A criminal act is called an offence; a civil act is a wrong. In a criminal case a person can be found guilty, whereas in a civil case a person may be made liable. A person is prosecuted in a criminal case but sued in a civil case. The two parties in a criminal trial are the prosecution and the accused (or defendant); in a civil trial they are the plaintiff (person bringing the complaint) and the defendant.

3.2.3 Method of case citation. A criminal case is written as *R* v *Greene* (*R* is short for *Regina,* Latin for Queen); a civil case will usually have the names of the two parties, e.g., *Smith* v *Jones.* Sometimes it may be written in the form: *Re McArdle* which means 'reference to' and this can arise if the parties ask the court to make a ruling on a particular matter.

3.2.4 Who brings the action? A criminal prosecution is brought on behalf of the state. It is usually started by the police and then, since the Prosecution of Offences Act 1985, it is taken over by the Crown Prosecution Service (CPS) who will decide whether to continue with the case. There are a number of other bodies who have power to prosecute for matters within their jurisdiction, like the Commissioners of Inland Revenue, the Commissioners of Customs and Excise, trading standards departments of local authorities, the Health and Safety Inspectorate, and the RSPCA.

In contrast a civil case is started by the plaintiff. However, in theory, anyone can bring a prosecution, except in certain specified cases, e.g., being given short measure in a public house when only the police or trading standards departments may prosecute. The difficulties of proof and the cost mean that in practice only a few private prosecutions are brought, for example, by the victims of crimes when the CPS have refused to act.

3.2.5 Stopping the case. As a general rule, once a criminal prosecution is started, then it cannot be stopped, even if the victim wants to stop it. However, it may be stopped by the judge for various reasons, like lack of evidence. A civil case may be stopped by the parties at any time. In 1992 269,668 writs were issued in the Queen's Bench Division of the High Court, 6,481 were set down for trial but only 928 cases went to trial. Settling out of court is the normal way.

3.2.6 Different courts. Cases are brought in separate courts. A criminal case will be tried in the magistrates' courts or the Crown Court. A civil case will normally be in the county courts or the High Court. However, there is a certain overlap as magistrates deal with some civil matters, appeal may be made on a point of law from a magistrates' court in a criminal case, to the Queen's Bench Division of the High Court which is a civil court. The House of Lords hears appeals in criminal and civil cases.

3.2.7 Intention. In a criminal case the prosecution has to prove that the defendant had *mens rea*, which means intention to do the act. This is not necessary in a civil case, although some element of fault must normally be proved.

The exception in both criminal and civil law is cases of strict liability where a person can be made liable without any fault or wrongful intention. For example, under the Weights and Measures Act 1985, s. 28, a trader giving short weight is strictly liable in criminal law. In the law of tort if someone publishes a defamatory statement about another person, that is libel irrespective of intention.

3.2.8 Standard of proof. In a criminal case the defendant is presumed to be innocent. The burden of proof is on the prosecution to prove its case and the standard required is to prove it *beyond all reasonable doubt.* The reason for such a high standard for the prosecution is that the defendant's liberty may be at stake if he is found guilty. In civil cases it is up to a party to prove their case on a *balance of probabilities*, which is much easier to discharge.

3.2.9 Evidence and procedure. The rules of evidence and procedure are strictly adhered to in criminal cases to protect the defendant. For example, the rule against hearsay, i.e., that only direct evidence of witnesses is allowed and not what someone told them, is strictly enforced. In civil cases the rules are relaxed. Another example is the use of confessions in criminal cases, which will be subject to close scrutiny, particularly after the activities of the West Midlands Serious Crimes Squad. By contrast, in civil cases admissions by one party are readily accepted.

3.2.10 Aims of the action. The aims of bringing a prosecution are usually a mixture of retribution, punishment, deterrence and rehabilitation, but the general principle is to punish. The main aim of a civil action is to gain compensation in the form of damages (money).

Since 1964 the victims of crimes of violence have been able to claim compensation from the Criminal Injuries Compensation Board, which is funded by the Government. Also since the Powers of Criminal Courts Act 1973, the criminal courts have had power to award compensation to the victim of an offence, payable by the convicted person. The courts have been reluctant to use these powers but the Criminal Justice Act 1988, s. 104, amends the 1973 Act and provides that if a court does *not* make such an order, it must give reasons for not doing so. Civil courts may, in rare instances, award 'punitive' damages to punish a defendant, see *Cassell & Co. Ltd* v *Broome* (1972).

3.2.11 Role of lay persons. Lay persons play a large part in criminal cases. Normally three lay magistrates will hear a minor case in the magistrates' courts, while in the Crown Court there will be a jury of lay persons. By contrast most civil cases are heard by a single professional judge. Civil juries are used mainly in cases of defamation or malicious prosecution.

3.2.12 Availability of legal aid. In *criminal* cases legal aid is free up to a disposable income of £47 per week and capital up to £3,000; above that contributions are payable on the basis of £1 for every £3 of income.

In *civil* cases legal aid is free up to a disposable income of £2,382 per year and capital up to £3,000. Payments are then made on a scale but legal aid is not available if disposable income is over £7,060 per year and disposable capital is over £6,750. For personal injury claims the limits are £7,780 for income and £8,560 for capital. If someone is receiving income support, they qualify for free legal aid in both criminal and civil cases. Legal aid is not available in certain types of cases, like defamation. These figures operate for 12 months from 11 April 1994. The net cost of legal aid (i.e. after taking into account contributions people make towards it) is likely to be over £1 billion for 1993/94.

3.3 Practical implications of the distinction

As we have seen, the relationship between civil and criminal law is not clear cut, and a further complication is added by the fact that one act may result in both civil and criminal liability.

Lane v Holloway (1967)

The plaintiff was 64 years old and the defendant 23. The old man came home from the pub one night and started chatting to a neighbour in the yard. The defendant's wife called out to him to keep quiet. He replied 'Shut up you monkey faced tart'. The defendant then came out and the plaintiff challenged him to a fight. The defendant went up to the old man, who struck the defendant a glancing blow on the shoulder. The defendant then hit him once in the face. The old man needed 19 stitches and was in hospital for a month.

The defendant was prosecuted in the magistrates' court, found guilty of unlawful wounding and fined.

The plaintiff then sued for trespass to the person in the county court and was awarded damages of £75, reduced because of his own behaviour. He appealed to the Court of Appeal. The court held that because the plaintiff was full of beer he had not consented to the assault. It also held that the defendant's blow was out of all proportion. Damages were increased to £300.

It is possible, therefore, for someone to become involved in two sets of proceedings over one incident. A conviction in the criminal courts can be used as evidence in a civil case, since the Civil Evidence Act 1968. As we have seen above, legal aid is rather more difficult to obtain in civil actions.

Lloyd v DPP (1991)

The defendant parked in a private car park, even though a notice warned that cars would be clamped and £25 charged for their release. The defendant refused to pay and later removed the clamps by cutting the padlocks. He was charged with criminal damage under the Criminal Damage Act 1971. The defendant claimed that he had an excuse as the landowner had trespassed on his car. The court held that he had consented to the clamping by parking in the private car park. Force could only be used if there was no reasonable alternative. He could have paid and sued for recovery in the county court. Therefore he was found guilty. The court said that it was not concerned with whether the defendant could sue the landowner for trespass as that was a matter for the civil courts. It is interesting to consider whether, if he had picked the locks without damaging them, he could have been convicted of anything.

EUROPEAN COMMUNITY LAW

1   Introduction

European Community law has been important in the United Kingdom since it joined the then European Community on 1 January 1973. Since the Treaty on European Union in 1992 (the Maastricht Treaty), the European Community has become the European Union. This section proposes to start by looking briefly at the origins of the former European Community before examining the work of the institutions of the European Union. It will then examine the role of the European Court of Justice in interpreting legislation and ensuring that the institutions and the members comply with Community law. Although on a political level the term 'European Union', or EU, is acceptable, it is not suitable for legal writing and reporting. This book will retain the use of the term 'Community law' which the authors believe is more likely to be generally acceptable. The European Court of Justice has no 'police force' to enforce its judgments but has relied on moral and political pressure and the co-operation of national courts. Under its new powers, it may now *fine* member states who do not fulfil their obligations under the Treaties. Finally, it will look at the types of Community legislation and their effect on English law. Community law has developed enormously in volume since the United Kingdom joined and continues to do so and this survey can only be a brief outline of the mechanisms and rules. Although the institutions of the European Union may seem far away, they are increasingly affecting the daily lives of the 350 million people within the Union; the creation of the internal market at the end of 1992 and the passing of the Maastricht Treaty, have both accelerated this process.

1.1   History of the European Community

The European Community had its roots in an agreement made after the Second World War, under which the USA agreed to provide economic aid if European countries co-operated with each other. Sixteen countries agreed to this and in 1947 the agreement, known as the 'Marshall Plan', was implemented. A united Europe was also seen as essential to maintain world peace, after two World Wars had started there within 25 years. These factors led to the creation of three separate communities (see below).

The original members of the European Coal and Steel Community in 1951 were France, Germany, Italy, Belgium, Luxembourg and the Netherlands. The European Economic Community and Euratom came into being in 1957 with the same six members. In 1973 the United Kingdom, the Republic of Ireland and Denmark joined; Greece joined in 1981 and in 1986 Spain and Portugal became full members. Negotiations are currently under way for Austria, Finland, Sweden and Norway to join in 1995 and Cyprus, Malta and Turkey have formally applied for membership. In April 1994 Hungary and Poland also applied to join the European Union.

1.1.1   The European Coal and Steel Community.   The Treaty of Paris 1951 set up the ECSC to rationalise these industries and to create a common market for coal and steel.

1.1.2   The European Economic Community.   The first Treaty of Rome 1957 set up the EEC with the aim of creating a common market for goods, labour and capital. The

Maastricht Treaty has, confusingly, changed the name of the European Economic Community to the European Community.

1.1.3   The European Atomic Energy Community (EURATOM).   This was created by the second Treaty of Rome, which was signed at the same time as the first Treaty. The object was to control the production of atomic energy and ensure it was used for peaceful purposes.

1.2   The Merger Treaty

Each Community had its own Council and Commission but shared one Parliament and one Court. A treaty was signed in 1965, the Merger Treaty, establishing a single Council and a single Commission, and this came into effect in 1967.

1.3   The Single European Act 1986

In 1986 the Single European Act was signed. This is not an Act of the United Kingdom Parliament but an international agreement between the member states. It was given effect in English law by the European Communities (Amendment) Act 1986, which came into force on 1 January 1987. It created an internal market within the European Union at the end of 1992, which allowed goods, services, capital and citizens of the Union to move freely between member states.

1.4   The Treaty on European Union

The Treaty on European Union was signed in Maastricht in February 1992 and came into force on 1 November 1993. It was implemented in English law by the European Communities (Amendment) Act 1993. The Treaty on European Union states:

   This Treaty marks a new stage in the process of creating an ever closer union among the peoples of Europe, in which decisions are taken as closely as possible to the citizen.

The Treaty expands the responsibilities of the European Union.

It introduces the idea of *Union citizenship*. This enables nationals of all member states to move and live freely within the territory of the Union. It also gives citizens of the Union the right to vote in local elections in any member state in which they reside, the right to diplomatic protection by any member state and the right to petition the European Parliament about any European matter which affects them directly.

The powers of the European Parliament are also increased, to give it a power of *co-decision* with the Council of Ministers on certain matters.

It emphasises the principle of *subsidiarity*, i.e. that the Union will only act in matters outside its exclusive jurisdiction if member states cannot achieve the objectives involved. In such matters the Union is subsidiary to the member state. Following this, the European Commission has withdrawn a number of proposals for legislation, to leave it up to individual member states.

A *Committee of the Regions* was also set up with 189 members. Membership is based on the size of the country, for example, the United Kingdom has 24 representatives and Ireland 9. This committee will be consulted by the Commission and the Council of Ministers on regional matters.

Other common matters including the social chapter, foreign and security policy and judicial affairs will be implemented separately from the Treaty, by agreement between governments, although the United Kingdom can 'opt out' of the infamous social chapter.

1.5   The importance of European institutions

The importance of the creation of these organisations is the effect they can have on the policies of member states and on the national laws of those states. Membership of the European Union involves giving up some powers to the institutions of that Union.

2   The institutions of the European Union

2.1   The European Parliament

2.1.1   Election of members.   Originally the members were appointed by their national parliaments, but since 1979 there have been direct elections, the most recent being in June 1994. Members of the European Parliament (or MEPs) hold office for five years. The system of election varies in each member state and seats are distributed roughly in proportion to the population of each state. The table below shows the number of seats in the European Parliament and how they are allocated.

MEMBERS OF THE EUROPEAN PARLIAMENT

Germany	99
France, Italy and UK	87 each
Spain	64
Netherlands	31
Belgium, Greece and Portugal	25 each
Denmark	16
Ireland	15
Luxembourg	6
Total	567

The members of the Parliament do not sit in national groups, but sit according to political allegiance, for example, all the Socialists sit together.

2.1.2   Powers of the Parliament

(a)   Generally the European Parliament has a right to be consulted on proposed legislation. The Commission will send a proposal to the Council, which will then send it to the Parliament, which may then give an opinion.

(b) The Single European Act 1986 increased the powers of the Parliament by introducing a 'co-operation procedure' to be used in certain cases. Under this procedure the Parliament is consulted in the normal way and the Council then confirms the measure, but it does not immediately become law. The Parliament has three months to consider it again and if the Parliament rejects the measure, the Council needs a unanimous vote to pass it.

(c) The powers of the Parliament were further increased by the Treaty on European Union 1992.

A 'co-decision' procedure was introduced which enables the Parliament to *amend* or *reject* decisions of the Council in certain matters, for example, training, education, health and consumer affairs.

If the Council approves a proposal from the Commission, it tells the Parliament. Parliament then has three months to approve it or do nothing and in either case the measure will be adopted.

If Parliament rejects the proposal by an absolute majority, the Council then convenes a 'conciliation committee' made up of equal numbers of the Council and Parliament. Parliament can then reject the proposal which effectively ends the matter. Alternatively, it may propose amendments and then the Council has three months to approve the amendments, in which case they are adopted. If the Council rejects them the 'conciliation committee' is formed again and has six weeks to agree. Failing agreement, Parliament has a further six weeks to reject the proposal finally.

Parliament has been given the right to initiate legislation; by a majority vote it may ask the Commission to prepare a proposal on laws it considers are needed to implement the Treaties.

Parliament must approve the European Commission as a body and the President of the Commission.

On the request of one quarter of MEPs, Parliament must set up a committee of inquiry to investigate a breach of Community law or maladministration.

The co-decision procedure is complex and could slow down decision making but by giving Parliament more powers this is a step towards democracy for the European institutions.

(d) Parliament's consent is needed for new members to join the Union.

(e) Parliament can submit questions to the Commission and the replies are published in the Official Journal.

(f) It can debate the Annual Report submitted by the Commission.

(g) It can dismiss the whole Commission by a motion of censure, if carried with a two-thirds majority. But Parliament does not appoint the new one.

(h) It may approve or modify the budget which is prepared by the Commission.

(i) It can take the other institutions to the European Court of Justice for breach of the Treaties.

(j) It is important to note that much of the work of the Parliament is done through its standing committees,e.g., the Agricultural Committee and the Legal Affairs Committee.

2.2 The Council of Ministers

2.2.1 Constitution. The Council of Ministers consists of twelve members, one from each member state, plus one observer from the Commission. The Council holds general meetings at which the representative is usually the Foreign Minister of each state, or specialist meetings at which an appropriate Minister will attend, for example, finance or social affairs. Meetings are held in private. Each member state acts as President of the Council for a period of six months. Because the Ministers also work for their own governments, they can only spend short periods in Brussels, so to provide more continuity a committee of permanent representatives (known as COREPER) was set up. This is composed of the ambassadors of the member states, who represent the interests of their own countries rather than Union interests.

2.2.2 Powers. The Council is the main decision making body in the Union. It is responsible for formulating policy, passing legislation, making agreements with foreign states and, together with the Parliament, agreeing the Union's budget. Note the new co-decision procedure outlined at *2.1.2(c)* above.

2.2.3 Voting. Article 148 of the EEC Treaty provides that the Council shall act by a majority unless otherwise provided. In fact most of the provisions of the Treaty need a qualified majority or a unanimous vote. For example, the admission of new members has to be by a unanimous vote. Other matters are by a qualified majority. Under Article 148 a system of weighted voting has been created. The number of votes allocated to each country is shown in the table below.

STATE	VOTES
UK, France, Germany, Italy	10 each
Spain	8
Belgium, Portugal, Greece, Netherlands	5 each
Ireland, Denmark	3 each
Luxembourg	2

A qualified majority is 54 votes from a total of 76. This means that the larger countries cannot out-vote the other members. In practice the Ministers often seek to obtain a unanimous vote, even if this is not required. This tends to slow down decision making.

When Sweden, Finland, Norway and Austria join, the possible number of votes in the Council of Ministers will be 90. The number for a qualified majority will then be 64.

2.2.4 The European Council. In 1974 it was agreed that the Heads of Government and Foreign Ministers of each state would meet each year to discuss community matters and political co-operation. These meetings became known as the 'European Council'. The Single European Act 1986 provides for the European Council to meet twice a year and two members of the Commission can attend. The European Council provides an opportunity to discuss political co-operation and foreign policy, with the aim of adopting common positions towards foreign states.

2.3 The European Commission

2.3.1 Constitution. The European Commission consists of 17 members appointed by the Governments of member states. Each appointment must be agreed by all member states. France, Germany, Italy, the United Kingdom and Spain have two members each; the others have one member. Commissioners are appointed for a period of five years (from 1995) and the whole Commission is re-appointed at the same time. On appointment, the President and members of the Commission are subject to approval, as a body, by the European Parliament. Meetings are held in private and decisions are made by a simple majority.

Each Commissioner is not regarded as a representative of their country. Article 10 of the Merger Treaty provides that they must be 'completely independent' in performing their duties. The President of the Commission is appointed from among the Commissioners for a term of two years and each Commissioner takes responsibility for a particular area, for example, economic affairs.

The Commission has a large staff of over 17,000 to assist it. There are 30 departments known as Directorates General which cover particular matters, e.g., competition, agriculture. Each department is under the control of a Director General.

The European Parliament may pass a vote of no confidence, by a two-thirds majority, to remove the entire Commission.

2.3.2 Powers. These are set out in the main in Article 155 of the EC Treaty and include:

(a)   The power to ensure that the Treaties, and all secondary legislation made under them, are applied properly.

(b)   The power to formulate and initiate policies authorised by the Treaties. In 1992 the Commission sent 651 proposals to the Council and 272 memoranda and reports.

(c)   The power to promote the interests of the Community both within the boundaries of the EC and abroad.

(d)   The power to act as the executive branch of the Community to ensure policies are implemented. This includes exercising powers delegated by the Council of Ministers, for example, the power to make detailed rules.

(e)   The power to take proceedings in the European Court of Justice:

(i)   against any member state which does not fulfill its obligations under the Treaties (Art 169, EC Treaty);

(ii)   against any institution of the Union which has acted outside its powers (Art 173, EC Treaty).

One problem the Commission has faced is what to do if a member state fails to comply with a judgment of the European Court of Justice. In 1992 there were approximately 100 instances of this. The Treaty on European Union 1992 has given the Commission greater powers. The Commission can give an opinion setting out how the member state has not complied with a judgment and giving the member state a time limit in which to comply. If the member state fails to do this, the Commission can bring the case to the European Court of Justice and suggest a *fine*, which the court can impose if it finds non-compliance. The United Kingdom has had a bad record in such matters in the past.

European Commission v *UK* (1985)

In 1981 the UK Government passed a statutory instrument which required clothes, shoes and electrical goods to be marked with their country of origin. The Commission believed that this would thereby increase the costs of such items and was effectively an import restriction, in breach of Article 30. The UK disagreed. The court delivered its opinion in 1985 and held that this was a breach of Article 30 by the United Kingdom. In March 1986 the statutory instrument was repealed.

3 The European Court of Justice

The European Court of Justice (ECJ) is officially called the Court of Justice of the European Communities and it sits in Luxembourg. It is important to note that it has no connection with the European Court of Human Rights which sits in Strasbourg. The ECHR was set up under the European Convention on Human Rights (1950) to supervise the rights given under the Convention. It has no jurisdiction over the laws of the European Union.

The European Court of Justice consists of 13 judges, the odd number being needed to avoid a tied vote when the full court is sitting. The quorum for the court is seven. At least one judge must come from each member state and Governments of member states must agree to the appointment of each judge. The judges hold office for six years, on a staggered basis, with a specified number retiring every three years. The judges elect a President who holds office for two years.

The judges are independent of their respective Governments. Decisions are made by a majority vote, but only one judgment is given, without any dissenting judgments. The judges are assisted by six Advocates General whose role, which is unknown in English law, is to present an impartial case to the court after the parties have presented their case. The object is to help the court in making its decision.

3.1 Types of actions

A distinction is made between direct actions and preliminary rulings.

(a)   Direct actions are actions started in the ECJ which also end in the ECJ.

(b)   Actions referred to the ECJ for a preliminary ruling arise when a national court refers a matter of European law to the ECJ. The ECJ makes its ruling on the point of law and the case goes back to the national court for the decision to be made in the light of the ruling.

3.2 Outline court procedure

3.2.1 Direct actions.   These are started with a document called an 'application' in which the applicant (or plaintiff) sets out his claim. This is sent to the ECJ which serves it on the defendant who then lodges his defence. The next stage is the preparatory inquiry by the ECJ which decides what evidence is needed to determine the facts. This may involve calling witnesses. The judge issues a summary of the facts and arguments. The hearing which follows is not as important as in an English court. Both sides present their case including any comments on the summary they have been given. Finally, the court gives its judgment, which is always reserved, i.e., it is never given straight away but after a period of time.

3.2.2   Preliminary rulings.   It is up to the national court to make an order for reference to the ECJ, the parties to the case have no say in the matter. The ECJ gives copies of the reference to the parties involved, Member States, the Commission and the Council (if it concerns a Council measure) and any of them may make observations and attend the hearing.

3.3   Jurisdiction of the ECJ

The jurisdiction means those matters with which a court has been given power to deal. The cases may be put into three categories, namely: contentious cases; preliminary rulings; and plenary matters.

3.3.1   Contentious cases.   Actions may be brought against member states and institutions of the European Union by other members or institutions. Individuals (whether natural or legal persons) cannot bring a direct action against a member state, but they may bring an action against an institution of the European Union if certain conditions are fulfilled.

   (a)   Member states.
A case may be brought against a member state for being in breach of Community law by another member or by the Commission (acting on behalf of the European Union) (Art 170, EC Treaty). The member state bringing the action must tell the Commission first, so that it may give an opinion, before the action can continue. A similar procedure is followed by the Commission in that it gives the member state notice and an opportunity to follow its opinion, before court action is taken.

   (b)   Institutions.
Action may be taken against institutions of the European Union on the grounds that any regulation, directive or decision is invalid. Claims may be based on the institution having done something it should not have done (Art 173, EC Treaty) or on having failed to act (Art 175, EC Treaty). Action may be taken by another European Union institution, a member state or an individual (natural or legal). An individual must show that the particular act is of 'direct and individual concern' to the applicant before he is permitted to commence such an action.

3.3.2   Preliminary rulings.

   (a)   Referral.
Art 177, EC Treaty gives the ECJ jurisdiction to make preliminary rulings on matters relating to:

   (i)   interpretation of Treaties of the European Union;
   (ii)   the validity of acts of institutions of the European Union.

Any national court or tribunal (like the Employment Appeal Tribunal) may ask the ECJ to give a *preliminary ruling*, if the national court believes a question of Community law is relevant to its decision. Any national court from which there is no appeal (like the House of Lords) must refer such matters to the ECJ.

Costa v ENEL (1964)

A case from an Italian magistrate involved less than two pounds in money, but under Italian law because of the small amount there was no right of appeal. It was held that it was a fit case to be referred under Art 177.

A national court need not refer a matter if the legal point has already been decided by the ECJ.

(b)   Effect of ruling.

A preliminary ruling is only binding on the court which referred the matter to the ECJ. The practical effect, however, is that such a ruling, in an English case, will be treated as a precedent in English law and will be followed throughout the European Union.

(c)   General points.

The ECJ does not determine matters of compatability between Community law and national law, that is for the national court to decide. There is no appeal against decisions of the ECJ. The ECJ does not have to follow the doctrine of precedent although it generally follows earlier decisions, unless, for example, the circumstances have changed.

3.3.3   Plenary matters.   These are cases in which a party is claiming damages for unlawful acts by institutions of the European Union. Examples include actions in tort, and actions by staff against the institutions.

3.4   The Court of First Instance (CFI)

In 1987 a total of 527 cases was referred to the ECJ. Because of this increasing workload, the Single European Act 1986 authorised the Council of Ministers to set up a Court of First Instance. This was established in 1988 and 12 judges were appointed in 1989 to hold office for six years.

The jurisdiction of the CFI is limited to:

(a)   actions by staff of the institutions;
(b)   actions against the Commission under certain Articles of the ECSC Treaty;
(c)   actions against institutions relating to competition policy.

The CFI cannot hear cases brought by member states or institutions of the European Union, nor can it deal with questions submitted by national courts through the preliminary ruling procedure. Appeals from the CFI to the ECJ can only be made on a point of law.

4   Community legislation

A distinction is made between primary sources of Community law and secondary sources.

4.1   Primary

These sources are the three Treaties setting up the three Communities, plus other treaties amending them from time to time, for example, the Treaty on European Union 1992 or when a new member joins. The Treaties set out principles of Community law which can have direct effect and give power to the institutions of the European Union to make laws. In addition to these three treaties are treaties with foreign states outside the European Union and agreements made between members of the European Union.

4.2   Secondary

The Council of Ministers and the European Commission can pass secondary legislation. Article 189, EC Treaty provides for three forms of such legislation:

4.2.1   Regulations.   These have general application throughout the European Union. They also have direct applicability, which means that they automatically apply within member states, without the states taking any action. (Article 189 provides that regulations shall be 'directly applicable in all member states'.)

4.2.2   Directives.   These are addressed to a member state or states. They cannot be addressed to individuals ('individuals' includes natural and artificial legal persons). Directives do not normally have direct applicability, it is left up to individual states to bring them into effect as they wish. In the United Kingdom this may be done by Act of Parliament or statutory instrument.

Example

The Directive on Unfair Terms in Consumer Contracts (93/13) which was published in April 1993 and must be given effect to by 31 December 1994.

4.2.3   Decisions.   These may be addressed to member states and individuals and are only binding on those to whom they are addressed.

There are also recommendations and opinions, but these do not have binding force.

4.3   Direct effect

Because regulations apply directly, individuals may rely on rights created by them in their national courts. Directives and Treaty provisions do not normally create rights until they have been incorporated in national law, but they may be treated as having direct effect if they have not been brought into effect within the prescribed period. However, recent developments have shown that the doctrine of direct effect can now be used to give rights to individuals (see *Effect of Community law on English law* section 5.2 below).

Van Duyn v Home Office (1974)
In this case the ECJ said that a Council directive permitting free movement of persons which had not been implemented in UK law could have direct effect. The reasons given were that the wording was clear and nothing needed to be done to implement it.

5   Effect of Community law on English law

5.1   Sovereignty

By joining the European Community the United Kingdom, along with the other member states has had to give up some of its sovereignty. The Union has power to pass laws on matters covered by the Treaties but the United Kingdom is still sovereign as regards matters of a purely domestic nature. There is no express provision in the Treaties dealing with the question of supremacy between Community and national law. Art 5 of the EC Treaty merely imposes an obligation on member states to adopt measures to follow their obligations under the Treaties. The ECJ has made its view clear in a number of cases.

Costa v *ENEL* (1964)

In this case the question arose whether an Italian statute passed after the Treaties took precedence over the Treaties. The ECJ said that Community law prevailed, whether the statute was passed before or after the Treaties.

The problem faced by the United Kingdom courts is that the Treaties do not have direct applicability in English law, but have to be given effect by Act of Parliament. The European Communities Act 1972 gives effect to the Treaties. This contrasts with countries whose constitution provides that international treaties take precedence over national law. Any Act of Parliament before 1972 would be overruled by the EC Act, but any later Act would take precedence.

In *Shields* v *Coomes Ltd* (1979) Lord Denning said that if there were any inconsistencies between English law and Community law, then Community law should prevail. But he added, that if Parliament deliberately passed an Act to contradict Community law, the courts would have to follow that Act.

5.2   Precedence of Community law

The problem of precedence arose in the following case.

R v *S of S for Transport ex p Factortame Ltd* (1990)

Under the Merchant Shipping Act 1988 the Secretary of State made regulations that fishing boats on the British register had to be 75 per cent British owned. The Spanish applicants claimed that the regulations contravened Article 52 of the (now) EC Treaty because they discriminated against other EC nationals. The House of Lords asked the ECJ for a preliminary ruling on whether a national court had to provide a remedy to protect rights with direct effect, if a party would suffer irreparable damage. The Spanish applicants would suffer financial damage if they could not use their boats.

The ECJ, giving a preliminary ruling said that in the circumstances the national court did have to set aside such a national law. When the case was referred back to the House of Lords, they ruled that a court should not set aside a law unless the challenge to it was a strong one. In this case it was, so the Act could be set aside.

The final ruling on the substantive question was given in *R* v *S of S for Transport ex p Factortame Ltd* (1991). The ECJ said, that in making rules for registration, a member state must comply with Community law. The Merchant Shipping Act 1988 was discriminatory on the grounds of nationality and was in breach of Art 52 of the (now) EC Treaty.

The relevant sections of the Merchant Shipping Act 1988 had been suspended but the Merchant Shipping (Registration etc.) Act 1993 now repeals those sections and provides for a new system of registration. The Spanish owners of the fishing boats have started an action for damages in the High Court. The *Factortame* case gave a right to relief against a national law which contravened Community law. The legal effects of unimplemented directives were considered in the following cases.

Marleasing v La Comercial (1990)

M claimed that the memorandum of La Comercial was a nullity under Spanish law because it had no legal purpose. La Comercial argued that the first Company Law Directive did not give lack of legal purpose as a ground for nullity. Spain had not implemented this directive, even though the date to do so had passed. The ECJ said that a private party could rely on an unimplemented directive against a member state if it was precise enough, but not against another private party (as here). However, national courts had to interpret national law in the light of the words and aims of the directive. The Spanish court was obliged to interpret Spanish law to conform with the directive, so that La Comercial's memorandum could not be a nullity.

The effect is that the directive gives rights to individuals through interpretation by the court as national law.

Francovich v Republic of Italy (1991)

An Italian company went into liquidation, owing Francovich wages. A 1980 directive required member states to have a compensation scheme for such employees but Italy had not implemented this. Francovich sued the Italian state for compensation. The ECJ held: (a) this directive did not make it clear the state had to pay compensation and so it could not have direct effect; (b) with a breach of Art 189 there was a right to compensation if three conditions were met:

    (i)   the directive gives rights to individuals;
    (ii)   the content of those rights is clear from the directive;
    (iii) there is a 'causal link' between the breach by the state and the damage suffered by the individual.

These conditions were met in this case and Francovich was entitled to compensation from the state.

This is a significant decision as it makes the state liable in damages for failure to implement Community law, if the above conditions are met.

The effect of Community law on member states has been gradual and mainly in areas like agriculture, trade, transport, company and competition laws and free movement of labour, services and capital. The Treaty on European Union has extended the areas in which the European Union is involved to include environmental, health, research and technology, employment, education, training and consumer matters. In spite of the United Kingdom being able to 'opt out' of the social chapter and the principle of subsidiarity, the influence of Community law will extend into these new areas and the European Union will move towards closer integration. Although under the theory of Parliamentary supremacy, Parliament could pass another Act overriding the European Communities Act 1972, the reality is that the law of the European Union now prevails.

LEGAL PERSONALITY

1 Introduction

This section looks at the concept of legal personality, i.e., who the law recognises as a person and the legal consequences of this, as regards rights. It will examine the importance for the legal system of knowing who is a legal person and the extent of their rights. There are many contemporary legal and ethical problems in this area, some of which will be briefly explored.

The law is a set of rules regulating the relationships between people in society. Those rules create both rights and duties. The question then arises as to who is entitled to claim such rights and duties? To answer this another legal concept needs to be examined, that of legal personality.

Who does the law regard as a legal 'person'? The law recognises two types of legal person, natural persons and artificial persons.

2 Natural persons

This includes all human beings. Although this seems relatively straightforward, it poses difficulties in determining when life begins and when it ends.

2.1 Life

Life begins when the child has emerged from the womb and has an independent existence from the mother. The problem of whether an unborn child has a legal personality arose in the case concerning the drug thalidomide. Pregnant women who had taken the drug thalidomide later gave birth to deformed children; but the point concerning the legal personality of an unborn child was not settled as an out of court settlement was made.

The Congenital Disabilities (Civil Liability)Act 1976 gave a right of action to a child who is born disabled because of prenatal injuries caused through negligence.

C v S and Others (1987)
S was a pregnant single woman who had been advised to have an abortion. The father sought an injunction against S and the health authority, to stop the abortion. The court held that, on the evidence, the foetus was incapable of breathing and could not be born alive, thus the abortion was not an offence under the Infant Life (Preservation) Act 1929. Therefore the woman could have an abortion. The importance of this case is that the father had to bring the action because the foetus had no legal personality.

A similar problem arose in the following case, with a rather different result. Note that the CD(CL) Act 1976 did not apply.

B v Islington Health Authority (1991)
The defendants operated on the plaintiff's mother in September 1966, when she was pregnant. The plaintiff was subsequently born in April 1967 with numerous abnormalities

and later claimed that the defendants had been negligent in operating, without checking if the mother was pregnant. The defendants argued that the plaintiff was an embryo at the time and had no legal status to sue. The court held that the person injured by the negligence did not have to have legal rights at the time of the negligent act. The plaintiff acquired legal rights at birth and could sue for injuries caused before birth. The defendants ought to have foreseen an operation would damage the embryo, and they were liable.

2.2   Death

Although at common law, death ended claims by or against the deceased, statute now generally allows claims by or against the estate.

A dead person has limited legal rights, like the right to have their property disposed of according to their will. A problem the law does have to tackle, however, is deciding when death occurs. There is no legal definition of death and if there was, it would be quickly overtaken by advances in technology. The medical profession has adopted the concept of 'brain death'. When there is no activity in the brain stem, a person can be certified as dead by two doctors. This may happen even if the body can be kept functioning by artificial means.

R v *Malcherek, R* v *Steel* (1981)
In both cases the victims had been attacked and so seriously injured that they had to be put on life support machines. These machines were later switched off and the question arose as to what had caused their death? Was it the original acts of the attackers or that of the doctors in switching off the machines? This question is examined in Chapter 3, Criminal Law. For present purposes, the cases are important for the acceptance by the trial judge in *Malcherek* that, once brain death is established, a person is dead for the purposes of the law of homicide, even though the heart still beats. (See Homicide section 1.3.2.)

2.3   Associated problems

Difficulties arise over the question of abortion, particularly at what stage in the development of the foetus the abortion should be performed. The legal time limit is the 24th week of gestation (Human Fertilisation and Embryology Act 1990).

The problems of sex changes were considered in the following case.

Cossey v UK (1990)
Cossey was born a male but had undergone a sex change operation before working as a female model. Cossey then 'married' Mr X, but the High Court declared the marriage void because the parties were not male and female. The case was then referred to the European Court of Human Rights, claiming a breach of Article 8 of the Convention that everyone has the right to 'respect' for their private and family life. Because the UK would not issue a new birth certificate showing Cossey as female, she had to disclose personal details whenever she needed to show a certificate. The court held that to maintain the secrecy of such a change, the UK would have to alter the present system of public access to the register but as it did not have to do this its action was not a breach of Article 8.

2.4 Status

All natural persons do not have the same rights and duties. Some classes of person are restricted or protected by the law.

(a) Minors, who are persons under 18 years old, cannot make valid contracts except for necessaries or contracts of employment for their benefit, neither can they own land in their own name or make a will.

(b) Persons under 16 years of age cannot marry.

(c) Persons of unsound mind cannot be convicted of a criminal offence.

(d) Anyone who cannot pay their debts and who is made bankrupt under the Insolvency Act 1986 cannot borrow more than £250, without declaring that they are a bankrupt, nor can they act as directors of a company, without permission of the court.

(e) Aliens (i.e., foreign nationals living in this country) cannot vote at elections or become Members of Parliament. (But see European Community Law section 1.4 above.)

3 Artificial persons

The law recognises artificial persons as having legal personality. They are known as corporations and there are two types of them, i.e., corporations sole and corporations aggregate.

3.1 Corporations sole

A corporation sole is one person who holds an office of some kind. Examples include Bishops of the Church of England, and the Crown. On the death of the holder the office still continues.

3.2 Corporations aggregate

These consist of more than one person, and examples include companies and local authorities. In the nineteenth century the development of large industries, particularly the railways, required investment on a grand scale, but people were reluctant to put money into risky ventures if they could be made fully liable for debts. The idea of the limited liability company solved the problem as investors were only liable for the amount of money they invested. Limited liability companies are classed as corporations aggregate.

Such corporations could be formed through Royal Charter, Act of Parliament or under the Companies Acts. The vast majority are now created under the Companies Acts, which require registration with the Company Registrar and the submission of an annual report. This has also become a way of controlling the activities of such organisations.

3.3 Corporations and unincorporated associations

The contrast is made between corporations (bodies which have been incorporated) and unincorporated associations (groups which have not been incorporated). The latter are groups of people who are following a common purpose, whether this be a business or recreation. They do not have a separate legal personality like a corporation (see 4.1.1

below). The law treats them as individuals in the normal way. The result is that such organisations face a number of difficulties, including who is responsible for running the organisation: this will normally be a group of people, for example, a tennis club committee. Further, all the individual members are legally liable for the acts of the organisation.

Example

Partnerships, trade unions, sports clubs. It should be noted, however, that a trade union is something of an anomaly as it can sue in its own name.

4 Implications of being a corporation

There are many advantages for individuals in forming a company to run a business but it creates problems of control for the legal system.

4.1   Advantages

4.1.1   Separate legal personality.   Once a corporation has been formed, it is a separate person, distinct from the people who formed it. The classic example is to be found in the following case.

***Salomon v Salomon & Co. Ltd* (1897)**
Salomon ran a cobbler's business and decided to form a company with his family. He sold the business to the company in return for shares. Salomon owned 99 per cent of the shares. Later the company got into financial difficulties. The liquidator claimed that Salomon should pay the debts of the company because really he and the company were the same person. The House of Lords held, that the company had been properly formed and was a separate person from Salomon. Salomon was not liable for the debts, the company, Salomon & Co. Ltd, was so liable.

4.1.2   Limited liability.   The members are not liable for the debts of the corporation, see *Salomon* above. They are only liable for the price of their shares in the company. If they have paid for their shares in full, they are not liable if the company gets into debt. It is possible to have corporations with unlimited liability, but these are rare.

4.1.3   Perpetual succession.   A corporation cannot die and will continue until it is wound up. If the members die this does not affect it, as long as there are at least two members left.

4.1.4   Ability to act in own name.   Companies can sue people and be sued in their own name. This is more straightforward than some unincorporated bodies, who normally have to sue and be sued through committees.

4.1.5   Own land.   They can own land in the corporate name. This is a great advantage over unincorporated associations, who have to own property through a trust.

4.2   Some problems with corporations

4.2.1   Ultra vires.   The term *ultra vires* means 'beyond the powers'. It is used in a number of areas of law. In relation to companies it means that a company cannot do anything outside the powers it has been given in its 'objects clause'. This is found in the Memorandum of Association which is sent to the Registrar when the company is formed. Problems arose if people made a contract with a company which acted outside its powers. Such an act was *ultra vires* and void, which meant the company was not bound by the contract. The Prentice Report in 1985 suggested abolishing the *ultra vires* rule and the Companies Act 1989 has effectively abolished the rule for those dealing with the company (outsiders), but the members can still bring proceedings to stop an *ultra vires* act by the company. The Companies Act 1989, s. 110 states that it is sufficient for the memorandum to state that the object of the company is to carry on a business as a general commercial company. This will allow the company:

(a) to carry on any trade or business; and
(b) to do anything incidental or conducive to carrying on a business.

It remains to be seen how far companies will adopt this provision.

If the company has already done an *ultra vires* act, then even the members cannot change this.

4.2.2 The corporate veil. Because a company has a separate legal personality from its members, an outsider cannot sue the members directly, but must sue the company. The same applies to companies in a group, i.e. the outsider must sue the group and not the individual companies.

Sometimes the courts have been prepared to 'lift the corporate veil', for example, if there has been fraud. In such a case, the courts go behind the legal personality of the company and let the members be sued.

Adams v Cape Industries PLC (1990)
The defendants headed a group of companies which mined asbestos and sold it throughout the world. Employees in America sued the company, who allowed judgment to be given against them in the American courts because they had no assets in America. The plaintiffs then tried to get the English courts to enforce the judgment, as other companies in the group had assets here. The court held that the business of a subsidiary company was not the defendants' business. The court could not disregard the principle in *Salomon* and lift the veil to make the defendants liable. The defendants had a right to use the law so that liability would be on another company in the group, and therefore the defendants were not liable.

4.2.3 Criminal liability. It is well established that a company may be vicariously (i.e., 'in place of') liable for torts which are also criminal offences committed by its employees in the course of employment: *Lloyd* v *Grace, Smith & Co.* (1912). But can a company be made liable in criminal law for the acts of its employees? If the offence is one of strict liability, there is no need to prove fault and the company can be convicted, even though it must do the act through human agents. But if the offence required *mens rea* (guilty mind) the difficulty was how to prove that the company had the necessary intention. A number of successful prosecutions of companies took place in the 1940s for offences like tax evasion.

Tesco Supermarkets Ltd v Nattrass (1972)
Tesco were prosecuted under the Trade Descriptions Act 1968 for selling washing powder at a different price from that marked. They put forward as a defence the fact that the act

was done by another person, the store manager and not the company. It was held that the manager was a separate person from the company, therefore Tesco were not guilty.

The case is important for approving an earlier case in which Lord Denning had compared a company to a human body, saying that it had a 'directing mind', i.e., the directors and managers. If they can be shown to have *mens rea*, then the company can be convicted.

Following the Zeebrugge Ferry disaster, a prosecution was brought in 1990 against P & O Ferries Ltd for manslaughter. To establish the company's guilt, the prosecution had to prove that one of the directors had the necessary *mens rea*. As this was unlikely to be proved, the judge directed that the prosecution case should be ended.

With other disasters, e.g. Piper Alpha (oil rig), the Marchioness (pleasure boat), the canoeing accident in Dorset in March 1993 and deaths at work, e.g. Denis Clarke who died from fumes from a cleaning agent in Dudley in 1992, the feeling is that justice is not being done. There is a growing demand for manslaughter charges to be brought against companies for grossly negligent acts. The company which organised the canoeing, Active Learning and Leisure Limited, has been charged with manslaughter and if the test of 'directing mind' was widened, such prosecutions would have a greater chance of success.

THE REDRESS OF GRIEVANCES

1   Introduction

When people talk about the courts, it will invariably be about the criminal courts, perhaps as a result of a case highlighted in the media. The impression given by the media is usually exciting, e.g., the cut and thrust of cross-examination, the accused cracking and admitting guilt, the sensational jury verdict and the sentence of life imprisonment. The reality, as anyone who has sat through a case will know, is generally rather different. Court business progresses slowly, if not boringly. One reason for this is the nature of court proceedings, based on oral argument and evidence, which all takes time.

The distinction between criminal and civil law was noted in *Classification of Law,* section 3, above. This distinction is to some extent mirrored in the court structure. The distinction is not, however, watertight and there are a number of discrepancies, due to the haphazard development of the courts. There is also a difference between courts of first instance or trial courts and those which hear appeals. Again, these are not watertight categories, for example the Crown Court acts both as a trial court and as an appeal court. The main trial courts in criminal cases are magistrates' courts and the Crown Court. In civil cases the trial courts are county courts and the High Court.

The main aim of providing a system for settling grievances, whether in criminal or civil law, is to stop people taking matters into their own hands. The State therefore provides ways for disputes to be settled in a relatively civilised manner. The State itself takes the leading role in criminal matters through the Crown Prosecution Service. In civil cases the State provides the mechanisms for people to use. The present century has seen the development of alternatives to the courts like tribunals, arbitration, conciliation and the Ombudsmen, perhaps tending to show that the courts are not always the best place to settle disputes. The Civil Justice Review highlighted problems in the civil courts and the Royal Commission on Criminal Justice has identified problems in the criminal courts and put forward a range of recommendations, such as the defendant losing the right to choose trial by jury in either way offences, and the abolition of committal proceedings. The launch of the Courts Charter in 1991 sets standards of service the public can expect from court staff. The court system has always had problems, because as soon as procedures are set up they become bureaucratic and cumbersome. The challenge faced by the courts is to be constantly receptive to change and to meet the needs of society, which is after all their purpose.

2 The court system

2.1 The criminal courts

These are the magistrates' courts, the Crown Court, the Court of Appeal (Criminal Division) and the House of Lords.

2.1.1 Magistrates' courts.

These are governed mainly by the Magistrates' Courts Act 1980. A magistrates' court may consist of between two and seven magistrates; usually it is three. They make decisions by a majority. Magistrates were originally known as Justices of the Peace (JPs). These courts are administered locally and do not come under the control of the Lord Chancellor like other courts. There are two types of magistrates.

(a) Lay magistrates.

On 1 January 1994 there were 30,054 lay magistrates. They are appointed by the Lord Chancellor on the advice of local advisory committees from each county. These committees are appointed by the Lord Chancellor. Many appointments of magistrates are related to political affiliations. In recent years advertisements have been put in the press to encourage people to apply, in an attempt to get more young people, women and those from ethnic minorities to become lay magistrates.

Lay magistrates are not legally qualified and do not get paid, although they can claim loss of earnings and expenses. They must live within 15 miles of the court in which they sit and at 70 years of age they are put on the 'supplemental list' and carry out limited functions. They receive approximately one week's training, supplemented by occasional weekends and sessions in court. Training is now under the supervision of the Judicial Studies Board.

Magistrates sit for approximately 15 days a year. They are assisted by the Clerk of the Court, who has had legal training, and who advises them on law and procedure. The powers of magistrates are limited. They can impose a sentence of up to six months' imprisonment and/or a fine of £5,000. If there are two or more offences, they can impose 12 months' imprisonment.

There are special magistrates' courts, youth courts, which deal with those under 18 years of age (Criminal Justice Act 1991, s. 70 (formerly known as juvenile courts)). The magistrates are from a special panel and there must be at least one man and one woman on the bench. They must retire at 65 years of age. The public are not allowed to attend the hearings of a youth court and there are restrictions on press reporting.

(b)   Stipendiary magistrates.

These are qualified barristers or solicitors, of at least seven years' standing. They are full-time and are paid a salary. There are about 80 stipendiaries, many of whom are based in London, with the remainder in large cities such as Liverpool. Only one sits to deal with cases and they have the same powers as a 'bench' of lay magistrates. They can usually dispose of cases more quickly.

Before looking at the work of magistrates' courts, it is worth briefly mentioning that criminal offences may be put in three categories:

(a)   summary offences which are minor offences which may only be tried by magistrates;

(b)   either way offences which may be tried by magistrates' courts or the Crown Court;

(c)   indictable offences which may only be tried by the Crown Court.

The two main functions of magistrates' courts are:

(a)   Preliminary investigation.

Virtually all serious criminal cases have to be brought before the magistrates, to determine whether there is sufficient evidence against the accused person. These proceedings are known as 'committal proceedings'. The case is then sent to the Crown Court for trial.

Example

Murder.

If the defendant has been charged with sexual or violent offences involving children, then before the magistrates investigate, the Director of Public Prosecutions can transfer the case to a Crown Court with live television links (Criminal Justice Act 1991, s. 53).

(b)   Trial.

Even though the magistrates are at the bottom of the hierarchy and they are not professionals, their importance must not be underestimated. They actually deal with 97 per cent of all criminal offences. They try summary offences and most of those in the 'either way' category. With the latter offences, if the magistrates think it suitable for trial in the Crown Court, they will send it to the Crown Court. They must hear representations from the prosecution and defence before doing so. If they think it suitable for summary trial they must tell the accused that he has the choice of mode of trial. They must also tell him that the magistrates can send him to the Crown Court for sentence.

Example

Theft is an either way offence.

Magistrates have other functions, which include granting bail, issuing warrants for arrest, and making criminal supervision orders over children under 17 years of age under the Children Act 1989.

2.1.2   The Crown Court.   The Crown Court was created by the Courts Act 1971 to replace the Assizes and Quarter Sessions. The court is now governed by the Supreme Court Act 1981. The jurisdiction of the Crown Court is not local, it may sit anywhere in the country. The Supreme Court Act 1981, s. 78, states:

> Any Crown Court business may be conducted at any place in England and Wales, and sittings of the Crown Court may be continuous or intermittent or occasional.

There are currently about 90 Crown Court centres. The judges in the Crown Court may be High Court judges, circuit judges or Recorders.

The main work of the court is to try indictable offences and those either way offences sent up by the magistrates' courts. It may also deal with summary offences if they are linked to trial on indictment (CJA 1988). It also hears appeals from the magistrates and cases sent for sentencing. In 1992 the Crown Court dealt with 100,742 cases.

Offences are divided into four classes, depending on their seriousness, and this will determine which classification of judge can try them. The most serious offences, like murder and treason, will generally be tried by a High Court judge. Usually one judge sits, with a jury of 12.

In 1956 Lord Devlin remarked that juries were 'male, middle-aged, middle-minded and middle class'. The intervening years have seen perennial complaints about juries and some tinkering with the system. A problem at one time was jury vetting, the procedure by which the prosecution could obtain evidence about the background of jurors, to see if they were 'suitable' for the case, i.e., likely to favour the prosecution!

The right of the defence to challenge jurors (i.e., to stop them taking their place in the jury box) was being abused in some instances mainly to produce juries favourable to the defence. This right of 'peremptory challenge' was abolished by the Criminal Justice Act 1988. Now any challenge by the defence must be based on a reason (cause), for example, that the juror knows the defendant. The proposal to stop jury trial in minor theft cases was dropped after a public outcry. The Roskill Committee recommended in 1986 that the jury should be replaced in fraud trials, because jurors would have difficulties following the evidence. Another complaint was that juries did not reflect the racial balance of the population. Cases showed that judges had varying views as to whether juries should reflect this. Juries have also been criticised for bringing in perverse verdicts against the evidence.

Since 1967 juries have been able to give majority verdicts of ten to two, if they have deliberated for at least two hours. If they cannot reach agreement, a new trial may be ordered. Suggestions have been made to give juries more help with written documentation and to have panels of trained jurors.

All the complaints about juries should be seen in the light of their function in criminal trials, i.e., to decide questions of fact such as, is the defendant telling the truth? Do jurors need legal knowledge or training to do that? Even in complex cases juries are still making that basic judgment. The influence of the judge must also be remembered. At the end of the prosecution evidence on a submission by the defence of no case to answer, the judge may direct the jury to acquit. The judge can also influence the jury in his summing up at the end of the trial and they must take directions on the law from the judge.

Assessing the value of juries is difficult because they do not give reasons for their decision. Further, the Contempt of Court Act 1981 makes it an offence to obtain or disclose anything said by jurors in the jury room. Attempts to study how juries work have been made by using shadow juries. They sit in on a real case and then make a decision, under observation. Such studies have generally been in favour of juries. The strength of the jury lies in the group nature of its decision making, which enables a balanced view to be taken and its role in providing lay participation in the legal system, which gives the system public credibility.

In June 1991 the trial took place of Pat Pottle and Michael Randle, who were charged with helping the spy George Blake to escape from prison in 1966, after he had been sentenced to 42 years' imprisonment. They defended themselves and, although they admitted the charge, told the jury they were right to break the law and reminded the jury of the refusal of nineteenth century juries to convict of sheep stealing, when it was a capital offence. This did the trick and they were found not guilty.

Lord Devlin in 'The Conscience of the Jury', (1991), *LQR* vol. 107, p. 398 (at p. 403), says that such perverse verdicts are '. . . a struggle between what the law demands and what conscience urges'.

Juries are only used for indictable offences where a 'not guilty' plea is made and in 1992 defendants pleaded 'guilty' in 69 per cent of Crown Court cases, so juries are the exception rather than the rule.

Among the proposals from the Royal Commission on Criminal Justice were removing the right to jury trial in either way offences; giving documents to the jury in complex cases and in exceptional cases allowing either side to select a jury with up to three people from ethnic minorities. A watch should be kept for any development of these proposals.

2.1.3 The Court of Appeal (Criminal Division). The Supreme Court Act 1981 governs this court and provides that the Supreme Court consists of the Court of Appeal, the High Court and the Crown Court. The head of the Criminal Division is the Lord Chief Justice and the judges are known as Lords Justices of Appeal. Normally three will hear an appeal, and they may be assisted by High Court judges. They hear appeals from the Crown Court and courts-martial, and appeals may be against conviction or sentence. In 1992 there were 7,077 appeals registered.

2.1.4 House of Lords. When the House of Lords sits as a court, only Lords of Appeal in Ordinary, known as the Law Lords, may sit. Normally five will hear an appeal, which in criminal matters is on a point of law only, and their decision is by a majority. The appeals are not heard in the main chamber of the House of Lords but in a committee room. They hear appeals from:

(a)   the Court of Appeal, with leave of the Court of Appeal or the House of Lords;
(b)   in some cases the High Court direct;
(c)   civil cases from Scotland.

In 1992 of 96 appeals entered, 12 were from the Criminal Division of the Court of Appeal.

It should be noted that the House of Lords 'hands down an opinion', it does not 'give a judgment'.

2.2 The civil courts

2.2.1 Magistrates' courts. So far as the civil law is concerned, magistrates are mainly concerned with family matters when they sit as family proceedings courts. There must be at least one man and one woman on the bench and they are selected from a 'family panel', who have had special training. They can make maintenance, adoption, personal protection and exclusion orders. Magistrates also deal with the recovery of debts in respect of income tax, national insurance, council tax, the supply of water, gas and electricity; and they grant licences for selling alcohol and betting.

2.2.2 The county courts. They were first set up in 1846 but are now governed by the County Courts Act 1984, as amended by the Courts and Legal Services Act 1990. There are 270 county courts all of which deal with the following matters:–

   (a)   claims in contract and tort;
   (b)   claims for the recovery of land;
   (c)   matters about equity and trusts and contested (i.e., disputed) probate matters.

Some county courts also hear:

   (d)   admiralty matters;
   (e)   divorce matters: which include residence of children, maintenance, domestic violence, adoption;
   (f)   bankruptcy and insolvency;
   (g)   claims under the Race Relations Act 1976.

In 1992 3,741,804 cases were started in the county courts.

The High Court and County Courts Jurisdiction Order 1991, made under the CLSA 1990, made new arrangements for the distribution of proceedings between the High Court and county courts. It did not affect family or admiralty matters. The Civil Justice Review had said that too many unsuitable cases were being brought in the High Court and were slowing down its work. The Order abolished financial limits on all claims to do with debt, personal injury and possession of land. For actions in equity and probate matters the claim must be for more than £30,000 for the action to be heard in the High Court.

Actions for less than £25,000 must normally be tried in the county courts. A transfer may be made taking the following factors into account:

   (a)   amount of the claim;
   (b)   whether the action is important for others who are not a party to the case, or for the public generally;
   (c)   complexity of facts or legal issues;
   (d)   would it achieve a speedier trial?

Actions for £50,000 or more must be tried in the High Court.

Actions for amounts between £25,000 and £50,000 may be dealt with in either court depending on certain factors. See also 2.2.3(a), below. County court judgments of £5,000 or more must be enforced in the High Court while judgments under £2,000 must be enforced in the county court. Amounts in between may be enforced in either court.

From 1 July 1991, the date when the 1991 Order came into force, the jurisdiction of district judges (formerly known as county court Registrars) is £5,000 for general trial jurisdiction and plaintiffs may issue proceedings in any county court, there no longer being a need for some connection through residence or the place where the matter arose. Under CLSA 1990, s. 9, the Lord Chancellor may give directions in family proceedings that cases be allocated to specified judges. This will enable some judges to specialise in such matters. There are over 150 statutes which give the county courts exclusive jurisdiction, for example, the Consumer Credit Act 1974.

2.2.3 The High Court.   The High Court may sit anywhere in England and Wales. Most business is conducted in London but there are about 25 regional centres. The High Court is divided into three divisions, the Queen's Bench Division, the Family Division and the Chancery Division. At the end of 1993 there were 95 High Court judges, most of whom were attached to the Queen's Bench Division.

The vast majority of civil cases are heard by a single judge. However, before 1854 most civil cases in the common law courts had to be tried before a jury. Acts of Parliament limited this right and the position is now governed by the Supreme Court Act 1981, s. 69. This gives a right to jury trial in cases of libel, slander, malicious prosecution and fraud, although this right can be refused if the trial involves the prolonged examination of documents. In all other cases the judge has a discretion to allow jury trial. In *Ward* v *James* (1966), which concerned a negligence claim arising from a car accident, Lord Denning said that trial by a single judge was more acceptable. The reasons were that judges were better able to assess the level of damages and their judgments provided uniformity and predictability.

H v *Ministry of Defence* (1991)
The plaintiff was a soldier who had Perone's disease, a curvature of the penis which made intercourse difficult. As a result of tests the penis became infected and an operation was needed, and during the operation it became necessary to amputate it. The plaintiff suffered psychological damage and now applied for trial by jury. It was held that justice required a consistent approach and juries were not suitable for deciding conventional scales of damages. Although the injuries were unusual, the same could be said of other cases of mutilation, or of quadriplegia. There had not been a jury trial in a personal injuries action for over 25 years. Trial by a judge was ordered.

Awards by juries in defamation cases have included initially £600,000 to Sonia Sutcliffe and £1.5 million to Lord Aldington. The Courts and Legal Services Act 1990, s. 8, provides that the Court of Appeal has power to order a new trial where the damages awarded are excessive, or to substitute a sum which is proper. Esther Rantzen was awarded £250,000 damages by a jury, following a newspaper article which claimed she had not told a school about a teacher she knew was a pervert. The Court of Appeal exercised its power under s. 8 to substitute an amount of £110,000 (*Rantzen* v *Mirror Group Newspapers* (1993)).

(a) Queen's Bench Division.

The main work of this division is actions in contract and tort, but there is also a Commercial Court and an Admiralty Court. The QBD hears appeals in criminal matters, on a point of law from magistrates' courts and the Crown Court. It exercises supervision over inferior courts by means of the prerogative orders of certiorari, mandamus and prohibition, to ensure that they do not exceed their powers. This division administers the Official Referees who hear cases involving technical matters.

The QBD issued a *Practice Direction* in June 1991 to take effect from 1 July 1991 as regards transfer of proceedings to the county court. All cases will be reviewed within seven days of being set down for trial, to see if they are suitable for transfer, taking into account matters specified in the Jurisdiction Order issued under the CLSA 1990. See also 2.2.2 above. The following types of case may be suitable for High Court trial: (1) professional negligence; (2) fatal accidents; (3) fraud or undue influence; (4) defamation; (5) malicious prosecution or false imprisonment; (6) claims against the police.

An action is started by the issue of a writ. In 1992 269,668 writs were issued and of these 51,927 were judgments by default, which means that there was no trial, just an order against the defendant. Only 6,481 cases were set down for trial, 4,381 fewer than in 1991, thus showing the effect of the new rules on place of trial. Under the CLSA 1990, s. 4, costs may be reduced by 25 per cent if an action should have been started in the county court. The court may also disallow 'wasted costs' if there have been unreasonable or negligent acts or even make the legal representative pay them!

(b) Family Division.

The Head of the Family Division is known as the President. The division deals with all matters concerning the family including some defended divorces, legitimacy, wardship, guardianship, residence, maintenance, adoption, domestic violence and other proceedings under the Children Act 1989. It also deals with uncontested probate matters.

(c) Chancery Division.

This comprises the Lord Chancellor, the Vice Chancellor and a number of High Court judges. Most business is dealt with in London, but there are eight regional centres. The division deals with sales of land; redemption of mortgages; trusts; contentious (disputed) probate actions; business matters including partnerships; revenue matters; bankruptcy; planning. The division includes the Companies Court and the Patents Court.

2.2.4   The Court of Appeal (Civil Division).   This hears appeals from the High Court, the county court and certain tribunals. Normally three judges will sit to hear an appeal. The number of appeals lodged in 1992 was 884.

2.2.5   The House of Lords.   As to the function of the House of Lords as an appellate court, see 2.1.4, above. It is to be noted, however, that in civil matters the appeal does not have to be on a point of law, although the majority are.

2.3   Other courts

2.3.1   The Judicial Committee of the Privy Council.   Originally part of the Privy Council, it was formally established by Act of Parliament in 1833. The judges are Law Lords and other Privy Councillors, who hold or have held high judicial office. Normally five sit to hear appeals by doctors from their disciplinary bodies, but it acts mainly as a final court of appeal from Commonwealth countries and dependent territories, dealing with between 50 and 70 cases each year. So far as the overseas jurisdiction is concerned, the Privy Council may still allow someone to be hanged, if their appeal is turned down. In *Pratt* v *Attorney General of Jamaica* (1993) the Privy Council granted Pratt's appeal against the death penalty, because allowing his execution after 14 years on 'death row' would have been inhuman.

2.3.2   The Restrictive Practices Court.   The court is made up of High Court judges and lay members and cases are heard by one judge and two other members. The court deals with applications under the Restrictive Trade Practices Act 1976 and the Fair Trading Act 1973.

2.3.3   Coroners' courts.   These courts are governed by the Coroners Act 1988. A coroner must have five years' experience as a barrister, solicitor or a medical practitioner. Coroners' courts investigate any violent, unnatural or suspicious deaths or sudden deaths without an obvious cause. A coroner has a discretion to summon a jury of between 7 and 11 people. In some cases, for example deaths in prison or police custody, a jury must be summoned. Inquests must normally be held in public. Coroners' courts also decide if items are treasure trove and therefore belong to the Crown.

3   Civil and criminal trials

This topic will be fully covered in the Practice section of the syllabus, so it is proposed to give only a brief outline here. Civil and criminal trials both follow the adversary system. This means that each side puts its case and the judge acts as a referee. This is in contrast to the inquisitorial system favoured in most European countries, under which the judge takes a leading role in the trial.

3.1   Criminal trials

The Prosecution of Offences Act 1985 established a national prosecution service. The police still make the initial decision to prosecute but the case is then passed to the Crown Prosecution Service (CPS). The police do not have to start a prosecution for every offence committed but have a discretion to caution someone instead. This will normally be used for minor offences or for those involving young persons.

There are two ways of starting a prosecution:

(a)   lay an information: this is done before the magistrates, setting out the alleged offence and they issue a summons, which is served on the defendant.

(b)   make a charge: this is usually used after someone has been arrested and taken to the police station. The charge is written down and the accused may then be detained or released on bail.

3.1.1   Summary trial.   If the offence is a summary one, or an either way offence to be tried summarily, it will go to the magistrates for trial. The defendant may plead guilty by post for any offence with a maximum sentence of three months but must inform the Clerk of the Court of this. A person cannot be imprisoned or banned from driving in his absence.

If the defendant does appear he may plead 'guilty' or 'not guilty'. The prosecution starts the case with a brief opening speech. Witnesses are called and they take an oath or affirm that they will tell the truth. The defence may then cross-examine them. At the end of the prosecution case, the defence may submit that there is no case to answer; essentially this is saying that the evidence does not amount to an offence. If this is not accepted the defence puts its case in the same manner as the prosecution has put its case. The magistrates then retire to consider their verdict. They must be sure that the defendant is guilty 'beyond all reasonable doubt'. If he is found guilty, then sentence is passed.

3.1.2 Trial on indictment. Serious offences will have been through committal proceedings in the magistrates' court, before being tried at the Crown Court, except for serious fraud cases which may go direct to the Crown Court. The indictment will state the offence(s) with which the defendant has been charged. This is read out at the start of the trial and if a 'not guilty' plea is made, the trial commences. A jury is selected from the jury panel by the Clerk of the Court. The prosecution begins the case with an opening speech and then calls witnesses. At the end of the prosecution case the defence may submit that there is no case to answer. If this submission is dismissed the defence may then present its case and each side makes a closing speech, the defence last. The judge then gives his summing-up, in which he reviews the evidence and may direct the jury. If a guilty verdict is returned, then the judge will sentence the defendant. Before this, defence counsel will put the defendant's background, employment history, and domestic circumstances to the court, a social inquiry report may be given by the probation officer, and a plea in mitigation may be made by counsel.

3.2 Civil trials

3.2.1 County court. The person making the claim will ask the court to issue a summons. This is sent to the defendant and a plaint (statement of claim) is entered in the court records. The summons may be for:

(a) a fixed date action which involves more than payment of money, for example, a claim over land. A date is fixed at the start;
(b) a default action.

A pre-trial review will take place before a district judge to determine what issues are contested. At the trial each side puts its case and calls witnesses. They then make closing speeches. A trial is unusual. In 1992 3,741,804 plaints were issued but there were only 26,722 trials.

In default actions most judgments are entered by default. Either the defendant does not reply to the summons within 14 days or makes an offer to the plaintiff which is accepted. In 1992 86 per cent of the actions taken were default actions. There are various methods of enforcing judgments, the usual ones being a warrant of execution against the debtor's goods or an attachment of earnings order.

3.2.2 High Court. Proceedings are similar to the county court. They are started by the issue of a writ which is sealed in the court office. The writ must then be served on the defendant, by the plaintiff, within four months. It will normally contain a statement of claim which sets out the facts and the damages suffered. The defendant then serves a defence in reply. The next step is the summons for directions, which is the equivalent of the pre-trial review. The case is then set down for trial. Trial is by a single judge and each side puts its case and calls witnesses. In 1992 269,668 writs were issued in the QBD but there were only 2,691 judgments.

4 Appeals

4.1 Criminal cases

4.1.1 Appeals to the Crown Court. A person convicted in the magistrates' courts may appeal to the Crown Court as of right:

(a)   against sentence if they pleaded guilty;
(b)   against conviction and/or sentence if they pleaded not guilty.

They must give notice of appeal within 21 days of the magistrates' decision. The appeal will be heard by a circuit judge and between two and four magistrates. Appeal against conviction takes the form of a re-hearing of the case and both sides may call witnesses. If the Crown Court convicts it may impose any sentence which the magistrates could have imposed. On appeals against sentence, the Crown Court may impose any sentence the magistrates could have given.

4.1.2 Appeals to the High Court. Either the defence or the prosecution may ask the magistrates (or the Crown Court hearing an appeal from the magistrates) to state a case for the Divisional Court of the Queen's Bench Division, on the grounds that the decision of the court below is wrong in point of law or the court has acted in excess of its jurisdiction. This is an appeal by way of 'case stated'. The court below must then provide a statement of the facts, agreed by both parties and the question of law at issue. The appeal does not involve re-hearing the case, but is by examination of the written statements. The Divisional Court may reverse, affirm or amend the decision or remit the case to the magistrates with its opinion.

A further appeal is possible to the House of Lords, if the Divisional Court certifies that a point of law of public importance is involved and the Divisional Court or House of Lords gives leave.

4.1.3 Appeals to the Court of Appeal (Criminal Division). A person convicted in the Crown Court may appeal to the Court of Appeal (Criminal Division):

(a)   as of right on a point of law;
(b)   with leave of the Court of Appeal on a question of fact or mixed law and fact;
(c)   against sentence, with leave of the Court of Appeal or the judge who passed the sentence.

Alternatively a person may ask the Home Secretary to refer the case to the Court of Appeal. The Home Secretary also has power to refer a case without an application having been made to him. The Court of Appeal may allow an appeal against conviction if it:

(a) is unsafe or unsatisfactory;
(b) is wrong on a question of law;
(c) contains a material irregularity.

It may allow an appeal against sentence:

(a) if the sentence is wrong in principle;
(b) if the sentence is manifestly severe.

Under the Criminal Justice Act 1988 the Attorney General may refer the case to the Court of Appeal, with its leave, if the sentence is too lenient. The Court of Appeal may impose such sentence as it thinks appropriate.

The Court of Appeal examines the transcript of the case from the court below, to see if the trial was properly conducted, the evidence was rightly admitted and that the jury were properly directed on the law. The decision to convict will be set aside only if it is unsafe or unsatisfactory. Under the Criminal Appeal Act 1968, s. 2(1), even if the appeal would be decided in favour of the appellant, there is a proviso that the Court of Appeal may dismiss the appeal if it is satisfied that no miscarriage of justice has occurred. The prosecution cannot appeal. One of the recommendations made by the Royal Commission on Criminal Justice was to widen the ground for appeal, so that the court should consider whether the conviction 'is or may be unsafe'. In 1992 the Court of Appeal (Criminal Division) dealt with 2,157 appeals against conviction and sentence, of which nearly 60 per cent were successful.

4.1.4 Appeals to the House of Lords.   An appeal may be made from the Court of Appeal or a Divisional Court to the House of Lords. An appeal lies if the Court of Appeal or Divisional Court certifies that a point of law of general public importance is involved; and either the Court of Appeal or the Divisional Court or the House of Lords gives leave to appeal. In 1992 there were 12 appeals from the Court of Appeal (Criminal Division).

4.2 Civil appeals

4.2.1 Appeals to the High Court.   An appeal may be made from the magistrates by way of case stated, to a Divisional Court of the QBD. The court makes a decision based on the written evidence. The court also hears appeals from the Crown Court and certain tribunals. In family matters appeal from the magistrates' courts is to a Divisional Court of the Family Division. A Divisional Court of the Chancery Division hears appeals in bankruptcy and insolvency matters from the county courts. Further appeals may be made to the Court of Appeal and the House of Lords.

4.2.2 Appeals to the Court of Appeal (Civil Division).   From the county court an appeal may be made on law or fact, to the Court of Appeal. In some cases leave of the county court or Court of Appeal is needed. The decision is made on the basis of notes made at the trial. The Court of Appeal may affirm, vary or reverse the county court decision.

THE STRUCTURE OF THE CRIMINAL COURTS

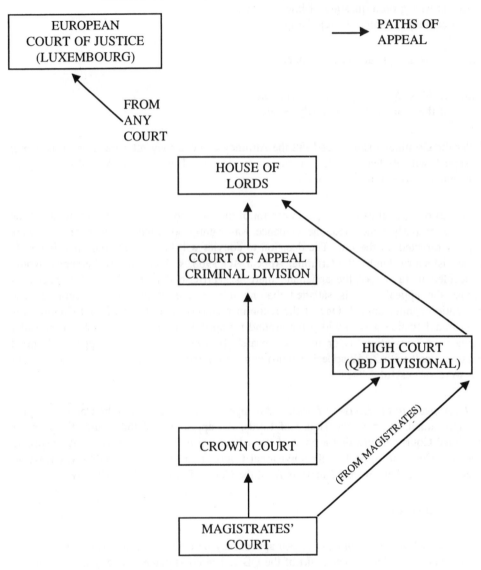

From the High Court there is an appeal, as of right, to the Court of Appeal. The application must be made within four weeks of judgment. The appeal is by way of a re-hearing, but this does not involve all the evidence again. The court will rarely upset the trial judge's finding of fact but they may order a new trial. In 1992 884 appeals were set down.

4.2.3 Appeals to the House of Lords.   If both parties consent and the House of Lords Appeal Committee gives its permission, an appeal may be made direct from the High Court to the House. This is known as a *leapfrog* appeal. In 1992 there were no such appeals.

An appeal may be made from the Court of Appeal on a point of law, with the permission of the Court of Appeal or the House of Lords. In 1992 58 appeals were entered and 73 appeals were determined but there were 72 appeals pending at the end of the year, so the House of Lords was still a year behind in its work!

THE STRUCTURE OF THE CIVIL COURTS

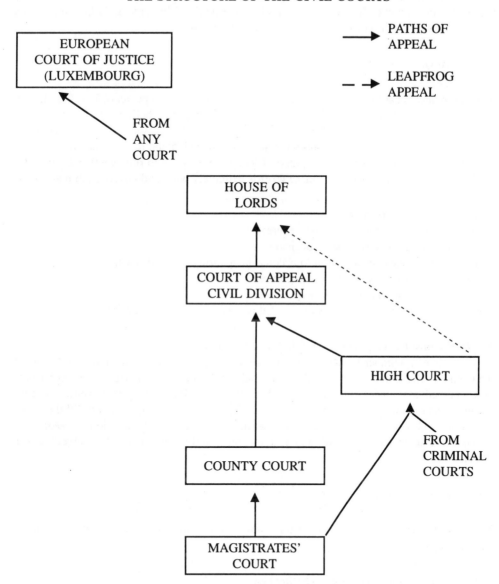

5 Judicial review

In a complex modern society many administrative decisions have to be made by central and local government. These decisions are often based on policy reasons and may affect a large section of society, for example, whether or not someone is entitled to a disability living allowance. However, if the decisions are made illegally or the correct procedure is not followed, then the courts can intervene. The individual affected may apply to a Divisional Court of the Queen's Bench Division for judicial review. This remedy is concerned with the legality of the decision-making *process*, as distinct from the *merits* of the decision. Under this process the court has the power to review the decisions of inferior courts, tribunals, Government Ministers and administrative bodies. This process is in contrast to a normal appeal, which will involve a re-hearing of the case.

5.1   Ultra vires

Judicial review is based on the doctrine of *ultra vires* (beyond the powers). This has already been explained in *Delegated Legislation*, 4.2 above. Any public body acting under powers given by Parliament must not act outside those powers. If it does, then it is said to act *ultra vires* and any such acts are void and have no legal effect. Judicial review may also be used for some acts under the Royal Prerogative. It is up to the courts to rule whether a particular act is *ultra vires* . The concept of *ultra vires* is extremely wide and covers such matters as:

(a)   the wrong person acting;
(b)   not following the correct procedure;
(c)   making the wrong type of decision;
(d)   taking irrelevant matters into account or ignoring relevant ones;
(e)   using powers for an improper purpose;
(f)   acting in an unreasonable way;
(g)   acting in bad faith. An example of this was seen in the following case.

R v Derbyshire CC ex p Times Supplements Ltd (1990)
The owners of a number of newspapers published a defamatory article about the leader of the Council. The Council then decided not to advertise in those newspapers. The applicants now claimed that under the Education Act 1986 the Council had to advertise teacher vacancies where they will be brought 'to the notice of persons . . . qualified to fill the post'. The court held that the general ban on advertising was not for any educational reason. The Council had acted with bad faith and vindictiveness and its decision not to advertise was quashed.

5.2   The rules of natural justice

The common law developed what became known as the 'rules of natural justice'. These are outlined below.

5.2.1   Everyone has a right to a fair hearing.

Ridge v Baldwin (1964)
The Chief Constable of Brighton was acquitted of charges of corruption. The Watch Committee (of the Council) had power to dismiss if they thought someone was unfit. They dismissed Ridge without giving details of the charges or notice of the meeting. The court held that the Committee had acted *ultra vires*. The Committee had to say what the charges were and give Ridge an opportunity to put his case.

5.2.2   No one can be judge in his own cause.

R v *Bristol Crown Court ex p Cooper* (1989)

The Crown Court dismissed a licensing appeal from the magistrates' court. A magistrate who had heard the case in the magistrates' court also heard the appeal. The court said that the test was whether a reasonable man, knowing that the magistrate had already rejected the application, might think that the magistrate was biased. It held, therefore, that judicial review would be granted.

In the past, courts have made a distinction between:

(a) *acting judicially*, i.e., like a court, when the rules of natural justice must be followed; and

(b) *acting administratively*, i.e., making a decision involving policy and having an element of discretion, when the rules need not be followed. In recent years, however, the courts have moved away from this distinction. In *Council of Civil Service Unions* v *Minister for the Civil Service* (1985) Lord Roskill stated that natural justice should be 'replaced by speaking of a duty to act fairly'. Thus the modern test is whether the particular body was acting fairly in all the circumstances.

5.3   Applying for the remedies

5.3.1   Application for review.   The procedure is governed by the Supreme Court Act 1981, s. 31. The first stage is that permission must be obtained to apply for judicial review, usually from a single judge. The aim of this is to see that claims are genuine. The second stage is the application for judicial review. The applicant may ask for an order of certiorari, prohibition or mandamus, or a declaration or injunction. The court may award any combination which is appropriate and award damages. The orders are available only in the case of the exercise of public power. Matters of private law like contract and tort are not covered.

R v *Jockey Club ex parte Aga Khan* (1992)

The Aga Khan, as a racehorse owner, had to register with the Jockey Club, which controls racing in Great Britain. By registering he agreed to follow the rules of the Jockey Club. In 1989 one of his horses won a race but a prohibited substance was found in a urine sample and, following a Jockey Club enquiry, the horse was disqualified. The Aga Khan argued that the Jockey Club was exercising a public function in controlling horse racing and sought judicial review of its decision, claiming it was damaging to his reputation. The Court of Appeal held that judicial review was not available as the Aga Khan had a contract with the Jockey Club and could pursue a remedy in private law.

5.3.2   Time limits.   The Supreme Court Act 1981, s. 31(6), provides that the court may refuse an application for review on the ground of undue delay, if granting a review would cause substantial hardship or substantially prejudice a person's rights or be detrimental to good administration. This must be read along with Order 53, Rule 4 of the Supreme Court Rules which provides that an application must be brought promptly and in any event within three months from when grounds arose. The courts use these powers to stop cases being re-opened after a period of time, especially if people's rights would be affected or it would lead to a flood of similar applications. It is possible for an application to be refused within the three month period if there has been undue delay.

5.3.3   Standing (locus standi).   The Supreme Court Act 1981 provides that judicial review is only available if a person has sufficient interest in the matter. This does not necessarily mean that their legal rights are affected.

R v *Secretary of State for the Environment ex p Rose Theatre Trust* (1990)
A group of people (RTT) tried to get the Secretary of State to use his powers to make the site of an Elizabethan theatre in London an ancient monument, to stop building on the site. The Secretary of State refused and the group claimed judicial review of this refusal. The court held that RTT did not have sufficient standing and the application was refused. The court said that the function of review was to provide redress for individual grievances and no one could show this here.

5.4   The prerogative orders

These are certiorari, prohibition and mandamus.

5.4.1   Certiorari.   This is used to quash the decisions of inferior courts, Ministers etc. It is then up to the body concerned to reconsider the matter. It may be used if a body has acted *ultra vires* or in breach of the duty to act fairly.

5.4.2   Prohibition.   This is granted to stop a body exceeding its jurisdiction. It cannot be used if the final decision has been made. It may be obtained if a local authority is going to act *ultra vires*. Failure to obey is contempt of court.

5.4.3   Mandamus.   An order telling a body to carry out a public duty. Failure to obey it is contempt of court. It may, for example, be used to make a local authority carry out a duty such as making by-laws.

5.5   Prerogative writ

The court may also issue the writ of *habeas corpus* (produce the body). This is used to obtain the release of someone who has been unlawfully detained, for example wrongfully arrested.

5.6   Non-prerogative orders

5.6.1   Declaration.   This is simply asking the court to make a ruling on what the law is. It is used in both public and private law and is available in wider circumstances than the prerogative orders.

Gillick v *West Norfolk Health Authority* (1986)
In this case it was used to determine the lawfulness of a DHSS circular. This stated that doctors could give girls under 16 years of age contraceptives. The court declared that this was legal.

5.6.2 Injunctions. These are normally a private law remedy but they may be used against public bodies. They can be obtained by local authorities, individuals or the Attorney General acting on behalf of the public (known as a relator action).

5.7 Damages

The court may award damages if it is satisfied that, had a claim been made in an ordinary action, damages would have been awarded.

5.8 Use of judicial review

In 1992 there were 2,439 applications for judicial review. Immigration cases take up about one third of the total and the use of judicial review has increased markedly over the last twenty years. The importance of these cases is not just for the applicant, but for the future policy of the Minister or body concerned. They will invariably review their practice for the future and so the rights of every citizen are safeguarded. However, a balance must be maintained, so that administrators do not become so worried about the prospect of review that they take too long in making decisions.

6 The Ombudsmen

The idea of an *ombudsman* originated in Sweden as an independent person who could investigate complaints by citizens against the state. The first one in this country was appointed in 1967 to investigate actions of the Government. There are currently eleven ombudsman schemes, which are a mix of statutory and private schemes. Their common factor is that the ombudsman is *independent* of the organisation that they investigate. The statutory schemes cover the Parliamentary Commissioner for Administration, local government, the health service, legal services, building societies, pensions and Northern Ireland. Voluntary schemes deal with banking, insurance, corporate estate agents and investment. In March 1993 the United Kingdom Ombudsman Association was formed to promote standards of good practice in both the public and private sectors.

6.1 The Parliamentary Commissioner for Administration

The office of Parliamentary Commissioner for Administration, popularly known as the Ombudsman, was first established by the Crown under the Parliamentary Commissioner Act 1967. The job of the Ombudsman is to investigate all complaints of injustice arising from *maladministration*. This term was not defined in the 1967 Act but is regarded as including matters such as bias, neglect, inattention, delay, incompetence and arbitrary decisions. The Parliamentary Commissioner has no control over the *merits* of a decision.

The Parliamentary Commissioner may investigate all Government departments plus a number of other authorities including the Inland Revenue, the Charity Commission, tourist boards, some tribunals and the administrative action of court staff. The Parliamentary Commissioner cannot investigate matters if a person:

(a) has a remedy in a court or tribunal, although this can be waived if it is not reasonable for the individual to take action;

(b)   has a remedy against health authorities;

(c)   is involved in any contracts or commercial matters;

(d)   has a complaint as an employee of the Crown.

Any individual or body may complain, but not a public authority. A written complaint must be made to an MP who then refers the matter to the Parliamentary Commissioner. There is no direct access to the Parliamentary Commissioner because it was felt that this would detract from the individual's right to complain to MPs. The Parliamentary Commissioner does in fact send direct complaints to an individual's MP, who may then continue with the case if the individual wishes. A complaint must be made within 12 months.

The Parliamentary Commissioner must tell the department concerned if an investigation is made and give it the opportunity to comment. The Parliamentary Commissioner's staff have wide powers to question Ministers and civil servants and to obtain documents. Crown privilege and official secrets legislation do not apply. After investigating, a report is made and copies sent to the MP, the department and any individuals concerned. If maladministration has been found, the report will suggest what action should be taken and may make suggestions for administrative changes. The Parliamentary Commissioner does not have power to enforce his report.

The Parliamentary Commissioner must also present an annual report to Parliament. In 1992 945 complaints were examined and of these only one quarter were accepted for investigation, the remainder mostly being outside the Parliamentary Commissioner's jurisdiction. In 177 cases the complaint was found to be wholly or partially justified. Most complaints were about the Benefits Agency (formerly DSS) and IR. The Parliamentary Commissioner cannot start an investigation, but must receive a complaint. In spite of the restrictions, there has been some success in obtaining financial compensation for those making complaints and getting departments to change their procedures.

6.2   The Health Service Commissioners

In 1973 two Health Service Commissioners were established, one for England and one for Wales. They investigate failure to provide a service or any other action taken by a health authority. They have similar restrictions to the Parliamentary Commissioner, as to what they can investigate, but their remit includes complaints about delays in admission to hospital, and inadequate follow up of complaints by hospitals, but not diagnosis, treatment, family doctors or dentists.

The complaint is made direct to the Health Service Commissioner, although the health authority must have been notified first and been given the opportunity to reply. An annual report must be presented to Parliament. About 1,000 complaints a year are received, with three quarters being outside the jurisdiction of the Health Service Commissioners.

6.3   The Local Commissioners

The Local Government Act 1974 provided for the establishment of four Local Commissioners; three for England and one for Wales. Their aim is to investigate complaints of injustice arising from maladministration by local authorities, police authorities, fire authorities and National Park Boards. They have similar restrictions on what they can investigate as the other ombudsmen, plus matters affecting all the inhabitants of an area and certain education matters.

A complaint originally had to be made through a councillor but since the Local Government Act 1988, an alternative is to make a direct complaint. The council must have been given the opportunity to investigate first. The local ombudsman then produces a report. If this is not acted on, a further report may be made. In some cases the local authority has not complied with the report. Most complaints are about housing and planning matters. Approximately 10,000 complaints are received annually and in 1992 381 findings of maladministration were made.

7 Tribunals

7.1 Introduction

The word 'tribunal' in its wider sense means any body which makes decisions, including courts. Here it means bodies which make decisions outside the normal courts. Tribunals developed along with the increased role of the state in controlling people's lives. Many regulations involve policy decisions, which courts are not geared to determining, and in other areas tribunals were better suited to make decisions than courts. These tribunals usually involve an element of public law although some tribunals decide disputes between individuals.

7.2 Domestic tribunals

A distinction is made between the above and domestic tribunals. These are bodies appointed within an organisation to decide disputes.

Example

The Disciplinary Committee of the General Medical Council, which controls the professional activities of doctors.

7.3 Inquiries

Tribunals may be contrasted with inquiries. A tribunal is a way of settling a dispute, whereas an inquiry is an investigation to ascertain facts, rather than to make a decision, and is used, for example, to investigate accidents.

7.4 Constitution of tribunals

There is a bewildering array of over 2,000 tribunals which have grown up to meet needs as they arose. A recent example is the Child Support Appeal Tribunal, set up under the Child Support Act 1991, to deal with disputes over the maintenance of children. The one common element is that they are all created by statute.

Example

The Office of Social Security Commissioners was originally created by the National Insurance Act 1946. They hear appeals from Social Security Appeal Tribunals who in turn hear appeals from decisions of the Department of Social Security. In 1992 the Commissioners dealt with 3,517 cases.

Tribunals may consist of one person but usually there will be three members. The chairman is independent and must be qualified in accordance with the CLSA 1990, s. 71. The other two members represent the two sides in a broad sense. For example, in an Industrial Tribunal which is hearing a claim of unfair dismissal, one member may be from a trade union and another from an employers' organisation.

7.5   The Franks Committee

The Franks Committee on Tribunals and Inquiries in 1957 made a number of proposals to improve the system:

   (a)   a need for settled rules of procedure;
   (b)   the need to give reasons for decisions;
   (c)   the right to legal representation;
   (d)   a proper system of appeals.

Franks said that the procedure of tribunals should be characterised by 'openness, fairness and impartiality'. Openness requires public hearings and reasoned decisions. Fairness dictates that parties must know the case they have to meet; they must have an opportunity to put their case; and a right of appeal. Impartiality demands that members of tribunals must be seen to be independent and not, for example, to be connected to a Government department involved. The Lord Chancellor should appoint chairmen.

7.6   Tribunals and Inquiries Act 1992

The Tribunals and Inquiries Act 1958 implemented many of the recommendations of the Franks Committee. The governing Act is now the Tribunals and Inquiries Act 1992. A Council on Tribunals keeps under review the constitution and working of tribunals. There are 20 members of the Council who are all part time. The Council meets once a month and has a permanent staff of 13. The powers of the Council on Tribunals are:

   (a)   to report on tribunals under its supervision and any matters referred to it by the Lord Chancellor;
   (b)   to receive and investigate complaints about tribunals; but there is no power to alter tribunal decisions;
   (c)   to make an annual report to the Lord Chancellor;
   (d)   to be consulted before Ministers make procedural rules for tribunals;
   (e)   to make recommendations on the appointment of members of tribunals.

The Lord Chancellor draws up lists of those suitable to act as chairmen and the Minister can choose from the lists. Legal representation is normally allowed. Judicial review is available against decisions of tribunals.

7.7 Advantages

The advantage of a tribunal is that it is:

(a)   quick with no long waits for the case to be heard and it is dealt with speedily;

(b)   cheap, as no fees are charged;

(c)   staffed by experts who specialise in particular areas;

(d)   characterised by an informal atmosphere and procedure;

(e)   allowed not to follow its own precedents, although tribunals do have to follow court precedents.

7.8 Disadvantages

The disadvantages of tribunals are that:

(a)   some are becoming more formal;

(b)   they are not always independent of the Government;

(c)   some tribunals act in private;

(d)   they do not always give reasons, although under the 1992 Act, s. 10, tribunals listed in the Act must give a written or oral statement of reasons, if asked to;

(e)   legal aid is not generally available, except for the Lands Tribunal and the Employment Appeal Tribunal;

(f)   There is no general right of appeal to the courts: it all depends on the particular statute. The 1992 Act gives a right of appeal on a point of law to the High Court from specified tribunals.

7.9 Examples of tribunals

7.9.1 The Lands Tribunal.   This was set up under the Lands Tribunal Act 1949 to determine a wide range of matters relating to the value of land, the discharge of restrictive covenants, valuation of land for taxation, compulsory purchase and compensation for subsidence from coal mining. In 1992 it received 2,489 cases and determined 474. At the end of 1992 there were 3,215 cases pending, nearly double the number at the start of the year.

7.9.2 Vaccine damage tribunals.   The Vaccine Damage Payments Act 1979 set up a compensation scheme for those damaged by vaccination which had been recommended by a public authority. Anyone refused payment by the Secretary of State may apply for review by a medical tribunal. The amount payable in compensation is £30,000.

7.9.3 Transport tribunal.   This was originally established by the Railways Act 1921 and is now under the control of the Lord Chancellor's Department. It deals with appeals from licensing authorities concerning the grant of licences for goods vehicles and public service vehicles' licences. It has a president, three lawyers who may be chairmen and five expert lay members.

7.10 Evaluation of tribunals

They do a useful job in taking some types of work away from the courts and dealing with specialised matters, less valuable claims and matters involving the exercise of a discretion.

It has been estimated that they deal with over *one million* cases a year (Partington, Martin, 'The Future of Tribunals', *Legal Action*, May 1993, p. 9). Problems remain over lack of standard rights, like the right of appeal, and procedures. In many instances they make important decisions affecting people's livelihoods and quality of life. The Council on Tribunals has begun to investigate the use of precedent, the establishment of a standard complaints procedure and the training of tribunal members. Its influence is hampered through lack of funds and having part time members. Some tribunals, for example the Lands Tribunal, have a backlog as large as the ordinary courts.

8   Arbitration

The parties to a dispute may choose arbitration as an alternative to a normal court action. This is only available in civil law. There are various types of arbitration.

8.1   Commercial arbitration

The parties to a contract can agree that any dispute should be settled by arbitration. This form of arbitration is governed by the Arbitration Act 1950 as amended. This is commonly used by national and international businesses rather than going to court.

8.2   Consumer

Individuals may choose to make agreements, in which provision is made to go to arbitration if there is a disagreement. Many codes of practice provide for disputes to be settled by arbitration, for example, in the motor trade. Under the Consumer Arbitration Agreements Act 1988 an agreement to submit to arbitration by a consumer will not be enforced where the claim is for a sum under £500.

8.3   Court arbitration

In the High Court a case may be dealt with by Official Referees who are two circuit judges nominated by the Lord Chancellor to deal with matters of a technical or scientific nature.

In the county court, the District Judge may deal with matters under £1,000 under the arbitration procedure. There is no need for legal representation and each side pays its own costs. The Lay Representatives (Rights of Audience) Order 1992 made under the CLSA 1990, s. 11, gives lay representatives rights of audience in cases dealt with by the arbitration procedure, but the person represented must attend the hearing. In 1992 over 80,000 cases were disposed of by arbitration or small claims procedure as this procedure is known in the county court.

8.4   General points about arbitration

Arbitration will usually be cheaper, quicker, handled by experts, informal and held in private. By going to arbitration the parties may maintain a business relationship. Choosing an arbitrator may cause disagreement, so this can be done in advance of any dispute or it may be agreed that the Chartered Institute of Arbitrators will appoint someone. An arbitrator is not bound by precedent but must follow the rules of natural justice. The decision of an arbitrator is called an award and it is final. Under the Arbitration Act 1979 an appeal to the High Court may be made on a point of law, with the consent of both parties or with the leave of the High Court, if the High Court considers that the point could substantially affect the parties. Under the Courts and Legal Services Act 1990, the High Court may deal with a case subject to arbitration, if both parties agree. Further, an arbitrator is given power to dismiss a claim for want of prosecution.

In April 1991 Arbitration Forum Ltd, a private company, was formed to assess damages in personal injury cases, where liability has been admitted. A fee of between £1,000 and £2,000 is charged and a decision given within six weeks. This is both cheaper and quicker than getting the courts to assess damages, but it remains to be seen if plaintiffs will use it.

9 Other means of resolving disputes

The fear of going to court, the cost, the delay and the uncertainty of the outcome are well documented. The parties to any dispute, be it matrimonial, an accident claim or a commercial matter, must realise that sooner or later they will have to reach a settlement. In reality the vast majority of cases do not go to trial and it is always open to the parties to reach an out of court settlement. Perhaps more effort should be made at highlighting and developing other ways of solving disputes. Such schemes may not always please lawyers, as it is probably difficult to help the poor and make a profit, but they could be beneficial to the prospective litigant. They are sometimes referred to as 'alternative dispute resolution'.

9.1 Payment into court

The existing system of payment into court is sometimes used, under which the defendant pays a sum to the court in settlement. The judge does not know the amount. If the award is less than this sum, the plaintiff has to pay the defendant's costs from the date of payment into court. This system can operate unfairly in forcing plaintiffs to accept smaller amounts than they would otherwise obtain.

9.2 Mini trials

This is a system used in the USA, under which the case is presented by lawyers to a neutral observer. This is at least in private and cheaper but the parties may then go to court in the normal way if no settlement is reached.

9.3 Class actions

If a number of people have suffered at the hands of a big company or the state, then rather than act independently they can act together. This is a relatively recent phenomenon and has developed with disaster claims like the Zeebrugge Ferry claim and the Piper Alpha claim. It poses particular problems as regards eligibility for legal aid and limitation periods for the individuals. Since June 1992 the Legal Aid Board has been able to make contracts with solicitors to do the common work for class actions involving personal injury. Under the guidance of pioneers like Rodger Pannone such actions have shown their benefits in complex cases. The Piper Alpha claims were settled within two years.

9.4   No fault schemes

To establish legal liability a plaintiff must usually show that someone is at fault, which may prove difficult. If someone can be made liable without proving they are at fault, this will save time or even save going to court. One example is that, under the Consumer Protection Act 1987, the producer of a defective product is liable for personal injury and damage caused by that product, irrespective of fault.

9.5   Mediation

The idea behind mediation or conciliation is that someone helps the parties to reach a settlement. The nature of the adversarial system does not lend itself to this. Mediation is more suited to some types of case, for example, divorce. It has happened in divorce cases that the parties' joint assets have just covered their legal costs which is obviously an unjust outcome! Mediation will play a major role in the family courts in the future.

9.6   Self help

It has been estimated that legal aid is now available to less than half of the population. It is possible to take out legal insurance for limited purposes, to cover legal costs. Anyone who is not eligible for legal aid, or who has a small value claim, or who is getting divorced should be encouraged to take their own case. Public libraries, law departments in universities and colleges, and large firms of solicitors could, with a little thought and planning, provide facilities and limited help for people, to enable them to prepare their case. This should become a priority as legal fees escalate, with partners in provincial firms charging £100 per hour and London rates up to four times that amount.

9.7   The 'family doctor' system

The system of general practitioners operated under the National Health Service could be used as a model for a similar system of legal advisers. This could be funded by a national insurance levy, lawyers would be paid a salary and advice would be limited to areas of law which are likely to affect people directly, e.g., family, criminal and property matters etc. Normal channels of legal advice would still be available to those prepared to pay or for more specialised matters like international patent applications.

9.8   Free help schemes

There are a variety of Law Centres and Citizens Advice Bureaux which give free legal advice. There is also a Free Representation Unit, set up by Bar students in London and with some regional units. Some lawyers, to their credit, have joined *pro bono* schemes under which they represent someone without charging.

10   Remedies available to the courts

There would not be much point in taking action in the courts unless the plaintiff got something out of it, apart from winning the case. The courts have a wide range of remedies to meet particular situations. Common law remedies of damages and repudiation are available, as of right. Equitable remedies, including specific performance, injunctions and rescission are discretionary, which means that the courts will not give them automatically, but will take into account the conduct of the parties etc. The main remedies will be looked at here but only briefly, as they will be examined in detail in the substantive areas like contract, tort and property. The courts have a wide range of particular orders which they may grant in helping parties obtain their legal rights.

10.1 Damages

Damages is the legal term for compensation. In most cases the payment of money will redress the wrong.

In contract the aim of damages is to put the innocent party in the same position as if the contract had been carried out, but the law will not pay damages for all the consequences of a breach, which could be endless. The principle of remoteness of damage was laid down in *Hadley* v *Baxendale* (1854) and this limits claims to (1) loss arising in the natural course of things; or (2) loss in the contemplation of the parties at the time the contract was made.

Example

Tim agrees to buy a new car to be delivered on 1 August. The garage sell the car to someone else. He was due to go on a motoring holiday but this has to be cancelled. Tim will be entitled to damages to put him in the same position as if he had got his new car. If he buys a new car elsewhere for a higher price he will get the difference. But he will not get compensation for loss of the holiday unless the garage knew about it.

In tort the aim of damages is to put the innocent party in the position in which they would have been, if the tort had not been committed. Obviously, money is of limited value in the case of personal injuries such as losing a leg, but it is probably the best solution available.

10.2 Repudiation

In the case of a breach of an important term in a contract, i.e., a condition, the innocent party may reject the contract, which means they do not have to carry out their part of it.

10.3 Specific performance

This is a court order telling someone to carry out their contract. It will normally only be granted if damages would not be adequate. In most consumer sales a party can quite easily obtain the goods somewhere else, so damages are suitable. This would not be the case if someone agreed to sell you a famous painting but then refused to hand it over. Specific performance will not be granted in certain circumstances, e.g., enforcing a contract of employment.

10.4 Injunctions

The courts have a general power to grant injunctions under the Supreme Court Act 1981, s. 37. There are a wide variety available and some of the main ones are as follows.

(a)   Interlocutory. These are granted to an applicant before the trial, to stop the other side doing anything to worsen the applicant's position. An example is a Mareva injunction (see *Classification of Law*, 2.5.2(a) above).

(b)   Prohibitory. These stop a party from doing a particular act.

(c)   Mandatory. These are used to make someone do a particular act.

In tort injunctions can be used to stop a nuisance. In contract they will normally only be used to stop someone from breaking an agreement not to do something.

Lumley v *Wagner* (1852)

A singer agreed to work for the plaintiff and not to sing anywhere else for three months. An injunction was granted to stop the singer working for someone else.

10.5   Rescission

The aim of rescission is to put someone back in their original position before the contract was made. An example of when rescission is available is if a misrepresentation has been made before a contract and it induced the contract.

QUESTIONS

ENGLISH LEGAL SYSTEM

Part A

1. What are the advantages and disadvantages of the doctrine of precedent?

2. Distinguish between Common Law and Equity.

3. When interpreting statutes, what 'rules' can judges use?

4. Briefly explain the system of appeals in civil cases.

Part B

5. Why are changes in the law needed and how are such changes made?

Outline answer

(a) Identify reasons why the law has to change. These would include the following:
— changes of Government, to reflect different policies
— public opinion and social attitudes, e.g. abortion
— technological change
— the wider needs of society
— because of the vast bulk of law, that some will always be out-of-date
— changes imposed by the European Communities.

(b) Explain the various mechanisms for making such changes. Here the emphasis should not be on the fine detail of the procedures but on when they will be used for particular types of change. Current examples should be given to illustrate these:
— case law, both first instance for new decisions and the higher courts
— statutes: briefly explain the process of bills becoming Acts. Emphasise that this is the most important method of change and mention pressures like the Law Commission
— delegated legislation: including explanation of when this would be used
— European legislation.

(c) Conclude by highlighting the most important points.

6. The Government decides to introduce legislation to ban the drinking of alcohol in public places. Explain the difficulties which might arise both in passing and enforcing such a law.

7. What effect has European Community law had on English law?

8. Does a court always have to follow an earlier precedent?

TWO

THE LAW RELATING TO LAND

INTRODUCTION

Land has always had an important place in the social and political history of English law. From Norman times the ownership of land has been equated with wealth and power, and it is perhaps only this century that its importance has diminished in that respect. At the same time, however, its importance has increased for a large proportion of the population, as home-ownership has become more prevalent. Inflation and several dramatic increases in house prices have meant that a significant section of the population now own an asset of considerable value. As that asset is not only the most valuable item that they own, but also their home, its importance to them cannot be exaggerated. On the other hand, as property prices have fallen, many people have found themselves with 'negative equity', as the market value of their homes has fallen below the amounts owing on the original loan taken out to buy the property. This phenomenon has emphasised the need for a good understanding of the interrelationship between the law and practice relating to mortgages.

The law relating to land is therefore particularly important to a practising lawyer, as it underlies the everyday conveyancing transactions which are often almost a matter of routine in a busy office. Each of those transactions however involves a large sum of money, as well as an asset which is of enormous value to the client in many ways. Despite the importance of the subject matter, much of conveyancing practice may seem to be a matter of completing the right form at the right time, in a standard manner. However, a knowledge of the reasons for the forms and the routine procedures is essential. An apparently innocuous point can otherwise be overlooked easily, with disastrous consequences. This chapter is therefore closely related to the Conveyancing Practice Syllabus, and every opportunity is taken to explain the relevance of the law to the type of work that a practising lawyer will encounter most frequently and typically.

The law relating to land can appear to be difficult because it is often technical in nature. These technicalities are rarely encountered in practice, or if they are, they are veiled in standard procedures and precedents that have been worked out over the years. For example, the procedure known as 'exchange of contracts' is so common-place as to seem hardly worthy of comment. However, there is a simple legal reason for the procedure, which may cast new light on it for you! Furthermore, the necessity in some circumstances for your clients to insure the property as soon as they have exchanged contracts for its purchase can easily be overlooked, but the importance of this step is rooted in a basic principle of land law. Similar principles will also help you to anticipate potential difficulties over such mundane items as garden furniture or fitted decorations in the house, and ensure that the 'standard' pre-contract enquiries are answered carefully and correctly in your client's interests.

The law is also very logical for the same reason that it is technical, namely that it has been constructed over the years to simplify the transfer of property, and therefore to a certain extent has been adapted to modern conditions. The reforms in this area started largely in 1925, when a completely new body of legislation was enacted, and that legislation has stood the test of time, with a few refinements. By working hard at the basic concepts therefore, you should be able to develop a good understanding of the law, and be able to apply it to everyday conveyancing practice. The standard forms and procedures will become that much clearer, and you will minimise the danger of overlooking any small defect which is not covered by them.

NATURE AND CLASSIFICATION OF PROPERTY

1   Real and personal property

1.1   The history of property

The simplest way to classify property would be to divide it into two categories. The first category would be immovable property (i.e., land) and the second would be movable property (i.e., everything else). Unfortunately English law is peculiar in that it has two artificial categories deriving from the ways in which the courts used to enforce a person's right to possession of property. If a person's property was taken by somebody else, the courts could only order its return if it was freehold land. The action that had to be brought to achieve this was known as a *real action* (in Latin, an action *in rem*). All other property was regarded as personal property and the owner was only entitled to financial compensation for its loss. Furthermore, leases were regarded as purely contractual arrangements between the freehold owner and the tenant and therefore fell into this category of *personal action* (in Latin, an action *in personam*). As a result, there were two categories of property: *realty* (i.e., freehold land) and *personalty* (i.e., all other property, also known as chattels, and including leases of land). This classification was always unnaturally artificial, however, and it became even more so from the 1600s onwards, as leases were gradually recognised as genuine interests in the land itself rather than mere contractual arrangements between the freehold owner and the tenant. Eventually this similarity between leases and realty was further recognised by sub-dividing personalty into *chattels real* (i.e., leases) and *chattels personal* (i.e., ordinary chattels), but the original classification and terminology has persisted to this day.

1.2   Tangible and intangible property

A more natural distinction is that between property that can be touched (tangible or corporeal property) and property which has no physical existence (intangible or incorporeal property). The meaning of 'land' is discussed below (*Introductory Principles*, 1.1) but it is sufficient for the moment to note that it includes not only the earth and the buildings on it, but also 'rights' over the earth, such as rights of way. In the eyes of a land lawyer the person who has a right of way also has 'land', just as much as the person who owns the earth and buildings that the right of way crosses. The difference of course is that the right of way has no physical existence, although there may be physical evidence for its existence in the form of deeds, a footpath or a stile. Similarly, personal property can exist in intangible forms. Property which cannot be taken into possession physically can only be claimed by taking court proceedings, although again there may be physical evidence of its existence in the form of a written agreement or certificate.

Examples

Copyright in a book, film or computer program. A patent on an invention. Shares in a limited company. The right to collect a debt. Where intangible property derives from a person's brain-work (i.e., copyrights or patents) it is often called intellectual property. All these are property, but can only be enforced by bringing an action in the courts. They are thus known as *choses in action* ('chose' from the French word meaning 'thing'). Goods which can be possessed in a physical way (furniture, cars, animals etc.) are known as *choses in possession*.

1.3   Modern property

There is little significance nowadays in the distinction between realty and personalty, and the phrase 'real property' is always taken to mean any legal interest in land, whether freehold or leasehold. To that extent therefore this chapter will cover the law relating to both freehold and leasehold interests in land. However, the technical distinction still exists, and therefore a will that left 'all my realty to my daughter' would not transfer a leasehold interest to her. The other distinction, that between tangible and intangible property, is only important in that it helps to develop an understanding of the wider, legal meaning of words such as 'property' and 'land'. The diagram on the facing page is included to outline all the different classifications in a visual form, and to summarise this section.

INTRODUCTORY PRINCIPLES

1   The meaning of 'land'

1.1   Introduction

The word 'land' has always had an extended meaning for the purposes of the English law. The common law principle was *cuius est solum eius est usque ad coelum et ad inferos*, a Latin maxim meaning that whoever owns the surface owns everything up to the heavens

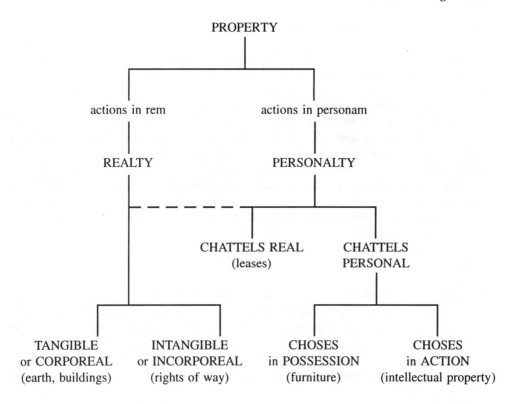

(*ad coelum*) and down to the depths (*ad inferos*). That approach was confirmed by the definition of 'land' set out in the Law of Property Act 1925, s. 205(1)(ix). This is a complex definition but it is clearly stated that it 'includes . . . mines and minerals . . . buildings or parts of buildings . . . and an easement, right, privilege or benefit in, over or derived from land'. In simple terms, this extended meaning of 'land' therefore covers everything attached to the area in question and is usually a matter of commonsense nowadays when the transaction concerns that most common of transfers of 'land', the sale of a dwelling-house.

Example

If a house-owner says to a potential purchaser 'I am selling my house', this is taken (quite correctly) to include the earth beneath the house, the air-space around it, the surface on which it is built, the plants in the garden, the right of way out of the back gate, and the garage and outbuildings.

For typical conveyancing purposes it is usual to speak of selling the house itself. However, legally the transaction is concerned with the sale of land, and the address of the house is merely a convenient method of identifying the area of the land. Thus the contract for the sale in practice will refer to 'all that property known as 27 High Street . . .'. This can have important legal effects, especially as far as the insurance on the house is concerned. Thus, if there is a contract to buy a house and the house is destroyed in a fire, strictly speaking the contract is still valid. The land that is the subject of the contract is still in existence, after all. Therefore a prudent purchaser will insure the house itself as soon as a binding contract is entered into, unless the contract specifically states that the seller retains the risk until completion (as in the Standard Conditions of Sale, covered in the Conveyancing syllabus).

1.2 The legal definition of land

The items referred to in the last example are themselves all examples of the various elements which make up the legal definition of land. They are all items which are attached in one way or another to the area in question, and can conveniently be placed under six headings. With a little ingenuity these can be made to spell out the word *magpie*:

- **M**ines and minerals under the surface

- **A**ir-space above and around the surface

- **G**round which is the visible surface area

- **P**lants and anything growing in the ground

- **I**ncorporeal rights attached to the land

- **E**rections on the land, including buildings and other fixtures.

Each of these items needs further explanation, as there are various exceptions to the general rule in every case.

1.3 Limitations on ownership of land

There are limits to the extent to which the owner of land automatically owns all of the items listed above.

1.3.1 Mines and minerals. Certain minerals are reserved for Crown ownership by statute (in particular coal, gas and petroleum) or at common law (gold and silver). Gold or silver bullion or items which were deliberately hidden on land are known as *treasure trove* and also belong to the Crown if the owner is unknown.

1.3.2 Air-space. Any wrongful intrusion into the air-space above the surface of property will amount to trespass. Typically this rule prevents an adjoining land-owner from erecting a building which projects over the boundary, and entitles a land-owner to remove over-hanging tree branches. However it also prevents even temporary intrusions as shown by the following case.

Anchor Brewhouse Developments v Berkley House (Docklands Developments) (1987)
The defendants were using a sky-crane. The plaintiffs obtained an injunction to prevent the jib of the crane swinging over their property, although this occurred at a great height and was not damaging their property or interfering with the normal use of the land.

There is a modern problem concerning the extent of the ownership of airspace, as in theory any passing aircraft, spaceship or satellite could trespass on the land of several thousands of householders. The Civil Aviation Act 1982 allows unrestricted rights of access to aircraft 'at a height above the ground, which . . . is reasonable' (s. 76). Other users of airspace are free to use it at a height which is beyond the limits of the usual use and enjoyment of the land-owner.

Lord Bernstein of Leigh v *Skyviews and General Ltd* (1978)

The defendants had flown over the plaintiff's land in order to take aerial photographs, with a view to selling them to land-owners. The plaintiff objected and asked for an injunction to prevent them doing it again, and damages for trespass. The court held that no trespass had been committed as the flight was too high to interfere with the plaintiff's use of his land.

1.3.3 Ground.   The visible surface area will include the bed of a river or lake on the property. However tidal rivers belong to the Crown, and the water which flows along a river bed can only be used for ordinary purposes, such as watering cattle. Extraction for commercial use is governed by the Water Resources Act 1991, and usually a licence must be obtained.

1.3.4 Plants.   All plants, trees, flowers etc. growing upon the property are included, whether cultivated or not. However under the Theft Act 1968 it is not theft to pick wild mushrooms, flowers or foliage from a tree or plant for private use (see Chapter 3, *Offences under the Theft Acts 1968, and 1978*, 2.6). Crops which have been specifically cultivated to be harvested within a year (such as wheat) are not automatically included in the sale of land.

1.3.5 Incorporeal rights.   The most peculiar feature of the definition of land is that it includes certain intangible rights enjoyed by the owner of the property, as well as all the physical aspects. The most important types of incorporeal rights are studied later (see 2.4 below and also *Legal and Equitable Interests*), but the typical example is the right of way. Thus if the owner of land enjoys the right of access over adjoining land, that right will automatically be transferred to a purchaser.

1.3.6 Erections.   The buildings erected on property are often the major reason for a purchase, and are included in the definition of land. However, problems arise with other objects which are only partially attached to the ground or a building. If the object is clearly part of the property it is known as a *fixture*. If it is merely a separable item which the seller will take away, it is known as a *fitting*. The distinction can often cause arguments between the sellers and buyers of domestic houses as well as commercial premises. Certain items such as curtains, carpets and furniture are clearly fittings, and are often dealt with by the insertion of a specific clause in the contract for sale. Other items are more contentious, and it is important to be aware of the potential problems which may be caused by 'fitted furniture', greenhouses, garden sheds and garden furniture. In domestic conveyancing practice it is usual to list every item which could conceivably give rise to a dispute, typically in replies to formal pre-contract enquiries. There is rarely a clear-cut answer to every item, as the test requires two factors to be considered. First, the extent to which the item was attached to the property; the more securely an item has been fixed, the more likely it is to be regarded as a fixture. Secondly, the purpose of the attachment must also be considered. Thus the key issue will be the extent to which there was an intention to improve the land, rather than merely to benefit a specific occupier. The application of these two factors can be seen in the following cases.

Leigh v Taylor (1902)

A tenant had fitted a tapestry inside a house by using a wooden frame nailed to the wall. However it was clearly his intention to use this method so that he could enjoy the look of the tapestry himself, and therefore the court held that it was not a fixture.

D'Eyncourt v Gregory (1866)

Various statues and vases in a house, and stone seats in the grounds, were not attached other than by their own weight. Nevertheless the court ruled that they were all part of a unified architectural design, and were therefore to be regarded as fixtures.

1.4   The definition of land and its effects

It is therefore vital in any contract for the sale of property to ensure that items which may be within the scope of the definition are dealt with according to the owner's real wishes. On the other hand, it should also be noted that the broad scope of the definition enables property to be divided up in a variety of ways. Not only can it be divided into plots according to ground area, but it can also be divided horizontally, and intangible rights sold separately. Thus the ground under the surface can be sold in layers, perhaps to allow veins of minerals to be worked or pipes to be laid. Even the airspace can be divided into layers, as when a house is divided into flats on different floors. Occasionally the upper floors of a house will (legitimately) overhang neighbouring land. That 'slice' of neighbouring airspace is known as a *flying freehold*, and is quite logical if the broad nature of the definition of land is understood.

2   Ownership of land

2.1   Introduction

To a certain extent this sub-heading is misleading. Land cannot be 'owned' in English law in the same way that a car or a book can be owned. As a result there are complicated rules governing the transfer of land, and the creation of interests in land. It is therefore important to develop an understanding of the unusual concepts underlying the ownership of land, before looking at the rules themselves. This section is an introduction to the basic concepts and terminology.

2.2   The doctrine of tenure

Following the Norman conquest in 1066, a feudal structure was imposed upon the English people. One result of this was that all land was deemed to belong to the Crown. Individuals could therefore only hold land by permission of the monarch, and in return were obliged to perform certain services. These services were the *tenure* of the land, i.e., the conditions under which the land was held. Typically the holder of the land would have to perform military service when called upon (by providing a specified number of armed men for a limited period of time). William I divided up the whole country between his principal followers, who were known as *tenants-in-chief*. Each tenant-in-chief was then entitled to 'sub-let' (technically *sub-infeud*) that land to lesser men, and in theory this sub-division of the land could continue until a vast pyramid was constructed, with the King at the top.

Example

Roger of London as tenant-in-chief is obliged to provide fifty armed men for service with the King. Roger sub-divides the land and grants an area to each of three sub-tenants (Alan, Bertram and Cedric) on tenure of ten armed men, thus effectively reducing his liability to his feudal Lord, the King. Each of those tenants could then sub-divide his plot along similar lines, and so on.

By the 1200s this continual sub-division of land was leading to much confusion! Accordingly a statute was passed in 1290 providing that there could be no more sub-infeudation. Instead, the last tenant in the pyramid could only transfer his land to another person, who would then take his place in the pyramid.

Example

Alan sub-infeuds to David part of the land he has been granted by Roger. In 1300 David's descendant grants that land to Eric. Eric will now hold that land directly from the descendant of Alan, and David drops out of the picture altogether.

The different types of tenure were gradually dispensed with by converting them into *freehold tenure* (the last few by the Law of Property Act 1922). This meant that all services were abolished (the land was 'held free') and replaced by the payment of a fixed sum of money. However, inflation soon rendered that sum meaningless, so that the only effective transaction became that between the last 'tenant' and the person who was taking his position in the pyramid. Thus the tenure system is still technically in existence, but in effect every holder of land now holds it from the monarch, free of services. Note that the word 'tenant' (from the French word 'tenir' meaning 'to hold') has acquired a different meaning nowadays, although it will still be encountered in its original sense on occasions (see for example *Co-ownership of Land*, 2.1).

2.3   The doctrine of estates

Far more important now than the concept of tenure is the doctrine of *estates*. Remember that it was not possible for anyone other than the monarch to 'own' land. Therefore anybody who held land could only do so for a certain period of time, depending on the exact terms of the grant from the monarch. As the tenure of the land described what services had to be performed for the feudal lord, so the *estate* which was granted described for how long the 'tenant' could hold the land. This specialised meaning of the word must therefore not be confused with its everyday use to mean an area of land (as in 'housing estate') or its use to represent the possessions of a deceased person. An estate could be limited in various ways.

2.3.1   For a life.   If it was granted only for the lifetime of the tenant, it was an *estate for life*. If it was to last for the life of another person, it was an *estate pur autre vie*. This situation would of course arise if a person with an estate for life sold that estate to somebody else.

2.3.2   Inheritability.   If the tenant was able to pass the land onto his heirs, then it was an *estate fee*. Even this could be limited however, by restricting it to direct descendants only (i.e., children, grandchildren etc.,), or even to only male or female descendants. Such estates were known as *estates tail male (or female)*. If an estate could be inherited by any heir without restriction, it was a *fee simple*.

2.3.3   Conditions.   Conditions could be attached to an estate, for example by stating that it would not commence until, or that it would terminate upon, a specified event. For example, a grant to Alan 'when he marries' or 'until he marries, and then to Bertram'. If an estate was free from any conditions it was *absolute*.

2.3.4   Commencement.   It was also possible to grant an estate to take effect immediately (*in possession*), or in the future (*in remainder*). In addition, if the land was to revert to the grantor after a period of time, then the grantor would have an estate *in reversion*.

Example

Roger of London grants an estate for life to Alan. Alan sells this estate to Cedric. Cedric will have an estate pur autre vie in possession (i.e., for the lifetime of Alan), while Roger will have an estate in reversion (i.e., the land will return to him upon Alan's death). Roger could also grant an estate to David (in effect, his right to re-possess the land after Alan's death). David would then have an estate in remainder, to take effect after Alan's death.

2.3.5   Certainty of duration.   Finally, it should be recalled that leases were eventually accorded recognition as an estate (see *Nature and Classification of Property*, 1.1). Thus in addition to the estates described above (which may be called the *freehold estates*), it was also possible to lease land, and thus have a *leasehold estate*. Both of these estates were a form of ownership of land, but the crucial distinction was that a freehold estate was for an indefinite period, whereas a leasehold estate was either certain or capable of being rendered certain. If the freehold estate was for life or pur autre vie, nobody could say in advance how long the 'tenant' would live. Even if it was an estate fee, it would not be certain that the 'tenant' would have any heirs, or that his heirs would have heirs. However, a lease was either for a fixed term, or for a period that could be made certain by giving notice. Thus even if it was for a recurrent period ('from year to year' or 'monthly' for example) the maximum term for each period was certain (i.e., one year, one month etc.), and could be brought to an end by giving the required notice (see *Estates in Land*, 2.3).

To summarise this section it should be noted that the estate that was nearest to full ownership was the *fee simple absolute in possession*. However any one piece of land could give rise to several co-existing estates, as there could be a reversionary estate, an estate in possession, an estate in remainder, and a lease, all at the same time.

2.4   Interests in land

The doctrines of tenure and estates apply to describe the extent of a person's ownership of land. However, a person may also have an interest in land belonging to somebody else. Some of these will be dealt with in detail in *Legal and Equitable Interests*. However, it is useful to consider briefly five particular interests at this stage.

2.4.1   Easement.   This is the right to do something on another person's land, for example, to walk or drive over a pathway; to run cables or pipes over or under the land (sewage, gas, electricity for example); to receive light across the land.

2.4.2   Profit à prendre.   This is the right to take something from another person's land, for example, to mine minerals, or even to hunt or fish.

2.4.3   Mortgage.   This is the right to have another person's land as security, in the sense that the interest will only be enforced if a specified sum of money is not paid. This arises most typically when a building society or bank lends money to the purchaser of a house, and is granted a mortgage on the property in return (see 2.8 below).

2.4.4   Restrictive covenant.   This is the right to restrict the way in which another person can use the land. Covenants are often entered into by purchasers of new houses on housing estates. Thus the builder will ensure that no house-owner (for example) will build walls or fences in front of the house, or run a business from the house.

2.4.5   Licence.   This is the right to use or remain on another person's land, although a full easement has not been granted. This arises every time that a person is sold a ticket to a concert, cinema, football match etc. This right is only a contractual matter between the parties to the agreement, and cannot be transferred to another person. The difficulty arises if the grantor seeks to terminate the right in breach of the agreement, for example, by telling a spectator to leave before the end of a performance. It seems that the licence cannot be revoked in this way, but there is some doubt as to whether this has the effect of giving the licensee an interest in the land, rather than just a special type of contractual right. If the licence is merely permission without any consideration, it is known as a *bare licence*. If it is coupled with a legal interest such as profit à prendre, it is enforceable along with that interest.

The importance of these types of interest in land is that they are attached to the land that they affect. Thus (subject to certain rules as to notice, which will be dealt with in *Registered and Unregistered Land*) any person who purchases the land will be bound by the interest. Similarly, if the interest is for the benefit of another specific piece of land (such as a right of way), then the purchaser of the land will also purchase the benefit of the interest.

2.5   Law and equity

The development of the English Legal System was dealt with in Chapter 1, and the difference between common law and equity explained in detail (see in particular *Classification of Law*, 2). For the purposes of land law, the development of the trust meant that any estate or interest could exist in equity as well as in common law. Estates that were recognised by the common law are known as *legal estates* or *legal interests*, to distinguish them from *equitable interests*.

Example

Roger grants a fee simple estate in land to Alan, but on trust for Celia for her life and thereafter in fee simple to David. Alan would thus have a legal estate in fee simple in possession. However the courts would recognise Celia and David's interests in equity. Celia would thus have an equitable life estate in possession, and David would have an equitable fee simple estate in remainder.

The key distinction between legal and equitable rights is that legal rights are *in rem* ('in the thing itself') and thus automatically enforceable against any other person. Equitable rights however are *in personam* ('against the person who granted it'), and thus only enforceable against other persons in particular circumstances. Normally therefore an equitable interest will only be enforceable against a third party who had notice of the interest in some form.

Example

If, in the example above, Alan sold the land to Bertram, Celia and David would only be able to enforce their interests under the trust if Bertram had notice of them.

The doctrine of notice is complex and will be dealt with later (see *Registered and Unregistered Land*, 3.6). To a large extent it has now been replaced by registration, and this determines the priority of equitable interests if there are more than one (see *Registered and Unregistered Land*, 3.3).

2.6   Deeds

There are various formalities that must be complied with before a legal estate or interest in land can be created. This requirement was introduced into English law as long ago as the Statute of Frauds 1677, and shows how land has always been regarded as a special type of commodity. The title of the 1677 statute is also an indication of the main reason for the introduction of formalities. One particular formality is that the final transfer of the estate or interest must be by *deed*. In everyday conveyancing terms, the deeds of a property are taken to be the bundle of miscellaneous documents which relate to it. However, strictly speaking a deed is a document that has been created in a particular way. Recent changes in the law have meant that there are now two sets of rules for the creation of a deed.

2.6.1   Common law.   Until 1989 a deed was a written document which had been *signed, sealed and delivered*. This meant that the person creating it had to sign it and make some sort of impression on it at its foot (typically by affixing a wax or self-adhesive seal). Historically the 'signature' would often be of little importance, as a large proportion of the population were illiterate and could only make a cross or mark. The seal would then be more relevant, as it would typically be done by impressing a special symbol into hot wax, thus making a mark which would be clearly identified with that person in particular. In modern times the seal has become a meaningless ritual of sticking a small red paper circle next to the person's signature. After signing and sealing, the document would not become a deed until the person creating it then performed some act to show that it was to take effect. Physically handing over the document could be sufficient, but need not be so. It has always been possible for a person to make it clear that the document will not become a deed until a certain event occurs. Such a document is said to be an *escrow*, or *in escrow*. Nowadays the transfer for the sale of a house is often signed several days before the transaction is to be completed. However, it is in escrow (and can even be sent safely to the solicitor acting for the purchaser for signature by the purchaser) until the day fixed for completion, when the purchase money will be handed to the seller.

2.6.2   Law of Property (Miscellaneous Provisions) Act 1989.   As from 31 July 1990 a deed can now be created merely by signing a written document which on the face of it is intended to be a deed. Thus a document which uses the words (for example) 'this deed...' need only be signed by the person executing it, and sealing is no longer necessary. Instead the document must now be witnessed, which has long been standard practice. The rules as to delivery still apply.

In a strict sense, therefore, the deeds to land are the various documents which have transferred the land from one person to another throughout the years, together with any documents which have created interests or estates affecting the land (for example, rights of way or leases). These documents were the best way of proving ownership of land, as the present owner could produce them to show how the land had been passed from hand to hand, ending in a legal transaction which transferred the land to him. If the purported owner of land could not produce the deeds, this would cast real doubts on the legitimacy of his ownership. This may still have to be done even now, although the registration of land has made it unnecessary in most cases (see *Registered and Unregistered Land*, 2.1). However under the Law of Property Act 1925 (as amended) a land-owner need now only produce the deeds showing ownership of the land back to a transaction at least fifteen years old.

2.7   Contracts for the sale of land

There are also formalities concerning agreements for the sale of land. Normally an agreement can be a legally binding contract even if it is purely verbal. However, since the Statute of Frauds 1677 there have always been special provisions concerning contracts for the sale or disposition of land or any interest in land. For many years these rules were set out in the Law of Property Act 1925, s. 40, and these rules still apply to contracts entered into on or before 27 September 1989. Since that date the Law of Property (Miscellaneous Provisions) Act 1989, s. 2 applies, and therefore both statutes need to be looked at in turn, as well as some other special rules relating to contracts for the sale of land.

2.7.1   The Law of Property Act 1925, s. 40.   Under this statute, a contract for the sale or other disposition of land or of an interest in land had to be evidenced in writing. The document had to include a note of the parties, the property, and the price ('the three Ps') and be signed by the person against whom it was to be enforced. This gave rise to the standard conveyancing practice of preparing duplicate contracts and exchanging them when the contract was intended to become binding. Under this system each party would have a document signed by the other party, setting out all the agreed terms. However, s. 40 expressly preserved the doctrine of part-performance. This doctrine allowed a contract to be enforced if the other person had peformed some act which showed that an agreement had been entered into. Thus, for example, if a person had moved into an empty house and started decorating it, that would be evidence of a contract relating to the house. Further evidence could then be admitted (including oral evidence) as to the precise terms of the contract.

2.7.2   The Law of Property (Miscellaneous Provisions) Act 1989, s. 2.   The formalities for all contracts entered into after 27 September 1989 are much stricter as a result of this Act. Firstly, non-compliance will render the contract void. Previously it would only have been unenforceable, so that any deposit paid by the person denying the existence of the contract could not be recovered. Secondly, both parties must sign the same document unless there is the traditional exchange of duplicate contracts. Thirdly, the doctrine of part-performance has been abolished. Finally, all the terms must be in the document, not just 'the three Ps' as before. This has proved to be the most contentious aspect of the Act, but the courts have adopted a common-sense approach which has reduced its potential severity. An agreement connected to the sale will still be valid therefore if it can be regarded as a separate 'collateral' contract.

Record v *Bell* (1991)

A contract for the sale of land was about to be entered into by the usual exchange of duplicate contracts, signed by the respective parties. By exchange of letters, the purchaser then formally accepted a guarantee by the seller as to the details of his ownership (a matter that would normally be dealt with after the contract had been entered into, as explained in the Conveyancing syllabus). When the purchaser subsequently sued him under the contract for sale, the seller claimed that the contract was void as it did not contain details of the additional agreement, but the court ruled that it was a separate and binding contract in its own right, and therefore outside the terms of the 1989 Act.

It is even possible to have a separate agreement which governs when the main contract can be finalised.

Pitt v *PHH Asset Management Ltd* (1993)

Mr Pitt had made several increased offers to buy a property, only for each offer to be bettered by another interested purchaser. Eventually, on the other purchaser outdoing him with another increased offer, he reached an agreement with the seller that the property would be sold to him at the agreed price if he exchanged contracts within fourteen days. Needless to say, before the end of the fourteen days, the seller stated that he would only proceed if the price was increased by another £10,000. When Mr Pitt refused, the property was sold to the other purchaser, and Mr Pitt sued for breach of contract. The Court of Appeal ruled that the agreement to 'lock out' further purchasers for fourteen days was valid, and awarded Mr Pitt damages. The agreement was not covered by the 1989 Act as it was not an agreement to sell, but merely a promise not to sell to anyone else.

2.7.3 Deposits. It is customary for a purchaser of land to pay a deposit to the seller as soon as the contract is entered into, and for this deposit to be forfeited if the purchaser breaks the contract by failing to complete the purchase. This is contrary to normal rules which state that a deposit can only be forfeited if it is a genuine pre-estimate of the losses that the innocent party will suffer as a result of the breach. The Privy Council have confirmed that the practice is valid, as an exception to the general rule, but that it is limited to a figure of 10% of the purchase price.

Workers Trust and Merchant Bank Ltd v *Dojap Investments Ltd* (1993)

The bank sold a property at auction in Jamaica to the defendants, with a clause in the contract providing for the payment of a deposit of 25% of the purchase price. When the defendants failed to complete the purchase (i.e., by paying the rest of the purchase price) within the time limit also stipulated in the contract, the bank forfeited the deposit and cancelled the contract. As the deposit amounted to nearly three million Jamaican dollars, and the delay was only a few days, the case was destined for the appeal courts! After over three years of court proceedings the case reached the Privy Council, where it was ruled that only a deposit of 10% can be forfeited as of right. As even this is by way of long-established exception to the usual law, they considered that any figure in excess of that amount can only be justified in exceptional circumstances. Accordingly the clause in the contract was held to be void, and the whole deposit had to be refunded.

2.7.4   Timeshares.   A recent innovation in conveyancing is the sale of one property to several people by dividing it into different annual time-slots. After mounting concern over the sales methods used by some unscrupulous companies, the Timeshare Act 1992 was passed. Any person selling a timeshare in the course of business within the UK (i.e., even if the property is in another country and therefore not governed by English law) must not only inform the customer that the contract can be cancelled after a fourteen day 'cooling off' period, but also provide a blank 'Notice of Cancellation' form. Failure to comply with the Act is a criminal offence, and will usually mean that the agreement is unenforceable against the customer.

2.8   Land as security

As mentioned above at 2.4.3, it is possible for a land-owner to raise money by using the land as security, i.e., by granting a mortgage. This can be done either by granting the lender a long lease which will terminate when the loan is paid back, or by way of legal charge in a deed (which is now the most common method). First mortgages are usually also protected by depositing the title deeds with the lender. If a loan is protected merely by the title deeds being deposited, or the mortgage is created in a document which does not meet the proper formalities, an equitable mortgage arises. There are three important implications of a mortgage on land.

2.8.1   Redemption.   Once a mortgage has been created, the land-owner has the right to cancel it by paying off the outstanding amount of the loan. This right is known as the *equity of redemption.* At common law the right to redeem would be lost for good once the date for repayment of the mortgage passed, but equity allows the right to be exercised until the lender has enforced his rights under the mortgage. Any provision in a mortgage which purports to block the right to redeem is known as a clog on the equity, and is void.

2.8.2   Enforcing a mortgage.   Lenders can enforce their rights in two ways. Usually a court order will be obtained to evict the land-owner, and the land will then be sold. The proceeds of sale will be applied to repay the loan, and any balance will be returned to the land-owner. If the proceeds of sale are inadequate, the lender can still sue the land-owner for the balance which is why the owners of houses with 'negative equity' (see *Introduction*) are in such a difficult position. Alternatively the mortgage can be foreclosed by obtaining a court order formally terminating the right of redemption.

2.8.3   Priority of mortgages.   If there is more than one mortgage on a piece of land, the proceeds of sale will be applied to pay them off in order of priority. Thus the first in order will be paid off in full before the funds are available for the second, and so on. The way in which priority is determined is complex, and is based on the date of the creation of the mortgage or its registration where applicable (see *Registered and Unregistered Land*, 2.4 and 3.4). The following table outlines the order:

First   Legal or equitable mortgages (title deeds deposited)

Second   Legal mortgages (no title deeds) i.e., puisne mortgages (see *Registered and Unregistered Land*, 3.4)

Third   Equitable mortgages (no title deeds).

ESTATES IN LAND

1 The 1925 legislation

By 1925 the traditional methods, doctrines and rules for dealing with land were proving too cumbersome for a modern society. In particular the easy transfer of land, and the simple creation of interests in land, were being hampered in three ways. First, owners of estates and interests had no simple way of protecting their rights if they were equitable. Secondly, potential purchasers of land were always in danger of buying land unaware of 'hidden' legal estates. Thirdly, the practice of placing land in trust meant that the land concerned (*settled land*) could not be transferred to anybody else, whether the person in possession wanted to work the land or not. The combined effect of these obstacles was that it was becoming increasingly difficult to transfer land freely, which in turn was having a stultifying effect upon the nation's economy. The answer was to be a complete reform of the law of property, so that in 1925 six important statutes were passed:

- Law of Property Act
- Land Registration Act
- Land Charges Act
- Administration of Estates Act
- Settled Land Act
- Trustee Act

This section will look at the effects of this legislation in reducing the number of legal estates and interests, and in simplifying the nature and administration of settled land. However, the legislation also set up systems of land registration, which started the process whereby the ownership of every piece of land in England and Wales would be recorded in a central register. In addition (and with immediate effect) these systems had the dual effect of enabling purchasers to buy land in the certain knowledge that there were no hidden equitable interests, and allowing owners of such interests to protect them easily. These registration systems will be looked at in the next section, *Registered and Unregistered Land*.

2 Legal estates and interests

2.1 Introduction

It has been explained already how the tenure system had withered away by the twentieth century, but that instead the number of legal estates had proliferated (see *Introductory*

Principles, 2.3). In addition there were several ways in which a person could hold a legal interest in another person's estate (for example, a right of way over the land). The principal innovation of the Law of Property Act 1925 was to reduce dramatically the number of estates and interests which were capable of being legal, as opposed to equitable, rights. Under the Law of Property Act 1925, s. 1:

The only estates which are capable of subsisting or being conveyed or created at law are:

(a)   an estate in fee simple absolute in possession;
(b)   a term of years absolute.

Further, only five interests are capable of existing at law:

(a)   an easement right or privilege in or over land equivalent to one of the two legal estates;
(b)   a rentcharge;
(c)   a legal mortgage;
(d)   charges imposed on land by statute;
(e)   a right of re-entry annexed to a legal term of years absolute or a legal rentcharge.

These interests listed above were deemed to be the minimum number of rights over land that could be given the benefit of being legal rights (i.e., enforceable against a third party regardless of notice or registration). Generally speaking all these rights would either be apparent from the title deeds, from a prudent inspection of the land (a right of way, for example), or by some other method (the retention of the title deeds by a mortgagor, for example). As a result all other estates and interests can now only take effect as equitable interests, and are therefore subject to the rules regarding notice and registration before they can be binding on, for example, any purchaser of a legal estate or interest. Note however that the Law of Property Act 1925 also set out certain formalities which must be followed before a legal estate or interest can be created or transferred. It is therefore necessary to deal with the effects of the Law of Property Act 1925 in five sections. First, an explanation of the estate fee simple absolute in possession. Secondly, an explanation of the estate term of years absolute. Thirdly, a brief consideration of the five legal interests. Fourthly, a look at the necessary formalities for the creation and transfer of legal rights. Fifthly, a summary of the various equitable interests that are still possible.

2.2   Fee simple absolute in possession

All of the terms used in this phrase derive from the traditional common law estates, and have already been explained (see *Introductory Principles*, 2.3). The meaning of each term can be remembered by one or two complementary words:

Fee	INHERITABLE
Simple	ALL HEIRS
Absolute	NO CONDITIONS
In possession	IMMEDIATELY

It should be recalled that under the doctrine of estates these terms are meant to describe the length of time that a person would be able to hold the land from his feudal lord. The overall effect of the phrase therefore is that the 'tenant' (and the 'tenant's' descendants) can hold the land, free from services or conditions, as long as there is an heir to inherit it. The Administration of Estates Act 1925 reformed the law on inheritance and set out a definitive list of the classes of persons who could inherit property. Distant relatives are not entitled to inherit at all, and it is thus quite feasible that one day a 'tenant' will die leaving no legal heirs. In that situation the land will revert to the Crown. Bearing in mind that possibility, an estate fee simple absolute in possession is the nearest that a person can come to absolute ownership of land in English law, and it is this which is known nowadays as *freehold*.

2.3   Term of years absolute

This is the *leasehold* equivalent of the fee simple absolute in possession. The phrase 'term of years' under the Law of Property Act 1925, s. 205, means any period with a fixed minimum duration, and therefore includes leases for less than a year, or on a periodic basis (i.e., weekly, monthly etc.). The duration of the lease must be certain in the sense that there is either a definite limit to the length of the term (i.e., a period fixed at the outset), or the limit can be set by either party in a clearly defined manner (i.e., a periodic tenancy). This principle seemed well-established after the case of *Lace* v *Chantler* (1944), where a lease 'for the duration of the war' was held to be void. A succession of Court of Appeal decisions in recent years have cast some doubt on it, however, with the result that the House of Lords had to restate the principle.

Prudential Assurance Co. Ltd v *London Residuary Body* (1992)

The Prudential had granted a lease to a local council that was to last until the council required the land for road-widening. The court ruled that the lease was void for uncertainty. The fact that the tenancy could be terminated by notice was irrelevant. Periodic tenancies are valid because, in effect, they consist of a succession of 'certain' periods (e.g., one month at a time).

The word 'absolute' does not seem to have any meaning here, and it certainly does not mean 'no conditions'. The Law of Property Act 1925 makes it clear (s. 205(1)(xxvii)) that a lease will still be a legal estate even if it can be brought to an end by notice or by re-entry if a condition is breached. However the Act goes on to state that a lease which is to come to an end on the death of any person cannot be a legal estate. There are four particular points concerning leases which should be borne in mind.

   (a)   A lease need not be 'in possession', unlike the legal freehold estate. Thus a lease which is granted to take effect in weeks, months or even years, will still be a legal estate. Note however the maximum of twenty-one years fixed by the Law of Property Act 1925, s. 149.
   (b)   A lease can be bought and sold just like a freehold estate.
   (c)   A lease grants exclusive possession of the land to the tenant. Anything less is only a licence (see *Introductory Principles*, 2.4.5). However the owner of the freehold estate still has a legal estate in reversion, and that estate can also be bought and sold quite freely.
   (d)   The everyday terms 'tenancy/tenant' are interchangeable with 'lease/lessee', and have no different legal meaning. Thus the weekly tenant of a flat has just as much a legal estate as the owner of a ninety-nine year lease on a house.

2.4   Legal interests

These five legal interests defined by the Law of Property Act 1925 are the only legal rights over another person's land that can now exist. Each can be briefly explained as follows.

2.4.1   Easements, rights and privileges.   The precise nature of these interests will be considered in *Legal and Equitable Interests* later in this chapter. However, it should be noted for the time being that they include three types of interest. First, positive interests such as rights of way, rights of drainage, rights to run pipes or cables over land etc. Secondly, negative interests such as the right to receive light over another's land. This right prevents one land-owner from stopping light reaching the land of another. Thirdly, profits à prendre such as the right to remove minerals from land, collect firewood etc. It should also be noted that, in order to be legal interests, these rights must be granted for a period equivalent to one of the two legal estates. Thus the grant must be either for a fixed period (term of years absolute) or for an unrestricted indefinite period (fee simple absolute in possession).

2.4.2   Rentcharges.   A rentcharge is the right to receive a sum of money periodically from the owner of the land. This right is secured on the land and will usually include the right to re-enter and take possession of the land if the rentcharge is not paid. However, under the Rentcharges Act 1977, with some exceptions, all existing rentcharges are to be extinguished at the expiry of sixty years from the date of the Act (22 July 1977) or the first date at which the rentcharge became payable, whichever is the later. In addition, no new rentcharges can be created, and existing rentcharges can be discharged by payment of a sum (calculated under the Act) to the rentcharge holder.

2.4.3   Mortgages.   A mortgage by way of charge upon the land (see *Introductory Principles*, 2.8). In order to be a legal mortgage, the charge must be in a certain form.

2.4.4   Statutory charges.   This class of legal interests has always consisted of some exotic matters, and is now of little importance.

2.4.5   Rights of entry.   Both leases and rentcharges give the holder a right to re-enter and take possession of the land, should the land-owner not pay the rent or rent-charge, or otherwise breach the terms of the lease.

2.5   Creation of legal estates and interests

Under the Law of Property Act 1925, s. 52, a legal right in land can only be conveyed or created by deed. The practical steps which must be taken to do this are covered in the conveyancing syllabus when the subject matter is a house, but it should be noted that this basic requirement applies to every legal estate and legal interest. Thus a legal easement can only be created by deed, and anything less will at best only give rise to an equitable interest. There are some exceptions to this basic rule, most of which are of a technical nature. However, one important exception concerns the creation of leases. If a lease meets the following criteria, it will be a legal estate even if created verbally.

(a)   Taking effect in possession (i.e., immediately). Note that 'in possession' means immediate legal entitlement to the estate. Thus, if the land is subject to an existing lease, the grant may merely entitle the new 'owner' to receive the rent on the land.

(b)   For a term not exceeding three years (even if the term can be extended). Thus a weekly, monthly or yearly tenancy will come within this definition, even though such a lease may last for several years in practice.

(c)   At a full market rent without a fine (a lump sum payment).

The typical example of such a lease is the weekly or monthly tenancy granted on a flat or house. Note however that it is not a legal estate until the tenants are entitled to move in immediately. Furthermore, a lease which falls within this exception can only be *created* verbally. If it is to be transferred, it must be done by deed (*Crago* v *Julian* (1992)).

2.6   Equitable interests

As a result of the Law of Property Act 1925 there are three principal categories of equitable interest. First, those interests which were recognised by equity even before 1925. Secondly, those interests which can now only exist in equity because of the Law of Property Act 1925. Thirdly, those estates and interests which can exist at law and equity.

2.6.1   Equitable interests pre-1925.

The two most significant are interests under a trust, and restrictive covenants. These have already been explained (see *Introductory Principles*, 2.5), and restrictive covenants will be looked at in detail later in this chapter under *Legal and Equitable Interests*.

2.6.2   Interests existing only in equity.

Prior to 1925 there were many types of legal estate that were possible (see *Introductory Principles*, 2.3). Now all except the two legal estates defined in the Law of Property Act 1925, s. 1, can only exist in equity. Thus it is still possible for land to be entailed (i.e., inheritable only by direct descendants, possibly restricted to male or female descendants) or granted for life only, or granted in remainder (to take effect in the future). However, these interests are now merely equitable. The combined effect of the Law of Property Act 1925 and the Settled Land Act 1925 is that these types of interest, relating as they do to the ownership of the land, take effect as trusts. Thus the grant of a life 'estate', or an entailed 'estate', will create a *settlement* of the land. This will be explained in more detail in 3.1 below, but the effect in simple terms is that a trustee must be appointed, to hold the full legal estate (fee simple absolute in possession). The legal estate can then be bought and sold, whereupon the equitable interests will be transferred to the proceeds of sale. Similarly, now only five strictly defined legal interests can exist. Thus an easement which is subject to conditions (i.e., which is not 'absolute') or which is granted for life only, can only take effect in equity. These types of equitable interest in land belonging to another person must be protected by registration (see *Registered and Unregistered Land*, 3.4).

2.6.3   Interests which can exist in law and equity.

The two legal estates and five legal interests which are possible since 1925 must be created by deed (see *Introductory Principles,* 2.6). Therefore any attempt to create such an estate or interest merely in writing will only create an equitable interest.

2.7   Successive and concurrent rights in land

An appropriate summary of this section is a look at the ways in which the two legal estates, five legal interests and numerous equitable interests can affect the same piece of land either in succession or at the same time.

2.7.1   Successive rights in land.   With the abolition of the system of tenures, all legal and equitable rights can now be transferred so that the previous owner loses all rights over the land, except those which have been specifically retained. Note, however, that some rights are restricted by their nature to certain classes of person, typically adjoining land-owners whose land can benefit from the right (see *Legal and Equitable Interests*, 2.1 and 3.6). Furthermore, the necessary formalities must be complied with to effect the transfer, as explained in 2.5 above. Successive rights in land can be created in advance by means of a trust. This means that the land will be held by one or more persons for a specified period (typically for so long as they live), and will then be transferred automatically to another person or persons. The persons who stand to benefit from the land, now or in the future, will not have a legal estate but only an equitable interest. The legal estate must therefore be held by trustees. There are two principal ways in which this arrangement can be created, viz a *strict settlement* or a *trust for sale*. Both of these will be explained in more detail (see 3 below).

2.7.2   Concurrent rights in land.   Both legal estates can exist over the same land at the same time. Indeed, there can also be successive leases, so that in theory there can be an infinite number of legal estates affecting the same piece of land.

Example

Roger has an estate fee simple absolute in possession over a piece of land. He grants a fifty-year lease to Celia, who in turn grants a forty–year lease to David. David is the 'owner' on the face of it, as he is physically in occupation of the land. However, he has a term of years absolute lasting for forty years. Roger has the fee simple absolute in possession in reversion, and Celia has a term of years absolute in reversion (i.e., for the time left after David's lease has expired). There is, of course, nothing to stop David granting a lease to another person, as long as it is for less than the remaining term of his estate.

At the same time any number of legal or equitable interests can affect the land. In the example above, all of the estate owners may have borrowed money and granted mortgages to the lenders. There may be rights of way crossing the land, and restrictive covenants affecting it. It is the job of the conveyancer to ascertain all of these rights, and to be able to assess and explain their importance and potential impact to the prospective purchaser.

3   Trusts and settled land

3.1   Introduction

It was explained in 2.7.1 above that a trust can be used in order to create successive interests in land. However, it has also been explained that this would tend to defeat the object of the 1925 legislation in promoting the free and simple transferability of land (see 1 above). The Law of Property Act 1925 and the Settled Land Act 1925 therefore have provisions to ensure that the full legal estate in any land subject to a trust can still be bought and sold quite freely. The basic principle concerned is that of *overreaching*. This means that the equitable interests in the land (i.e., the interests of the persons who benefit from the land under the trust) are transferred from the land itself to the proceeds of its sale. There are two ways in which a trust of land can be created, viz the *strict settlement* and the *trust for sale*.

Each will be considered in turn, but that basic principle underlies the rules affecting each type.

3.2 Strict settlements

The general policy of the Settled Land Act 1925 was to ensure that 'owners' of land who were restricted in any way from dealing with the land, would in fact have wide powers to work it, mortgage it or even sell it. This situation arose frequently before 1925, especially under 'family' trusts which were designed to keep land within the control of a particular family after a marriage or death. The most usual devices were the life interest or the entailed interest (see *Introductory Principles*, 2.3). Under the Settled Land Act 1925 any such arrangement creates settled land, and the person who has the immediate benefit of the land is known as the *tenant for life*. This is a technical term and should not be confused with the use of the word 'tenant' in other contexts. It merely denotes the person who is 'holding' the land under the settlement for the time being, and that person may be in actual occupation, or entitled to receive the rent from the land if it is subject to a lease. There will, of course, in addition be other beneficiaries under the settlement, usually those who have an interest in remainder.

Example

Roger of London grants his land to Cedric for his life, and thereafter to David in fee simple. Roger is now known as the *settlor*, as he has created a settlement under the Settled Land Act 1925. Cedric is the tenant for life, as he has the immediate benefit of the land. David has an equitable interest which is also protected by the provisions of the Act.

Normally a settlement will be created by the execution of a trust deed or in a will. This is known as the *trust instrument*, and it will set out the trustees, the terms of the trust, and the persons who are intended to benefit under it. Under the Settled Land Act 1925, s. 4(1), such a deed must be executed before a legal estate can be created. However, the courts have been ready to find a settlement in informal arrangements.

Ungarian v *Lesnoff* (1989)

The two parties were an unmarried couple living together as husband and wife. The woman had left her home and job in Poland to come to England and live with the man in his house. There was an understanding that she could live there indefinitely, but when the relationship broke down the man sought to remove her. The court held that a constructive trust had been created and that therefore the woman was now tenant for life. (A constructive trust is an exception to the rule that trusts of land must be created in writing; see *Co-ownership of Land*, 3.1.)

3.3 Effects of a settlement

Once a settlement has been created there are several consequences, as follows.

3.3.1 Vesting the legal estate. The tenant for life is entitled to have a *vesting deed* (or *vesting assent* if the settlement was by will) executed in his name. This will set out a description of the land and the names of the trustees, and other basic information concerning the trust. However, the full details of the terms of the trust will not be mentioned.

3.3.2   The powers of the tenant for life.   The tenant for life will now be able to deal with the land in the same way as the owner of the full legal estate, subject to various conditions and restrictions under the Act. In particular the tenant for life can sell, exchange, lease or mortgage the land. Under the Settled Land Act 1925, s. 106, any provision in the settlement which tends to prevent or discourage the tenant for life from exercising these powers, is void.

3.3.3   The duties of the tenant for life.   The legal estate is vested in the tenant for life, but his position is almost equivalent to that of a trustee, so that he must have regard to the interests of other persons entitled under the settlement. The main effect of this is that he must obtain the best reasonable price if the land is disposed of, and pay any money received to the trustees.

3.3.4   The purchaser from the tenant for life.   A purchaser of the settled land is only entitled to see the vesting deed, as this is sufficient evidence of the title of the land. The effect of the purchase is to transfer the full legal estate, free from the other interests under the settlement. Those interests are 'overreached', and from then on will attach to the sale moneys. A purchaser acting in good faith does not need to be concerned with the formalities with which the tenant for life should have complied (such as giving notice to the trustees), nor with the sufficiency of the price paid, or to where the money is going. However, if the transaction is one which is not authorised by the Settled Land Act 1925, it will be void (s. 18).

3.3.5   The trustees of the settlement.   Their functions are to protect the interests of all the beneficiaries under the settlement. To this end they will act as 'owners' of the land, should the tenant for life be unable to (for example, if the tenant for life is a minor), and receive and deal with any capital money arising from a disposition of the land. They also have to be given notice of, or give consent to, certain transactions.

3.4   Trusts for sale

This is an alternative device for creating successive interests in land. However under the Law of Property Act 1925 it must be 'an immediate binding trust for sale' if the result is not to be a strict settlement. Thus the trustees must have a duty to sell the land (not merely a power to sell it), and must be able to sell it immediately. A grant to trustees 'to sell the land when Cedric is twenty-one . . .' would be a strict settlement. Trusts for sale can be created expressly or by operation of statute. There are thus three typical situations where they will arise.

(a)   Express trusts. The legal estate in the land must be conveyed to the trustees, together with a statement of the terms of the trust. There is no need for two documents, as for settled land, but in practice it is wise to keep the terms of the trust separate from the legal estate, and thus away from the eyes of any future purchaser of the land. The trust instrument may be in a will, or there may even be an unwritten constructive trust (see *Co-ownership of Land*, 3.1).

(b)   Co-ownership. Under the Law of Property Act 1925, ss. 34–36, a conveyance of land to two or more persons will operate as a trust for sale. The effect of these provisions is that the first four persons named in the conveyance will hold the land as trustees for themselves and any others named. This will give rise to either a *joint tenancy* or a *tenancy in common*. These terms will be explained in more detail later (see *Co-ownership of Land*, 2.1) but it should be noted that the word 'tenant' is being used in the technical sense of the 'holder' of land, as in 'tenant for life' (see *Introductory Principles*, 2.2).

(c)   Intestacy. Under the Administration of Estates Act 1925, s. 33, all land which is left by a deceased person on intestacy is held by the personal representatives on trust for sale.

3.5   Effects of a trust for sale

Although trusts for sale are not regulated by the Law of Property Act 1925 as closely as is settled land by the Settled Land Act 1925, there are nevertheless several statutory regulations, as well as consequences which have arisen in subsequent court cases.

3.5.1   Trustees' powers.

The most important of these is the power to postpone a sale under the Law of Property Act 1925, s. 25. It is this power which makes the trust for sale a reasonable alternative to a strict settlement, as it gives the trustees a discretion as to when they can sell the land. However, all trustees must agree to the postponement. In *Re Mayo* (1943) the court ordered a sale even though it was only a minority of the trustees who wanted it. Note that the power to postpone sale can be excluded by the terms of the trust, in which case the trustees must sell the land as soon as is reasonable. Otherwise the trustees have all the powers of a tenant for life and trustees under the Settled Land Act 1925.

3.5.2   The interests of the beneficiaries.

The immediate effect of the trust is that the beneficiary's interest in the land is converted into an interest in the proceeds of sale, having thereby the same effect as 'overreaching' in the case of settled land. However, the desires of the beneficiary concerning the land can be given more weight than in the case of a settlement. Thus in a statutory trust for sale the trustees must consult the beneficiaries and give effect to the wishes of the majority (Law of Property Act 1925, s. 26(3)). The courts have also been willing to refuse a sale where the sale would defeat the objects of the trust. This has arisen most frequently in the case of a matrimonial home.

Jones v Challenger (1961)

A house was conveyed into the joint names of a husband and wife, thus creating a trust for sale. The wife left when the marriage broke down, and they were divorced. Eventually the wife applied for an order that the house be sold and the proceeds of sale be divided between them. The Court of Appeal held that the purpose of the trust was to provide a home for the family, and as that purpose could no longer be pursued (the children had left the house as well), a sale could be ordered.

Note that the terms of the trust can specifically state that the trustees should consult the beneficiaries, or even that consents should be obtained before the sale can take place (Law of Property Act 1925, s. 26). As a result, the trust for sale can be extremely effective as a way of preventing the sale of land, possibly even rendering it unsaleable.

Example

Roger transfers his land to trustees on trust to sell it, for the benefit of Cedric for his life, then to David absolutely. However he indicates a wish that Cedric and David should be able to live in the house built on the land and stipulates that both their consents are necessary before the land can be sold. In this situation the courts are not going to order a sale unless both beneficiaries consent.

3.5.3 The purchaser of land subject to a trust for sale. The purchaser need not be concerned with the terms of the trust under the Law of Property Act 1925, s. 27, as long as the purchase moneys are paid to two trustees or a trust corporation.

REGISTERED AND UNREGISTERED LAND

1 Introduction

1.1 The nature of land registration systems

The legislation of 1925 introduced a system of registration of title to land, and expanded the system of registration of interests in land. Registration of title was introduced by the Land Registration Act 1925, and meant that ownership of every parcel of land would eventually be recorded in the central Land Register. In addition this Register would record all the interests affecting that land. However, registration of title could only proceed slowly, and therefore in the meantime a comprehensive system of registration of interests in land was set up by the Land Charges Act 1925. This meant that particular rights over another person's land had to be recorded in the central Land Charges Register. There are thus two distinct systems for conveyancing purposes. If land is registered under the Land Registration Act 1925, all the information concerning that land (including the name of the owner) will be recorded in the Land Register. All a purchaser needs to do is to search the Register by sending in a request with a note of the title number of the piece of land in question. If land is not registered, the purchaser needs to do two things. Firstly, the seller's ownership of the land must be checked, by inspecting the title deeds (see *Introductory Principles*, 2.6). Secondly, the Land Charges Register must be searched to ensure that there are no interests recorded which affect the land. This is done by searching against the names of the existing and previous owners of the land.

1.2 The two systems in practice

The existence of these two systems means that there are two procedures to be followed by conveyancers, and two sets of forms to be used, depending on whether the land being sold is registered or unregistered. These practical matters are covered by the Conveyancing Practice Syllabus, but it is important to proceed from an understanding of the law which underlies each system. It is also easy to confuse the different terminology, unless there is an easy familiarity with the legal principles involved. For example, the Land Register (for registered land) has three sub-registers, including a Charges Register. This, however, is a completely different set-up from the Land Charges Register (for unregistered land). Each register is physically distinct, contains different information, and is regulated by different rules. It is not too difficult to confuse the Land Register's Charges Register with the Land Charges Register! Other terminology is not so crucial, but should also be used carefully so as not to cause misunderstanding. For example, the document which formally transfers ownership of registered land is called a *transfer*, whereas in the case of unregistered land it is a *conveyance*. Although they have the same effect, there are some technical rules as to the format that should be used for a registered land transfer.

1.3 The objects and principles of land registration

The basic principle in both systems is that an interest in land is not valid unless it is recorded in the appropriate register. The onus of recording an interest is on the owner of that interest, and a failure to do so means that a purchaser of the land will not be bound by it. This achieves neatly the dual objects of simplifying the transfer of land while protecting the owners of interests in land. The owner of an interest need only register it to be certain of protection. The potential purchaser need only search the appropriate register to be certain of knowing what interests affect the land. The uncertainty is taken out of conveyancing, and the necessity for long and complex checks on the status of the land and its owner is done away with. Unfortunately, neither system quite achieves this ideal. The gaps and anomalies in the systems must therefore be noted carefully as they are encountered throughout this section, and each system will be looked at in turn.

2 Registered land

2.1 Introduction

Under the Land Registration Act 1925 the whole of England and Wales will eventually be divided into parcels of land, each parcel with its own title number. On a central register (the *Land Register*) will be recorded the owner of the land, together with all interests affecting or benefiting the land. A purchaser of the land in question can therefore ascertain a complete and up-to-date picture of the land from a legal point of view, although an inspection of the property and enquiries of the owner will still be necessary to ascertain the physical state of the land. All land which is situated in a part of the country which has been denominated an area of *compulsory registration* must be registered by the new owner within two months of a *specified transaction*. Since 1 December 1990 the whole of England and Wales has been an area of compulsory registration. A specified transaction is one where there is a sale of the freehold, or of a lease having more than twenty-one years to run, or where a lease for more than twenty-one years is granted. The new owner must prove to the Land Registry that the transaction created one of the two legal estates under the Law of Property Act 1925 (see *Estates in Land*, 2.1). This is done by producing the title deeds to prove the chain of ownership of the land back to a transfer at least fifteen years old. In addition all interests affecting the property must be disclosed, by producing searches against all the previous owners of the land. This is substantially the same procedure that must be followed whenever unregistered land is transferred (see 3.2 below). In this way the complete picture is built up and recorded on the Land Register forever, so that a future purchaser need not follow this complicated and time-consuming procedure all over again. The owner of the land receives a document from the Land Registry called a *Land Certificate*. This effectively replaces the deeds as evidence of ownership, but it is not so important as it is merely a copy of the Land Register as at the date it is issued (which is marked inside).

2.2 The Register

The Land Register is divided into three sections.

2.2.1   The property register.   This contains a description of the land by reference to an annexed plan. It describes the estate for which the land is held, together with any easements or covenants which benefit it.

2.2.2   The proprietorship register.   This states the name and address of the owner, and occasionally sets out restrictions on the owner's right to deal with the land. These may arise because of the necessity to protect a possible interest in the land (a *caution*), or because certain conditions must be complied with by the owner (a *restriction* or *inhibition*). These methods of protecting interests will be explained later (see 2.5 below). The proprietorship register also specifies the nature of the owner's estate according to certain categories set out in the Land Registration Act 1925. The category to which an estate is assigned depends upon the extent to which ownership can be proved, and it can be upgraded in the future if circumstances change. The highest category is *absolute title*. This may be either freehold or leasehold and denotes that there is no doubt about the owner's title. If it is a leasehold title this means that the owner will have produced satisfactory evidence that the lease was validly granted. If the owner of a leasehold estate cannot prove that the person who granted the lease had the right to do so, then title will be classified as *good leasehold*. If there is any other reason to doubt the effectiveness of the registration the classification will be as *qualified title*, but this is unusual. It is more likely that it will be classified as *possessory title*, which arises where the estate owner can only prove possession of the land (perhaps because title deeds have been lost), and therefore indicates that the existence of an estate or interest in the name of another person cannot be guaranteed. After twelve years of uncontested possession a qualified freehold can be upgraded to absolute title, and qualified leasehold can be up-graded to good leasehold.

2.2.3   The charges register.   This contains entries of incumbrances on the land, such as mortgages and restrictive covenants.

The register is always the definitive statement as to the title and rights affecting the land (subject to overriding interests: see 2.6–2.7 below). Any person can now inspect the register by applying for office copies of it. The Land Registry will send a certified copy of all existing entries, and this can be updated, shortly before the transaction is completed by an official search of the register. The official search will reveal any entries made since the date of the office copies, and will give the searcher a protected period in which his transaction can be completed without the risk of any other interests being registered in the meantime. However, rectification of the register is possible. The register can be rectified under the Land Registration Act 1925, s. 82, if there has been fraud or error, and compensation paid for any losses incurred because of the inaccuracy. This will not be done, however, if it would be 'unjust' to do so, which means that registration can sometimes give a person better title to property than that to which they are legally entitled.

London Borough of Hounslow v Hare (1992)
The defendant had purchased property and her title was registered, although unknown to her the sale was void because the land was subject to charitable trusts. The court refused to rectify the Land Register (thus allowing her to retain a legal estate) because compensation would not give her the same quality of life if she were to lose her home.

2.3   Protection of third party interests

The interests of other persons over registered land are protected in four ways. First, certain legal estates can be registered separately with their own title number (for example, leases for more than twenty-one years). Secondly, a mortgage must be protected by registration as a charge in the charges register of the land in question. Thirdly, the majority of interests (known as *minor interests*), must be protected by registration of a caution, notice, inhibition or restriction. Fourthly, certain special rights are known as *overriding interests* and do not need to be registered at all. Apart from the separate registration of leases, each of these categories needs further explanation. However, it should be noted that a registrable interest which is not registered is void against a purchaser of the registered title (but not against a person who receives the title as a gift).

2.4 Mortgages

Under the Land Registration Act 1925, s. 106, a legal mortgage of registered land will only take effect as an equitable interest (and therefore would need protecting as a minor interest) until it is registered in the charges register. This is therefore an important exception to the basic rule that a legal estate or interest is always good against third parties. If a mortgage is registered against registered land, the owner of the land receives a *Charge Certificate* instead of the usual Land Certificate, kept by the mortgagee along with the deeds. This is in exactly the same form apart from its title. Accordingly it is again merely a copy of the Land Register as at the moment that it is issued.

2.5 Minor interests

Any other interest which must be registered can be protected in one of four ways. There are prescribed forms and procedures for each of these methods.

2.5.1 Notice. If the owner of the land consents, the interest can be recorded by notice in the charges register of the Land Register (not to be confused with the Land Charges Register, which is only appropriate for unregistered land). This procedure, however, merely serves to protect the holder of an interest against purchasers.

Mortgage Corporation v Nationwide Building Society (1993)
The plaintiffs had a charge against the property and had taken possession to recoup the amount of the loan. Because it was not registered in the charges register the charge was only classed as an equitable interest (see 2.4 above), and furthermore would not have been enforceable against a purchaser because it was not protected by a notice. The defendants also had a charge, which had been created later, but which they had protected by a notice. There was only enough money from the proceeds of sale to satisfy one charge, and the court ruled that the plaintiffs' charge took priority as it had been created first.

Normally the Land Certificate must be produced, but an exception is made in the case of a spouse who wishes to protect the right to reside in the matrimonial home under the Matrimonial Homes Act 1983.

2.5.2 Caution. This enables any person claiming an interest in the land to register a caution in the proprietorship register. The cautioner will then be notified of any proposed dealing with the land and given an opportunity to object. This will usually take the form of a hearing to decide the validity of the interest claimed should it be disputed by the owner of the land. The cautioner will possibly also need to take further action to preserve the priority of the interest, for example by registering a notice, as the caution is only a procedure for giving warning, and not protection in itself.

Clark v Chief Land Registrar (1993)

The plaintiff held a charge over a house and registered a caution to protect it. The house owners then subsequently created a legal charge in favour of another person. When this was registered in the charges register, the Land Registry neglected to give the plaintiff the warning to which he was entitled and when the property was subsequently sold there was not enough money from the proceeds of sale to cover both charges. The court ruled that the registered charge should be paid first, but that the Land Registry would have to compensate the plaintiff for his losses (see 2.2 above).

This case has since been followed by *Chancery plc* v *Ketteringham* (1993), but as both are only decisions of the High Court there is still some lingering doubt as to the position.

2.5.3 Restriction. Occasionally the powers of the registered owner to deal with the land may be limited. This situation will typically arise where the registered owner is a trustee, a tenant for life under a settlement, or a charity. The proprietorship register will contain an entry stating that no disposition of the land can be registered unless (for example) the purchase money is paid to the trustees of the settlement (see *Estates in Land*, 3.3.5), or (in the case of a charity) without the consent of the Charity Commissioners.

2.5.4 Inhibition. This is an unusual entry in the proprietorship register and prevents any dealing in the land whatsoever. It typically arises when the owner has been adjudicated bankrupt.

2.6 Overriding interests

Under the Land Registration Act 1925, s. 70(1), there are twelve groups of interests which will bind a purchaser of the land, whether they have been registered or not. To a limited extent they are equivalent to the legal interests recognised by the Law of Property Act 1925, but there are many discrepancies. It is best therefore to recognise them as similar in principle to legal interests, in the sense that they are interests which should be identifiable in some other way and which it is inappropriate to expect the owners to have to register. Of the twelve, only six are commonly encountered.

(a) Easements and profits à prendre. As the principal category of legal interests, it is perhaps to be expected that these would be so protected. They should be identifiable by an inspection of the property, or by careful enquiry of the owner.

(b) Leases for less than twenty-one years, if granted at a full market rent without taking a fine (see *Estates in Land*, 2.5). Other leases must be registered as a separate title to the land, and will thus be automatically noted on the register of the freehold title.

(c) 'Squatters rights'. More technically, these are rights of prescription, or in the process of being acquired under the Limitation Act 1980. A person who has been in possession of land for a certain period of time (usually twelve years) will eventually obtain ownership of the land. It is clearly impractical to expect such a person to register this process, and their occupation should be obvious to a prudent purchaser in any event.

(d)   Local land charges. Rights which are protected as local land charges until they are registered in the prescribed manner.

(e)   Limited titles. If the registered title is only 'good leasehold', or a possessory or qualified title (see 2.2.2 above), any rights not affected by registration are protected, otherwise there would be little point in limiting the registration of the title.

(f)   Rights of a person in actual occupation of the land. This is the most contentious provision under s. 70(1) and is worthy of special consideration.

2.7   Rights of persons in actual occupation

This provision protects any interest in the land 'save where enquiry is made of such person and the rights are not disclosed' (Registered Land Act 1925, s. 70(1)(g)). Thus a prudent purchaser should be able to ascertain that somebody is 'in actual occupation', and make careful enquiry of that person. There are principal elements which must be considered: the 'rights' which are capable of protection; the meaning of 'actual occupation'; and the nature of the enquiry which may protect a purchaser.

2.7.1   Protected rights.
The right must be in reference to the land, rather than a personal right such as a right to occupy the house because of marriage to the owner (see also *City of London Building Society* v *Flegg* (1988) below). The typical situation is that of a beneficial interest under a trust, particularly where the trust has arisen out of a domestic relationship (see *Co-ownership of land*, 3.1). The principle in this context was finally established in 1981.

Williams and Glyn's Bank Ltd v *Boland* (1981)
Mr and Mrs Boland were married and lived in a house which was in the sole name of Mr Boland. However, because Mrs Boland had contributed to the purchase moneys, a constructive trust arose so that she had an equitable interest in the land. Mr Boland then borrowed money from Williams and Glyn's Bank for his business, and granted the bank a mortgage on the house by way of security. His business eventually went into liquidation, and the bank claimed possession of the house to pay off the loan. Mrs Boland, however, claimed that the mortgage was granted after her interest arose, and that therefore the bank was not entitled to gain possession from her, only from her husband. The House of Lords ruled that she had an effective overriding interest which bound the bank, and that therefore she was entitled to remain in possession of the house.

2.7.2   Actual occupation.
In Mrs Boland's case there was no doubt about this, as she had been living in the house for many years before the mortgage was granted by Mr Boland. More difficult questions arise when the 'occupation' is a more fleeting presence. This may occur when the house is not being lived in.

Lloyds Bank PLC v *Rossett* (1990)
A semi-derelict farmhouse was purchased by a married couple, but in the sole name of the husband. The wife did not contribute to the purchase price or the mortgage payments, but used her skills as a trained decorator by working on the house for two months before they moved in. When the bank claimed possession under the terms of the mortgage, the question arose as to whether the wife had an overriding interest. The courts held that she was in

actual occupation although she had not moved into the house, but that she had no equitable interest (see *Co-ownership of Land*, 3.3).

However, the more typical situation is where a mortgage is granted when a house is being purchased. The 'occupation' may be slight (i.e., moving in the furniture) and the only time when it is contemporaneous with the interest in the land is after the land has been transferred to the new owner. It is only at that point that the owner can be said to be holding it in trust for the person claiming an interest, but in practice the owner grants a mortgage to the lender (the bank or building society) at the precise moment that the purchase is completed. Is there a real moment of time between the completion of the purchase and the granting of the mortgage? Certainly the mortgage cannot be granted before the purchase is completed because a person cannot mortgage land unless he owns it. However, in reality the purchaser needs the lender's money in order to pass it on to the seller, and thus complete the purchase, and the lender will not release the money until a mortgage is granted. In this everyday situation there is a clear conflict between the technical position and the reality of practice, which has had far-reaching implications.

Abbey National Building Society v *Cann* (1990)
The background to this case is complex, and involves a fraud practised upon Mr and Mrs Cann by their son. However, in simple terms, when the house in question was purchased by the son, Mr and Mrs Cann had an equitable interest in it because a constructive trust arose. They lived in the house thereafter, and thus had an overriding interest. Their son had granted a mortgage to the Abbey National Building Society in order to obtain the funds for the purchase, but subsequently defaulted on the mortgage. The building society then sought possession of the house in order to sell it and clear the loan, but Mr and Mrs Cann claimed a right to continue in occupation because of their overriding interest. The House of Lords granted possession to the building society. First, they said that there was insufficient occupation as Mr and Mrs Cann had merely moved in some furniture and possibly made a cup of tea. Secondly, in reality the mortgage and purchase took place simultaneously, and therefore there was no 'gap' when their interest and occupation could take effect before the building society's rights arose under the mortgage.

2.7.3   Protection by enquiry.   Following the case of *Williams and Glyn's Bank Ltd* v *Boland* the major institutional lenders (banks and building societies) adopted a procedure to avoid the consequences of the House of Lords decision. When a sole owner applied for a loan by way of mortgage, the lender would require a written statement that no other person over the age of eighteen would reside in the property to be mortgaged, or to list those who would. Any persons thus revealed would have to sign a formal disclaimer of any interest in the property, thus excluding themselves from the protection of s. 70(1)(g). However, this procedure would not be taken where the proposed purchase is in the names of two people. In that situation, the lender can rely instead on the principle of overreaching (see *Estates in Land*, 3.1).

City of London Building Society v *Flegg* (1988)
A Mr and Mrs Brown purchased a house ('Bleak House') in their joint names. Mrs Brown's parents (Mr and Mrs Flegg) contributed towards the purchase price, and the intention was that they would all share the house. Thus a trust for sale was created, both on the face of the transaction (a purchase in joint names) and in equity to protect the interest of Mr and

Mrs Flegg. Subsequently Mr and Mrs Brown defaulted on the mortgage and the building society claimed possession. Mr and Mrs Flegg claimed a continuing right to occupy because of their overriding interest. The House of Lords ruled that their equitable interest under the trust for sale was overreached because the mortgage moneys had been properly paid to two trustees, as required by the Law of Property Act 1925, s. 27. Thus their rights now attached to the proceeds of sale, and so they had no interest *in the property* which could form the basis of a claim under s. 70(1)(g).

2.7.4   A limited equitable interest.   The courts have, however, developed a new principle to give some protection to mortgagees where an interest arises under an implied trust and the holder of the equitable interest knew of the mortgage and benefited from it. This principle was first suggested in *Bristol and West Building Society* v *Henning* (1985), and given some support by the House of Lords in *Abbey National Building Society* v *Cann* (1990). The principle has been confirmed by the Court of Appeal in no uncertain terms, however, and extended to the situation where the first mortgage is replaced by another one.

Equity & Law Home Loans v Prestidge (1992)

A man and woman were living together in a house which was held in the sole name of the man, subject to a mortgage of £30,000. The woman had contributed towards the purchase price, however, and thus had a substantial equitable interest under a resulting trust. Unknown to the woman, the man remortgaged the house by taking out a mortgage of £42,000. This enabled him to pay off the first mortgage, and to disappear with the balance of £12,000. Inevitably he failed to keep up the mortgage payments and the mortgagees claimed possession of the house in order to sell it and pay off the mortgage. As this was an entirely new mortgage, it should have been subject to the woman's equitable interest, as she was in occupation of the house. However, the Court of Appeal ruled that, because she had consented to the first mortgage for £30,000, and benefited from it by living in the house, the first £30,000 of the remortgage would take priority over her interest.

The full extent of this decision has yet to become clear, especially with regard to the question of what amounts to a 'benefit' from the mortgage.

Example

Often remortgages or further mortgages are raised for extensions or improvements to the property. Would it depend on the extent to which the holder of the equitable interest used the improvement? A kitchen would benefit both the cook and the consumer of the food, presumably. What about a study? Garage? Hobby room?

On the issue of consent it is, however, clear that this needs a full knowledge of the consequences of agreeing to the mortgage.

Skipton Building Society v Clayton (1993)

The owners of a house sold it for one-third of its value, but retained the right to live there for the rest of their lives. Two months later the purchaser persuaded them to consent to a mortgage on the house by assuring them that it would not affect their right to live there. He failed to keep up the payments, however, and the building society claimed possession on the basis that their rights took priority over those of the occupants because they had explicitly consented to the mortgage. The Court of Appeal ruled that the occupants could not be treated as having consented because they misunderstood the way in which their rights would be affected.

2.8 Effects of registration

(a)   The register becomes the repository of all information concerning the land. Thus the title number (and to a lesser extent the Land Certificate) replaces the title deeds as evidence of ownership. In addition, this information is available to the public in a way that title deeds are not.

(b)   Dealings in land (if a specified transaction) have no legal effect until registration is completed.

(c)   Any rights affecting the land which are not registered are unenforceable against purchasers (unless they are overriding interests).

(d)   The state guarantees that the register is an accurate reflection of the title to the land, to the extent that compensation will be paid if rectification is necessary.

(e)   A purchaser is protected against any interests other than those revealed on the register (and overriding interests), including those that arise during the protected period of the official search.

3 Unregistered land

3.1 Introduction

Although the whole of England and Wales is now in an area of compulsory registration, there will still be many transactions which fall outside the registered land system. This is because many areas have only become areas of compulsory registration within the last few years, and therefore much land in those areas will not yet have been subjected to a 'specified transaction' which necessitates registration. It will be necessary to know the principles of unregistered conveyancing well into the next century. The system is the same in that it seeks to satisfy the purchaser that the correct person owns the land, and that there are no unforeseen interests affecting the land. However, it is different in that two separate procedures must be followed, rather than the single inspection of the Land Register which reveals both title and interests in the case of registered land. First, in unregistered land transactions the title must be established by inspection of the title deeds. This procedure is basically unchanged since before the 1925 legislation. Secondly, interests affecting the land are mostly revealed by searching a special Land Charges Register (separate and distinct from the Land Register). This system was partly in operation before 1925, but was greatly extended by the Land Charges Act 1925. That Act has now been replaced by the Land Charges Act 1972 but the basic principles remain the same. However there are still gaps in the protection afforded by registration, and therefore consideration must also be given to the *doctrine of notice* (see 3.6, below), which governs the way in which non-registrable equitable interests are binding.

3.2 Proof of title

The importance of the title deeds in this respect has already been explained (see *Introductory Principles*, 2.6). Under the Law of Property Act 1925, s. 44 (as amended), the owner of the land must produce these to the purchaser to enable the chain of ownership to be checked back to a *root of title* at least fifteen years old. A root of title at common law must be a transaction which deals with the whole legal estate, contains an adequate description of the land, and contains nothing to cast doubt on the title. This is looked at in more detail in the Conveyancing Syllabus, but the typical root of title will be a conveyance on sale of the land in question. In the first place the purchaser is not entitled to see the deeds themselves, and traditionally the seller would produce instead an *abstract of title* which is a short-hand transcription of every deed relating to the title. Nowadays either an *epitome of title* will be produced, consisting of photocopies of the relevant deeds, or even the deeds themselves. The deeds must at the latest be produced when the transaction is to be completed so that they can be checked against the abstract before the purchase moneys are handed over.

3.3   Land charges registration

Since 1925 most equitable interests and one legal interest must be registered by the owner of that interest at the Land Charges Registry. Under the Land Charges Act 1972, s. 4, failure to register a registrable interest means that it is void as against a purchaser of the land, and cannot then be revived against future purchasers. In addition, interests take priority according to the date of registration, rather than the date of creation.

Example

Roger grants an equitable mortgage to Celia. The following day he grants a further equitable mortgage over the same land to David. David registers his mortgage before Celia. If the land is sold, David's mortgage will be paid off from the proceeds of sale before Celia's mortgage. If there is insufficient money to pay off both mortgages, then Celia will suffer the consequences of delaying the registration of her mortgage.

Charges are recorded against the name of the owner of the land in question (not against the land itself, as in registered land practice). A potential purchaser must therefore search the register against all the owners of the land since 1925. However, in practice a purchaser will only know the names of owners from the root of title to the present day. Accordingly compensation from central funds for undetected rights is payable under the Law of Property Act 1969, s. 25 (this being the statute which reduced the period for the root of title from thirty to fifteen years). The searcher will receive a certificate detailing all entries against the names cited, with a note in each case of the land against which the charge has been entered. This certificate also gives a searcher priority over applicants to register charges for a period long enough to allow for completion of the purchase.

3.4   The Land Charges Register

There are in fact five registers kept under the Land Charges Act 1972:

(a)   register of pending actions;
(b)   register of annuities;
(c)   register of writs and orders affecting land;
(d)   register of deeds of arrangement;
(e)   land charges register.

Under the Land Charges Act 1972, s. 2, the Land Charges Register itself is divided into six classes of charge denominated A through to F, with several different types of charge under each classification. A charge is registrable if it falls into one of the categories thus described. Fortunately only six are of everyday importance, and will serve as examples. Roman numerals are used to distinguish the types of charge within each classification.

(a)   Class C I. Puisne mortgages. These are legal mortgages, and this is the only legal right that requires registration. Usually a mortgagee of unregistered land will take the title deeds to the land to ensure that his mortgage is protected. If this is not possible (for example, where it is a second mortgage) then it is classed as a puisne (pronounced 'puny') mortgage and requires registration to protect its priority over possible subsequent mortgages (see *Introductory Principles*, 2.8).

(b)   Class C III. General equitable charge. A residual category, such as equitable mortgages.

(c)   Class C IV. Estate contracts. A binding agreement to transfer or create a legal estate in land. Any contract for the sale of land is registrable, but this is rarely done in practice as the time between entering into the contract and completing the transaction is usually only four weeks at the most. However an option to purchase, or an option to renew contained in a lease, should be registered. When the option is exercised (i.e., by the holder of the option calling on the estate owner to sell) it is merely a continuance of the original contract.

Armstrong & Holmes Ltd v Holmes (1994)

The plaintiff had been granted an option to purchase property, registered it as a Class C IV land charge, and in due course exercised it in writing to the defendant. The defendant sold the property to another person, however, and then claimed that the letter exercising the option should also have been registered in order for it to be binding. The High Court ruled that the original option was the only estate contract involved, and therefore nothing else needed to be registered (nor was there any need for the exercise of the option to comply with the Law of Property (Miscellaneous Provisions) Act 1989, s. 2; see *Introductory Principles*, 2.7.2).

(d)   Class D II. Restrictive covenants entered into after 1925.

(e)   Class D III. Equitable easements created after 1925.

(f)   Class F. The sole charge under this classification is the right to occupy the matrimonial home granted to a spouse under the Matrimonial Homes Act 1983. This arises when the home is in the sole name of one spouse.

3.5   Other equitable interests

There are two categories of equitable interest that are not registrable.

3.5.1   Trusts.   It should be recalled that under the Law of Property Act 1925 all estates other than the two allowed by the Act could only take effect as equitable interests (see *Estates in Land*, 2.6.2). The effect of this step and the Settled Land Act 1925 was that interests such as life interests or entailed interests became interests under a trust. These are thus protected by the principle of overreaching, so that a purchaser will automatically take free of them if the purchase money is paid to two trustees. The interests then attach to the money, and are protected by the law relating to trusts.

3.5.2   Pre-1925 interests.   There still remain other equitable interests which have no protection at all under the 1925 legislation. Examples have already been given by implication in 3.4 above, such as restrictive covenants or equitable easements created before 1926. Whether these (admittedly rare) interests bind a purchaser of the land depends upon the doctrine of notice.

3.6   The doctrine of notice

This was the fundamental principle which applied to equitable interests before the 1925 legislation extended the system of registration. The courts wished to ensure that it was possible to buy land safely, as otherwise the free transfer of land would be hindered. On the other hand, it would not be fair to deprive the owner of an equitable interest merely because the land-owner had sold to somebody else. This doctrine was therefore developed as the best way of deciding between two innocent parties, i.e., the owner of the equitable interest and the innocent purchaser. The doctrine states that an equitable interest will be binding on everybody except a *bona fide purchaser for value of the legal estate without notice*. Once such a person has acquired an estate free from the interest, everybody who subsequently holds the land through that person will also hold it free from the interest, even if they themselves have notice of it. There are thus five essential elements.

(a)   Bona fide. A latin phrase meaning 'in good faith'. The purchaser must therefore have not been acting fraudulently, although in effect this only serves to stress the necessity for there to have been no notice.

(b)   Purchaser. Thus the land must have changed hands because of an agreement between the parties, and not merely by operation of law. Therefore the automatic transfer of property to the next of kin on an intestacy, or the vesting of property in the trustee for bankruptcy, are not 'purchases'. However, a gift or a specific bequest in a will are purchases in this context (but would fall foul of the 'for value' provision).

(c)   For value. There must have been some valuable consideration for the transaction, whether it was money or money's worth. The consideration can be nominal, as long as it has some value in law. Thus it could be 'in consideration of marriage', but not 'in natural love and affection'.

(d)   A legal estate. If the purchaser only acquires an equitable interest, then he is bound by existing equitable interests. The principle is that 'where equities are equal the first in time prevails'.

(e)   Without notice. There are three possible ways in which a purchaser could have notice. First, *actual notice*, as when the purchaser knew of the existence of the interest. Secondly, *constructive notice* which can arise if a purchaser does not make the proper and usual enquiries, or is negligent in so doing. Under the Law of Property Act 1925, s. 44, a purchaser must investigate the title to land for a specified period (now fifteen years: see 3.2 above). In addition there may be particular circumstances which merit investigation, such as the presence of another person on the land (see *Kingsnorth Trust* v *Tizard* (1986) and *Co-ownership of Land*, 3.5). Thirdly, *imputed notice* where a purchaser employs an agent (such as a solicitor). Anything that the agent discovers is deemed to be passed on to the actual purchaser, whether the agent does so or not.

3.7   The doctrine of notice and the 1925 legislation

It is worth reconsidering the impact of the 1925 legislation on the doctrine of notice. The effect of the Land Charges Act 1925 and the Land Registration Act 1925 was to substitute registration for actual notice. Thus a purchaser would thereafter be deemed to have notice of an interest if it was registered, whether he knew of it or not and whether he had searched the appropriate register or not. Conversely, if a registrable interest was not registered, a purchaser would be deemed to be innocent and ignorant even if he knew all about it! The key issue now therefore is whether an interest is registrable or not.

4   Registration and protection of rights in land

A summary of the consequences of the 1925 legislation can be encapsulated by noting the various categories of interests in land that do not require registration before they are protected as against a purchaser of the land. The first question of course must be whether the land in question is registered land. It is important to note carefully and to contrast what are overriding interests in the case of registered land, and what are non-registrable legal estates and interests in the case of unregistered land. Easements and profits à prendre are in each category, as are leases to a certain extent. After that the differences are substantial. It should then be borne in mind that if the land is unregistered, there are a few rare instances of non-registrable equitable interests which are still affected by the doctrine of notice. Finally, there is that small category of equitable interests which are not registrable whether the land is registered or not, because they are covered by the principle of overreaching. A few important examples from each of these categories of interest can be noted under the following headings.

(a)   Registered land: overriding interests. Easements and profits à prendre. Leases under twenty-one years. Rights of an occupier.

(b)   Unregistered land: legal rights. Easements and profits à prendre. Leases. Mortgages (unless puisne).

(c)   Unregistered land: non-registrable equitable interests. Pre-1925 restrictive covenants and easements.

(d)   Registered or unregistered land: overreachable interests. Interests under a settlement or a trust for sale.

The first task therefore is to check whether the land is registered or unregistered. Thereafter, if an interest does not fall into one of these categories, it must be registered in the appropriate register. Now, is that the Land Charges Register, or the charges register of the Land Register . . .?

CO-OWNERSHIP OF LAND

1   Introduction

1.1   Concurrent interests in land

It is possible for two or more persons to have the legal right to enjoy the same piece of land at the same time. Such persons are said to have *concurrent interests*, and if they both have the same legal estate they are known as *co-owners*. This situation must be distinguished from successive interests in the same piece of land, as when there is a life interest and an interest in remainder (see *Estates in Land*, 2.7).

Example

Roger grants a piece of land to Celia for life and thereafter to David in fee simple. Successive interests have been created (and the land becomes settled land in this particular example). Roger grants another piece of land to Celia and David jointly. They each have an immediate right to full possession of the land, and are therefore co-owners.

Technically there are four types of co-ownership : coparcenary, tenancy by entireties, joint tenancy and tenancy in common. In practice the only types that need be considered are joint tenancy and tenancy in common. The difference between these will be looked at in detail later (see 2 below).

1.2   The creation of concurrent interests

Co-ownership in land can be created expressly (as when land is transferred to two or more people on sale, or under a will), or by implication (where one person is sole owner of the legal estate but another person has an interest in it). Under the Law of Property Act 1925, ss. 34–36, this always creates a trust for sale (see *Estates in Land*, 3.4). Furthermore, under the Law of Property Act 1925, s. 53, an express trust must be created in writing. However an exception is made for resulting, implied or constructive trusts, and these will be considered later (see 3 below). The effect of these provisions is that whenever two or more persons become entitled to a concurrent interest in land, the legal estate is held by trustees on a trust for sale. In addition the Law of Property Act 1925, ss. 34(1) and 36(2), stipulate that the trustees themselves will hold the legal estate as joint tenants, although the equitable interests under the trust may be either joint or in common. The trusts thus imposed by the Act are known as the statutory trusts.

1.3   The statutory trusts

Under the Law of Property Act 1925, s. 34, the legal estate can only be held by a maximum of four persons. Where more than four persons are named in a grant, the first four of full age will be the trustees. Those four will thus hold the legal estate on trust for themselves and the others named in the grant. The trust will be a trust to hold the rents and profits pending sale, and to sell the land and to hold the proceeds of sale for the benefit of the various persons entitled to a share in them. The effects of a trust for sale have already been described (see *Estates in Land*, 3.5). It should be noted however that typically the co-owners themselves will be both the trustees and the beneficiaries under the trust. They will thus be able to postpone the sale under Law of Property Act 1925, s. 26(3), as long as they are in agreement. If the trustees/beneficiaries do not agree then normally the land must be sold. However, under s. 26(3) the trustees must consult with and give effect to the wishes of the beneficiaries 'or, in the case of a dispute, of the majority'. Thus in effect the majority of the trustees/beneficiaries (by value of their respective shares in the proceeds of sale) could still decide to postpone the sale. In addition, the court can refuse to order a sale if it considers that the purpose of the trust would thereby be defeated. This may be particularly relevant in the case of a matrimonial home (cf *Jones* v *Challenger* (1961), *Estates in Land*, 3.5.2).

2   Joint tenancies and tenancies in common

2.1   Introduction

As explained above, the equitable interests under the trust may be either joint or in common. In this context the word 'tenancy' derives from the French word 'tenir' meaning 'to hold', and should not be confused with its modern meaning of an interest under a lease (see *Introductory Principles*, 2.2). A joint tenancy means that each of the owners is entitled to the whole of the estate. It is as if two people are holding a single six-foot plank of wood. It is impossible to say that one is holding the first four feet of the plank and that the other is holding the remaining two feet (or any combination whatsoever). If one of them left, the remaining person would be in the same position, except that his arms might ache a little more! A tenancy in common however means that each person has a specific share in the estate, even though the shares have not yet been divided up. A tenancy in common is therefore sometimes known as an undivided share in land, the key distinction being that it is a share in the land, rather than an entitlement to the whole of the land. To continue with the above analogy, it is possible for each of them to leave with his part of the plank!

2.2   The nature of a joint tenancy

There are two crucial features of a joint tenancy, the principle of *survivorship* and the *four unities*.

2.2.1   Survivorship.
On the death of a joint tenant his interest in the land passes automatically to the others. If only one is left alive, then that one person now holds the whole land. This process is sometimes known by the Latin phrase *ius accrescendi*. The process is best thought of as the deceased tenant dropping out, rather than his share being transferred. The plank of wood is merely being supported by one less person, until eventually just one person is left holding it. This means that the rights of the remaining tenants cannot be affected by the deceased's will or intestacy, and the land is not inherited in the sense of being transferred as part of the deceased's estate. For conveyancing purposes, therefore, a survivor under a joint tenancy only needs to prove the death of the other joint tenant(s) to be able to transfer the land freely. Under the Law of Property (Joint Tenants) Act 1964, s. 1(1), if the land is unregistered, a surviving joint tenant is deemed to be solely entitled if he conveys as 'beneficial owner'. If it is registered land, then there must be a restriction on the proprietorship register before the other tenants in common are protected (see *Registered and Unregistered Land*, 2.5.3).

2.2.2   The four unities.
These were not in fact invented by PITT the Younger (or Elder!), although their initial letters spell out his name. A joint tenancy cannot exist unless all four of these unities also exist. They are first, the unity of *possession*. All co-owners (including tenants in common) must be entitled to every part of the land and thus one co-owner cannot be guilty of trespassing on any part of the land. Secondly, the unity of *interest*. Each joint tenant must have the same interest in the same estate: there cannot be joint tenants where one has a fee simple and the other a term of years. Thirdly, the unity of *time*. The interest of each must arise at the same time. This unity is perhaps doubtful as a certain test (see 2.3.3 below). Fourthly, the unity of *title*. The interest of each joint tenant must derive from the same document (for example, a conveyance) or act (for example, possession under

the Limitation Act 1980). Thus if one joint tenant assigns his interest to another person, that person must hold under a tenancy in common (see however 2.3 below for further clarification of this situation).

2.3   Creation of a joint tenancy

In conveyancing practice the purchasers prepare the transfer or conveyance, for approval by the seller. Therefore it will be the co-purchasers who decide whether they wish to hold as joint tenants or to have separate shares in the land, and there should be a clear statement to that effect. In the standard form of registered land transfer to co-owners there is a printed clause giving the option as to whether the survivor can give a valid receipt for capital moneys raised on the land in the future (typically upon a future sale of the land). Although only a survivor under a joint tenancy can do this (see 2.2.1), even this is not a clear enough statement as to the status of the beneficial interests, and more specific wording should be used (*Huntingford* v *Hobbs* (1993)). If there is a clear statement of the trusts, this will be conclusive between the co-owners should there be any dispute in the future. Thus a statement such as 'as joint tenants in law and equity' will create a joint tenancy. If words are used which imply a severance of the interests in the estate, then a tenancy in common will be created. For example, words such as 'in equal shares', 'amongst', even 'equally'. The point is that any word which implies that each person does not have a right to the whole of the estate, is inconsistent with a joint tenancy. Unfortunately there is not always a clear statement in this way, particularly where the transfer has not been drafted by the co-owners themselves. Therefore certain rules have been developed to ascertain the position where there is any doubt.

2.3.1   Provisions in the document effecting the grant.   Occasionally an ambiguous phrase will be encountered, such as 'as joint tenants in equal shares'. The courts have sometimes taken this to show a joint tenancy (*Joyce* v *Barker Bros* (1980)), and sometimes a tenancy in common (*Martin* v *Martin* (1989)). However, the context of the document as a whole may provide evidence of the grantor's intention.

Re North (1952)
A bequest of land to two beneficiaries was coupled with a condition that they should pay in equal shares the sum of £10 per week to a third person. It was held that this obligation to pay separate shares in one lump sum must correspond to the terms of the gift of the land, and that therefore a tenancy in common had been intended.

2.3.2   Presumptions of equity.   If there is a simple transfer to two or more people, with no surrounding circumstances as mentioned above, the presumption will be that the grant creates a joint tenancy in equity to correspond with the legal estate (which must be a joint tenancy. See 1.2 above). However, in three situations there will be a presumption of a tenancy in common. First, where the co-owners provided the purchase money in unequal proportions. As this is the case in most domestic conveyancing transactions, it is vital that the conveyancer ensures that the co-owners' intentions are accurately reflected in the transfer to them. Secondly, where the co-owners are mortgagees, whether they have lent the money in equal or unequal shares. It is assumed that each means to lend and take back his own money, rather than have a right to the whole amount. Thirdly, where the co-owners are partners in a business sense and the land is part of the business's assets. The principle of survivorship is not seen as appropriate to commercial transactions.

2.3.3   Reference to the 'four unities'.   It is sometimes said that the lack of one or more of the unities of 'interest', 'time' or 'title' means that a tenancy in common must exist (unity of possession must of course be present whenever there is co-ownership). However, this adds little to the equitable presumptions stated above, and will normally be a matter of common sense. If there are different 'interests' then, by definition, the co-owners cannot be joint tenants. If the interests were created at different 'times', they could still in theory be joint tenants if the grant so states. Therefore it is the grant and its construction which is all important. If the interests derive from different 'titles', a tenancy in common is created because this amounts to a *severance* (see 2.4 below), not because of the formalism of the 'unities'.

2.4   Severance of a joint tenancy

A joint tenancy can be converted into a tenancy in common, and in some circumstances such a conversion is obligatory. This only affects the equitable interests, however, as the legal estate must always be held as a joint tenancy (see 1.2 above). This conversion is known as *severing* the joint tenancy because the process has the effect of dividing it into individual shares. A joint tenant whose interest is severed should protect himself by recording that fact. If the land is unregistered, this should be done by endorsing a notice on the deed which conveyed the land to the joint tenants. If it is registered land, a restriction should be placed on the proprietorship register. There are five ways in which a severance can happen.

2.4.1   Mutual agreement.   The joint tenants can agree to a severance, and such an agreement will take effect even if it is not legally binding.

Burgess v Rawnsley (1975)
The joint tenants were a couple whose relationship had broken down. They agreed that the man would buy the interest of the woman for £750. Unfortunately the man died, and therefore there was a dispute as to whether the survivorship rule would operate in favour of the woman. As the agreement was only verbal, it was unenforceable under the Law of Property Act 1925, s. 40, but still a valid agreement (see *Introductory Principles*, 2.7 and note that the agreement would now be void). However, the Court of Appeal held that it still had the effect of severing the tenancy.

The principle would seem to be that it is the conduct of the parties which is important, rather than the agreement itself. In that respect this type of arrangement could perhaps be placed under the next heading, although it is regarded by the courts as a distinct category.

2.4.2   Conduct.   Any behaviour or dealing with the property which shows an intention that there be separate shares in the estate will operate as a severance. Thus if one tenant sells her interest, the purchaser will hold a share as tenant in common while the remainder of the estate will still be held by the others as joint tenants. If one tenant acquired an additional estate or interest in the land, this would have the same effect.

Example

Bertram, Celia and David hold a lease as tenants in common. Celia sells her interest to Erica, who will now be a tenant in common for a one-third share. The remaining two-thirds will still be held by Bertram and David on a joint tenancy. If Bertram were now to buy the freehold reversion, this would merge with his leasehold interest and sever the remaining joint tenancy.

This situation differs from the 'agreement' principle in that the conduct must be irrevocable in its effect. Thus a contract to sell could operate as a severance, as it is legally binding. A gift in a will however will not operate as a severance, as it has no effect until the testator's death and is revocable until then.

2.4.3 Homicide.   This could also be regarded as an extreme example of the principle of conduct operating as a severance! However, there is a well-established principle that a person cannot benefit from his crime, so that if one joint tenant unlawfully kills another he cannot be allowed to benefit from the survivorship rule. If there are several joint tenants, the effect will be the same as the sale of one interest.

2.4.4 Involuntary alienation.   The bankruptcy of a joint tenant will have the same effect as a sale of her interest, as it will vest in the trustee in bankruptcy.

2.4.5 Notice in writing.   Under the Law of Property Act 1925, s. 36(2), any joint tenant can sever the tenancy by giving notice in writing to the other tenants. This takes effect as soon as it is posted, even if it is not received. It need not be in any particular form, as long as the intention is clear.

Re Drapers Conveyance (1969)
A matrimonial home was in the joint names of the husband and wife. The wife issued a summons under the Married Women's Property Act 1882 asking for the house to be sold and the proceeds divided. It was held that this amounted to a severance.

This case should be regarded as an extreme example. Usually a proper notice should be served, and certainly any other form of unilateral declaration or conduct will not operate as a severance.

Harris v Goddard (1983)
In this case the wife had issued a divorce petition. In the prayers in the petition was the standard application for a transfer of property or property adjustment order. The Court of Appeal ruled that this was not a severance.

2.5   The distinction between joint tenancies and tenancies in common

A useful way to summarise this section is to compare joint tenancies and tenancies in common under four headings.

(a)   Shares. A joint tenant has a potential share in the proceeds of sale, as they must be divided equally when a sale takes place. A tenant in common has a share already, although it has not yet been divided. In practice, of course, this distinction has little effect. However, tenants in common need not have equal shares.

(b)   Transfer of interests. A joint tenant's interest cannot be transferred without creating a tenancy in common. On death the principle of survivorship will operate, which is not a transfer as such. Tenants in common can transfer their shares freely, for example, under their wills.

(c)   Four unities. The unity of possession applies to both. The other three unities (interest, time and title) only apply to joint tenancies.

(d)   Conversion. A joint tenant can convert his joint tenancy into a tenancy in common by severance. Tenants in common must all agree and execute a new document to convert their interests into a joint tenancy.

3   Implied co-ownership

3.1   Introduction

The situation often arises that the legal estate is in the sole name of one person, although another person is clearly meant to have an interest in it. This situation is most common when a house is the matrimonial home for a husband and wife or an unmarried couple. However, other forms of relationship can give rise to the same problem, and often involve several people (see, for example, *City of London Building Society* v *Flegg* (1988) and *Abbey National Building Society* v *Cann* (1990) in *Registered and Unregistered Land*, 2.7). The non-owner who is a spouse has a right to occupy the house under the Matrimonial Homes Act 1983, and can protect that right by registration. However, the right of occupation has no effect upon the equitable interests in the proceeds of sale of the house, although it is often used as an informal bargaining counter! In any event, a spouse always has the option of taking divorce proceedings, whereupon the divorce court can be asked to grant or transfer property rights, regardless of the legal or equitable interests. The problems caused by sole ownership with 'hidden' interests are therefore most likely to cause difficulties where the house is lived in by an unmarried couple, or is shared with parents as in the two cases mentioned above. In that situation it may be that the non-owner has contributed towards the financial costs of buying or running the home, and wishes to claim that the owner holds the property on trust for them both. The basic rule is that a trust in land must be in writing (Law of Property Act 1925, s. 53). The only way therefore that an interest in property can be obtained is where the couple are married and one of them has made a substantial contribution in money or money's worth to the improvement of the property. Under the Matrimonial Proceedings and Property Act 1970, s. 37, the courts will treat such a person as having acquired a share or an increased share, in proportion to the amount by which their contribution has increased the value of the property. More importantly, however, there is a specific exception in the Law of Property Act 1925, s. 53(2) for *'resulting, implied or constructive trusts'*. This terminology is confusing, as the courts have failed to distinguish clearly between the three terms. However, it seems to be the position that the word 'constructive' is a catch-all term to mean any type of co-ownership which is implied by the courts rather than created expressly. Accordingly there are two clear categories of *resulting* and *implied* trust which can be applied to assist any person in the situations described above.

3.2   Resulting trusts

A resulting trust arises when one person purchases property at least partly with another person's money. In this situation it is presumed that the person providing the funds for the purchase is to be entitled to a share proportionate to the size of the contribution. Thus the legal estate will be held on trust, unless it can be proved that some other result was intended.

Sekhon v Alissa (1989)

A woman gave her daughter some money to buy a house. The daughter obtained a mortgage and bought the house in her own name. The court ruled that this arrangement created a trust, as the daughter was unable to prove that the money from her mother was intended to be a gift.

3.3   Implied trusts

The courts will also impose a trust where there is some other evidence of an intention that a non-owner was meant to have an interest in land. There are several decisions of the courts which sometimes conflict, but it now seems that this intention can be inferred from an express agreement or from the conduct of the parties.

Lloyds Bank plc v Rossett (1990)

A semi-derelict farmhouse was purchased by a married couple, but in the sole name of the husband. The wife did not contribute to the purchase price or the mortgage payments, but used her skills as a trained decorator by working on the house for two months before they moved in. Unfortunately the bank had to claim possession under the terms of the mortgage (see *Introductory Principles*, 2.8), and the question arose as to whether the wife had an overriding interest. As this could only be established if she had an equitable interest (see *Registered and Unregistered Land*, 2.7), the House of Lords had to rule on her position. They held that her contributions were not sufficient to infer a trust, and confirmed that only two situations would give rise to such an inference; there must have been either an agreement relied upon by the non-owner to her detriment, or conduct showing that ownership was to be shared. In the second situation, however, only certain conduct could give rise to the inference, such as a contribution towards the purchase price.

The decision of the House of Lords in *Lloyds Bank plc v Rossett* was based on developments of the law through earlier court decisions. As these also illustrate the typical situations in which an implied trust will take effect, each will now be looked at in turn.

3.3.1   Express agreement.

There are two distinct elements to this situation. First, there must be a verbal agreement that the non-owner is to have a share in the property. In *Grant v Edwards* (1986), the case which established this principle, there was a clear agreement that the house would be placed in the man's name so that it would not complicate the woman's divorce proceedings. The agreement may be less clear cut than that, however.

Hammond v Mitchell (1992)

Ms Mitchell moved in with Mr Hammond, a married man. After two years they had had a child, and Mr Hammond decided to purchase another house. This was in his sole name and with no financial contributions from Ms Mitchell, but there were discussions beforehand about the tax advantages and the potential difficulties with his divorce. The court ruled that this amounted to an understanding that the beneficial interest in the house would be shared between them, and awarded Ms Mitchell a half share.

Secondly, there must be evidence that the non-owner relied upon the agreement to her detriment. This could be simply by paying towards household expenses, as the woman did in *Grant v Edwards*. In *Hammond v Mitchell* the woman signed an agreement allowing Mr Hammond to take out an increased mortgage, and helped out in his business.

3.3.2 Conduct of the parties. The conduct must be related to the purchase of the property, and therefore only a direct contribution to the purchase price in money or money's worth will be clear evidence of an intention that a non-owner has an interest. Contributions towards the mortgage payments would come under this heading, but no other contributions, no matter how substantial.

Gissing v Gissing (1971)

A house was purchased by a married couple, but conveyed into the sole name of the husband. The husband provided all the deposit, and paid the mortgage. The wife bought various items of furniture and paid for the lawn to be re-laid, and also spent her earnings on clothes for herself and their son. The House of Lords held that there was no implied trust.

Physical assistance in building the property could create an implied trust as this is a contribution in money's worth:

Cooke v Head (1972)

The plaintiff formed a relationship with a married man (the defendant). While they were waiting for his divorce, they purchased some land to build a bungalow. The land was conveyed into the sole name of the defendant, and he paid the deposit and mortgage payments. However, the plaintiff used a sledgehammer to demolish old buildings, operated the cement mixer and barrowed away rubble. The relationship terminated before they could move into the bungalow, but the Court of Appeal ruled that the plaintiff was entitled to a one-third share in its value.

There may be difficulties where the contribution to the purchase of the property is more indirect. The situation often arises where one party pays the mortgage, while the other pays for food, clothing or other household bills. The courts may infer a trust if this is part of a special arrangement.

Hazel v Hazel (1972)

A husband and wife lived in a house conveyed into the sole name of the husband. The husband paid the mortgage, but when the wife obtained a job he reduced the housekeeping which he regularly gave her out of his wages. She continued to pay all of the household expenses, apart from the mortgage. The Court of Appeal ruled that she was entitled to a share in the house under an implied trust.

3.3.3 Quantifying the non-owner's interest. Once an implied trust has been established, the court may go on to look at all the circumstances to enable it to determine the terms of the trust (i.e., the respective shares). The extent of the non-owner's interest will always depend upon the terms of the agreement, rather than the value of their contributions; but on the other hand the value of the contributions may be the best evidence of the intended extent of the non-owner's interest!

Stokes v Anderson (1991)

A man lived in a house which was in the joint names of himself and his wife. His wife left and they were divorced. He then formed a relationship with another woman and decided to purchase his ex-wife's interest in the house. The woman contributed various sums, both immediately and subsequently, and also worked on the house and the garden. Their relationship then broke down and he applied for an order to remove her from the house. The Court of Appeal ruled that there was an implied trust because of her contributions to the purchase of his ex-wife's share, and looked at all the conduct after that point to decide that she was meant to have a half share in the half share that was purchased (i.e., a quarter of the total value of the house).

In *Hammond* v *Mitchell* the court even took into account the effort that Ms Mitchell put into Mr Hammond's business, as this showed that they regarded all their enterprises as jointly owned in practice.

3.4 Summary

If the legal title to land is in the sole name of one person, but there is evidence to suggest that another person or persons may wish to claim an interest in that land, the following questions should be asked one after the other.

Trust agreement in writing?	EXPRESS TRUST
Purchase with non-owner's money?	CONSTRUCTIVE TRUST
Other financial contribution by non-owner?	CONSTRUCTIVE TRUST
Verbal agreement and reliance by non-owner?	CONSTRUCTIVE TRUST
None of these applies	NO TRUST

Do not be misled by a situation which seems to demand a constructive trust for the sake of 'fairness'. The following two cases illustrate how unfair the law can be on occasions.

Burns v Burns (1984)

A couple lived together for nineteen years. The man owned the house and paid the mortgage. The woman brought up their two children, was known as his wife, and when she was in employment she paid for many household expenses. The Court of Appeal held that she was not entitled to a share in the house.

Thomas v Fuller-Brown (1988)

An unmarried couple lived together in a house which was in the sole name of the woman. The man made no contribution towards the purchase price. The woman obtained an improvement grant and the man designed and built a two-storey extension. He also did electrical and plumbing work, landscaped the garden, laid a drive and carried out various other repairs and improvements. The Court of Appeal held that this work could merely have been instead of paying rent, and that therefore it was not evidence of an intention that he was to have a share in the house.

3.5 Protection of implied co-owner

An equitable interest which arises under a constructive trust cannot be registered. A person with such an interest must therefore rely for protection against third parties on the doctrine of notice if the land is unregistered.

Kingsnorth Trust Ltd v *Tizard* **(1986)**

A man told the surveyor for the plaintiff company that he was single. The plaintiff lent him money on the security of a house which was in his sole name. However the man's wife was in occupation, and the court ruled that the plaintiff had notice of her interest as a result. The only other enquiry that the plaintiff made was an inspection by appointment on a Sunday afternoon, and therefore it had constructive notice of her interest (see *Registered and Unregistered Land*, 3.6(e)).

If the land is registered, then the interest may be an overriding interest (see *Registered and Unregistered Land*, 2.6). Whether the land is registered or unregistered, however, care must be taken when applying the basic rule, as the courts have gone some way to reducing the effectiveness of the protection when the third party is the mortgagee of the property. Refer back to the section concerning the rights of persons in actual occupation (*Registered and Unregistered Land*, 2.7), and note again the effect of *Abbey National Building Society* v *Cann* (1990) and *City of London Building Society* v *Flegg* (1988). In particular it should be noted that an implied trust may be subject to a subsequent mortgage if the mortgage was with the knowledge, and for the benefit, of the holder of the interest, under the special rule in *Equity & Law Home Loans* v *Prestidge* (1992).

LEGAL AND EQUITABLE INTERESTS

1   Introduction

There are many ways in which land owned by one person can be subject to rights owned by another person. One recent innovation is a statute which enables the courts to make an order allowing a land-owner who needs to carry out essential repairs to their property to have access to another person's land in order to carry out the work properly (the Rights of Access to Neighbouring Land Act 1992). More important, however, are the different legal and equitable interests which are part and parcel of normal land ownership, and with which the conveyancer has to have an easy familiarity. The five legal rights possible under the Law of Property Act 1925 have been explained already (see *Estates in Land*, 2.1). In addition there are certain equitable interests that must usually be protected by registration (see *Estates in Land*, 2.6 and *Registered and Unregistered Land*, 3.4). Of the legal interests, mortgages are encountered most frequently by the practitioner as nearly every domestic house sale or purchase will be subject to a mortgage. This aspect of land law is dealt with in the Conveyancing Practice Syllabus.

The *servitudes* (easements and profits à prendre) are also important, as they can operate both for the benefit of, or as an incumbrance on a piece of land. Easements are probably encountered most often in everyday conveyancing practice. Most properties need the main services such as gas, electricity and sewerage and the appropriate pipes and cables may have to run under adjoining land. Whenever this happens there must be an easement in favour of the land being 'served'. In older properties it is not uncommon for rights of way to exist to enable access to be gained to the rear of the land. As well as advising a prospective purchaser of the various rights affecting the land, the conveyancer must also ensure that the appropriate easements have been granted for its benefit, and that the terms of the grant are sufficient for the owner's purposes. A right of way for pedestrians is not much good for the land-owner who wants to have access by car or lorry!

Of the equitable interests, the rules relating to *restrictive covenants* are perhaps the most complex. Most land is subject to restrictions imposed by previous owners. In the case of domestic housing, these restrictions will often have been imposed by a land-owner who sold the land to a developer but who wanted to protect a special interest. Thus, for example, in areas of the Midlands many houses have a specific restriction forbidding them from being used for the sale of alcohol, because the original land-owners were companies which owned breweries and public houses of their own. Similarly the developers themselves may impose restrictions in order to enhance the value of the housing on the estate that they are building, and thus enable them to sell the houses at a higher price. Thus many modern housing estates are 'open plan', and no house-owner is permitted to erect a fence or wall at the front of the house. Covenants may be even more vital where the land is being used for commercial purposes, as they could effectively prevent the very business that the land-owner has in mind.

All servitudes and restrictive covenants are therefore limits on the freedom of successive land-owners to deal with the land, and persons having the benefit can bring court proceedings to prevent their rights being infringed. There are thus strict rules as to the extent to which such restrictions can be imposed and the way in which they can be created.

2 Servitudes

2.1 The nature of easements

An easement is a right attached to a specific piece of land whereby another piece of land of different ownership is utilised for its benefit. The land which has the benefit of the easement is known as the *dominant tenement*, and the land over which the easement is exercised is the *servient tenement*. The right can be positive or negative in nature. A positive easement is the right to do something on the servient land, such as walk over it. A negative easement restricts the servient owner in some way, such as preventing a right of light from being blocked. The parties to the agreement must intend the right to be attached to the land, however, rather than just a personal right. If a land-owner merely wants to allow another person to use their land under a personal agreement, the right granted will typically be called a 'licence'. If a deed uses this term, therefore, that will usually preclude the existence of an easement.

IDC Group Ltd v *Clark* (1992)

The owners of adjoining houses entered into a formal and professionally drafted agreement, described as a 'licence', whereby an opening was made in the party wall as a fire escape route from one house into and through the other. Twenty years later the properties had changed hands, and after the defendant had blocked up the doorway, the plaintiffs claimed a continuing right of way in accordance with the original agreement. The Court of Appeal ruled that, as a licence, the agreement did not give rise to an easement. The use of the word 'licence' did not necessarily preclude the agreement amounting to the grant of an easement in fact, but the circumstances at the time did not suggest that the parties intended anything other than a purely personal agreement.

Once an easement is established it will affect both dominant and servient tenements until it is extinguished, and can therefore be enforced by successive owners of the dominant land against successive owners of the servient land. However, not all rights can amount to easements.

Re Ellenborough Park (1956)

Several people owned houses which adjoined a park. They had all been given the right to 'full enjoyment' of the park when they purchased their houses. The Court of Appeal held that this was an easement, but that in different circumstances the mere privilege to use an area at will would not be so regarded.

Therefore, the distinction between what can and what cannot be an easement is not always clear. The Court of Appeal in *Re Ellenborough Park* laid down four essential elements.

2.1.1 A dominant and servient tenement. The right must be connected to land. A right which is independent of ownership of land is said to be *in gross*, and can only be enforceable as a personal agreement between two people.

London & Blenheim Estates Ltd v Ladbroke Retail Parks Ltd (1993)

The plaintiff had purchased land together with a right of way over and a right to park on land retained by the seller. The transfer also purported to allow these rights to be exercised for the benefit of any other land purchased by the plaintiff within five years, as soon as written notice was given to the seller. The retained land was eventually sold to the defendant. The plaintiff in due course purchased some more adjoining land, but the defendant refused to allow the easements to be used for its benefit. The Court of Appeal ruled that the rights could not be extended to the new land as it was not (part of) the dominant tenement at the time that the easements were granted.

2.1.2 Accommodation of the dominant tenement. It is not sufficient that the right is notionally connected to land, as it must actually benefit that land as well. Usually this will mean that the servient land is adjacent, but that is not strictly necessary as long as the dominant tenement is thereby made a better property. The crucial distinction is always going to be whether the right is merely a personal benefit to the occupier of the dominant tenement, or whether the land itself is improved. However, as the improvement of land is usually for the increased enjoyment of the occupier, this distinction is often a difficult one. Any increase in the value of the land is irrelevant in itself, as it is the use of the land which must be benefited. Rights of access or light are usually beneficial to the use of any land. A right which benefits a specific and well-established business on the land may also amount to an easement.

Moody v Steggles (1879)

The dominant tenement was a public house, with a right to attach advertising signs to the wall of an adjoining property (the servient tenement). This was held to be an easement.

However, note that the business must itself be closely connected to the dominant tenement.

Hill v Tupper (1863)

The owner of a canal leased land to the plaintiff together with the sole right to put pleasure boats on the canal. The defendant was the landlord of a nearby public house who also started to run pleasure boats. The court ruled that the plaintiff had not been granted an easement, but only a personal licence which was only enforceable against the canal-owner. The right to use pleasure boats was an independent business enterprise, with no real connection to the land in question.

If the dominant tenement is a domestic dwelling, it is sometimes difficult to distinguish between rights which are merely recreational and therefore personal to the occupier, and rights which amount to an improvement in the facilities of the land. This will often involve an assessment of what types of facilities are integral to everyday domestic arrangements.

Example

A right to the owner of land to have free access to the local football ground would probably not amount to an easement. However in *Re Ellenborough Park* a right to use a park 'for such domestic purposes as taking out small children in perambulators . . . is clearly beneficial to the premises' (per Evershed MR).

2.1.3 Different owners. Rights exercised by an owner over his own land cannot be easements unless one tenement is occupied by another person, for example, under a lease granted by the owner.

2.1.4 The right is capable of being granted. There are three possible ways in which a right may not qualify. First, there must be a capable grantor and grantee. Certain corporations may not be allowed to grant or receive an easement, and a fluctuating body of people is not capable of benefiting from a grant. Secondly, the right must be definite. Thus a right to 'privacy', or a 'view' would be too vague to be capable of being an easement. Thirdly, the right must be one that has the characteristics of rights recognised by the courts as amounting to easements. In other words, there are certain recognised categories of easements (rights of way, water, light and support) and the courts are wary of allowing anything which does not fall into one of those categories. As any easement acts as a restriction on the use of land, and therefore on the free development or transfer of that land, the courts' policy is to limit new types. One basic principle is that a right cannot be an easement if it effectively allows the dominant owner to share possession of the servient tenement.

Copeland v Greenhalf (1952)
The plaintiff owned an orchard. Access was by a strip of land, with a wide entrance where it joined the main road. The defendant was a wheelwright with premises opposite the entrance, and he proved that he had used the strip of land for fifty years as storage for vehicles awaiting his attention. The court ruled that this could not amount to an easement as the right claimed was too extensive.

This problem has frequently arisen in modern times in connection with parking rights. The approach to be taken was clarified by the High Court in *London & Blenheim Estates Ltd* v *Ladbroke Retail Parks Ltd* (1994) (2.1.1 above), which ruled that a right to park can be an easement as long as it relates to the servient tenement generally (i.e., is not restricted to a defined space). It will be a question of degree in every case, therefore, whether the right granted is so extensive as to amount to possession of the land rather than an easement over it.

2.2   The nature of profits à prendre

A profit is the right to take something off another person's land which is either part of the soil or produce of the soil. This definition includes minerals, crops or wild animals or fish. A profit will run with the land affected and is therefore enforceable against successive owners of the land, in the same way as an easement. The important distinction between a profit and an easement is that a profit can exist in gross, or be attached to a dominant tenement. If it is attached to a dominant tenement it is said to be a *profit appurtenant*, and must therefore be for the benefit of the dominant tenement. The principal consequence of this is that the profit will be limited in its extent.

Example

A profit appurtenant to take fish from a servient tenement will not allow the dominant owner to take fish for the purposes of resale. The fishing must be limited to an amount sufficient for the needs of the dominant tenement alone. However, if the profit was in gross, then there would be no restriction unless one was imposed under the terms of the grant.

It is also possible (and usual) for a profit to be enjoyed by several people, as long as they are a definite class. It is then said to be a profit (or right) *in common*. The servient tenement is known as *common land*, and details of the land and the rights attaching to it have to be registered under the Commons Registration Act 1965. If undeveloped land is being purchased in a rural area, a search of the Commons Register should be made by the purchaser, as well as the normal pre-contract searches.

2.3   Creation of servitudes

Easements and profits must have their origin in a specific grant. This will usually be an express grant. However the courts sometimes have to deal with situations where a right clearly exists, but no express grant can be traced. In such cases they may declare an implied grant, or a presumed grant. There are thus three basic methods whereby a servitude can be recognised by the courts, and each must be considered in some detail. Usually the same rules will apply to both easements and profits, but the occasional differences should be noted carefully.

2.4   Express grant

There are four ways in which a servitude may be expressly created. They will be considered individually below.

2.4.1   Statute.   An Act of Parliament may allow public utilities to lay pipes or cables over land. This will have the effect of creating an easement, although there is no dominant tenement as such.

2.4.2   Deed.   To be a legal interest an express grant by one person to another must be by deed and be for a term equivalent to one of the two legal estates (see *Introductory Principles*, 2.3). Otherwise the right will only be an equitable interest, and must be registered. The terms of the agreement may even indicate that the parties intended nothing more than a purely personal agreement, and not an easement at all (see *IDC Group Ltd* v *Clark* (1992), 2.1 above). The terms of the original grant will govern the extent of the interest for as long as it exists. The difficulty often arises, however, of construing the extent of the original easement where there is a substantially increased use of the right. The general rule is that an express grant in general terms will allow the grantee to exercise the right in any way, as long as it is lawful. A distinction must therefore be drawn between a use which is different in kind from that originally granted; and the same use, but in a different way.

Example

A grant of a right of way 'by foot' will not allow a future owner of the right to have access with a vehicle. A general right of way, even if granted before the days of motorised vehicles, will support access by cars or lorries, but will not necessarily permit them to park on the land. In practice the distinction is not always easy to draw, as the following two cases show.

Alvis v *Harrison* (1990)

The defendant had a general right of way over the plaintiff's land, but as the nature of his business changed, large articulated lorries began to pass over it with increasing regularity. Eventually he laid tarmac to make access for the lorries even easier, at which point the plaintiff tried to limit use to ordinary vehicles. The House of Lords ruled that, as the grant was express and in general terms, increased use (albeit in a different manner and with different vehicles) could not be prevented.

White v *Richards* (1993)

The defendant purchased land with a right to 'pass and repass on foot and with or without motor vehicles' over a dirt track belonging to the plaintiff. At the time of the grant the track was about nine feet wide, and the plaintiff's house stood only nine feet away from it and facing it. The defendant started using the track for heavy lorries, so that eventually fourteen lorries were passing over it every day. The Court of Appeal granted an injunction restricting use to vehicles nine feet wide and under ten tons laden weight.

The proper construction of the terms of the grant must also look carefully at the full circumstances surrounding the grant, as ancillary rights such as parking may be implied in certain situations (see 2.5.2 below).

Example

A right to park on a right of way may be necessary to allow loading and unloading if the right was granted to allow access for that purpose, but only if there is no other land available. A right of way 'on foot' leading from a car park to a supermarket may permit access with a supermarket trolley, and for the trolleys to be parked there for unloading and later collection by supermarket staff.

It is common for such rights to be created by reservation. This arises when a land-owner sells part of his land, and under the Law of Property Act 1925, s. 65, may be included in a conveyance without any need for execution by the purchaser.

Example

Celia sells part of her land to Roger. However, she needs to have a right of way over it to gain access to the part she has retained. In the conveyance, therefore, there will be a clause 'reserving' such a right.

The distinction between a *grant* and a *reservation* is important. Normally any ambiguity in the terms of the servitude will be construed in favour of the grantee. However, a reservation is deemed to operate by way of re-grant to the seller of the land. In the example above, therefore, any ambiguity in the terms of the right of way will be construed in favour of Celia.

2.4.3   The Law of Property Act 1925, s. 62.   Under this section, every conveyance of land will automatically transfer (unless there is a contrary intention expressed in the deed) 'all easements, rights and advantages whatsoever appertaining or reputed to appertain to the land . . . or enjoyed with the land'. This only applies where the land being sold (the dominant tenement) is already being occupied by a different person from the occupier of the land over which the right is enjoyed (the servient tenement).

Example

Roger sells his house to David, but retains an adjoining piece of land for his own use. Roger has always used that piece of land to gain access to his house. The Act will not operate to transfer that right of way to David (but see 2.5 below). However, if the house had been occupied by a tenant, who was allowed across Roger's land to get to it, the conveyance to David would include that right of way without it being mentioned.

This rule will therefore have the effect of converting a revocable licence into a legal right.

***Wright v Macadam* (1949)**
A land-owner leased adjoining premises to a tenant. He then allowed her to store coal in a bunker on his land. When the lease was renewed, it operated to grant the tenant an easement to use the bunker to store coal which could not now be revoked.

2.5   Implied grant

The courts may sometimes decide that the parties to a transaction would have expressly agreed a servitude (typically an easement) if they had given proper thought to the situation. The underlying principle is that of *non-derogation from grant*, i.e., that the terms of a grant should not usually have the effect of nullifying the usefulness of the land being transferred. The courts will therefore imply terms into a grant in such a situation, which arises in three typical sets of circumstances.

2.5.1   Implied reservation.   If a person sells part of a piece of land and retains the remainder, the courts may allow an easement of necessity. This is strictly limited to rights without which the land could not be used at all, and only considering the situation as at the time of the transaction.

Corporation of London v *Riggs* (1880)

The defendant had sold land to the plaintiff, but had retained a piece which was completely surrounded by it. Initially this piece was used for agriculture, but the defendant then started to bring building materials across the plaintiff's land. The court ruled that there was a right of way of necessity, but only for the purposes of agriculture.

However, it seems that the basis of the principle is not one of public policy, but that of the presumed intentions of the parties. Thus the 'necessity' of the right is evidence that the parties would have agreed such a right if they had given proper thought to it. There may be other situations where the real intentions of the parties can be ascertained, regardless of the issue of necessity

2.5.2   Implied grant.   Where a right is claimed by the purchaser of the land, the courts are more inclined to imply one. In *Pwllbach Colliery Co. Ltd* v *Woodman* (1915) the House of Lords stipulated that this could occur in two ways. First, if the easement was necessary to give effect to the express terms of the grant. This is a strict test in that it would usually only apply to allow (for example) access to the land. Secondly, if the easement is necessary to give effect to 'the common intention of the parties'. This could depend on the circumstances in which the grant was made rather than its precise terms, and the person claiming the easement must prove both the existence of a common intention, and that the easement is necessary to give effect to it.

Stafford v *Lee* (1993)

The plaintiff owned a plot of woodland that had originally been conveyed with no express right of way to it. The defendants owned a road that had also belonged to the original owner of the woodland, and which was the only practical means of access to it. The plaintiff now wished to build a house on the land, but the defendants refused to allow access along the road for any purpose other than to use the plot as woodland. This would obviously prevent construction vehicles using the road, for example. The Court of Appeal noted that there was originally a common intention that the woodland would be built on, as two similar plots adjoining it (which were also shown on the plan attached to the conveyance) had already been built on before the date of the conveyance. The easement claimed by the plaintiff would be necessary to give effect to that common intention, and therefore would be implied into the grant.

2.5.3   Quasi-easements.   These are practices which the land-owner was accustomed to exercise over the land conveyed while it was still in his ownership, and which benefit the land retained by him. In the example in 2.4.3 above, Roger's custom of crossing the land to his house could amount to a quasi-easement (right of way) for the purposes of this rule. The rule itself was formulated in the case of *Wheeldon* v *Burrows* (1879) and was stated as being that a conveyance of the quasi-dominant tenement (i.e., the land which benefits from the right) will pass 'all those continuous and apparent . . . quasi-easements . . . which are necessary to the reasonable enjoyment of the property granted and were actually enjoyed prior to the conveyance'. There are thus four distinct requirements. First, that it was 'continuous'. This is not applied strictly, and means permanent rather than incessant, so that regular use over a substantial period of time would suffice. Secondly, that it was apparent. Visible pipes or cables, or a worn pathway would fit this requirement. Thirdly, it is 'necessary to the reasonable enjoyment of the property'. Therefore it does not need to be one without which the land could not be used at all, but it must benefit the land in some way. Fourthly, it was 'actually enjoyed prior to the conveyance'. Again, the courts are not too strict about this, so that in *Costagliola* v *English* (1969) an established access was not prevented from being a quasi-easement merely because it had not been used for ten months before the conveyance. A hypothetical situation can show how the rule would operate in practice, and the importance of thinking carefully about all the circumstances of a case.

Example

Roger owns Lodge Farm. The farmland has a separate building on it called Rose Cottage where Roger used to live, but he has now built a new house for himself. Roger sells Rose Cottage to Celia, together with a right of way along the farm-track to the main road. There is also an overhead electricity cable and an underground sewer running to the main road. A footpath crosses Roger's fields as a short-cut to the main road, and Roger used to collect water from a spring in one of the fields. First, these various 'rights' can only be quasi-easements if Roger was still using them at the time of the conveyance. This may depend on whether he had moved in to his new house or not. Secondly, how 'apparent' are they? The electricity cable clearly is. Is there an obvious footpath to the road and the spring? Are there man-hole covers for the sewer? Thirdly, are they all 'necessary'? Electricity and sewerage certainly are necessary but the short-cut is probably not. The use of the spring is only necessary if there is no other water supply.

It should be noted that this rule does not apply to profits à prendre.

2.6   Presumed grant

If a servitude is enjoyed for a long period of time, it might give rise to the creation of a legal right. There are three methods whereby this can occur. The principle was developed first at common law, and eventually a separate mechanism was devised by the courts known as the fiction of *lost modern grant*. A statute was enacted to rationalise the process, but with little success! In each case the basic criteria are that the right was exercised *nec vi nec clam nec precario*, i.e., that it was not obtained by force, nor secretly, nor with permission. Thus, if the land-owner is aware that another person is using the land in some way, great care must be exercised to ensure that a servitude does not develop.

2.6.1   Common law.   Originally it had to be proved that the right had been enjoyed since time immemorial. This was fixed as 1189 (the beginning of the reign of Richard I), but the courts would presume that it had existed for that long if it could be shown that the right had been exercised for 20 years. However, that presumption could be rebutted by evidence to the contrary, for example that the land had been under water until 1200.

2.6.2   Lost modern grant.   As the strict common law rules could disallow a right even if it had been exercised for hundreds of years, the courts developed a fiction that enjoyment for a lengthy period must mean that a right had been granted, but that the deed has since been lost. Unfortunately this rule has never been consistently applied and therefore cannot be relied upon, but it can still form the basis of a valid claim as the following case shows. Contrast the decision as to the extent of the easement with the courts' approach in the case of express grants (see *Alvis* v *Harrison* (1990), 2.4.2 above).

Mills v *Silver* (1991)

The plaintiff owned a hill-farm in Herefordshire and the owners of adjoining land had used a rough track over the farm on and off for 40 years. The defendants had purchased the land in the belief that they could use the track, but when it became impassable one winter, they repaired it with 700 tons of stone without seeking the permission of the plaintiff. The court ruled that a right of way existed, but that its extent was limited in that use of it must be restricted to the manner in which it had been used to date (i.e., the type of use which had given rise to the presumption of a grant). The use of stone went beyond mere repair and was therefore a trespass on the plaintiff's land.

2.6.3 Statute. Under the Prescription Act 1832 there are complicated and confusing rules laying down various ways in which a right can be established by long use. The basic period is twenty years, and if this is established then a right is acquired regardless of events before that time, as long as *nec vi nec clam nec precario* applies. After 40 years of use the claim can only be defeated by showing it was exercised with written permission. Oral permission will therefore not defeat a claim under the longer period. The period must have been uninterrupted. An interruption must be for a full year, showing that the right is disputed. Finally, the right does not exist until a court has ruled that the criteria have been complied with. Other complications are the existence of different rules for calculating the 20-year and 40-year periods. Rights of light are dealt with separately (for example, an oral permission will not defeat a 20-year claim). There are also different periods for profits à prendre (basically, 30 and 60 years). Note also that a profit in gross cannot be obtained under the Act, although it can by the other methods of prescription. Overall, the Act is badly drafted and uncertain in its effects.

2.7 Extinguishment of servitudes

There are various ways in which this can occur.

2.7.1 Express release. A deed should be executed. However an informal agreement will be effective in equity, either where consideration is given for it, or if the servient owner has relied upon it to his detriment.

Example

Roger has a right of light over David's land. Roger agrees to release it, whereupon David builds a house which blocks out the light. Roger will not be allowed to enforce the easement, and it will effectively cease to exist.

2.7.2 Implied release. The conduct of the dominant owner might show an intention to abandon a servitude. Non-user in itself will not be enough unless combined with a particular act.

Example

Celia has a right of light to her house over Roger's land. She bricks-in all the windows on the side facing Roger's land, and does nothing more for several years. She might then be unable to prevent Roger building so as to block the light.

2.7.3   Change of circumstances.   If circumstances are such that the servitude will never be able to be exercised in the future, this might extinguish it. Thus in *London & Blenheim Estates Ltd* v *Ladbroke Retail Estates Ltd* (1993) (2.1.1 above) the High Court stated that the right to park on the defendant's land would cease if the special areas allocated for parking were removed for any reason.

2.7.4   Unity of ownership and possession.   If one person acquires ownership and possession of both the dominant and servient tenements, the servitude will be extinguished. It will not revive should the land-owner subsequently sell one of the tenements.

2.7.5   Statute.   Note the effect of the Commons Registration Act 1965 on profits in common (see 2.2 above).

3   Restrictive covenants

3.1   Privity of contract

A covenant is simply an obligation contained in a legally binding agreement which is in the form of a deed. The law of contract is therefore the first stage in any consideration of covenants. This states that only the parties to the contract can sue or be sued under the terms of the agreement; this is known as the doctrine of privity of contract. However, the benefit of the agreement can be transferred to another person in some circumstances (assignment of a chose in action), whereas the burden must always remain with the original party to the agreement. The details of these rules must be left to the study of the law of contract itself, but the operation of the basic principles can be seen in the two situations in land law where covenants are typically entered into.

(a)   Landlord and tenant. When a lease of land is granted, the basic agreement will be for the landlord to allow the tenant to have exclusive possession of certain land, and for the tenant to pay a specific amount of rent in return. Unless the lease stipulates otherwise, the landlord can sell the freehold, and the tenant can transfer the right to possession of the property. However, the original obligations under the lease must remain with each of them, so the tenant will always be liable for the rent until the original tenancy is terminated. The same principle applies to any other terms included in the original agreement.

Example

Roger leases a grocery shop to Celia for one year at a rent of five hundred pounds per month. The lease contains a covenant by Celia to keep the property water-tight, and a covenant by Roger to sell the freehold to Celia if she requests it. Roger sells the freehold of the shop to David, and Celia sells the lease to Bertram. Bertram is now entitled to use the shop, but Celia will still be liable for the rent for the remainder of the one year of the lease, and to pay for any repairs needed to keep the shop water-tight. This could be important for Roger or David if Bertram abandons the shop and disappears.

In *Norwich Union Life Insurance Society* v *Low Profile Fashions Ltd* (1992) the Court of Appeal ruled that this liability would extend to losses caused by any future assignees of the lease, even though the original lessee has no control over such assignments. However, the harshness of the rule has at least been mitigated in situations where the lease has been extended under statutory provisions protecting business tenants (see the Conveyancing Practice syllabus).

City of London Corporation v *Fell* (1993)

A firm of solicitors entered into a ten year lease of business premises, and after three years they assigned the lease to a company for the remainder of the term. At the expiry of the term the company obtained an extension of the lease under the provisions of the Landlord and Tenant Act 1954, but subsequently went into liquidation owing over £30,000 in rent. The landlords sued the solicitors for the rent arrears, but the House of Lords ruled that the liability of the original tenant ceased with the expiry of the contractual term of the lease.

   (b)   Transfer of ownership. If land is transferred, both parties might enter into various covenants. Typically this will happen when land is sold, whether it is the freehold or a leasehold estate which is being transferred.

Example

When Roger sells the freehold of the shop to David, he agrees that he will not open another shop within a one mile radius. David agrees that he will only sell groceries in the shop and that he will not allow the boundary wall to fall down. If David now sells the freehold to Bertram, he will still be liable to Roger should Bertram start selling fast-food, or knock down the boundary wall.

3.2   Privity of estate

It has been shown that the basic rules of contract apply to both landlord and tenant agreements, and agreements for the transfer of land. However, these basic rules are not totally satisfactory for these particular situations. It is of little use to Roger to sue Celia for the rent if it is Bertram who is using the shop, and Celia has disappeared. Similarly, Roger will want to stop Bertram selling fast-food rather than having to sue David for breach of the agreement, particularly as David by now will be living elsewhere, and may not be traceable. Thus the law relating to land has had to develop certain principles to extend the law of contract, by enabling certain covenants to be enforced by successive owners of the land in question. The crucial issue will usually be whether the covenant *runs with the land*. This means that it can be enforced by or against the present owner, regardless of the normal rules of the law of contract. In the case of landlord and tenant agreements, the common law doctrine of privity of estate states that the benefit and burden of all covenants which touch and concern the land (i.e., which are not merely personal arrangements) will be enforceable against the current landlord or tenant, as well as against the original parties to the lease. Thus in the examples above, Roger will be able to claim the rent from Bertram while he owns the freehold, or even against Eric, should Bertram transfer the lease to him. At the same time he could claim the rent against Celia if he so choses, under their original contract. However Celia will not be able to enforce her option to purchase against David, as this is only a personal agreement with Roger which is not connected to the land. An option to purchase should in fact be registered as a C IV land charge (see *Registered and Unregistered Land*, 3.4). Furthermore, to protect herself against a claim by Roger for the rent or costs of repairing the property, Celia should ensure that Bertram covenants to indemnify her against any such claims. If Bertram transfers the lease to Eric, he should obtain a similar indemnity. The combined operation of these contractual principles and the doctrine of privity of estate can be visualised as follows.

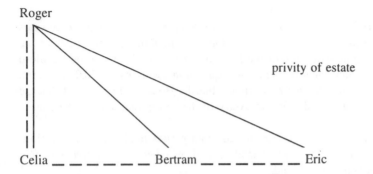

The dotted lines show the contractual relationships, and the solid line represents privity of estate.

3.3   Covenants between land-owners

In the case of covenants in an agreement for the transfer of land, the situation is much more complex, and will be dealt with in detail in this section. In this respect there are different rules for positive covenants and for restrictive covenants. A positive covenant is one which requires action for it to be complied with, no matter how it is worded. Thus Celia's covenant to repair and David's covenant not to allow the boundary wall to fall down are both positive covenants. Roger's covenant not to open another shop, and David's covenant only to sell groceries are both restrictive covenants, as they can be complied with without any action being taken. The significant difference here is that Celia's covenants are in a lease, and therefore run with the land whether they are positive or negative. David's covenants are subject to the complex rules concerning covenants between land-owners, which must now be looked at in detail. Unfortunately there are different rules for the benefit and the burden of restrictive covenants, and different rules at common law and in equity.

3.4   Covenants between land-owners at common law

3.4.1   The benefit of a covenant.   The benefit of a covenant will pass if it touches and concerns the land of the person benefiting under it (as for landlord and tenant covenants in 3.2 above), whether it is positive or restrictive. If the covenant is pre-1926, the new land-owner must have the same legal estate as the person who entered into the original agreement. However under the Law of Property Act 1925, s. 78(1), this rule does not apply to covenants entered into after that date.

Example

Roger sells a freehold house to Celia and imposes covenants on her to keep in repair the boundary wall between the house and land retained by him. If Roger grants a lease of his land to David, David will be able to enforce the covenant against Celia as long as it was entered into after 1925.

Thus there are three crucial elements. First, Roger retains land which can benefit from a covenant. Secondly, the covenant touches and concerns that land. Thirdly, s. 78(1) applies if a different legal estate is conveyed.

3.4.2   The burden of a covenant.   It was ruled by the courts in *Austerberry* v *Oldham Corporation* (1885) that the burden of a covenant cannot run with the land at common law. The only exception is where a land-owner seeks a benefit under a covenant which also brings with it an obligation.

Halsall v *Brizell* (1957)

Land was sold together with the right to use a road over land retained by the seller. However, the purchaser covenanted to contribute to the upkeep of the road. The land changed hands again. The court ruled that the new owner could not be obliged to contribute unless he used the road. The choice was therefore up to him, either he was to use the road and pay, or he was not to use the road at all.

At common law, therefore, there could be difficulties in transferring the benefit of a covenant if it is pre-1925. The burden of a covenant can only be transferred directly by granting a lease of the land instead of selling it. The burden can be transferred indirectly by creating a chain of indemnity, whereby every seller of the land includes a covenant that the purchaser will meet the costs of complying with the covenant should the original land-owner bring proceedings for its breach. However, if the chain is broken in any way, this will be ineffective. If only one intermediate purchaser is not asked to give an indemnity, or disappears, the present owner will be protected from action. The original land-owner may be able to obtain damages, but it is more likely that he will want to stop the breach.

Example

The covenant seeks to prevent the keeping of live-stock on the land. The present owner sets up an exceedingly smelly chicken farm. The original land-owner still lives in an adjoining house, and is more concerned to stop the smell rather than tracking down the original purchaser and claiming damages from him.

It is in these situations that the equitable rules might grant a remedy to the original land-owner if the covenant is restrictive rather than positive in nature.

3.5   The benefit of restrictive covenants between land-owners in equity

The benefit of a restrictive covenant will pass with the land in three situations, as long as it touches and concerns that land.

3.5.1   Annexation.   It will run with the land if it can be shown that the wording of the covenant made it clear that all subsequent owners of the land were intended to benefit. Thus the covenant should refer to the subsequent owners ('the vendor his heirs and assigns and others claiming under them') and to the land itself ('for the benefit of their adjoining land'). However, under the Law of Property Act 1925, s. 78, a covenant shall be deemed to be made with the covenantee and his successors in title and the persons deriving title under him or them, and shall have effect as if such successors and other persons were expressed.

Thus precise words may not be necessary unless it is intended that the benefit should not pass automatically.

Roake v *Chadha* (1983)

A covenant was entered into to prevent the building of more than one house on a plot of land. The agreement specified that the covenant would not 'enure for the benefit of any owner or subsequent purchaser . . . unless expressly assigned'. There had been no specific assignment, and the court held that the covenant could not be enforced.

3.5.2   Express assignment.   This must be at the same time that the land is transferred. In *Re Pinewood Estate, Farnborough* (1958) it was ruled that it must also be assigned in all subsequent transfers. However it would seem that, because of the Law of Property Act 1925, s. 78, this will only be necessary where the original agreement so stipulated, as in *Roake* v *Chadha*.

3.5.3   Development scheme.   Where land is developed in several plots, so that each plot is to be part of an overall plan, it is possible to impose mutual obligations on all subsequent purchasers of the plots. Thus each plot-owner can sue and be sued by other plot-owners.

Example

A builder creates an open-plan housing estate, with clusters of twelve houses grouped together in a cul-de-sac. One cluster is called Brookside Close. Each purchaser covenants (inter alia) not to erect a fence or wall around the front garden, or to park any vehicle other than a standard car in front of the house. One house-holder runs a mobile fruit and vegetable business. Any of the other house-holders could bring proceedings to prevent him parking his van in the Close.

The rules as to when such a scheme exists were laid down in the following case.

Elliston v *Reacher* (1908)

The court set out five conditions. First, the area of the development scheme was a clearly defined estate (in the sense of an area of land). Secondly, this estate was divided into different plots (even if purchasers were able to chose the precise area of their respective plots). Thirdly, the same person (i.e., the original developer) imposed the covenant on each plot of land. Fourthly, each purchaser entered into the covenant on the basis that it would be enforceable by every other purchaser. Express words are usual, but the circumstances of the purchase may be sufficient (e.g., if it was made by reference to an estate plan). Fifthly, the original seller intended that the covenant would be for the benefit of all the plots sold.

The formal requirements in *Elliston* v *Reacher* have been relaxed by the courts as housing estates have become more common, and their nature more accepted as part of everyday life. Thus in the following case the court stressed that the vital elements are the existence of a scheme in a broad sense, and an intention that covenants should bind all purchasers mutually.

Re Dolphin's Conveyance (1970)

Several sellers had imposed the covenants in question, and the land had never been laid out in plots. Nevertheless the court ruled that there was a valid scheme.

This type of scheme is frequently encountered with new houses, and often there are several covenants involved. It is a vital part of modern conveyancing practice to ensure that a potential purchaser is fully aware of the implications of such covenants, before the contract is entered into.

3.6   The burden of restrictive covenants between land-owners in equity

The rules which govern whether the burden of a restrictive covenant will run with the land were formulated in the following case.

Tulk v Moxhay (1848)

A purchaser of land in Leicester Square in London knew that there was a covenant to maintain the garden in the centre 'in an open state, uncovered with any buildngs'. The court granted an injunction to prevent him from building on the garden, and ruled that covenants would be binding on purchasers in equity in particular circumstances.

The judgment in Tulk v Moxhay laid down five criteria which a covenant must satisfy before it will run with the land.

(a)   Restrictive nature. A positive covenant (see 3.3 above) will not run with the land. Note that the covenant in Tulk v Moxhay was expressed in positive terms, but was ruled to be restrictive in nature.

(b)   Intention to benefit. It must have been intended to benefit specific land retained by the original land-owner. The benefit of the covenant will then run with that land (the dominant land), subject to the rules in 3.4.1 or 3.5 above.

(c)   Actual benefit. It must touch and concern the dominant land (see 3.2 above). Normally this will mean that the original landowner retained adjoining land, and proximity is a key factor. There are certain exceptions under statute, e.g., the National Trust can impose binding restrictions under the National Trust Act 1937, and under the rules relating to development schemes (see 3.5.3 above).

(d)   Intention to burden. It must have been intended to burden the land in question. Under the Law of Property Act 1925, s. 79, this will be presumed unless a contrary intention is expressed. For covenants before 1926, there must be words in the agreement which show this intention, although the wording of the covenant itself may be sufficient.

(e)   Notice. Under Tulk v Moxhay the covenant could not be enforced against a bona fide purchaser of a legal estate without notice of it. Since the 1925 legislation, if the land is registered the covenant must be protected as a minor interest. If it is not registered land, the covenant must be registered as a Class D II land charge (see Registered and Unregistered Land, 3.4).

The effect of Tulk v Moxhay, therefore, is to create a type of equitable interest. Subject to notice or registration (whichever is applicable), this interest can thus be enforced against all owners and occupiers of the land, whatever their estate or interest. The usual equitable remedy will be an injunction to prevent the covenant being breached, and damages in addition or in lieu at the court's discretion.

3.7   Modification and discharge of restrictive covenants

As with a servitude, a restrictive covenant will be extinguished and cannot be revived, when the same person acquires both the dominant and the servient land (apart from the special situation of development schemes, see 3.5.3 above). If there is any doubt as to the validity of a covenant, the court can make a declaration under the Law of Property Act 1925, s. 28(4). However, if a covenant is valid, it is quite likely that circumstances have changed so much that it is undesirable that the land should still be burdened with it!

Example

In 1926 Roger sells farmland to Celia. It is next to his sixteenth century manor, and is several miles from the nearest town, a small place called Birmingham, so he imposes a covenant that the land can only be used for agricultural purposes. By 1990, the manor house has long fallen down and been replaced by a warehouse. The small town of Birmingham has swallowed up the area so that all around it are factories. Yet the present owner of the ex-manor house can still prevent any building on the ex-farm-land!

In these circumstances an application can be made to the Lands Tribunal under the Law of Property Act 1925, s. 84(1). The Tribunal can modify or discharge the covenant in four situations.

(a)   Obsolescence. Changes in the character of the property or neighbourhood have made the covenant obsolete.

(b)   Impedance of development. The continued existence of the covenant prevents a reasonable use of the land, and it is either of no practical benefit to the land any more, or is contrary to the public interest.

(c)   Agreement. The persons entitled to its benefit have agreed to its discharge or modification.

(d)   No disadvantage. The proposed modification or discharge would not injure the person entitled to its benefit.

It is to be noted that restrictive covenants will frequently cover the same activities as planning controls. A typical restriction on a private dwelling house is that it canot be used to run a business, and planning regulations will almost certainly prohibit that as well. If a land-owner wishes to discharge the covenant, it will still be necessary to obtain planning permission (and vice versa).

3.8   Summary

The interplay of the various rules governing covenants is confusing. However, there are certain key questions that can be asked, which should at least enable the student to ascertain what the problem is about!

(a)   Are the parties the original parties to the agreement containing the covenant? If so, the simple rules of contract will apply.

(b)   Is one (or both) of the parties a subsequent land-owner? If so, then the doctrine of privity of contract applies, and there must be a special rule to allow the covenant to be enforced.

(c)   Was the original agreement in a lease, and the present relationship one of landlord and tenant? If so, the doctrine of privity of estate applies.

(d)   Is the present relationship between two land-owners? If so, first work out the nature of the covenant at issue, i.e., is it positive or restrictive? Is it a benefit or a burden?

(e)   If it is the benefit of the covenant at issue, do the common law rules apply? If not, e.g., it does not benefit land of the covenantee, is it restrictive? If so, an equitable rule may apply (cf the Law of Property Act 1925, s. 78, or development schemes).

(f)   If it is the burden of the covenant at issue, the common law is of no help unless there is a chain of indemnity or *Halsall* v *Brizell* applies. Even the former is only of partial assistance. Consider finally therefore the rules under *Tulk* v *Moxhay* if the covenant is restrictive.

(g)   Reasoning must be double checked. Is it a positive covenant? If so, the equitable rules cannot apply whether it is the benefit or the burden which is at issue.

There is no doubt that the rules concerning covenants are complex and, to a certain extent, anachronistic. In recent years the courts have been forced to use their ingenuity to adapt the law to modern conditions, as in the rules relating to housing developments. The basic rules are well-established, however, and the House of Lords recently confirmed that the burden of a positive covenant could not be enforced against a successor in title to the original covenantor.

Rhone v *Stephens* (1994)
The defendant bought a house subject to a covenant to keep the roof in good repair, as the roof extended over the adjoining house owned by the plaintiff. The House of Lords ruled that the covenant could not be enforced because of the old rule concerning positive covenants, and that the rule in *Halsall* v *Brizell* (3.4.2 above) did not apply.

The Court of Appeal in *Rhone* v *Stephens* were very critical of the old rule and suggested that the principle in *Tulk* v *Moxhay* (3.6 above) should be extended to positive covenants. The House of Lords considered the arguments, but were not prepared to overrule a principle which had been relied on by sellers and buyers for over one hundred years. They pointed out that even legislation on the issue would require careful consideration, and so perhaps the time is ripe for a complete review of such basic principles of land law.

QUESTIONS

THE LAW RELATING TO LAND

Part A

1. Explain the concept of 'land' in the law relating to land.

2. Distinguish between registered and unregistered land in respect of the ways in which rights in land are protected.

3. Explain how a trust which is not in writing may still be valid. Illustrate with examples.

4. Distinguish between legal and equitable interests in land.

Part B

5. Albert, Bernardette, Cecil, Daphne and Elizabeth purchased a piece of land known as 'Blacklands' in 1989. In 1990 Albert died. In 1991 Bernardette sold her interest to Fred, and shortly after that Cecil entered into a verbal agreement to sell his interest to Greta.

Advise Cecil, Daphne, Elizabeth and Fred of the position regarding the legal estate and equitable interests in 'Blacklands'.

Outline answer

(a) Introduce your answer by explaining the legal background. Thus explain briefly the concepts of co-ownership, trusts for sale and joint tenancies/tenancies in common. Cite the Law of Property Act 1925, and the relevant sections.

(b) Apply the rules concerning trusts for sale. The first four trustees hold the legal estate (if of full capacity) in trust for themselves and Elizabeth and Fred. The legal estate is held by them as joint tenants.

(c) The equitable interests depend on the rules relating to joint tenancies/tenancies in common. Consider the status of the initial purchase. Explain briefly the four unities and the possibility of severance.

(d)   Apply the rules concerning joint tenancies/tenancies in common to Albert's death (noting the effect of the 'survivorship' principle), and to Bernadette's sale (noting its effect as a severance).

(e)   Consider the effect of Cecil's agreement with Greta. Is it an act that amounts to a severance? Cite *Re Draper's Conveyance* (1969) and *Burgess* v *Rawnsley* (1975). Note however, the possible effect of the Law of Property (Miscellaneous Provisions) Act 1989 (verbal agreements for the sale of an interest in land are now void, not merely unenforceable).

(f)   Conclude by summarising the position. If the original purchase created a joint tenancy, after Albert's death, Bernadette, Cecil and Daphne held the legal estate on trust for themselves and Elizabeth (each thus having a potential one-quarter share). Bernadette severed the joint tenancy as far as her share was concerned, so that after the sale to Fred he became entitled to a one-quarter share as a tenant in common with Cecil, Daphne and Elizabeth (who were thus entitled to the remaining three-quarters as joint tenants). It is doubtful whether Cecil's verbal agreement acted as a further severance.

6.   Anthea and her husband Bob own Whiteacre as joint tenants. Anthea has recently purchased a considerable number of antique statues and urns which she intends to have placed in the garden as part of a landscaping project. She also has a fifty-year lease on Blackacre.

Anthea recently executed a homemade will leaving 'all my realty' to her friend Clarence. She now asks your advice concerning the effect of this will on her death, assuming that Bob would not take court proceedings to circumvent it.

7.   Anne has died leaving a house which was in her sole name. Her will states 'I would like my husband Bill to live in the house as long as he wishes, but then for it to go to my son Claude'. Explain the effect of this provision as far as Bill and Claude are concerned.

8.   Anton's house is in the middle of several acres of land, all of which is also owned by him. There is a track which leads to the main road. In 1989 Anton sold the house and some surrounding land to Bettie, but retained a large area himself. Bettie has since sold the house and land to Cynthia.

Anton now wishes to build another house on the land he retained. Advise him as to his right to use the track as access, and the effect of the term in the conveyance to Bettie that he would only use the land for agricultural purposes.

THREE

CRIMINAL LAW

INTRODUCTION

The criminal law syllabus starts by looking at the basic principles of criminal law and then goes on to cover various specific crimes. Most of these crimes will be encountered in everyday practice and therefore a knowledge of them will be of direct benefit to the criminal practitioner. Some, such as murder and manslaughter, are more unusual, and it may be thought that there is little point in studying them in detail. However, it is vital to assimilate the basic principles of the criminal law, not only by studying those principles in theory, but also by applying them to specific offences. The crimes covered by the syllabus are therefore more valuable as an opportunity for you to train yourself to analyse the elements of criminal offences in general, than as a source of knowledge about specific crimes.

The practitioner usually only encounters the criminal law in minor matters, and the headline grabbing crimes are few and far between. All criminal cases (with rare exceptions) start in the local magistrates' court, and solicitors have an important role there as advocates. They often represent a defendant through the whole process, including the trial itself. Serious crimes are not dealt with by the magistrates but instead are transferred to the Crown Court where the Crown and the defendant are usually represented by Counsel. You will have to understand how the process works, and the procedure whereby cases are transferred, or 'committed', to the Crown Court, for the Criminal Procedure examination. Thus the legal executive engaged in criminal practice is typically involved in preparing cases for a solicitor to present in the magistrates' court, or in briefing Counsel to appear in the Crown Court. Most of the preparation will involve practical matters such as applying for legal aid, interviewing the defendant and witnesses, and advising the defendant on the next step in the proceedings. What use therefore is a detailed knowledge of the principles of the criminal law?

First, it is important to remember that even the most minor of criminal offences can involve complex problems arising out of the basic principles. A typical example is the defendant charged with shoplifting who says: 'I want to plead guilty because I did take the packet of peas out of the shop without paying; but I want you to explain that I had forgotten that it was in my bag'. A knowledge of the basic principles of criminal law, and of the law of theft in particular, will enable you to advise the defendant that a plea of 'not guilty' must be entered if that was the situation. Thus your knowledge of the criminal law will be working hand in hand with your understanding of criminal procedure.

Secondly, on occasions a case can give rise to a point of law requiring an appeal to a higher court. Some seemingly minor cases have even reached the House of Lords, such as *Alphacell Ltd* v *Woodward* (1972) (a case concerning river pollution). The system of appeals is covered in the Criminal Procedure syllabus, and you will see that there are various choices open to the practitioner. You must be aware of the importance of the issues involved as the choice of court to which an appeal must be directed may depend on this.

Finally, the everyday work of a criminal lawyer involves advising clients on a myriad of technical offences, which are often set out in complex statutes or statutory instruments. Your knowledge of the basic principles will enable you to be able to read through unfamiliar regulations, to decipher them, and to advise your clients with confidence.

PRINCIPLES OF LIABILITY

1 Elements of a crime

Every criminal offence can be divided into two elements. This is usually stated by the Latin maxim *Actus non facit reum nisi mens sit rea. Actus* (the act) and *mens* (the mind) are easily translated; *reum/rea* means 'wrong' or 'criminal'. Thus the complete phrase can be translated as meaning that a crime is only committed when a person performs a prohibited act in a guilty state of mind. The Latin phrase is shorter, and also provides the phrases describing the two elements: *actus reus* (the prohibited act) and *mens rea* (the guilty state of mind). The definition of a criminal offence will describe both the actus reus and the mens rea for that particular crime. The definition will be set out either in a statute or in the decisions of judges in past court cases. It is important to remember both the definition of a crime and its source.

Example

The definition of theft is 'to dishonestly appropriate property belonging to another with the intention of permanently depriving the other of it'. The actus reus is 'appropriate property belonging to another'. The mens rea is 'dishonestly . . . with the intention of permanently depriving'. The source of the definition should be cited as 'Theft Act 1968, s. 1'. The definition of murder however is 'unlawful killing of a human being under the Queen's Peace with malice aforethought' contrary to common law.

Both elements must be present for a crime to have been committed. Thus in the example of the shoplifter given in the introduction to this chapter, the crime of theft will not have been committed because the prohibited act (taking the packet of peas) was not accompanied by a 'guilty mind' (knowledge that the packet was being taken out of the store without being paid for i.e., 'dishonestly ... with the intention of permanently depriving'). Criminal offences are usually defined by stating first the prohibited act, and then setting out the state of mind that is necessary for the person to be guilty of a crime. Therefore when considering a problem you should first explain what crime may be involved, and then discuss whether the actus reus of that crime has been fully committed. Only then should you go on to consider the mens rea for the crime. This is also the most logical way of approaching a problem. It does not matter how disreputable a person's motives are if they have not actually done something wrong to start with!

Example

A woman sees her worst enemy falling over a cliff. She hopes that he will be seriously injured, and in fact he is killed. It is pointless discussing whether she has the mental element for murder unless she actually caused the fall in the first place. If it was a pure accident, then she cannot be responsible for the injuries suffered.

2   Actus reus

2.1   Elements of the actus reus

The definition of the actus reus of a crime will typically include a combination of three elements, but not necessarily all three. The three elements are conduct, consequences and surrounding circumstances. The actions of a defendant to a criminal charge must be carefully studied to ensure that they meet each part of the definition of the appropriate crime.

Example

The actus reus of the crime of murder requires conduct (an act such as stabbing), consequences (the death of the person stabbed) and surrounding circumstances (for example, that the victim was not an enemy in time of war). The actus reus of the crime of perjury merely requires conduct (making a statement not believing it to be true) and surrounding circumstances (while under oath in judicial proceedings).

The prohibited actions must also have been those of the defendant. The actus reus of a crime will therefore only have been committed if the defendant was acting voluntarily.

Leicester v *Pearson* (1952)
A car driver was prosecuted for failing to give precedence to a pedestrian on a zebra crossing, but was acquitted when it was established that his car had been pushed onto the crossing by another car hitting it from behind.

2.2   Criminal omissions

The conduct element must usually have consisted of a positive act by the defendant. In English law it is not a crime to fail to do something.

Example

A man sees a person drowning and refuses to help, even though he could easily do so at no risk to himself by stretching out his hand or throwing a lifebelt. He will not be legally responsible if the person drowns.

There are three main exceptions to the general rule that it is not a crime to fail to act. First, a statute may so define the actus reus of a crime as to make it clear that an omission is an offence. Secondly, a person may already be under a legal duty to do something. Thirdly, a person's previous behaviour may give rise to a moral duty to act which the courts will recognise as imposing a legal duty.

2.2.1 Statutory duties.   Statutory duties are imposed in various situations. Under the Road Traffic Act 1988, s. 6(4), it can be an offence for a driver of a motor vehicle to fail to supply a specimen of breath. Some crimes are even defined so that a 'state of affairs' amounts to the actus reus. Under the Road Traffic Act 1988, s. 4(2), it is an offence to be unfit to drive through drink or drugs 'when in charge of' a motor vehicle. The courts may have to decide if a statute imposes liability whether the defendant had failed to act or not.

R v *Larsonneur* (1933)
The defendant had been refused permission to land in the United Kingdom but was forcibly deported from Ireland to England by the Irish police. She was still convicted of being 'found' illegally in the United Kingdom.

2.2.2 Legal duties.   Legal duties can be imposed in other ways than directly under the criminal law. In those situations a failure to carry out the duty may have such a harmful consequence that a criminal offence has been committed.

R v *Pittwood* (1902)
A level crossing keeper failed to shut the gates when a train was coming, with the result that a man was hit by a train and killed. Although his duty to shut the gates was only owed to his employers under his contract of employment, he was still convicted of manslaughter.

R v *Gibbins and Proctor* (1918)
A man was convicted of murdering his seven-year-old daughter. The woman who was living with him and looking after the children in the house had starved the child to death. The court held that the father was under a positive duty to care for his child, had deliberately not interfered in what was being done, and therefore was legally responsible for its death.

2.2.3 Moral duties.   A moral duty can give rise to a legal duty where the defendant has behaved in such a way that it can be said that a responsibility has been voluntarily assumed. This can arise deliberately.

R v *Stone and Dobinson* (1977)
The defendants took in Stone's adult sister and started to look after her. However the sister became completely bed-ridden, the defendants gave her less and less attention, and the sister eventually died. Both defendants were convicted of manslaughter.

A similar situation can even arise accidentally.

R v *Miller* (1983)

The defendant was sleeping in an empty house and awoke one night to find his mattress on fire from the cigarette he had been smoking. He merely moved to another room and went back to sleep, leaving the fire to take hold and damage the house. The House of Lords ruled that he was properly convicted of arson under the Criminal Damage Act 1971 as he had started the chain of events and was therefore under a duty to counteract any danger as far as it was in his power to do so.

2.3   Observations

There is no doubt that the law in this area is uncertain and still being developed by the courts. In the example given in 2.2 above, presumably the onlooker would be under a duty to act if he was the father of the swimmer and the swimmer was a child; also if he had taken the swimmer into the water in the first place, perhaps to give swimming lessons. However, there is doubt as to whether he would be under a duty to save his adult child, or his father. It is also difficult to see where exactly his duty would start, if for example he had merely pointed out to the swimmer where he could get into the water, or told him how to swim. It seems clear however, that English law will not impose a general duty to help others, unlike many continental jurisdictions.

3   Mens rea

3.1   Introduction

The mens rea required before a person can be convicted of a crime is specified in the definition of every crime. Thus the prosecution must prove that the defendant committed the actus reus while in a certain state of mind. The definition of the crime must therefore first be considered carefully in order to identify what state of mind it is necessary to prove before the defendant can be convicted.

English law recognises three mental states which may form the basis of criminal liability. These are *intention, recklessness* and *negligence*. In addition the definition of a crime may require 'knowledge', 'belief' or some other specific state of mind.

Example

The crime of handling is defined in the Theft Act 1968, s. 22, as 'dishonestly receiving stolen goods knowing or believing them to be stolen'. The mens rea is defined by the word 'dishonestly', but obviously also requires the prosecution to prove 'knowing or believing'.

Sometimes the definition will make it clear which of these three mental states is appropriate, but sometimes it is necessary to be aware of court decisions which explain the requirements of the definition more precisely.

Example

The definition of theft in the Theft Act 1968, s. 1, includes the words 'with the intention of permanently depriving'. This clearly requires *intention*. The definition of a serious assault under the Offences against the Person Act 1861, s. 20, uses the words 'maliciously inflict grievous bodily harm'. The word 'malicious' has been clarified by the courts as meaning *reckless* (*R* v *Cunningham* (1957); see 3.6.1 below).

3.2 The hierarchy of mental states

The three states of mind which are recognised for the purposes of criminal liability are in effect in a hierarchy. Thus it is more difficult to prove *intention* than it is to prove *recklessness*, and *negligence* is the easiest of the three to prove. Therefore the most serious crimes, which carry the most severe punishments, tend to require the prosecution to prove at least *recklessness*, and often *intention*. Minor crimes often require no mens rea at all and are known as crimes of *strict liability*.

Example

It is not a defence to most traffic offences to say that you did not realise that you were doing something wrong. You will be guilty of speeding, for example, even if you had not noticed the speed restriction signs. (Note, however, that regulations require those signs to be properly placed so that they are visible to the driver.)

This hierarchy can be visualised by constructing a table as shown below. The criminal offence that you are considering can then be 'placed' on the table according to the requirements of its definition. The prosecution must prove that the accused's mens rea 'reached' at least as high as that point.

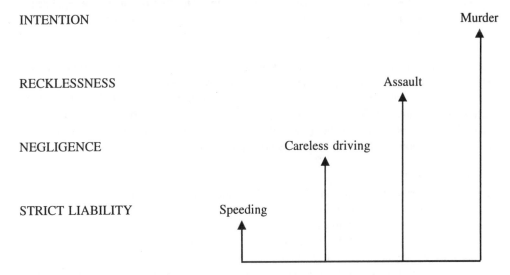

INTENTION — Murder

RECKLESSNESS — Assault

NEGLIGENCE — Careless driving

STRICT LIABILITY — Speeding

Obviously if the prosecution can prove that the accused's state of mind 'reached' even higher than the required point then the accused is still guilty! If that situation occurs it probably means that the accused was not charged with a serious enough crime.

Example

A man is arrested after breaking another man's arm. He is charged under the Offences against the Person Act 1861, s. 20, with 'maliciously inflicting grievous bodily harm' which carries a maximum penalty of five years' imprisonment. This crime only requires reckless-ness but the prosecution is able to prove that he *intended* to break the other man's arm. He is convicted but is fortunate, as he could have been charged under the Offences against the Person Act 1861, s. 18, 'with the intention to cause grievous bodily harm'. This crime carries a maximum penalty of life imprisonment!

3.3   Intention

The word *intention* seems at first sight to be self-explanatory. However, as with many expressions used in law, it has a particular legal meaning, as well as its everyday meaning. In everyday use, if we say that something was 'intended' by a person, we understand that to mean that it was 'desired', and that it was that person's 'purpose' to do it. If that is the situation, then there is no difficulty in law. However it is possible for a person to have a specific purpose, while at the same time knowing that something else will inevitably happen. If that 'something else' is the actus reus of the crime with which a person is charged, can it be said to have been 'intended'?

Example

A woman places a bomb on an aeroplane. She wants to blow it up so that she can claim insurance on it. She knows that there are passengers on the 'plane and that they will certainly die, although she can honestly say that she does not want them to die, and would be delighted if they all survived! Does she 'intend' them to die? If not (in the legal sense) then she will not be guilty of murdering them, as the mens rea for murder is 'intending to kill or cause grievous bodily harm'.

There are thus in effect two types of intention. *Direct intention* is the typical situation when intention can be equated with purpose, i.e., when the consequences of a person's actions are desired. The second type arises in the situation depicted in the last example and is usually called *oblique intention*. The consequences (the deaths of the people on the 'plane) were not what the woman planned, but she nevertheless knew that they would inevitably follow from her actions in blowing up the 'plane. This principle was clearly stated in the following case.

***R v Moloney* (1985)**
A young soldier won a drunken challenge by loading a shot-gun before his step-father. When challenged to complete the contest by pulling the trigger, he did so, and killed his step-father. He claimed that in the heat of the moment he had not 'intended' to kill. The House of Lords stated that foresight of the consequences is evidence that those conse-quences were intended. Thus if Moloney knew that his step-father would be killed or seriously injured, that would be evidence that he had the mens rea for the crime of murder ('intention to kill or cause grievous bodily harm').

3.4   Foresight of consequences

The courts have stipulated that foresight of the consequences can only be evidence of intention if the accused knew that those consequences would definitely happen. Thus it is not sufficient that the accused merely foresaw a possibility of a particular occurrence, as that would only amount to recklessness (see 3.6 below).

R v *Nedrick* (1986)

The defendant had poured paraffin through a letter box and set fire to it. A child was killed in the blaze, but the defendant claimed that he only wanted to frighten the woman who lived there. The Court of Appeal stated that the defendant's knowledge that people might be injured would only be evidence that he 'intended' that consequence if he knew that the injury was inevitable barring some unforeseen intervention.

The Court of Appeal took a similar approach in the following case.

R v *Walker and Hayles* (1990)

The defendants had dropped a man from a third-floor balcony. He survived and the defendants were charged with attempted murder. The Court of Appeal stated that the wording used in *Nedrick* was preferable, but that a phrase such as 'very high degree of probability' was close enough to make no difference.

Clearly therefore the test is always going to be vague, as the form of wording used by the Court of Appeal ('inevitable' or 'highly probable') cannot be precise.

3.5   A summary of intention

The best way to summarise the law is by considering a hypothetical situation.

Example

A man sets fire to a house because he wants to injure the people inside. He will be guilty of murder if they die. However, could he be said to have *intended* to injure the occupants if he merely wanted to frighten them, as in *Nedrick*? Imagine three situations. First, he thinks that the occupants will escape easily because the house has smoke alarms and they sleep on the ground floor. Secondly, he knows that they might be injured because they sleep upstairs but thinks that there is a possibility that the alarm will awaken them in time. Thirdly, he knows that there is no possibility that they will escape because they sleep on the top floor and have no fire-escape or alarms. However, even in this last situation there is the theoretical possibility that, for example, a fire engine would pass by at just the right moment to save them.

In this example, only the last situation would be evidence of an intention to cause death or serious injury. The theoretical possibility of the miraculous fire-engine is so unlikely that death or serious injury can still be said to be inevitable for all practical purposes.

3.6   Recklessness

Recklessness concerns knowledge that there is a risk that a consequence will happen. It is easier to prove that a person was aware of a risk, than to prove that he knew that something would definitely happen. In the example given in 3.5, both the first and the second situations are examples of recklessness on the part of the man setting fire to the house in that he knew there was a possibility that people would be injured. Crimes which require intention are not established by proof of recklessness, but crimes which require the defendant merely to have been reckless will have been committed if the defendant actually 'intended' the consequence, as explained above in 3.2.

Example

It is an offence to cause damage to property recklessly under the Criminal Damage Act 1971. If a woman throws a stone at a window in order to break it (and succeeds), she will be guilty. If she also knows that there is a risk that the stone will hit somebody, and in fact a person is killed by it, she will not be guilty of murder. Murder requires 'intention to kill'.

Recklessness is usually seen as the minimum that is necessary before a person can be said to be guilty of a criminal offence. It is therefore sometimes called 'basic mens rea'. However, two different tests have been developed by the courts, the result of which is that recklessness now has two different legal meanings.

3.6.1 Subjective recklessness. The first test follows a subjective approach. The question that must be asked is 'was the risk in the defendant's mind at the time the crime was committed?'. This test was established in the following case.

R v *Cunningham* (1957)

The defendant tore a gas meter off a wall in order to obtain the money inside with the result that gas escaped and poisoned the woman next door. He was charged with 'maliciously administering a noxious substance' under the Offences against the Person Act 1861. The Court of Appeal decided that 'maliciously' meant 'recklessly' and that therefore Cunningham could only be convicted if it was decided that he had foreseen the risk of the gas escaping and reaching somebody.

3.6.2 Objective recklessness. The second test follows an objective approach. The question that must be asked is 'would a "reasonable man" have recognised the risk?'. In other words, even if the risk was not in the mind of the defendant, should it have been? This test was established in the following case.

R v *Caldwell* (1982)

After a dispute with the owner of a small hotel, Caldwell set fire to the hotel. He was charged with criminal damage 'recklessly endangering life' under the Criminal Damage Act 1971, as no one was actually injured by the blaze. The House of Lords decided that, in everyday language, the word 'reckless' includes the situation where a person should have recognised a risk which would have been obvious to the 'reasonable man'.

3.6.3 Excuses for reckless behaviour. Even if a defendant's mental state satisfies the appropriate test for recklessness for a particular offence, there may be circumstances which would amount to an excuse.

R v *Reid* (1992)

The driver of a car had crashed while overtaking on the inside lane of a dual carriageway, killing his passenger. He was convicted of 'causing death by reckless driving' under the Road Traffic Act, 1988, s. 1, an offence which has now been replaced by the Road Traffic Act 1991 with 'causing death by dangerous driving'. The House of Lords dismissed his appeal, but stated that there could be various situations where a driver might have taken a risk knowingly (subjective recklessness), or given no thought to an obvious risk (objective recklessness), and yet would not be guilty of the offence of 'reckless driving'. They also ruled that the precise meaning of the word 'reckless' would necessarily vary for different crimes. Driving offences, for example, often involve split-second decisions taken with almost no thought, but in circumstances where the driver knows all along that a potentially dangerous activity is involved.

It is important to try and derive some general rules from the judgment in *Reid*, but although four of the Law Lords gave reasons for their decision, each gave slightly different examples, most of which dealt with reckless driving. Perhaps the clearest examples, which could also be applied to other offences, were those given by Lord Keith of Kinkel.

Example

A jury may consider it not to have been 'reckless' where a driver acted under some understandable and excusable mistake; or because of a sudden dilemma created by the actions of others; or was unable to appreciate risks because of some condition not involving fault on the driver's part (such as an illness).

The main difficulty lies in defining what mistakes are 'understandable and excusable'. Until there are authoritative decisions on a range of 'reckless' crimes, the best way to approach specific offences involving recklessness will be a two stage process. First, decide on basic liability according to whether the crime requires subjective or objective recklessness. Secondly, decide if there are any special circumstances which could be an 'understandable' excuse, and qualify your answer accordingly!

3.7 Subjective or objective recklessness?

It is obviously necessary to know whether the definition of a crime requires the *Caldwell* or the *Cunningham* test. The objective test set out in *Caldwell* seems to be limited to crimes which are defined by a statute by the use of the word 'reckless' or 'recklessly'. Most other statutes use the word 'maliciously' and for those the subjective test set out in *Cunningham* must be applied. Common law offences are not defined so precisely but it would seem that the *Cunningham* test is the appropriate one.

Example

The crime of assault is usually defined as 'unlawfully causing a person to fear immediate personal violence'. In the case of *R v Parmenter* (1991) the House of Lords decided that the prosecution must prove that the defendant knew of the risk of assaulting the victim. This is clearly the *Cunningham* test.

3.8 Negligence

Negligence involves judging a person's actions by the standards of a reasonable person. The question to be asked therefore is 'should the defendant have realised that there was a risk'. It does not matter that the defendant was unaware that something dangerous might happen, if the 'reasonable person' would have realised the risk, and taken steps to avoid it.

Example

'Driving without due care and attention' is an offence under the Road Traffic Act 1988, s. 3 as substituted by the Road Traffic Act 1991, s. 2. A driver who forgets that the road is slippery from recent rain, and skids off the road after taking a corner too fast, would be guilty. It may be that the speed of the car would have been satisfactory in normal circumstances, but a reasonable driver would have remembered the rain, and taken extra care to avoid skidding.

It is not even relevant that this particular defendant could not reasonably have avoided the consequences which gave rise to the offence.

McCrone v Riding (1938)

A learner-driver was convicted of driving without due care and attention, despite the fact that it was accepted by the court that he had exercised all the skill that could have been expected from a driver of his limited experience.

Crimes which only require negligence can be classified under the heading of 'social expediency'. They are relatively minor offences in themselves but can have serious social consequences. The actual state of mind is less important than the fact that, for example, a driver was careless and endangered other road users, and it is argued that the prospect of being punished for errors should encourage drivers to think more carefully about their driving. The difficulty however is that there appears to be little difference now between negligence and the *Caldwell* type of recklessness. The only possibility seems to be that the behaviour in question must somehow be regarded as especially bad, or 'gross', before ordinary negligence can be regarded as recklessness.

3.9   Basic and specific intent

To summarise this section it must be recalled that criminal offences that require mens rea will only have been committed if the accused had *basic mens rea*, i.e., intention or recklessness. To confuse the issue slightly you may sometimes see recklessness referred to as *basic intent!* This is merely a way of stressing that it is the minimum degree of mens rea that is normally required for a criminal offence. Similarly crimes that require intention are sometimes referred to as crimes of *specific intent*. This distinction between basic and specific intent is particularly important when the defence of *intoxication* is considered (see *General Defences*, 3.3.2). However, some criminal offences are defined so that negligence is sufficient to establish liability, thus emphasising the importance of looking carefully at the definition of every criminal offence in order to clarify exactly what mental element is required for guilt to be established.

4   Strict liability

4.1   Introduction

For an offence of strict liability to be committed there is no necessity for mens rea and therefore the state of mind of the accused is never questioned. Guilt is established as soon as it is proved that the accused committed the actus reus. Offences of strict liability are often known as 'regulatory offences'. The actions that are being prohibited are not really harmful in themselves, but need to be regulated to ensure that everyday life can be carried on smoothly. The punishment is light (a small fine) and no stigma is attached to a person who is convicted of such a crime. On the other hand the nature of the offence and the number of people who tend to commit it make it unrealistic to allow arguments concerning the mental state of the accused.

Example

Parking a car on the side of the road is hardly an 'immoral' activity. However, there need to be regulations to restrict parking so that traffic can move freely and everybody can have the opportunity to visit the locality for shopping. A person who breaks those regulations will therefore have committed a criminal offence in the broad sense of the term. If the definition of the crime allowed an accused to argue that the signs or yellow lines had been accidentally over-looked, there would be too many contested hearings, very few convictions and a lot more congestion on the roads!

However not all strict liability crimes are so easily categorised. Some quite serious crimes are so defined that at least an element of the definition does not require mens rea.

R v *Prince* (1875)
The defendant had eloped with a 13-year-old girl. He was charged under the Offences against the Person Act 1861, s. 55, with unlawfully taking a girl 'under the age of sixteen out of the possession and against the will of her father or mother'. He knew that the girl's parents did not want her to go away with him, but he convinced the jury that he thought that she was 18. However the court decided that the defendant's belief as to the age of the girl was irrelevant as long as she was actually under 16.

Sometimes the offence itself is construed by the courts as being one of strict liability.

Alphacell Ltd v *Woodward* (1972)
A company owned settling tanks which overflowed into a river and polluted it. It could not be proved that anybody in the company knew that this could happen, or had even been negligent in any way. Nevertheless the House of Lords decided that a crime had been committed contrary to the Rivers (Prevention of Pollution) Act 1951.

4.2 Statutory interpretation

The main difficulty is that statutes do not state explicitly that a particular offence is one of strict liability. Often a statute will define a crime by using words that make it clear that mens rea is required before guilt can be established. Thus words such as 'intentionally', 'maliciously', 'recklessly' or 'knowingly' leave no room for doubt. However other words are ambiguous, for example, 'causing', or there may not be any indication at all. It will then be a matter for the courts to interpret the statute and decide whether mens rea is required or not. The courts have stated that there is a presumption that a statute requires mens rea for any crime created by it.

Sweet v *Parsley* (1970)
The defendant was charged with 'being concerned in the management of premises used for the purpose of smoking cannabis' under the Dangerous Drugs Act 1965. She was a teacher

who had let an isolated farmhouse and only visited it occasionally to collect the rent. It was accepted that she did not know what was going on when she was not there. The House of Lords decided that there was a presumption that mens rea was required and that therefore she should be acquitted.

This presumption can be rebutted if the court feels that there are good reasons for categorising the crime in question as one of strict liability. Clearly that was done in *Alphacell* v *Woodward*. The principal issue would seem to be whether the offence is truly 'criminal' or merely 'regulatory' (see 4.1 above).

Gammon (Hong Kong) Ltd v Attorney General of Hong Kong (1985)

The defendant company had constructed a building contrary to the strict terms of the approved building plan, but without realising that was what they were doing. The Privy Council decided that the presumption in favour of mens rea being required was not so strong for regulatory offences, especially when those offences were concerned with an issue of social concern such as public safety.

Therefore it would seem that truly criminal offences will always require mens rea, even if the statute in question is silent on the point. If the offence can be described as 'regulatory', then the courts may decide that it is an offence of strict liability if it deals with a matter of social concern. Matters clearly of social concern are: public safety; food regulations; pollution; use of motor vehicles. The difficulty is being able to say in advance with certainty that a particular statutory offence is 'regulatory' and a matter of 'social concern'.

4.3   The necessity for strict liability

To conclude this section it is worth considering briefly the reasons for creating offences of strict liability. In *Gammon* v *AG of Hong Kong* it was suggested that making an offence one of strict liability may encourage people to exercise greater vigilance. Certainly strict liability offences tend to be in areas where people voluntarily engage in a particular activity which automatically carries certain risks, e.g., driving a car, operating a factory next to a river, preparing food for public consumption, etc. In addition it is argued that it could be extremely difficult to prove mens rea in such cases, as the activities in question are so much under the private control of the operator.

Example

It would be impossible in practice to contradict a factory owner's explanation that the wrong valve had been opened by an unknown trespasser, causing unlawful pollution. However, if the owner knew that liability would arise anyway, perhaps more care would be taken to keep important valves under supervision?

A relatively modern development has been to allow the accused to avoid liability by proving that all reasonable steps had been taken to avoid breaking the regulations. The prosecution no longer has such an impossible job because the onus of proof is shifted onto the defendant. This has the effect of retaining the social benefits of having a strict liability offence, while mitigating the harshness of punishing a person who is not to blame in any way. However, this special defence is only possible if the statute specifically allows for it.

Example

Under the Licensing Act 1964, s. 169 (as amended by the Licensing Act 1988), it is an offence for a licensee to sell alcohol to a person under 18 regardless of whether the licensee knew the age of the person or not. However under s. 169 (4A) 'it shall be a defence for him to prove that he had no reason to suspect that the person was under eighteen'.

5 Vicarious liability

5.1 Introduction

It is possible for an employer to be guilty of committing a criminal offence even though the actual criminal acts were those of an employee. This can be seen as a type of strict liability, as typically the employer will have had no knowledge of the employee's actions, and therefore cannot be said to have the mens rea for the offence. The arguments in favour of vicarious liability are therefore similar to those for strict liability. It is seen as a way of encouraging employers to be more careful in the control that they exercise over their employees, especially in situations where employees are likely to be susceptible to their employer's instructions.

Example

The owner of a fleet of lorries will be liable for those lorries being driven with defective brakes, even if it is an employee who is actually driving the lorry at the time. The employer is thus encouraged to keep the lorries properly maintained, and the drivers are more likely to point out defects rather than to keep quiet for fear of being sacked for complaining too much.

There is no general principle for vicarious liability in criminal cases. However there are four situations where vicarious liability will arise: statutory provisions, delegated statutory duties, implied vicarious liability and corporate liability.

5.2 Statutory provisions

Sometimes a statute will make it clear that vicarious liability applies by using a phrase such as 'servant or agent'.

Example

Under the Licensing Act 1964, s. 163(1), it is an offence in some circumstances for a person with a liquor licence to deliver alcoholic liquor for sale 'himself or by his servant or agent'.

5.3 Delegation of a statutory duty

Under various statutes people are only permitted to carry on certain activities if they have a licence. One of the costs of obtaining the privilege of a licence is that the licensee has to comply with various regulations. Breaches of those regulations are then criminal offences, and often only the holder of the licence is bound to comply with them. However, in practice it would be impossible to expect the licensee to do all the work involved, and therefore the licensee will have many employees, who may do things which are contrary to the licensing regulations.

Example

Under the Licensing Act 1964, s. 172, 'the holder of a justice's licence shall not permit drunkenness or any violent quarrelsome riotous conduct to take place in the licensed premises'. It is likely that the licensee of a large public house would have employees serving drink in different bars. If one of those employees allowed an obviously drunk man to remain in the bar, it could not be said that the holder of the licence was permitting drunkenness; but neither is the employee committing an offence as he is not the licence holder.

The problem then is two-fold. First, the employee may not be committing an offence; and secondly the employee's breach of the regulations cannot be said to have been 'done by' the licensee. The effect therefore would be to make the regulations unenforceable, as the employer could simply hand over all the work to employees, who would not be bound by the regulations at all. The courts have therefore evolved the principle of *delegation* whereby the knowledge of the employee in such a situation is deemed to be transferred to the employer. The employer must have clearly delegated authority to the employee, even if it is only for part of the premises.

Example

If the licensee of a public house is looking after the same bar as the employee, or is sharing responsibility for two bars, or has only left the employee alone for a moment, then the employer is still 'in charge' and can only be convicted if he has the mens rea for the offence in question.

This can be illustrated by the following case.

Vane v *Yiannopoullos* (1965)
The restaurateur had given instructions to a waitress and had then gone to another floor of the building. The waitress sold alcohol to people who were not eating meals, in contravention of the Licensing Act 1964. The restaurateur was acquitted as there had not been full delegation of his responsibilities.

5.4 Implied vicarious liability

The courts have construed some statutes as having the effect of imposing strict liability on employers. Thus words such as 'sell' or 'use' are taken to mean that any sale or use will render the owner or licensee liable, even if it is somebody else who does the actual selling or using.

Example

The owner of the lorries in the example in 5.1 above is 'using' his lorries even though employees are driving them. Thus he will be guilty under the Road Traffic Act 1988 which states that it is an offence if a person 'uses on a road a motor vehicle . . . which does not comply' with Construction and Use Regulations.

This principle was used in the following case.

Coppen v *Moore* (1898)
The owner of several shops was convicted of 'selling' incorrectly described meat although it was a shop assistant working under a manager who had labelled some American ham as 'Scotch Ham'.

This approach is now commonly taken by the courts in cases involving pollution, as concern for the environment has increased.

National Rivers Authority v *Alfred McAlpine Homes East Limited* (1994)
The defendant company had been building houses next to a stream, and the site manager allowed wet cement to enter it, killing fish and generally polluting the stream. The company was charged with 'causing pollution to enter controlled waters' under the Water Resources Act 1991, s. 85. The Queen's Bench Divisional Court ruled that the company would be guilty of the offence if the pollution resulted from its own operations, carried out under its essential control, even though those in the company's Head Office had no direct part in the work. In this case, Morland J stated specifically that the principle of vicarious liability must apply to offences under s. 85, if it is to be 'an effective weapon' in the defence of the environment.

5.5   Corporate liability

A properly registered limited company is said to have 'legal personality'. This means that it can be treated by the courts in the same way as an ordinary person. Therefore a company can be convicted of a criminal offence, although the actions giving rise to criminal liability must obviously have been carried out by a living person. However, only certain individuals connected to a company can render that company guilty of a crime.

Tesco Supermarkets Ltd v *Nattrass* (1972)
The company was prosecuted under the Trade Descriptions Act 1968 because there was no washing powder on sale at a reduced price, despite advertisements to that effect. This was clearly the fault of the appropriate store manager and not the directors or senior executives of Tesco, who had issued proper detailed instructions to all store managers. The House of Lords acquitted Tesco and stated that a company can only be liable if acts are committed by someone who is its 'directing mind and will'.

It will therefore be a question of fact in every case as to whether the relevant person has sufficient control over the company's activities to amount to its 'directing mind'.

5.6   Strict liability and vicarious liability

To conclude this section it is important to stress the relationship between strict liability and vicarious liability. The effect of the two sets of 'rules' is that, if an offence is one of strict liability, then an employer will automatically be liable whoever has committed the crime (see, for example, *Alphacell Ltd* v *Woodward* in 4.1 above and the examples in 5.4 above). In that situation, therefore, the crime can be said to come under both categories by imposing strict and/or vicarious liability. It does not really matter which label is attached to it (especially to the person convicted). However if an offence requires mens rea, then an employer can only be convicted if the statute explicitly so allows (5.2 above); or authority was delegated to the perpetrator (5.3 above); or the perpetrator was the 'directing mind' of the employer company (5.5 above). It must always be clear therefore which rule is being applied to a given situation.

PARTICIPATION IN CRIME

1 Introduction

When a crime is committed there are often several people involved. The first party or *principal* will commit the actus reus of the crime, but several secondary parties may assist in various ways. If those other people are sufficiently connected to the crime they may be known as *accomplices* or *accessories* (the two words mean the same thing), and therefore be guilty of a criminal offence themselves.

Example

A shop called 'Julie's Jewels' is burgled. One man forces the security shutters with a crow-bar, smashes the shop window and takes out all the jewellery. The crow-bar had been lent to him by a friend who knew that it was for a burglary. Another friend keeps watch. A third friend is driving a get-away car. The first man is the principal and his three friends are all accomplices.

All of the persons who participate in a criminal offence can be convicted of the crime that is committed, as long as they have participated to a sufficient extent. This section will therefore look at the rules which govern responsibility for a criminal offence in these ways.

2 The principal

2.1 The main perpetrator

The person who directly brings about the actus reus of the crime, and is therefore the main perpetrator, is known as the *principal*. Thus the man who pulls the trigger of the gun which fires the bullet which kills the victim is the principal on a charge of murder (as long as he had the intention to kill or cause grievous bodily harm). It is possible to have more than one principal. Thus if two men attack another man and kill him by a variety of blows they will both be principals on a charge of murder. It is not necessary to decide which one struck the decisive fatal blow. There are borderline cases, however, where it will not be clear whether the second person was a joint principal, or merely assisting. In those cases it is a matter of looking carefully at the facts and deciding whether the second person did enough on his own to contribute directly to the actus reus of the crime.

Example

Two men attack a third man. One attacker holds the victim while the other strikes him. Both are clearly guilty of assault as principals, but the position would not be so clear if the victim had been stabbed to death and the charge was murder.

2.2   Innocent agency

There is a special situation known as *innocent agency* where a person who has not committed the actus reus of a crime will still be treated as the principal. This situation arises where one person arranges events so that the actus reus of the crime is carried out by another person who is totally innocent. This may be because the person committing the actus reus is under the age of criminal responsibility (ten years old), or is insane, or simply does not realise what is happening and therefore does not have the mens rea for the crime.

Example

A man instructs his eight-year-old son to take goods out of a shop without paying for them. The man will be guilty of theft as the principal, as his son is legally incapable of committing a crime because of his age.

This situation can arise where the person committing the actus reus is simply unaware of the facts which would render his actions criminal, i.e., he did not have the mens rea for the offence.

R v *Butt* (1884)

The defendant had deliberately given false information to the book-keeper of the company for which he worked, knowing that it would be entered into the accounts. As the book-keeper had innocently entered the wrong information, the defendant was convicted as the principal on a charge of falsifying the accounts.

3   Secondary parties

3.1   'Aid abet counsel and procure'

Under the Accessories and Abettors Act 1861 'whosoever shall aid abet counsel or procure' a criminal offence 'shall be liable to be tried, indicted, and punished as a principal offender'. Therefore if the assistance given to the principal comes within the definition 'aid abet counsel or procure', the persons who have assisted will simply be charged with the same offence as the principal and will be liable to the same punishment. However, the prosecution will obviously have to prove how they assisted the crime, in order to establish their guilt.

Example

The three friends in the example in 1 above will all be charged with burglary. The prosecution will have to prove that they assisted in a specific way, in order to secure their conviction. They will then be convicted of exactly the same offence as the principal ('burglary of Julie's Jewels on 1 April 1991') and liable to the same maximum penalty of ten years' imprisonment (although in practice they will possibly receive lesser sentences if the judge feels that their involvement was less blameworthy).

The phrase 'aid abet counsel or procure' describes four different ways of assisting in a crime. This was the opinion of Lord Widgery CJ in the following case.

Attorney General's Reference (No. 1 of 1975)

In this case the defendant surreptitiously added alcohol to a friend's drink with the result that when the friend was breathalysed on his way home he was over the statutory limit. The Court of Appeal ruled that the defendant could be convicted as an accessory to the offence of driving with excess alcohol. The court discussed the phrase 'aid abet counsel or procure', and was of the opinion that each word had a separate meaning.

Although the precise meaning of each word is not certain, probable definitions can be given.

(a)   To aid a crime. This is to assist during the commission of the actus reus, for example by holding the victim of an assault.

(b)   To abet a crime. This is to encourage the principal, for example by shouting favourable remarks to an attacker while he is assaulting his victim.

(c)   To counsel a crime. This means to give assistance or encouragement beforehand, for example by helping plan the offence.

(d)   To procure a crime. This was defined in *AG's Ref. (No. 1 of 1975)* as 'to produce by endeavour'. Thus the defendant in that case had 'procured' the crime of driving with excess alcohol by 'spiking' his friend's drink.

3.2   Actus reus of participation

It does not matter which part of the phrase applies in any given situation, but the defendant's behaviour must fit at least one of the four words. When answering a problem it is therefore best to state clearly which one is particularly relevant. However, it is important to remember that the definitions and examples are only approximations, and often the accomplice's activity can fall under two headings.

Example

In the example in 1 above the friend who keeps watch can be said to be aiding and/or abetting. He is ensuring that the principal can work undisturbed and is encouraging him by giving him moral support. The get-away driver is in a similar position, while the man who supplied the crow-bar was counselling the offence by giving assistance beforehand.

There must actually be conduct on the part of the accused before he can be said to be an accomplice. Thus it is not sufficient merely to know about a crime, or even to be present at it unless 'presence' can be seen as 'encouragement'.

R v Clarkson (1971)

Two soldiers watched while a woman was being raped in their barracks by their fellow soldiers. It was ruled that they were not accomplices without evidence that their passive behaviour had assisted in some way.

A similar situation arose in the following case.

R v Bland (1988)

The Court of Appeal ruled that the accused could not be guilty as an accomplice to drugs offences merely because she shared a flat with a person whom she knew bought drugs.

Therefore in such a situation only the accused who has a legal authority to control the principal will be an accomplice. This arose in the following case.

Tuck v Robson (1970)

A licensee of a public house watched while some customers carried on drinking after closing time. He was convicted as an accomplice to their offence of consuming alcohol after permitted hours on licensed premises contrary to the Licensing Act 1964, s. 59(1)(b) because he was entitled to eject them from the premises after ten minutes drinking up time.

3.3   The mens rea for an accomplice

This basically consists of the intention to assist in the commission of a crime, but it must be broken down into two separate elements. First, knowledge that a crime is to be committed; secondly, intention to assist the principal. Each of these elements can be problematical and therefore each needs to be considered separately.

3.4   Knowledge that a crime is to be committed

The accomplice need not know the exact crime as long as the type of crime is known.

R v Bainbridge (1960)

The defendant had lent cutting equipment to a man who had subsequently used it to break into a bank. The defendant claimed that he thought that it was going to be used to cut up stolen cars. The Court of Appeal stated that this would not have been sufficient to convict him as an accomplice, as robbery or burglary (breaking into the bank) are different types of crime from handling stolen goods or criminal damage (cutting up stolen cars). However, as nobody believed his story he was convicted anyway!

3.5   Intention to assist the principal

Normally this will be straightforward, but a problem may arise if the person charged as an accomplice was merely doing something that would usually be innocent.

Example

A man goes into a hardware store to purchase a crow-bar. Just before he buys it he mentions to the shop-keeper that he is going to use it for a burglary. Should the shop-keeper refuse to sell it to him?

It would seem that even an innocent transaction will render the seller liable as an accomplice if the illegal intentions of the purchaser are known.

National Coal Board v *Gamble* (1959)

A lorry driver had filled his lorry with coal at an NCB yard. The coal was formally transferred to his ownership after the lorry and its load had been weighed on the NCB's weighbridge. The weighbridge operator noticed that the lorry was overloaded but allowed it to proceed. The lorry driver was found guilty of using an overloaded lorry, and the NCB (as employers of the weighbridge operator) were convicted as accomplices.

An intention to assist may even be present where a person is legally obliged to perform the act in question, although there is some doubt as to whether this would apply in every case.

Example

A man has borrowed a crow-bar from his friend. The friend now asks for it back in order to kill his wife. If the man returns the crow-bar he would probably be convicted as an accomplice to the murder. Would the position be different if the crime was not so serious, for example, if the friend wanted the crow-bar to commit a burglary?

One case suggests that in this situation the person with possession of the goods must not hand them over, even to the rightful owner.

Garrett v *Arthur Churchill (Glass) Ltd* (1970)

The Divisional Court ruled that the defendant could be convicted of being knowingly concerned in the export of goods without a licence by handing over a goblet to the person who had employed him to purchase it. The original purchase was made innocently, but apparently the defendant should have refused to hand the goblet over to the legal owner as soon as he found out that it was about to be exported illegally.

3.6   Assistance after the crime

To conclude this section it should be noted that it is only assistance before or during a crime that can render a person liable as an accomplice. There is no longer such a concept as an 'accessory after the fact', as this was abolished in the Criminal Law Act 1967. There are, however, specific crimes that may be committed if help is given after a crime has been committed.

Example

A woman is driving along a street when she sees a friend standing by the kerb. She stops and the friend tells her that he has just burgled a shop and wants to get away quickly. If the woman drives him away she will be guilty of doing an act 'with intent to impede his apprehension or prosecution' under the Criminal Law Act 1967, s. 4. She would not be guilty as an accessory to the burglary as she did not help until after the crime was over (unlike the typical get-away driver, who is present during the crime as part of the plan).

INCHOATE OFFENCES

1 Uncompleted crimes

1.1 Introduction

It is possible to be guilty of a criminal offence even if the actus reus of the crime that had been planned has not been committed. This is to ensure that the police are able to take steps to prevent crimes when they learn about them in advance. Thus it is an offence to take the preliminary steps to commit a crime; to encourage another person to commit a crime; or to plan a crime with another person. The police can arrest and charge a person with *attempting* to commit a crime if they can catch him in the preliminary stages. They can charge him with *incitement* if they find out that he is encouraging somebody else to commit a crime. Or they can bring a prosecution for *conspiracy* against two or more people who have been planning a crime. All of these offences can be committed regardless of whether a full criminal offence has been committed. In fact if a full crime has been committed then everybody who was involved will usually be charged with that crime, as principal or an accomplice.

Example

Two men plan to break into Newtown Bank on 1 April and a third man encourages them to do so. On the day one man and a woman friend carry out the plan. The man and the woman are guilty as principals, and the other two men as accomplices because of their assistance and encouragement beforehand. If the man and the woman had been arrested just as they were breaking into the bank, they would be guilty of attempting the crime and probably also conspiracy to commit it. The other two men would be guilty of conspiracy and incitement respectively.

1.2 The distinction from liability as an accomplice

A key distinction between inchoate offences and liability as an accomplice is that an inchoate offence is charged as a crime in its own right, whereas accomplices are charged with the crime that is actually committed.

Example

In the example in 1.1 above, if the crime was prevented then the charges would read 'attempting/incitement/conspiracy to burgle Newtown Bank on 1 April 1991' depending on the person being charged. If the crime had succeeded, then each person would be charged 'did burgle Newtown Bank on 1 April 1991'.

Generally speaking the inchoate offences are statutory offences. *Attempting* a crime and *conspiracy* are specific crimes under Acts of Parliament. However, there are also two common law offences of conspiracy specifically preserved by statute, and *incitement* is still a common law offence although mode of trial (and maximum penalties to a certain extent) are fixed by statute. It is therefore necessary to consider each offence separately.

2   Attempting a crime

2.1   The definition

The Criminal Attempts Act 1981, s. 1(1), defines an attempt as follows: 'with intent to commit a crime. . . a person does an act which is more than merely preparatory to the commission of the offence'. Any attempt to commit a crime is therefore an offence in its own right and it is punishable in the same way as if the crime had been committed. However, this only applies to indictable offences or offences triable either way and not to summary offences. You should refer to the Criminal Procedure syllabus for more detail about the distinction between these categories, and the ways in which it affects the progress of a criminal trial.

Example

A woman is caught by a store detective as she is about to conceal some goods under her coat. When she is arrested she admits that she intended to steal the goods, but then tries to tear up the store detective's note-book. She will be charged with attempted theft and will be liable to a maximum penalty of seven years' imprisonment if convicted, although in practice she will probably only be fined. She cannot be charged with attempted criminal damage of the note-book, as minor criminal damage is only a summary offence.

2.2   Excepted offences

It should first be noted that certain crimes cannot be 'attempted'. Thus under the Criminal Attempts Act 1981, s. 1(4)(c), the following will not amount to a criminal attempt:

(a)   attempting to conspire;
(b)   attempting to aid abet counsel or procure;
(c)   attempting to assist an offender after the commission of a crime.

Note however that it is possible to attempt to incite. It may also be possible to attempt to aid and abet if there is a specific crime of aiding and abetting, such as 'a person who aids abets counsels or procures another to commit suicide' under the Suicide Act 1961, s. 2. There are also certain crimes which cannot be attempted in the criminal sense because of the nature of the crime, e.g., any crime which requires negligence, as it is not possible to try to do something carelessly!

2.3   Attempting the impossible

Under the Criminal Attempts Act 1981, s. 1(2), it is still a criminal attempt even if in that particular situation the crime would not have been possible.

Example

A man puts his hand into another man's pocket in order to steal his wallet. He is caught and would be convicted of attempted theft although the pocket was actually empty.

This was illustrated in the following case.

R v *Shivpuri* (1987)

The defendant was convicted of attempting to deal with prohibited drugs because he admitted that he had handled packets containing heroin. Much to his surprise an analysis of the contents of the packets showed that they only contained snuff, but the House of Lords decided that he was still guilty of a criminal attempt.

2.4 *The actus reus of a criminal attempt*

The relevant words in the definition are 'an act which is more than merely preparatory to the commission of the offence'. Thus it is not a crime merely to get ready to commit an offence, but the difficulty lies in deciding when the accused has passed that point.

Example

A man intends to shoot someone. Imagine the process in three stages. First he buys a gun and goes on a reconnaissance of the scene where the shooting will take place. Secondly on a certain day he lies in wait for his victim, loads the gun and aims it. Thirdly he pulls the trigger and the bullet hits the victim. The actions in the first stage are clearly 'merely preparatory' and not an attempt to murder. The actions in the third stage would just as clearly amount to attempted murder if the victim was not killed. Only the jury can decide where in the second stage the 'attempt' begins, by looking at the facts of the particular case.

R v *Campbell* (1991)

A man intending to rob a Post Office was arrested in front of it carrying an imitation gun and a threatening note. The Court of Appeal quashed his conviction for attempted robbery. They stated that it would be difficult to uphold a conviction for attempting a crime where the accused had not arrived at the place where the crime was to be committed, but that no firm rule could be laid down.

Two cases illustrate the difficulty further and show how important it is to look carefully at the facts of each case.

DPP v *Stonehouse* (1978)

The defendant was an MP who had taken out several insurance policies on his life in favour of his wife and then faked his own death by drowning. Although his wife had not had the opportunity of making a formal claim, the House of Lords decided that he was properly convicted of attempting to obtain the proceeds of the policies by deception.

However, a different result was achieved in the following case.

R v *Gullefer* (1987)

The defendant surprised the spectators at a greyhound race by jumping onto the track and waving his arms vigorously. He surprised the police even more by admitting that he was trying to get the race declared void so that he could get back his stake money (his chosen dog was performing particularly badly). He was acquitted of attempted theft as he had not yet tried to claim back his stake money.

The difference between these two cases would seem to be that Stonehouse had done everything in his power to enable his wife to make a claim, and therefore had to leave the rest up to her. Gullefer however had merely prepared the ground for his own claim.

2.5   The mens rea for a criminal attempt

This is indicated by the words 'intent to commit an offence'. Usually this will cause no difficulty but the effect may be that a higher degree of mens rea is required for an attempt than for the completed crime. For example, the mens rea for murder is 'intention to kill or to cause grievous bodily harm', but in *R* v *Walker and Hayles* (1990) (see *Principles of Liability*, 3.4) the Court of Appeal made it clear that the defendants must have intended to kill before they could be convicted of attempted murder. It would not have been sufficient for them to have intended to cause grievous bodily harm. Similarly it is not possible to be guilty of attempting to commit a strict liability offence unless the prosecution can prove that the results were intended, although obviously the offence itself requires no mens rea at all.

Example

A man could only be guilty of attempting to pollute a river if it could be proved that he intended to do so. However, if the pollutant had actually entered the river he would be guilty even if it was a pure accident (see *Alphacell Ltd* v *Woodward* (1972), *Principles of Liability*, 4.1).

There is also a difficulty with crimes that require an accused to have committed a central element together with knowledge of additional circumstances. Thus the crime of rape requires sexual intercourse (the central conduct) with a woman who is not consenting (the additional circumstances). The mens rea for the completed crime can be established by proving that the defendant had been reckless as to whether the woman was consenting or not. For the offence of attempted rape the question then arises as to whether the wording of the Criminal Attempts Act 1981 makes it necessary for the prosecution to prove that a defendant not only intended to have sexual intercourse (the central conduct), but also that he intended it to be without the woman's consent. In the case of *R* v *Khan* (1990) the Court of Appeal decided that to convict a defendant of attempted rape the prosecution need only prove that he intended to have sexual intercourse and that he was reckless as to the victim's consent. This would therefore presumably also be the case for similar crimes such as criminal damage 'being reckless as to whether the life of another would thereby be endangered' under the Criminal Damage Act 1971, s. 1(2), (see *Criminal Damage*, 4.1). A charge of attempting this crime would require an *intention* to cause damage (the central conduct), but only *recklessness* as to endangering life.

3   Incitement

3.1   Introduction

The crime of incitement is a common law offence. However under the Magistrates' Courts Act 1980 the mode of trial for criminal incitement must be the same as for the crime incited. Thus incitement to commit a summary offence is only triable in the magistrates' court; incitement to commit an offence which is triable either way can be tried by the magistrates or the Crown Court (for the way in which this is decided, refer to the Criminal Procedure syllabus); and incitement to commit an indictable offence can only be tried by the Crown

Court. The Act stipulates that crimes of incitement tried by the magistrates carry the same maximum penalty as the crime incited. Other crimes of incitement, however, have no limits at all in theory. Thus if a case is triable either way and is committed to the Crown Court for trial, or if it is an indictable offence, there is no maximum penalty!

Example

On a conviction for inciting someone to steal, the Crown Court would not be restricted to the maximum of seven years' imprisonment fixed for theft by the Criminal Justice Act 1991. However, if the case had been dealt with by the magistrates' courts the maximum penalty would be six months' imprisonment as that is the limit of the magistrates' jurisdiction.

3.2   The actus reus of incitement

This usually involves one person encouraging or persuading another to commit a crime. However threats or pressure may also amount to incitement.

Race Relations Board v Applin (1973)
The House of Lords was asked to make a declaration concerning the conduct of the defendant. He had written threatening letters, distributed circulars and held public meetings in an attempt to persuade a married couple to stop fostering non-white children. It was decided that this amounted to inciting the couple to break a section of the Race Relations Act 1968 which makes it unlawful to discriminate in the public provision of services.

It is also possible to be guilty of incitement by advertising an object to the public, if the advert suggests an illegal use.

Invicta Plastics v Clare (1976)
The defendant had advertised a device with a photograph showing a view of a speed restriction sign, implying that it could be used to detect police radar traps. As such a use would breach the Wireless Telegraphy Act 1949, the Divisional Court decided that it amounted to a criminal incitement.

It is vital, however, that the person being incited would be guilty of a criminal offence if the suggested acts were to be carried out.

R v Whitehouse (1977)
The crime of incest can only be committed by a woman if she is over the age of 16. The defendant had to be acquitted of the charge of inciting his daughter to commit incest with him as she was only 15, and thus would not have been committing a crime if she had gone through with it.

As a result of this case the Criminal Law Act 1977 had to have a special clause inserted to make it an offence 'for a man to incite to have sexual intercourse with him a girl under the age of sixteen whom he knows to be his granddaughter daughter or sister'. However, note that it would still not be a criminal incitement for a man to encourage a young girl to have incestuous sexual intercourse with another man.

3.3   The mens rea of incitement

This is an intention by the accused that the person incited should commit a crime. Thus the prosecution must prove that the accused knew that a crime would result.

Example

A woman tries to persuade her boyfriend to sell her television set. If she knows that it was stolen and tells him so, then she will be guilty of inciting him to handle stolen goods. However, she would not be guilty if she did not know that it was stolen, nor would she be guilty if her boyfriend was unaware that it was stolen, as he would only commit the crime of handling if he sells the television 'knowing or believing it to be stolen' (Theft Act 1968, s. 22(1)).

3.4   Incitement and counselling

To conclude this section it is useful to compare *incitement* with *counselling* (see *Participation in Crime*, 3.1). If the crime is actually carried out, then the inciter will usually be liable as an accomplice, and therefore charged with the crime itself. However, it does not follow that everything that amounts to counselling would also amount to incitement. Incitement implies something more positive, such as persuasion or 'talking him into it'. Lending a person a crow-bar for a burglary will be counselling, but it will not be incitement without an element of positive encouragement in addition.

4   Conspiracy

4.1   Introduction

Under the Criminal Law Act 1977, s. 1, it is an offence 'if a person agrees with any other person or persons that a course of conduct shall be pursued which will necessarily amount to or involve the commission of any offence by one of the parties to the agreement . . . if the agreement is carried out in accordance with their intentions'. This is the crime of *statutory conspiracy* and in simple terms is an agreement to commit a crime. However the Criminal Law Act 1977, s. 5 preserves the *common law conspiracies* of conspiracy to defraud and conspiracy to corrupt public morals or outrage public decency. There are thus two types of conspiracy, both only triable on indictment. The maximum penalties are those fixed for the intended crime.

4.2   Statutory conspiracy

There are three elements to the actus reus of a statutory conspiracy, and the necessary mens rea.

4.2.1   An agreement.   Under the Criminal Law Act 1977 it is not possible for a married couple to conspire, or for a person to conspire with a child under the age of ten or with the intended victim. In those situations there must therefore be at least one other 'qualified' person involved in the agreement. The agreement must then be concluded in the sense that a plan is formulated by the parties. A mere discussion or exchange of suggestions will not amount to a conspiracy.

Example

A married couple meet a 15-year-old girl and agree that the husband will have sexual intercourse with her (perhaps in return for payment). This would be a crime by the husband under the Sexual Offences Act 1956 if the plan were carried out as the girl is under 16, but there is no criminal conspiracy as spouses cannot 'conspire'. In addition the girl would technically be the victim of the husband's offence and therefore she cannot be part of the conspiracy either! It would only be a criminal conspiracy if another person became involved in the plan, such as the girl's 'pimp'.

4.2.2   A course of conduct.   This must result in a crime being committed. It is irrelevant that many things could go wrong before the plan would result in a crime, and in fact the Act stipulates that it is still a conspiracy if the crime would actually have been impossible to commit.

Example

Three men agree to travel to Newtown on Thursday afternoon and to steal goods systematically from every major department store. Obviously it is possible that their car may break down, or that they find nothing worth stealing, or that the stores' security systems are too good. Nevertheless they are still guilty of conspiracy to steal, and would be guilty even if (unknown to them) Thursday was early closing day in Newtown!

4.2.3   The committal of a crime by one (or more) of the parties to the agreement.

R v *Hollinshead* (1985)
The Court of Appeal said that it was not a statutory conspiracy to agree to sell devices which would enable people to use electricity without it being recorded by their meters. The crime of evading payment by deception under the Theft Act 1978, s. 2, would be committed by the person who used the device, who was not involved in the actual agreement. Unfortunately the case then went to the House of Lords who decided it on a different point, and therefore it is not certain that this is the effect of the wording in the Criminal Law Act 1977.

4.2.4   The mens rea.   This is an intention that a crime should be committed. It is specifically stated in the Act that an agreement to do something which is a strict liability offence cannot be a criminal conspiracy unless the parties intend to bring about the result.

Example

Two women agree to take a girl away from her parents without their consent. This is a crime under the Sexual Offences Act 1956, s. 20, if the girl is under 16, and in *R* v *Prince* (1875) it was decided that there is no need for knowledge of the girl's age (see *Principles of Liability,* 4.1). Thus if the two women thought that the girl was 17 and took her away, they would still be guilty. If they had only planned the crime, however, they would not be guilty of conspiracy.

4.3   Common law conspiracy

There are two types as explained in 4.1 above and these were retained because at the time of the Criminal Law Act 1977 it was felt that their abolition would leave a gap in the law.

It was intended to review the law on fraud and public morals and to enact a further statute to define specific offences. After 17 years this has still not been done, and it is thus necessary to consider briefly the offences of conspiracy to defraud and conspiracy to corrupt or outrage public morals.

4.3.1 Conspiracy to defraud. This offence must be charged where the effect of the agreement is to deprive somebody of something which belongs to them, in a dishonest way but without amounting to a crime. This is obviously a vague definition and it is difficult to lay down strict guidelines. An example can be seen in the following case.

Scott v Metropolitan Police Commissioner (1975)
The defendants paid the employees of cinemas to allow them to make copies of films being shown there. These copies were then distributed for their own profit. Although this clearly deprived the owners of the copyright in the films of their right to payment, it would not have amounted to theft or even deception. The defendants were convicted of conspiracy to defraud.

4.3.2 Conspiracy to corrupt public morals or outrage public decency. These are wide offences with no real definition and can be criticised as blurring the distinction between criminality and morality. Again it is only really possible to give an illustration of these offences rather than a proper definition.

Knuller (Publishing Printing and Promotions) Ltd v DPP (1973)
The owners of a magazine printed advertisements encouraging homosexuals to have sexual relations with each other. Since the Sexual Offences Act 1967 most homosexual acts in private were pefectly legal. However, the defendants were still convicted of a conspiracy to corrupt public morals.

The precise definition of the actus reus and mens rea for conspiracy which is set out in the Criminal Law Act 1977 does not apply to these common law conspiracies. There are therefore some slight differences in theory, but in practice the courts will follow the principles explained in 4.2 above.

4.4   Conspiracy with a foreign element

The law on conspiracy is complicated by the fact that the agreement and the criminal act may take place in different countries. In these situations different rules may apply depending on whether it is the agreement or the criminal act which takes place outside the jurisdiction of the English courts.

4.4.1 Agreements in England and Wales. Under the Criminal Law Act 1977, s. 1(4), an agreement to commit a criminal offence will only amount to conspiracy if the offence itself would be triable in England and Wales if committed as planned. Liability will therefore depend upon the English law relating to the crime in question.

Example

An agreement in England to damage property in Germany would not amount to a conspiracy in English law, because the criminal damage (if carried out) could not be tried by the English courts. An agreement to murder someone abroad, or to commit bigamy by marrying in another country, would both be conspiracies, because both murder and bigamy are crimes which can be tried in an English court although committed abroad (if committed by a British citizen).

The Act also states that an agreement to murder is included 'notwithstanding that the murder in question would not be so triable if committed in accordance with the intentions of the parties to the agreement'. Therefore, even if the parties to the agreement are not British citizens, and the murder is to take place abroad, the agreement will still amount to a conspiracy punishable under English law. The Criminal Justice Act 1993, ss. 5 and 6, has also extended the jurisdiction of the English courts to a variety of offences under the Theft Acts 1968 and 1978, and the Forgery and Counterfeiting Act 1981. Thus conspiracies in England to steal, defraud, blackmail or commit forgery abroad (for example) could all be tried by an English court. The main condition is that the planned act should be a crime in both England and the country where it is to be committed. This is known as the principle of 'double criminality'.

4.4.2   Agreements outside England and Wales.   The Act makes no specific reference to this situation, except that the provision relating to murder could mean that any agreement to murder could be prosecuted in England, even though the parties were not British and both the agreement and the murder itself were abroad. The more likely situation, however, is that where the agreement abroad is to commit an offence in England. The House of Lords in *DPP* v *Doot* (1973) ruled that such a conspiracy would be triable in England if the parties subsequently acted in England in pursuance of the agreement. However, the Privy Council in *Somchai Liangsiriprasert* v *United States* (1990) only required evidence that the conspiracy was continuing and was clearly connected to England, which need not necessarily be provided by an overt act in England. As this decision was followed by the Court of Appeal in *R* v *Sansom* (1991), it is likely that any agreement abroad to commit a crime in England will now be triable by the English courts. At the very least, this will now be the position for the categories of offences covered by the Criminal Justice Act 1993 (see 4.4.1 above), under s. 3 of that Act.

4.5   Conspiracy and liability as an accomplice

As with incitement, it is useful to conclude by stressing that if an agreement actually results in a crime, the parties to the agreement will almost certainly be guilty of the crime itself. A party to the agreement who takes no part in the criminal act will still have 'counselled' it, and will therefore be liable to conviction for the crime as an accomplice.

GENERAL DEFENCES

1   Introduction

1.1   Defending a criminal charge

The simplest way of denying a criminal charge is for the accused to say that the actus reus was not committed, i.e., 'I did not do it'. The next approach is for the accused to deny that the actus reus was committed with the appropriate mens rea. Precisely what this means will depend on the definition of the crime in question, but if the charge was one of theft, the accused could say 'I only borrowed the item'. As the definition of theft under the Theft Act 1968 includes the words 'with the intention of permanently depriving', this could amount to a good defence (see *Offences under the Theft Acts 1968 and 1978*, 2.12).

1.2   Mistake

Sometimes there may be no mens rea for the crime because the accused made a mistake. This will still be a good defence as long as the mistake was one of fact rather than law.

Example

Under the Offences against the Person Act 1861, s. 57, it is the crime of bigamy to marry a person while still married to someone else. If a woman has been separated from her husband for two years and goes through a marriage ceremony with another man, she will obviously be highly embarrassed if he turns up at the reception! However she would not be guilty of bigamy if she honestly believed at the time of the ceremony that her husband was dead. On the other hand, if she mistakenly believed that the crime of bigamy did not apply after two years' separation, she would be guilty.

The mistake does not even need to be 'reasonable', as long as it is honest.

DPP v *Morgan* (1986)
The defendants were soldiers who had been told by a friend that they could all have sexual intercourse with his wife. He told them further that she would pretend to resist to increase her own pleasure, but that really she would be consenting. When they were charged with rape they claimed that they honestly believed that they thought she was consenting, and the House of Lords stated that this could be a good defence, even though their belief was patently unreasonable.

This may seem grossly unfair on the victim. However, it is clear that if a defendant honestly believed that he was doing nothing wrong, then he would not have had the mens rea for the crime. The jury, of course, still have to believe his story, and in *DPP v Morgan* the House of Lords went on to say that no jury could possibly have believed the soldiers' story and that therefore their convictions would not be quashed.

1.3   The general defences

Even if the accused performed the actus reus and had the mens rea for the crime, there are various defences that can be raised. These are general defences that apply to any criminal charge and there are seven of them. Thus the defendant may be too young to be deemed capable of committing a crime. The defendant may have been acting involuntarily after suffering from concussion. The defendant may have been insane at the time the crime was committed, or so intoxicated that he did not know what he was doing. Another person, or circumstances beyond his control, may have forced the defendant to commit the crime; or the defendant may have been acting to defend himself or someone else from harm. Each of these will be looked at in more detail.

1.4 The burden and standard of proof

Finally it should be noted that it is for the prosecution to prove the defendant's guilt beyond reasonable doubt. This includes the obligation to prove not only that the defendant performed the actus reus of the crime, but also that the defendant had the necessary mens rea and that none of the general defences applied. In practice this means that the prosecution must prove the actus reus and mens rea, but only disprove any defence that is suggested during the course of the trial. The accused is thus said to have the *evidential burden.* The accused must ensure that the issue is merely raised (it could be by the accused's own evidence or by something that is said by another witness, for example) whereupon the prosecution must proceed to disprove the defence beyond reasonable doubt.

Example

A man is charged with the murder of his father. The prosecution call witnesses to prove that he was seen firing a gun at his father and that subsequently his father died from gun-shot wounds. The actus reus has thus been established, and the mens rea can easily be inferred from the defendant's behaviour. The prosecution do not need to do anything else to secure a conviction, but if one of their witnesses had said unprompted 'I saw the defendant taking drugs an hour previously', then they would have to prove that the defendant was not intoxicated at the time of the shooting. Similarly the defendant could say in his evidence that he had been knocked out beforehand and could not remember anything else. It would not be necessary for him to prove this, but the prosecution would have to disprove it.

The only exception to this rule is the defence of insanity, where the defendant has the *legal burden* of proving the defence on the balance of probabilities, and must therefore call evidence specifically to that end.

2 Age

2.1 Under ten

Under the Children and Young Persons Act 1963 it is conclusively presumed that a child under the age of ten cannot be guilty of a criminal offence. Thus even if there is clear evidence that the child knew that a crime was being committed, and no matter how serious the offence, the child cannot be convicted.

2.2 Under fourteen

Between the ages of ten and fourteen at common law a child is presumed not to know the difference between right and wrong. This presumption weakens as the child nears the age of fourteen, and may in any event be rebutted by evidence to the contrary. The evidence must show that the child knew that the act was seriously wrong, and not just naughty, although this may be inferred from the circumstances of the case.

J M v Runeckles (1984)

A 13-year-old girl had attacked another child with a broken milk bottle. She had then run away and hidden, but eventually made a statement which showed that she had the average mental ability of a 13-year-old. In those circumstances the Divisional Court decided that the magistrates had been entitled to convict her.

Doubt has now been cast on this principle, as the Divisional Court in *C* v *DPP* (1994) stated that it is no longer part of the law of England because changes in social conditions have made it unnecessary and contrary to common sense. There is undoubtedly now a need for the issue to be determined by the House of Lords.

2.3 Over fourteen

After the age of fourteen children are treated in the same way as an adult for the purposes of criminal responsibility. Thus evidence as to their understanding of the law is not relevant to their guilt, although it may affect their sentence. However children under the age of 18 must usually be dealt with by the youth courts, and there are restrictions on the punishment that can be imposed on them. In addition any child (including one under the age of ten) may be placed in the care of the local authority as an alternative to punishment, although this must be in the interests of the child and will be dealt with in separate proceedings before the Family Court under the provisions of the Children Act 1989.

3 Intoxication

3.1 Introduction

The law concerning intoxication (whether by alcohol or drugs) is complex because of the conflicting concerns that lie at the heart of the issue. There is no doubt that a person who commits a crime while intoxicated is probably doing something out of character, and possibly even without the mens rea required for the offence. However, it would not be socially acceptable to acquit automatically anybody who was intoxicated no matter what crime had been committed. In particular it would be offensive to most people to acquit a person who deliberately got drunk and then committed a crime. Complicated rules have therefore been formulated by the courts to try and meet both these concerns. The basic rule is that intoxication can only ever be a defence if it results in the accused not having the mens rea for the crime. Drink and drugs can remove normal inhibitions, impair judgment, or prevent people from thinking about the consequences of their actions. Those effects are irrelevant as long as the defendant was acting voluntarily at the time that the crime was committed. This basic rule must then be applied to the two different situations of voluntary and involuntary intoxication.

3.2 Involuntary intoxication

If the accused was so intoxicated that there was no mens rea for the crime, this will be a defence if the intoxication was involuntary. Thus if a person becomes intoxicated by drinking a soft drink spiked with vodka, or eating food containing LSD, the defence of intoxication will be available. However, there are limits to this aspect of the defence.

R v *Allen* (1988)
The defendant had drunk wine not knowing that it was extremely strong home-made wine. He then committed sexual offences, but claimed that he was so drunk that he had not known

what he was doing. The Court of Appeal decided that this did not amount to involuntary intoxication. He was thus treated as if he were voluntarily intoxicated.

On the other hand a person will be regarded as involuntarily intoxicated if it was as a result of drugs taken according to a prescription, or possibly unprescribed drugs that have had an unusual effect.

R v *Hardie* (1985)

A man was trying unsuccessfully to persuade his former girlfriend to go out with him again. She finally gave him some old tranquilliser tablets and left him alone in her flat, telling him that the tablets would only calm his nerves and could not hurt him. In her absence he set the flat on fire but claimed that he could not remember anything after taking the tablets. He was acquitted of criminal damage on the grounds that he could not be expected to anticipate that tranquillisers would have that effect upon him.

For many years it was thought that the basic rule set out in 3.1 above (i.e., that the intoxication must negative mens rea) would also apply to cases of involuntary intoxication. A recent Court of Appeal decision, however, has cast doubt on that.

R v *Kingston* (1993)

A man was prosecuted for indecent assaults upon a boy in another man's flat. He claimed, however, that the other man must have given him a drugged drink, and that he only gave in to temptation as a result. He admitted, however, that he knew what he was doing at the time of the assault. The Court of Appeal ruled that, where a person has committed a crime as a result of being intoxicated, there could be a defence if the intoxication was induced by a trick.

There seems no reason of principle why this decision should not be extended to cover other situations where the accused became intoxicated innocently, and committed a crime purely because of a lack of his or her normal inhibitions. The implications could be widespread (the decision has been described as 'astonishing' by commentators) and leave has been given for an appeal to the House of Lords.

3.3   Voluntary intoxication

There are two situations that must be looked at separately. First the so-called 'Dutch courage' situation, and secondly the situation where the accused did not consider the crime until after the drink or drugs had an effect.

3.3.1   The 'Dutch courage' rule.   This applies to cases where the accused decided to commit a crime and then got drunk. It derives from the following case.

Attorney General for Northern Ireland v *Gallagher* (1961)

The defendant had decided to kill his wife and so purchased a knife and a bottle of whisky, drank the whisky and stabbed his wife to death. He subsequently claimed that he was so drunk that he did not know what he was doing, or possibly even that the drink had brought on a latent psychopathic state so that he was insane at the time of the killing. The House of Lords decided that intoxication could not be a defence in either case as the intent had been clearly formed, albeit before the killing took place.

This situation is unlikely to arise very often in practice. The phrase 'Dutch courage' is really describing a situation where drink or drugs are taken to reduce a person's inhibitions. Such a person would still have the mens rea for the crime in any event, under the basic rule in 3.1 above.

3.3.2 Mens rea after intoxication. The more typical situation is where a person commits a crime without any prior planning and while so intoxicated that the mens rea for the offence cannot be formed. The approach to this situation was stated by the House of Lords in the following case

DPP v *Majewski* (1976)
The defendant was charged with assault after a fight in a public house. He claimed that he could remember nothing about the incident and that he must have 'blacked out' from the large quantity of drugs and alcohol that he had taken beforehand. The House of Lords stated that intoxication in those circumstances could only be a defence to crimes of *specific intent,* i.e., crimes where the mens rea involves a particular intention on the part of the defendant. If the crime was one of *basic intent* then the defendant must be convicted, as such crimes only require recklessness, and the defendant was reckless when getting intoxicated in the first place.

Example

The crime of theft requires the defendant to have acted 'with the intention of permanently depriving'; therefore intoxication can be a defence. However, the crime of criminal damage is committed by a person who acts 'intending to destroy or damage . . . or being reckless as to whether any such property would be destroyed or damaged'; therefore intoxication would not be a defence.

3.4 Criticisms of the Majewski rule

There are several inconsistencies in this statement of the law.

3.4.1 The specific/basic intent classification. In practice there is no clear distinction between crimes of specific and basic intent. For example, the courts will not allow intoxication as a defence to a charge of rape, although the definition requires the accused to have intended to have 'unlawful sexual intercourse'.

R v *Fotheringham* (1988)
A man got into his own bed after coming home from a party and forced the baby-sitter (who was already in the bed) to have sexual intercourse. He claimed that he was so drunk that he thought the girl was his wife. Until recently it was regarded as lawful for a man to force his wife to have sexual intercourse. The issue was therefore not concerned with his attitude to her consent (that only requires recklessness to sustain a conviction) but his knowledge of her identity. Nevertheless he was convicted and the Court of Appeal made it clear that this was for reasons of public policy.

In effect therefore the courts are deciding crime by crime whether intoxication should be allowed as a defence or not. The following table shows the effect of court decisions on some major crimes.

SPECIFIC INTENT	BASIC INTENT
Murder	Manslaughter
Wounding with intent	Malicious wounding
Robbery	Assault (including indecent assault)
Theft	Criminal damage
Handling stolen goods	Rape

3.4.2 Recklessness by intoxication. The other major difficulty with the decision in *Majewski* is the suggestion by the House of Lords that the mens rea for a crime of basic intent is supplied by the recklessness of the accused in getting intoxicated in the first place. However it is not always reckless to get intoxicated, and there is still no real connection between the decision to become intoxicated and the crime that is eventually committed, perhaps hours afterwards.

3.5   Conclusions

It is clear that in reality the courts are trying to achieve a balance between the conflicting interests mentioned in 3.1 above, and that logic has little to do with the rules they have formulated. The relevance of voluntary intoxication to other defences should also be carefully noted, and in particular in the section on *automatism* there is a separate note on how the courts deal with an accused who raises such a defence when intoxication is also an issue (see 4.3 below).

4   Automatism

4.1   Introduction

This defence arises when a person's body acts independently of the mind. It goes further than saying that the person did not have the mens rea for the offence by saying that in effect the person did not even 'act', as the mind was not in control of the body at all. The importance of the distinction is that automatism could possibly be a defence to a strict liability crime. The defence can be raised if the defendant was unconscious at the time that the crime was committed because of an external factor, such as a blow on the head. External factors such as alcohol or drugs are subject to the rules on voluntary intoxication (see 4.3 and 5.8 below), but any other events that cause a normal well-balanced person to act unconsciously may be valid.

R v T (1991)
The defendant claimed that she had committed a robbery in a dream-like state. There was medical evidence that she had been raped three days before the robbery, and that this may have caused her to enter a dissociative state caused by post traumatic stress. The judge at the Crown Court ruled that this could amount to the defence of automatism.

4.2   Limitations on the defence

The defence is limited in several ways.

4.2.1 Evidential burden. As explained in 1.4 above, the defendant has an evidential burden. In practice therefore there will have to be some medical evidence produced by the defence at least to raise the issue.

4.2.2   Unconsciousness.   The defendant must have been completely unconscious.

Broome v *Perkins* (1987)
The defendant had driven erratically while suffering from hypoglycaemia (low blood-sugar caused by excessive insulin in the bloodstream), but was convicted of driving without due care and attention because of evidence that he had controlled the car on occasions. He had been able to react consciously to imminent collisions by swerving, and was therefore deemed to be partially in control.

This decision seems very harsh, but it was recently confirmed by the Court of Appeal in even more extreme circumstances.

Attorney General's Reference (No. 2 of 1992)
A lorry driver apparently deliberately drove his lorry for nearly half a mile along the motorway hard-shoulder. Eventually he drove straight into a van and a recovery vehicle, both with flashing lights, killing two people. He was acquitted after a psychologist described a condition known as 'driving without awareness', a trance-like state induced by long journeys on straight, featureless roads. The Court of Appeal ruled that this could not amount to the defence of automatism, as this requires total destruction of voluntary control. The condition of 'driving without awareness' merely impairs or reduces the ability to control.

4.2.3   Insanity.   The court may rule that the defendant is in fact raising the defence of *insanity*. This can have serious consequences for the defendant, as although there will still be an acquittal, the court must treat an 'insane' defendant in special ways. The law on insanity means that defendants suffering from an internal disorder such as epilepsy, diabetes or sleep-walking, must be classified as insane in the legal sense (see 5.7-5.8 below).

4.3   Self-induced automatism

Finally it should be noted that self-induced automatism is not a defence. The typical example of this is automatism brought on by voluntary intoxication and in that situation the rules regarding intoxication and automatism overlap.

R v *Lipman* (1970)
The defendant took LSD and subsequently had hallucinations that he was being attacked by snakes. While in that state he killed his girl-friend by hitting her and pushing a sheet into her mouth, but pleaded that he was not in control of his body because of the effects of the drug. Nevertheless he was convicted of manslaughter.

5   Insanity

5.1   Introduction

There are three stages at which a person's mental capacity is relevant, and there are different consequences at each stage. First, a person may be mentally incapable of taking part in a trial. Secondly, a convicted defendant may be suffering from a mental disorder that needs to be taken into account when sentence is passed. Thirdly, an accused may have committed a crime when actually insane. It is important to distinguish carefully between these three possibilities, as the defence of *insanity* is only applicable in the third instance, and there are very specific rules that only apply to that defence. In the first situation the court is really not concerned with the crime but only with the accused's mental state. In the second situation the defendant has actually been convicted and will therefore have a criminal record, even though the sentence passed does not amount to punishment, but only treatment.

5.2 Mental incapacity at trial

If this is the case, then the trial will not take place as the accused person will be deemed to be *unfit to plead*. Under the Criminal Procedure (Insanity) Act 1964 the accused must be committed to a mental hospital at the discretion of the Home Secretary and the trial will not take place until he is capable of understanding the charge and properly conducting his defence. However under the Criminal Procedure (Insanity and Unfitness to Plead) Act 1991 the court will first have to hear evidence of the charges to decide if a crime had in fact been committed. If not, then the defendant's mental capacity cannot be questioned, and he must be released. The judge will also be able to choose from a wider range of orders should the accused be found to be unfit to plead, including supervision with a condition of medical treatment as an out-patient.

5.3 Mental disorder after conviction

Even if the defendant was mentally capable at the time the crime was committed, and was able to take part in the trial, the judge has a wide discretion when passing sentence. A probation order can be made with a requirement of medical treatment, or a hospital order under the Mental Health Act 1983 whereby the defendant is sent to a mental hospital with or without restrictions on a release date.

5.4 Insanity at the time of the crime

It is only in this situation that the defence of insanity can be raised. The rules governing the defence derive from the common law, although various statutes have laid down rules regarding the nature of the verdict. The Criminal Procedure (Insanity) Act 1964 states that if the defence is successful the verdict must be recorded as 'not guilty by reason of insanity'. Thus, although the defendant has been acquitted and may now be perfectly sane, the verdict is not a simple 'not guilty'. The Criminal Procedure (Insanity and Unfitness to Plead) Act 1991 now enables the judge to choose from a wider range of disposals, including supervision with a condition of medical treatment as an outpatient, but the defendant still carries the stigma of the 'insanity' verdict.

5.5 The definition of insanity

The rules governing the defence of insanity are called the *M'Naghten Rules*. In 1843 M'Naghten had shot and killed Sir Robert Peel's secretary but was acquitted of murder on the grounds of insanity. This caused an outcry and an attempt was made to clarify exactly what the defence entailed. The House of Lords therefore put a series of questions to the judges, and their answers provide the basis for the law on insanity even now. They are still called the M'Naghten Rules although they were not expounded during his trial, and in fact had no foundation in the system of binding precedent. However, they were subsequently adopted by the courts and are therefore now firmly part of the common law. It should be noted however that *insanity* is a strictly legal term in this context and has only a limited basis in medical science, let alone modern medical science! The M'Naghten Rules state that every person is presumed to be sane until he can prove that at the time of the offence 'he was labouring under such a defect of reason due to a disease of the mind as not to know the nature and quality of the act he was doing, or if he did know it, that he did not know he was doing what was wrong'. The first point therefore is that the burden of proof is clearly on the defendant, who must prove his own insanity on the balance of probabilities. This is the only general defence where the burden is not on the prosecution to disprove it, once it is raised. The second point is that there are three distinct stages in proving the defence. First, a 'defect of reason'; secondly, a 'disease of the mind'; thirdly, that the defendant did not know either the 'nature and quality' of his act or that he was doing 'what was wrong'. Each of these terms has a very specific meaning and must be looked at separately.

5.6   A 'defect of reason'

This means a complete loss of the power of reasoning, not merely confusion or absentmindedness.

R v *Clarke* (1972)

The defendant was charged with shoplifting and claimed that she took the goods without really thinking what she was doing, as a result of depression from which she was suffering at the time. The Court of Appeal ruled that this did not amount to a 'defect of reason'.

5.7   A 'disease of the mind'

This is not only a physical disorder of the brain such as inflammation, or a recognised mental illness such as schizophrenia, it also covers any internal disorder which affects the mental faculties, even if it is only short-lived.

R v *Sullivan* (1984)

The House of Lords ruled that the defendant was insane when he attacked a friend while suffering from an epileptic fit. This was so even though the epilepsy was controllable, the fit was over in moments, and the defendant's actions were an extremely unusual result of an epileptic fit.

A similar problem arose in the following case.

R v *Hennessey* (1989)

The defendant was a diabetic who was charged with taking a motor car without authority and driving while disqualified. He claimed that he was suffering from hyperglycaemia (excessive blood-sugar) at the time because he had not taken any insulin nor eaten properly for days, and as a result was acting unconsciously. The Court of Appeal held that this still amounted to a defence of insanity because the internal disorder of diabetes had caused the malfunctioning of his mind.

Finally, sleep-walking has always been thought of as a classic example of non-insane automatism. However a recent case has rejected that approach.

R v *Burgess* (1991)

The defendant had brutally attacked his female friend after an evening watching television. She managed to bring him to his senses, whereupon he voluntarily called an ambulance. He claimed that he was unaware of what he was doing and that he must have been sleep-walking throughout the attack. The Court of Appeal ruled that even sleep-walking amounts to insanity, as it must have been caused by an internal disorder.

5.8 *Insanity, automatism and voluntary intoxication*

External factors which cause a person to act unconsciously will not amount to insanity but will instead give rise to the alternative defence of automatism.

Example

While playing tennis a woman is struck on the head. This causes concussion and she thereafter carries on playing but unconsciously. She then leaves the court and drives off in somebody else's car. She could raise the defence of automatism to a charge of theft of the car and would be entitled to a full acquittal.

Drugs can come under this heading but again the rules relating to voluntary intoxication overlap. If the drugs had been properly taken for purely medical reasons then the court may have to consider exactly what caused the defendant's mental impairment.

R v *Quick* (1973)

The defendant was charged with assaulting a patient in the hospital where he worked. He was a diabetic and he claimed that he was acting unconsciously at the time because of hypoglycaemia. He had taken insulin but had not eaten properly, with the result that the excess of insulin in his bloodstream caused his blood-sugar level to fall. The Court of Appeal decided that he was not insane in the legal sense, because it was the drug that had caused the hypoglycaemia, not the diabetic condition.

Note in addition in *Quick*, that as the drug itself had been taken properly, it was not a case of voluntary intoxication; therefore the defendant was entitled to a defence of automatism and was acquitted. This case should be carefully contrasted with *Hennessey* in 5.7 above, to understand the relationship between diabetes and (legal) insanity.

5.9 *The defendant's state of mind*

The effect of the disease of the mind must be to cause the accused to fail to know either the 'nature and quality' of the act or that the act was 'wrong'. The law recognises only these two states of mind as being symptomatic of insanity, and the accused must prove that one or the other applies.

5.9.1 *'Nature and quality'.* By referring to the 'nature and quality' of the act the rule merely means that the accused did not know what he was doing.

Example

A woman would not know the 'nature and quality' of her act if she thought she was cutting a loaf of bread when in fact she was cutting somebody's throat.

5.9.2 'Wrong'. If the accused knew what he was doing then he would still be insane if he did not know that he was doing something 'wrong'. In the following case the court decided that this means legally wrong.

R v *Windle* (1952)

The defendant had been living with his mentally disturbed wife for so long that he became mentally ill himself and he poisoned her. However he was heard to say 'I suppose I shall be hanged for this'. Thus, despite the fact that he was so ill that he thought it was morally right to kill his wife, his defence of insanity did not succeed, as he clearly knew that he was committing a crime.

5.10 Discussion

It is clear from this outline of the law on insanity that the defence has many defects. First, the fact that a successful defence may result in the defendant being committed to a mental hospital means that most defendants would rather be convicted. Most of the leading cases in fact concern defendants who have pleaded automatism as a defence, only to withdraw their defence upon being told by the court that they are in law pleading insanity. In *R* v *Sullivan* for example, the defendant eventually pleaded guilty and agreed to a sentence of three years' probation. Similarly both Quick and Clarke changed their pleas to guilty when the trial judge ruled that they were pleading insanity, and then appealed against the ruling. They were fortunate in that their convictions were then quashed when the Court of Appeal overturned the original ruling. The 1991 Act may have removed some fears about committal to an institution, but the stigma of the verdict remains. Connected to this problem is the second area of difficulty, namely that the definition includes many disorders which are clearly not insanity in the medical sense, but at the same time excludes other states of mind where defendants are so mentally disturbed that they are not responsible for their actions.

Example

The courts have construed 'disease of the mind' to include epilepsy, diabetes and sleep-walking. By no stretch of the imagination can such people be deemed 'insane'. However, if a man thought that he was the reincarnation of Jack the Ripper and that God was ordering him to kill prostitutes, legally he would not be insane. He would know both the 'nature and quality' of his acts and that legally they were 'wrong'.

The combined result of these defects is that many people plead guilty to crimes for which they were not responsible, rather than suffer the indignity of being pronounced insane.

5.11 Insanity and diminished responsibility

Finally mention must be made of the special defence to murder of *diminished responsibility*, introduced in the Homicide Act 1957, which is looked at in more detail later (see *Homicide*, 3.3). This defence has a much wider definition than insanity and has the effect of reducing the charge to manslaughter. The judge is then able to impose any sentence on the defendant, including, for example, probation or a hospital order. Note, however, that the defendant will still have a criminal record, and that the defence is not available for any other charge.

6   Duress and marital coercion

6.1   Introduction

The defence of duress is a common law defence. It allows an accused to be acquitted of a crime if it was committed as a result of threats from another person. Unlike defences such as intoxication or insanity there is no doubt that the accused had the mens rea for the crime, but the law recognises that sometimes a person may have to choose to commit a crime because of the stronger influence of the desire for self-preservation. In effect therefore the law is making a concession to human weakness.

Example

A bank manager is ordered to open the bank's safe by thieves who are holding her husband hostage. The manager clearly knows that she is assisting in the theft of the money inside the safe, but makes a choice that the threats to her husband are more important. If she was charged with theft she would be able to raise the defence of duress.

Because the defence is only a concession to human weakness it is limited in application. First, the definition of the defence is strictly limited in a variety of ways. Secondly, the defence does not cover certain crimes or situations.

6.2   The definition

The definition of duress can be stated as an immediate threat of personal violence which was a reasonable cause of the accused committing the crime. There are thus three elements.

6.2.1   Immediate threat.
The threat must be immediate in the sense that it is operating upon the accused at the time that the crime is committed. Thus if the defendant could avoid the threat by escaping, or if the person making the threats is no longer nearby, then the defence will not be available. However, the courts have made it clear that the circumstances of every case must be looked at carefully to assess whether it was realistically possible for the threat to be avoided, and it does not matter that the threat would not be put into effect for some time afterwards.

R v Hudson and Taylor (1971)
Two girls told lies on oath in a criminal trial to protect the defendant. They were then charged with perjury but claimed that the defendant's gang had threatened them and were sitting in the public gallery during the trial. The Court of Appeal ruled that the defence of duress could have been open to the girls if they reasonably felt that the police could not have offered them satisfactory protection. It was also irrelevant that the threats could not have been carried out until after the trial.

6.2.2   Personal violence.
Threats against the accused's property would not be sufficient, and in the case of R v Singh (1973) the Court of Appeal ruled that a threat to expose the defendant's adultery would also not be sufficient grounds to plead duress. It is generally accepted that threats of violence to the defendant's family would suffice, and in the Australian case of R v Hurley (1967) the Supreme Court of Victoria allowed the defence

when the theats had been made towards the defendant's girlfriend with whom he was living at the time. This restriction to threats of violence, however, could be unfair in that it takes no account of the nature of the crime that the defendant was forced to commit.

Example

A man is told that his shop will be fire-bombed unless he takes a bottle of whisky out of a supermarket without paying for it. The threat is thus to destroy his home and his livelihood, and the crime he is being forced to commit is a minor theft. Nevertheless the defence of duress would not be available to him.

6.2.3 Causation. The threat must reasonably have caused the accused to have committed the crime. There are thus two distinct questions. First, did the accused commit the crime because of the threat? Secondly, would a person of reasonable courage have given in to the threat? The first question involves an assessment of the defendant's motives at the time, but it is possible for the threat of violence to be only one out of several factors.

R v Valderrama-Vega (1985)
The defendant had been involved in importing drugs under threats of violence towards him and his family as well as threats to expose him as an homosexual and to ruin him financially. The court held that the defence of duress was available to him as long as the threats of violence were the decisive factors, although clearly the other threats influenced his decision as well.

The second question involves an assessment of the reasonableness of the accused's actions in giving in to the threats.

R v Graham (1982)
The defendant had killed his wife under the influence of another man who shared their house and who was his homosexual lover. The Court of Appeal upheld his conviction for murder and stated that as a matter of public policy the defendant must have acted with the steadfastness of an ordinary citizen, although the court could take account of the defendant's personal characteristics such as his age. The fact that he was voluntarily intoxicated at the time however would be irrelevant and thus could not be taken into account (see 3.5 above).

6.3 Limitations on the defence

The defence is limited in extent in two ways.

6.3.1 Voluntary membership of a violent gang. This will disqualify an accused from pleading duress by threats from the other members of the gang. The key issue which the jury will have to decide is whether the accused knew from the beginning of the propensity to violence on the part of the other gang members.

R v Sharp (1987)
The defendant had entered into a conspiracy to rob and had been threatened when he tried to withdraw. He was charged with manslaughter when somebody was killed during the robbery, and the Court of Appeal upheld his conviction on the basis that the jury had

decided that he knew how violent the other members of the conspiracy were before he joined them in the plan.

This should be contrasted with the following case.

R v *Shepherd* (1987)

The defendant was part of a gang which was planning burglaries. The Court of Appeal stated that it was quite feasible that the defendant might not have anticipated violence. On that basis the defendant's plea of duress was accepted and he was acquitted.

6.3.2 Murder and treason. Duress cannot be a defence to a charge of murder, and possibly not to a charge of treason. For many years it was thought that the defence was available to an accomplice to murder. In *DPP for Northern Ireland* v *Lynch* (1975) the House of Lords acquitted a man who had been forced to drive the getaway car for an IRA gang who murdered a policeman. However in *R* v *Howe* (1987) the House of Lords reversed that decision and stated that the defence could never be available to a charge of murder no matter what the circumstances were. The reasoning would seem to be that in such a situation the accused cannot be allowed to place a greater value on his own life than on the life of the intended victim. The principal criticism of the decision is that the Law Lords glossed over the possibility that there might be a clear balance in favour of giving in to the threat, and were content to leave such situations to the discretion of the relevant authorities.

Example

A gang of terrorists threaten to kill several members of a man's family unless he drives them to the place where their victim is to be given a severe beating. If the victim dies then all of them will be guilty of murder, as the mens rea for murder is 'intention to kill or to cause grievous bodily harm'. But the man will have had the choice between seeing several people killed, or merely participating in an activity which may result in a serious assault, and only possibly result in one death. Nevertheless he would be convicted of murder as an accomplice and would receive the mandatory sentence of life imprisonment. The House of Lords felt that such a situation could satisfactorily be left to the discretion of the police not to prosecute the man; or to the discretion of the Home Secretary in recommending a pardon; or to the discretion of the Parole Board in granting the man early parole.

There are old authorities concerning the availability of the defence to a charge of treason, but these are not satisfactory for modern purposes. The general opinion is that the defence is not available, and this was stated obiter by Lord Goddard CJ in *R* v *Steane* (1947). In addition, in *R* v *Gotts* (1991) the House of Lords ruled that the defence could not be raised where the charge was one of attempted murder.

6.4 *Marital coercion*

Under the Criminal Justice Act 1925, s. 47, it is a defence for a woman to prove that she committed a crime in the presence of and under the 'coercion' of her husband. Murder and treason are specifically excluded. The defence is rarely used, as the defence of duress is just as effective, but under the statute the woman has the burden of proof. In the defence of duress the defendant only has to raise the issue by presenting some evidence, after which the prosecution has the burden of disproving it. It is possible however that 'coercion' is not restricted to threats of violence, and that in that respect therefore the defence could be wider than that of duress.

Example

A man threatens his wife that he will leave her and take the children unless she helps him commit a crime. There are no cases deciding whether this would amount to 'coercion' or not, but it would not amount to duress (see 6.2.2 above).

7 Necessity and duress of circumstances

7.1 Introduction

In the case of duress, the accused has the choice between committing a crime or suffering violence from another person. Sometimes the choice will lie between committing a crime or allowing some other harm to occur.

Example

A woman is rock-climbing when the man above her falls and causes her to fall as well. The rope holding them is attached to the rock, but it is not strong enough to bear the weight of both of them. If the woman cuts the rope so that the man falls, she will be saved but will be responsible for his death. If she does not, then they will both fall to their deaths.

There are three areas of case-law concerning necessity. First, several important cases suggest that it cannot be a defence at all. Secondly, however, there are cases which have allowed a plea of necessity in some circumstances. Thirdly, there have been recent developments which clearly allow such a defence in special situations called *duress of circumstances*.

7.2 The unavailability of necessity as a defence

The generally accepted position is that necessity cannot be a defence to a criminal charge. The principal case is from the previous century.

R v Dudley and Stephens (1884)

After a shipwreck the defendants had been adrift in a lifeboat for three weeks together with the ship's cabin-boy. They were eventually picked up alive, but minus the cabin-boy. It transpired that they had followed an old naval tradition of killing and eating the weakest person in order to stay alive. A jury refused to convict them of murder but a special court of the Queen's Bench Division stated that their obvious necessity was no defence, and they were convicted. However, the death sentence was commuted to six months' imprisonment.

Other cases have followed this decision albeit in not such dramatic circumstances. Thus in the case of *Buckoke* v *Greater London Council* (1971) Lord Denning MR stated obiter that the driver of a fire-engine would be guilty of breaking traffic regulations by crossing a red traffic light, even if it was to rescue someone in extreme peril. In *Wood* v *Richards* (1977) a police officer was actually convicted of driving without due care and attention despite the fact that he was driving in response to an emergency call.

7.3   The availability of necessity as a defence

In some special cases the defence has been allowed. In the civil case of *Leigh* v *Gladstone* (1909) it was held that prison officers could force-feed a prisoner when she was on hunger-strike, although legally this would amount to an assault. Similarly the defence of self-defence has always been allowed to a charge of assault or even murder, even where it was to defend another person or property (see 8.1 below). In *Re F (Mental Patient: Sterilisation)* (1989) the House of Lords recognised that acts can be justified if taken in the best interests of a person who cannot make the decision herself. These cases are limited however, and do not really cast doubt on the general principle that necessity is not a defence.

7.4   Duress of circumstances

Recently the courts have seemed ready to accept a special defence of *duress of circumstances*: two cases should be compared.

R v Conway (1988)
A man had driven recklessly because he thought he was being chased by some thugs who wanted to kill his passenger. In fact they were plain-clothes police officers. The usual defence of duress was not available, because the pursuers had not ordered the defendant to drive recklessly. However the Court of Appeal decided that there could be a defence even where it was circumstances rather than another person which had forced the defendant to choose to break the law.

R v Martin (1989)
The defendant had driven his stepson to work although he was disqualified from driving. He claimed that he had done this because his wife (the boy's mother) had threatened to commit suicide unless he did so, as the boy was in danger of losing his job if he was late. The Court of Appeal stated that the jury should have been allowed to consider whether the circumstances were such as reasonably to leave the defendant with no choice but to commit the crime.

7.5   Conclusions

It would seem that necessity can be a defence if it was particular circumstances rather than another person that forced the accused to commit a crime. However, this defence is restricted in the same way that the defence of duress is restricted, so that the threat to the accused must have been one of violence to him or his family, and the defence would not be available on a charge of murder or treason. The woman in the example in 7.1 would not be able to raise the defence of duress of circumstances, and would have to be convicted of murder.

8   Necessary defence

8.1   Introduction

If a person causes harm to another it may be a defence to plead that it was done to avert harm to oneself, to another person, to property, or to prevent a crime being committed.

There is also a specific statutory defence to a charge of damage to property under the Criminal Damage Act 1971 (see *Criminal Damage*, 3.3). In effect therefore there are three separate situations. First, self-defence and defending someone else; secondly, defence of property; thirdly, prevention of crime, which is covered by the Criminal Law Act 1967, s. 3.

8.2   Self-defence or defending another person

This defence is available even if force was used to protect a member of the accused's family or a complete stranger. The key question is whether the force used was reasonable. If the force was unreasonable then the defence fails completely.

Example

A man is punched by a boy and responds by knocking him to the ground and then beating him severely, clearly intending to cause him grievous bodily harm. He would have no defence to a charge of assaulting the boy, and if the boy died the man would be convicted of murder.

The question of what is reasonable force is purely a matter for the jury in all the circumstances of the case, but there are two principal issues. First the state of mind of the accused at the time, and secondly the exact situation that the accused was in.

8.2.1   The state of mind of the defendant at the time of the assault.   This is important because the defendant will be judged according to the circumstances that he believed existed.

R v Williams (1987)
The defendant had seen a man attacking a youth. He therefore assaulted the man, only to find later that the man had been trying to arrest the youth for theft. The defendant was charged with assaulting the man, but was acquitted by the Court of Appeal on the grounds that he should be judged by what he thought was happening to the youth, even if he had unreasonably jumped to the wrong conclusion.

Furthermore, in the case of *Palmer v R* (1971) the Privy Council stated that a person who is being attacked should not be expected to 'weigh to a nicety' what is required to protect himself, and that the heat of the moment could be taken into account in assessing whether the accused had reacted reasonably. This does not mean however that a person can be 'allowed' to lose his temper, as it is only his belief of what is necessary that is at issue.

Example

A woman is approached by a man. She unreasonably but honestly thinks that she is about to be attacked and so knocks him out before he can touch her. She could successfully plead self-defence if the blow was one of desperation in the heat of the moment, but not if the reason that she hit him so hard was because she thought he was a 'groper' and that caused her to lose her temper.

Finally, the defendant will not be guilty where he mistakenly believes that the circumstances call for a degree of force which, in fact, is not necessary.

R v Scarlett (1993)

The defendant was a pub landlord who had thrown out a drunk who had come in demanding drink well after closing time. The drunk was a large and aggressive man, and the defendant had had to bundle him through the exit door in order to get him out. Unfortunately the drunk fell down some steps and died from a fractured skull. The Court of Appeal ruled that there must be clear evidence that the defendant knew that the force he was using was unnecessary, and they quashed the landlord's conviction for manslaughter.

8.2.2 The precise circumstances of the attack. These are important in that they allow the jury to assess properly whether the defendant had acted reasonably. Thus it is not always necessary to try to run away when attacked, or even to have to wait for the expected attack to occur.

R v Bird (1985)

A woman was accosted by a man in a pub and hit him with a glass. The Court of Appeal quashed her conviction and ruled that in some circumstances it may be necessary to react immediately, without first demonstrating an unwillingness to fight.

Similarly, but more dramatically, the following case illustrates the principle in a different context.

Attorney-General's Reference (No. 2 of 1983)

The defendant was charged with unlawful possession of explosives after a cache of petrol bombs was found in his shop in Liverpool. He claimed that he intended to use these to keep rioters away from his shop, as there were serious disturbances taking place in Toxteth at that time. The Court of Appeal ruled that it could be possible to view the use of such weapons as self-defence even if an attack were only apprehended rather than in progress.

Note, however, that in *R v O' Grady* (1987) it was held that a mistake caused by voluntary intoxication should not be taken into account, on the grounds of public policy associated with the general rules on intoxication as a defence (see 3.5 above).

8.3 Defence of property

Again the key issue is one of reasonableness and possibly attitudes have shifted over the last 50 years, so that property is now seen as much less important than people. Certainly a person is entitled to use force to prevent a robbery or a burglary, but it is unlikely that killing a criminal or even causing serious harm would be justified, even if that were the only way that property could be protected.

R v Hussey (1924)

The defendant was barricaded in his room while his landlady and some accomplices were trying to break down his door to evict him unlawfully. The defendant had fired a gun through the door, and wounded one of them. He was acquitted of the wounding charge on the grounds of self-defence, but it is unlikely that this decision would be followed today.

8.4 Prevention of crime

Under the Criminal Law Act 1967, s. 3, a person may use 'such force as is reasonable in the circumstances' in three situations: prevention of crime, arresting or assisting someone to arrest an offender, or arresting an escaped prisoner. The courts' approach should be similar to the common law defence of self-defence, and in fact most cases will now fall under this heading anyway.

Example

A man is attacked. By defending himself he is also preventing a crime (a criminal assault, albeit upon himself) and therefore his actions will be covered by the Criminal Law Act 1967. However if the attacker were under ten years old, no crime would in fact be committed (see 2.1 above) and so he would have to rely on the common law defence.

With respect to the state of mind of the defendant, the same test applies as in the case of self-defence (see 8.2.1 above).

DPP v Morrow, Geach & Thomas (1994)
The defendants had been convicted of an offence under the Public Order Act 1986 after a demonstration outside a clinic where abortions were carried out. One of their defences was that they believed that illegal abortions were being performed, and that they wished to prevent them. The Divisional Court ruled that their honest belief was sufficient to form the basis of a defence under the Criminal Law Act 1967, but that the defence was not appropriate in the case of an aggressive demonstration which was meant to prevent lawful as well as unlawful abortions.

The courts have ruled that the circumstances may even justify killing.

Attorney-General for Northern Ireland's Reference (1977)
A soldier had been acquitted of murder after he shot dead a man who was running away from the scene of a burglary. It later transpired that the man was not a terrorist as the soldier believed him to be. The House of Lords were asked to consider the issue and ruled that the social harm of letting a suspected terrorist escape could outweigh the risk to the victim.

HOMICIDE

1   Unlawful killing

1.1   Introduction

It is not necessarily unlawful to kill another person. It is part and parcel of a war, and many countries still have the death penalty for certain crimes. There is a strict definition which must be applied to any act of killing before it can be classified as 'unlawful' and therefore a type of homicide. However there is no crime of homicide as such. Once it has been decided that a killing is unlawful, the next step is to consider whether it falls into the two categories of homicide recognised in the law of England and Wales. The first category is *murder*, which is seen as the most serious crime that can be committed, and which carries a mandatory sentence of life imprisonment. There are, however, three special defences to a charge of murder which allow the court to reduce the conviction to *manslaughter*. These three defences are *provocation, diminished responsibility* and *suicide pact*, and are known collectively as *voluntary manslaughter*. The second category of homicide is that of manslaughter. This category of homicide also has a detailed definition, separate to that of the three types of voluntary manslaughter just mentioned, and is known as *involuntary manslaughter*. It carries no fixed penalty because it covers such a wide range of offences, and therefore the judge has complete discretion as to what punishment can be imposed. It is easier to regard the defences known as voluntary manslaughter as being special situations where the judge will have a discretion as to sentence even though the defendant has been found guilty of murder. This section on homicide will follow the same pattern. This should also be seen as an indication of the process that should be followed when considering a killing. First, was the killing *homicide*? Secondly, if so did it amount to *murder*? Thirdly, if it was murder, is there a special defence leading to a reduction of the charge to *voluntary manslaughter*? Finally, if it was not murder, did the killing amount to *involuntary manslaughter*? This process can be visualised in the form of a flow-chart (below)

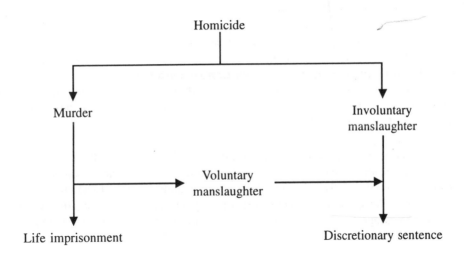

1.2   The definition

The first stage is to define homicide. This definition derives from the common law but is usually accepted as being 'the unlawful killing of a human being under the Queen's Peace, death occurring within a year and a day'. Each part of the definition requires some consideration, but in practice the crucial issue will often be whether the accused actually 'killed' the deceased, in the sense of being legally responsible for the death. This is known as the issue of *causation* and will be looked at last (see 1.3 below). The basic definition is thus the 'unlawful killing of a human being under the Queen's Peace', which contains four elements.

   (a)   The killing must be 'unlawful'. Thus the accused may be able to plead self-defence, or it may have been a legally authorised execution.
   (b)   The victim must have been a 'human being'. Normally this will be self-evident, but it is not homicide to kill a child if it is not fully born and physically independent of its mother. Those offences are covered by the law on abortion and child destruction.

(c)   The killing must be 'under the Queen's Peace'. The English courts have jurisdiction over any killing within England and Wales by any person, or by a British citizen in any country. Under the War Crimes Act 1991, British citizens or residents may also now be tried for homicides committed in German-held territory during World War Two if they were 'in violation of the laws and customs of war', no matter what their nationality was at the time.

(d)   There is then a further stipulation that the victim must have died 'within a year and a day'. This means that death must occur within a year and a day from the injuries which caused the victim's death.

R v *Dyson* (1908)

The defendant had injured a child in November 1906, and then again in December 1907. The child eventually died in March 1908, sixteen months after the first assault but only three months after the second assault. The Court of Appeal quashed the conviction for manslaughter because the judge had directed the jury that they could convict no matter which assault had caused the death. In fact the jury needed to be certain that it was the second assault that was the cause.

The rule is certainly still valid as a recent case shows.

R v *The Coroner for Inner West London ex p De Luca* (1988)

A boy died more than a year after he shot himself. The Divisional Court decided that the rule even applied to offences connected to suicide, and accordingly the boy's death could not be classified as a suicide by the coroner.

The original reason for the rule was that a death could not be traced with any certainty to a particular incident after such a long period of time. Medical science has now developed to the point where positive diagnosis after a year is quite possible. In addition victims may be kept alive for considerable periods of time by advanced techniques, thus enabling the criminal to escape full responsibility, even if a severe sentence can still be imposed for a different offence.

Example

A woman attacks a man and stabs him. He survives on a life-support machine for eighteen months before eventually dying. She can only be convicted for a serious assault rather than murder. Although under the Offences against the Person Act 1861, s. 18, this carries a discretionary maximum penalty of life imprisonment, the woman will still avoid the stigma of a murder conviction.

1.3   Causation

If the basic definition and the 'year and a day' rule are met, then the only remaining condition must be that the prosecution can prove that it was the act of the accused that caused the victim's death. This is not as simple a question as it may seem at first sight because there are often several acts which have combined to cause a death. The court will then have to decide whether the defendant was legally responsible or not.

Example

A man invites a friend to meet him. On the way to the appointment the friend is attacked and killed. Although he would not have been attacked if he had not been out on the street, the man who invited him cannot be blamed legally for his death. On the other hand, if the attacker leaves him lying in the road and he is then run over and killed by a car, the attacker will still be legally responsible for the death. Yet another issue would arise if the victim had been taken to hospital after the attack, only to die from clumsy medical treatment. On the one hand it was the attacker's fault that he was in hospital, but on the other hand the attacker was not to blame for the doctor's misdeeds.

There are various rules which the courts have devised to meet these situations, which must be considered in turn.

1.3.1   It must be the unlawful act of the accused which causes the death.

R v Dalloway (1847)

The defendant had run over and killed a child with his horse and cart, and there was clear evidence that he was driving carelessly at the time. His conviction for manslaughter was overturned by the Court of Appeal because the jury should have been told to consider whether the child would have been killed even if Dalloway had been driving properly.

1.3.2   The act need only accelerate death.   It is irrelevant that the deceased would have died anyway, even if it would have been only a matter of minutes later. This is subject to the maxim *de minimis non curat lex*, usually shortened to 'the de minimis rule'. This means that the law is not concerned with trifling matters.

Example

A man is dying in hospital from a serious illness. His wife switches off his life-support machine to prevent any further unnecessary pain. She would still be legally responsible for the death and it would probably amount to murder. However, if she had merely pricked him with a pin, although it could be argued that the loss of one drop of blood hastened his death, even by a fraction of a second, the courts would not accept that as grounds for legal liability.

A difficult problem arises when doctors give pain-killing drugs, knowing that these will also shorten the patient's life. In *R v Adams* (1957) the court ruled that this would not amount to homicide if it was proper medical treatment to relieve pain, but this situation must be distinguished carefully from the giving of drugs which merely hasten death, even though the motive is the same.

R v Cox (1992)

Dr Cox gave a lethal injection to a female patient who was on the verge of death, in intense pain and begging him to kill her. It was well established that no pain-killing drugs would reduce her suffering. Dr Cox was charged with attempted murder, apparently on the grounds that the exact cause of death could not be established because she had been cremated by the time that the incident was reported (see 1.3.1 above). He was convicted but only given a suspended prison sentence, whereas if he had been convicted of murder he would have received life imprisonment.

Advances in medical science have created particular problems. In *R v Malcherek*; *R v Steel* (1981) it was held that proper medical procedures as to determining death would not be questioned by the court, thus allowing doctors to switch off a life-support machine when all brain activity had ceased. The problem has now arisen as to how to deal with cases of 'persistent vegetative state', where a person has no brain function, but can survive (i.e., breathe) unaided as long as water, nutrition and medicine for infection are administered.

Airedale NHS Trust v Bland (1993)
Tony Bland had been crushed in the Hillsborough Stadium disaster four years previously, and it was accepted that he would never regain consciousness as his brain had been destroyed. The hospital, with the support of Tony's family, applied for a declaration that it would not amount to homicide if they stopped giving him nutrition, water and medicine for infection, although this would inevitably result in his death. The House of Lords gave the declaration as requested, but clearly felt that the issue should be resolved by Parliament. The House of Lords accepted that there was no difference in law between withdrawing life-sustaining treatment (see *Principles of Liability* 2.2.2 above) and giving an injection such as Dr Cox had done, and that in fact the latter would be the more merciful procedure. They reiterated, however, that any positive act to bring about his death would be homicide, and only the withdrawal of treatment could be permitted.

1.3.3   The accused must take the victim as he finds him.

R v Hayward (1908)
A man chased his wife into the street shouting threats and kicked her. She collapsed and died from a thyroid condition which made her peculiarly susceptible to physical exertion and fear. He was convicted of manslaughter.

This principle extends to aspects of the victim's personality.

R v Blaue (1975)
The defendant had stabbed a woman. She was a Jehovah's Witness and died in hospital after refusing a blood transfusion for religious reasons. Nevertheless the defendant was convicted of manslaughter.

1.3.4   Only unforeseeable intervening acts will relieve the defendant of responsibility for the death.   Usually this will be a matter of common sense.

Example

A man is attacked and left lying in the road. The attacker will be responsible for the death if the man dies from loss of blood, exposure, an infection of the wounds, or if he is run over by a car. However the attacker would not be liable if the man was struck by lightning or killed by another assailant.

Some more difficult situations have been highlighted by cases.

R v *Williams & Davis* (1992)

A hitch-hiker jumped from a car and died from head injuries. It was ascertained that he had been threatened by the driver and another passenger, the defendants, who were then charged with manslaughter. The Court of Appeal ruled that the defendants should be convicted if the victim's reaction was a foreseeable response to the threats, and that it would only absolve the defendants of liability for the death if it had been 'so daft as to make it his own voluntary act'.

R v *Pagett* (1983)

The accused knew that his flat was surrounded by armed police and so he went out holding his girlfriend in front of him. When he shot at the police they returned fire to defend themselves and killed the girl. The defendant was convicted of her murder as the Court of Appeal decided that his actions had forced the police to fire and had therefore caused the girl's death.

1.3.5 There is a particular problem when the victim of an attack has died after negligent medical treatment. The courts are loath to shift the blame for the death from the attacker onto the medical staff and will thus only do so in extreme circumstances. Two key cases can be compared.

R v *Jordan* (1956)

The defendant had stabbed a man who subsequently seemed to be making a full recovery. However, he was then given a drug to which he was allergic, together with other treatment that made his allergic reaction even worse. As a result he died and the defendant was acquitted by the Court of Appeal.

A different conclusion was reached in a similar case only three years later.

R v *Smith* (1959)

The defendant had stabbed a fellow soldier in a fight in their army camp. The victim was carried to the medical room but dropped twice on the way. He was then left for too long, and eventually given treatment which made his condition worse so that he died. Nevertheless the defendant was convicted and the court stated that if the original wound is still a substantial threat to the victim's life then any medical treatment will be irrelevant. Only if the original wound is merely part of the history of events and the treatment is completely overwhelming in its effects will it relieve the accused of responsibility.

It is likely that the approach in *Smith* will be preferred by the courts to the decision in *Jordan*, as presumably even there the wound was still a threat, otherwise no further treatment would have been necessary. Certainly, the courts are unable to specify exactly when a defendant's liability will cease, although the possibility has been left open.

R v *Cheshire* (1991)

The victim had been shot and had been given a tracheotomy (a hole cut in his windpipe to enable him to breathe) in the hospital. The gun-shot wounds were no longer life-threatening, but negligent medical treatment allowed the tracheotomy to close, so that he suffocated. The defendant's conviction for murder was upheld by the Court of Appeal, who stated that negligent treatment would only exclude the defendant from liability for the death if the treatment was 'independent of his acts, and in itself so potent in causing death'.

2   Murder

2.1   The definition

This derives from common law and is usually stated as being homicide with *malice aforethought*. The phrase *malice aforethought* denotes the mens rea for murder, but it is ambiguous in that it implies that an element of planning is necessary. The mens rea for murder is more accurately and simply stated as intention to kill or cause grievous bodily harm. If the accused had that state of mind at the time of the killing then it is properly described as malice aforethought, regardless of any other motive.

Example

All of the following persons would have the mens rea for murder. A woman giving her incurably sick husband an overdose of drugs at his request to put him out of his pain. A man who kills on the spur of the moment with only a second's forethought. Two climbers have fallen and the rope holding them is only strong enough for one. Just before it breaks the climber nearest the top cuts the rope below her, so that she is saved but the next climber falls to his death (see *General Defences*, 7.1 and 7.5).

It is therefore possible to be guilty of murder without having intended to kill. This was finally confirmed by the House of Lords in the following case.

R v Cunningham (1982)

The defendant had repeatedly struck his victim with a chair and the victim died from the injuries he received. The House of Lords stated that an intention to cause 'really serious injury' was sufficient to amount to the mens rea for murder, and would not attempt to define 'grievous bodily harm' further than that.

Thus it will amount to murder even if the accused had deliberately planned events so that the victim would live, as long as in the process a serious injury was caused.

Example

A terrorist group capture a suspected police informer and shoot him in the legs. Their intention is that the informer should live but be crippled, to act as a warning and deterrent to others. If the victim dies (perhaps because of an unsuspected heart complaint) the group members will be guilty of murder.

2.2   Intention

This has already been discussed at length (see *Principles of Liability*, 3.3–3.5). It should be recalled that the courts have ruled that the jury are entitled to infer that an intention to cause death or grievous bodily harm was present if the accused foresaw that it would inevitably happen as a result of his actions but carried on anyway. There are two particular difficulties however.

2.2.1   Contemporaneity. The intention to kill or cause grievous bodily harm must be contemporaneous with the actus reus. Usually this is a matter of common sense.

Example

A man goes out to look for his sworn enemy, but has only driven a few yards when he accidentally runs somebody over. On inspecting the dead body he notices that it is the man he was hunting and therefore expresses his delight at the death. The intention to kill was clearly present both before and after the actual killing, but not at the precise moment when the death occurred. Therefore there is no question of the accident amounting to murder.

However a difficulty arose in the following case.

R v *Thabo Meli* (1954)
The accused had attacked the victim as part of a plan to kill him, and then thrown the body over a cliff. It transpired that the attack had not killed him (which was when the intention was present) but that he had died from exposure (when the accused thought that he was merely disposing of a dead body). However the Privy Council disposed of this ingenious if unmeritorious argument by explaining that where there is a series of acts amounting to one transaction the accused need only have the mens rea at one stage of the process.

This decision was confirmed some years later in slightly different circumstances.

R v *Church* (1966)
The defendant had beaten up his girlfriend before throwing what he thought was her dead body into the river. In fact she was not dead and she died by drowning. The Court of Appeal ruled that the same principle applied although there had not even been a preconceived plan. The defendant had been convicted of manslaughter and was perhaps fortunate that he had not been charged with murder, as he clearly had intended to cause the woman serious harm in the first place.

2.2.2   *Transferred malice.*   An intention to injure one person will suffice even though the accused's act accidentally injures another person.

R v *Latimer* (1886)
The defendant had attacked another man with a heavy belt. A blow glanced off his intended victim and hit a woman standing nearby, wounding her severely.

2.3   *The punishment for murder*

This is fixed as imprisonment for life by the Murder (Abolition of Death Penalty) Act 1965. The definition of the offence remains as stated by common law however. The mandatory nature of the penalty has come under increasing attack in recent years, as it is seen as operating unfairly in areas such as mercy killing (see 1.3.2 above) and killing by battered women (see 3.2.2 below). First the House of Lords Select Committee on Murder and Life Imprisonment (1989), and then the Lane Committee on the Penalty for Homicide (1993) recommended that it should be replaced by a discretionary penalty, with life imprisonment as merely the maximum sentence. The Government has resisted the pressure, however, stating that it regards the mandatory nature of the penalty as necessary to stigmatize properly the crime which is regarded as the most serious possible crime.

3   Voluntary manslaughter

3.1   Introduction

If the accused had the mens rea for murder the charge may nevertheless be reduced to one of manslaughter if one of three special defences can be established. These defences are set out in the Homicide Act 1957 and do not apply to any crime other than murder, not even attempted murder. This is because the situations covered by these partial defences only really justify a reduction in the accused's sentence rather than a complete acquittal. Murder has a fixed penalty of life imprisonment, but in all other crimes (including manslaughter) the judge can consider the same issues when passing sentence. The three partial defences are *provocation, diminished responsibility* and *suicide pact*.

3.2   Provocation

This is a common law defence but is put in a statutory framework by the Homicide Act 1957, s. 3. This states:

> Where on a charge of murder there is evidence on which the jury can find that the person charged was provoked (whether by things done or by things said or by both together) to lose his self-control, the question whether the provocation was enough to make a reasonable man do as he did shall be left to be determined by the jury.

There are therefore three distinct stages in assessing whether an accused can succeed with a defence of provocation. First, is there some evidence of provocation? Secondly, did the accused actually lose self-control? Thirdly, would a reasonable man have lost self-control? It is important to follow this process of reasoning very carefully, as there are separate issues requiring consideration at each stage.

3.2.1   Evidence of provocation.   This can be provided by any witness at the trial, not necessarily by the defendant alone. Once the possibility of provocation has been raised the whole issue must be left to the jury. The courts are now extremely reluctant to direct the jury that the defence is not available. In addition almost anything can amount to provocation in the legal sense, as long as it falls within the description of 'things done or things said' in the Homicide Act 1957.

R v *Doughty* (1986)
A man had killed his baby and wanted to argue that he had been provoked by the child's incessant crying. The trial judge refuse to allow this as amounting to provocation, but the Court of Appeal ruled that the defendant could have raised the defence and therefore quashed the conviction.

It would seem that this covers words or acts by any person (not necessarily the victim) but would exclude naturally occurring acts. Even this wide definition could have unfair results.

Example

A man is so enraged by hearing a speech by an MP that he kills the nearest person he can find wearing the MP's rosette. A woman loses self-control on hearing that a storm has destroyed all the crops on her farm and shoots the local Farmers' Union representative. Whether either case deserves an excuse or not, the man could at least raise the defence whereas the woman could not.

3.2.2   The subjective test.   The next question is then to decide if the accused actually lost self-control. The link between provocation and a loss of self-control can be found in the following case.

R v *Duffy* (1949)
Devlin J stated that the provocation must cause 'a sudden and temporary loss of self-control, rendering the accused so subject to passion as to make him or her for the moment not master of his mind'.

There must be evidence that this actually happened, and the usual factors to be assessed are the accused's behaviour at the moment of the killing and the length of time that had elapsed since the provoking act. This 'cooling off' period is often the most crucial factor, and has caused some controversy.

R v *Thornton* (1992)
The defendant was married to a man who frequently beat her. After a series of arguments and threats she stabbed him to death while he was asleep on the sofa. The Court of Appeal ruled that she was not 'provoked' in the legal sense, and approved Devlin J's statement. The defendant had admitted that she had calmed down before fetching the knife and was therefore properly convicted of murder.

This has been criticised as failing to take into account the mental state of a weak person who has lived under the constant threat of violence by a stronger person, and who therefore cannot and will not react by losing self control suddenly. Instead such a person (typically a woman living with a violent man) will tend to react when it is 'safe' to do so. It is argued that the traditional rule is based on a male viewpoint of human behaviour and should therefore be extended, but the Court of Appeal has rejected this and once again approved the rule in *R* v *Duffy*.

R v *Ahluwalia* (1992)
The defendant had suffered years of physical and mental abuse from her husband. One night he went to bed saying that he intended to beat her again when he got up in the morning. She waited until he was asleep and then poured petrol over him and set it alight, as a result of which he died. She was convicted of murder, but after 18 months in prison she appealed with new expert evidence that she suffered from a psychological condition known as 'battered woman's syndrome'. This was rejected as being irrelevant to the issue of provocation, but was allowed as evidence of diminished responsibility (see 3.3 below).

3.2.3   The objective test.   If it is decided that the accused had been provoked into losing self-control, the jury must go on to determine whether a reasonable man would have reacted as the accused did. This entails an assessment of all of the accused's behaviour, including the extent of the reaction to the provocation.

Example

A man is slapped by another man. He loses his self-control (which may be seen as reasonable) but then attacks the other man with a knife (which would certainly be viewed as an over-reaction and therefore unreasonable).

The difficult issue is the extent to which the jury can take into account any particular characteristics that the defendant may have, as these may help explain why the provocation made him lose self-control.

Example

A woman calls a man 'baldy'. The reasonable man would be assumed to have a full head of hair and therefore would be merely bemused by the insult. If this man was bald, then obviously that would be a vital factor in assessing whether it was reasonable for him to lose self-control.

Two cases have formulated the guidelines on this point.

DPP v Camplin (1978)
The defendant was a 15-year-old boy who had been forcibly buggered by a middle-aged man. The boy claimed that the man had then taunted him so much that he lost his self-control and killed him by hitting him on the head with a heavy frying pan. The House of Lords decided that the jury should have been allowed to take into account the age of the boy when assessing whether it was reasonable for him to have reacted as he did, together with 'such of the accused's characteristics as they think should affect the gravity of the provocation to him'.

R v Newell (1980)
The defendant was in a sorry state. He was an alcoholic and was recovering from an over-dose of drugs, was emotionally distressed because his girl-friend had left him, and had been drinking heavily. A male friend made homosexual advances to him as a result of which he lost self-control and beat him to death with an ashtray. The Court of Appeal ruled that first, the jury could only take into account permanent characteristics, and that secondly such characteristics would have to relate to the actual provocation. Thus the effects of drink and drugs and his emotional state could not be considered, as they were only temporary. His alcoholism could possibly be relevant, but here it was completely unconnected to the provocation, which was directed towards his sexuality.

In R v Ahluwalia (1992) (3.2.2 above) the Court of Appeal recognised that 'battered woman's syndrome' could amount to a characteristic for these purposes, but it now seems likely that the courts will refuse to take into account the fact that the defendant was addicted to drink or drugs.

R v Morhall (1993)
The defendant was addicted to glue-sniffing and was nagged about it by a friend. A fight ensued, during which the defendant stabbed his friend to death. On his trial for murder the Court of Appeal ruled that a self-induced addiction such as glue-sniffing could not be taken into account as a characteristic for the purposes of a defence of provocation. They reasoned

that such addictions are inconsistent with the concept of 'the reasonable man', and would allow indulgence for all kinds of abuse.

3.3   Diminished responsibility

It states in the Homicide Act 1957, s. 2, that a person charged with murder shall be entitled to be convicted of manslaughter instead if 'he was suffering from such abnormality of the mind . . . as substantially impaired his mental responsibility for his acts'. This is much wider than the definition of insanity. For example, in *R* v *Ahluwalia* (3.2.2 above), the defendant's plea of diminished responsibility on the grounds of 'battered woman's syndrome' was accepted on her re-trial, and she was released.

R v *Byrne* (1960)
The defendant had killed while suffering from uncontrollable perverted sexual desires. He clearly knew what he was doing and that it was wrong. However the Court of Appeal ruled that the defence covered this type of situation.

The Homicide Act 1957 restricts the defence to abnormality caused by 'arrested or retarded development of mind or any inherent causes or induced by disease or injury'. Ordinary intoxication would therefore not suffice unless it could be proved to have actually damaged the mind.

R v *Tandy* (1988)
The defendant who was an alcoholic had strangled her 11-year old daughter after drinking a bottle of vodka. The Court of Appeal ruled that her alcoholism could only give rise to a defence of diminished responsibility if it compelled her to drink alcohol uncontrollably. She was convicted on the basis that she was in control when she started drinking and that therefore her state of mind at the time of the killing was merely induced by the alcohol.

Where the abnormality of the mind was caused both by alcohol and an admissible cause, the Court of Appeal ruled in *R* v *Egan* (1992) that the jury must ignore the effects of the alcohol. This will mean that the jury will have the seemingly impossible task of constructing a totally hypothetical situation; they must decide whether, if the defendant had not consumed alcohol, not only would he still have killed the victim, but also whether he would have been under diminished responsibility at the time.

3.4   Suicide pacts

This defence is in the Homicide Act 1957, s. 4. A suicide pact is defined as 'a common agreement between two or more persons having for its object the death of all of them'. If one party to the agreement then kills one or all of the others, a charge of murder will be reduced to manslaughter if at the time 'he has the settled intention of dying in pursuance of the pact'.

Example

Two lovers decide to die together. They both take sleeping tablets and the man turns on the gas-fire without lighting it. The woman is asphyxiated but the man is rescued still alive.

Technically he could be charged with murdering the woman, as it was his act which killed her and he intended to kill her. However as he also intended to die himself, he could utilise the defence.

3.5 The burden of proof

Of the three defences, the Act places the burden of proof on the defendant for both diminished responsibility and suicide pact. However, if there is some evidence of provocation the burden is then on the prosecution to disprove it.

4   Involuntary manslaughter

4.1 Introduction

This is the category of homicide which covers those unlawful killings which do not amount to murder. There is sometimes a temptation to slot crimes into this category merely because the facts in a problem do not appear to justify a conviction for murder. However, there are three types of involuntary manslaughter and the facts of a problem must be analysed so that if murder is dismissed as a possibility, these are then considered as alternative grounds for a conviction. The three types are *constructive manslaughter*, *reckless manslaughter* and *gross negligence manslaughter*, and each of these must be considered briefly in turn.

4.2 Constructive manslaughter

This type of manslaughter is committed when the defendant has caused the death of a person by an unlawful and dangerous act. There are thus two distinct elements.

4.2.1 There must be an unlawful act on the part of the accused.

R v Ariobeke (1988)
The victim had been electrocuted while crossing a railway line to avoid the defendant. There was evidence that the defendant had been looking for him, but no evidence of any assault or even sufficient acts to amount to an attempted assault. The Court of Appeal therefore acquitted the defendant.

4.2.2 The act must be dangerous in the sense that the average person would recognise that it could cause some harm to another person.   It therefore does not matter if the accused did not see the risk. However the harm must be some form of physical harm beyond mere discomfort.

R v Dawson (1985)
An attendant at a petrol station died of a heart attack shortly after a robbery. The Court of Appeal ruled that it was not sufficient for a charge of manslaughter that the defendants foresaw that their acts would cause emotional disturbance.

4.3 Reckless manslaughter

This type of manslaughter is committed by a person whose actions create an obvious and serious risk that somebody will be harmed. It is thus the category into which an accused would fall if there was not a clear intention for the purposes of a murder conviction.

Example

A woman sets fire to a house knowing that there are people in it and a man is killed in the blaze. If she knew that he would inevitably die or suffer serious injury, then that is evidence of intention for the purposes of a murder charge. However, if she only knew that there was a risk of serious injury, or that only slight injury would be caused, then that would only be sufficient for a manslaughter conviction (see *Principles of Liability*, 3.5).

This is illustrated in the following case.

R v *Pike* (1961)
The defendant had persuaded his girlfriend to inhale a drug before having sexual intercourse. He knew that the drug sometimes caused people to lose consciousness, but on this occasion she actually died as a result. He was convicted of manslaughter as he was aware of the risk that she could suffer some harm.

Note that the recklessness is *Caldwell* type recklessness (see *Principles of Liability*, 3.6.2), so that it may not be necessary for the accused to have personally recognised the risk if it was 'obvious'.

R v *Seymour* (1983)
The defendant and his girlfriend met in the street some time after they had had an argument. Her car was blocking the path of his lorry. When she got out of her car to carry on the argument he drove his lorry so that it crushed her to death. He claimed that he only meant to push her car out of the way, but the House of Lords upheld his conviction, as the risk of causing serious injury was obvious, even if he had not recognised it.

4.4   Gross negligence

This used to be regarded as the principal type of involuntary manslaughter. In *R v Bateman* (1925) it was defined as negligence that is so gross that it goes beyond the sort of behaviour that can usually be left to the parties involved to resolve by themselves (i.e., by suing in the civil courts for compensation). This definition is very vague, and for many years the courts seemed to be replacing it with the 'reckless manslaughter' test. In *R v Kong Cheuk Kwan* (1985) for example, the Privy Council applied the 'reckless manslaughter' definition, and stated that they viewed it as the comprehensive test for all unlawful killings which were not covered by murder or constructive manslaughter. The Court of Appeal, however, have now confirmed that there is an offence of gross negligence manslaughter in certain situations known as 'breach of duty'.

R v *Sulman* (1993)
Three separate appeals from convictions for manslaughter were heard by the Court of Appeal at the same time, so that general principles of liability could be established. Two cases involved doctors who had killed patients by negligent treatment, and the third concerned an electrician whose faulty wiring had caused a person to be electrocuted. The Court of Appeal ruled that a test of 'gross negligence' should be used where the defendant was under a special duty to take care because of the dangerous nature of the job and his particular expertise in that area. Negligence would only be classified as 'gross' if it was far

below the standards expected of experts in the appropriate area. Simple lapses of concentration would therefore not be enough to form the basis of criminal liability, but could result in the perpetrator being sued in the civil courts.

It is not clear whether there is still a test of gross negligence for other situations which are not 'breach of duty', and the case will undoubtedly be appealed to the House of Lords.

5 Other homicides

To conclude this section it should be noted that there are other crimes which involve unlawful killing, primarily under the Road Traffic Act 1991. First, under s. 1, the offence of causing death by dangerous driving, which replaces the former crime of causing death by reckless driving under the Road Traffic Act 1988. Secondly, under s. 3, the completely new offence of causing death by careless driving while under the influence of drink or drugs. There is also a special provision for increased punishment under the Aggravated Vehicle-Taking Act 1992 where a 'joyrider' is involved in a fatal accident. In addition there is the crime of *infanticide* under the Infanticide Act 1938. Under certain circumstances a woman who kills her own child within 12 months of its birth can either be prosecuted for infanticide, or plead it as a defence on her trial for murder. If convicted (or if her defence is successful) she will then be treated as if she had been convicted of manslaughter. However, the circumstances which can give rise to the defence would be covered by the defence of diminished responsibility and so it is rarely used.

OFFENCES UNDER THE THEFT ACTS 1968 AND 1978

1 The Theft Acts

1.1 Introduction

These two statutes cover not only the crime of theft but also a variety of other offences which involve dishonest dealings with property. Before 1968 there were several different statutes which in turn were rooted in old common law. The Theft Act 1968 not only codified existing law but also amended and modernised it. As a result it contains the definitions not only for theft itself, but also for such crimes as burglary, robbery, handling of stolen goods, blackmail and various types of deception. For the purposes of this section the two crimes to be considered in detail will be *theft* and *obtaining property by deception*. There were some problems with the working of the Theft Act 1968. In particular it transpired that not all acts involving dishonesty could be brought within one of the crimes defined in the Act.

Example

If a man consumes a meal in a restaurant and then leaves without paying, it would be very difficult to prove that he intended to do this from the start (he might not have realised until too late that he had no money). He would not have deceived anybody therefore, and by the time he finished the meal the food would belong to him anyway and he could not be said to be stealing it when he leaves. The restaurant would merely have the right to sue him for the bill.

It was therefore necessary to pass a further statute, the Theft Act 1978. This is a much shorter statute but contains three important crimes which will be considered in this section. They are *obtaining services by deception, evasion of a liability by deception* and *making off without payment.*

1.2   Problems with Theft Act offences

It is important to realise that each of these offences under the Theft Acts is an independent crime with its own precise definition. The number and variety of offences have caused some difficulties to prosecutors, who have to fit the facts of a particular crime to one of the specific offences as defined in the Acts. This has led to many cases where in effect the 'wrong' crime has been charged. As a result, either the court has had to strain the definition to fit the crime, or has had to dismiss the case. Neither result is satisfactory, as in the first situation the law becomes confused and complex, and in the second a potentially guilty person is acquitted.

2   Theft

2.1   Introduction

The definition of theft is set out in the Theft Act 1968, s. 1. A person is guilty of theft if 'he dishonestly appropriates property belonging to another with the intention of permanently depriving the other of it'. This definition is then broken down into its different parts and each part defined at length by ss. 2-6 of the Act. It should also be noted which parts relate to the actus reus and which to the mens rea. This can perhaps be best visualised in the form of a chart.

Part of definition	Section number	Actus reus/mens rea
'Dishonestly'	2	mens rea
'Appropriates'	3	actus reus
'Property'	4	actus reus
'Belonging to another'	5	actus reus
'With the intention . . .'	6	mens rea

In any particular problem the facts should first be scrutinised to ensure that the actus reus of theft has been committed, before the mens rea of the accused is considered. Accordingly the same pattern will now be followed, so the three elements making up the actus reus of the crime will be looked at first.

2.2 'Appropriates'

In the Theft Act 1968, s. 3, this is defined as 'any assumption by a person of the rights of an owner' and it specifically includes 'where he has come by the property (innocently or not) without stealing it, any later assumption of a right to it by keeping or dealing with it as an owner'. Thus although theft usually occurs when a person takes property belonging to somebody else, there are many other situations where it can arise.

Example

A woman lends a book to a friend. If the friend sells or gives the book away, or destroys the book, she will have appropriated it, and may therefore be guilty of theft. Only the owner of property has the right to do those things and she would therefore be treating the book as if she owned it.

Appropriation occurs as soon as there is an assumption of any of the rights of the owner.

R v *Morris* (1984)
In this case the House of Lords heard two separate cases involving theft from a supermarket. In each case the defendant had switched labels on goods so that a lower price was indicated. In one case the accused had been arrested after he had paid for the goods at the lower price. In the second case the accused had been arrested before he had got to the checkout. They were both convicted on the basis that the act of switching the labels was something that only the owner (the supermarket) was authorised to do. Therefore the appropriation had taken place at that moment.

For several years there was doubt as to the position where the defendant had the apparent consent of the owner, but had only obtained that consent by a trick or deception. These types of case should perhaps have been charged as 'obtaining property by deception' (see 3 below), but were frequently charged as theft instead.

Example

In a supermarket the customers are allowed to take goods from the shelves. This permission is only granted, however, on the understanding that they will subsequently pay for them at the checkout. A customer who takes goods from a shelf in order to steal them has not therefore got the true consent of the supermarket manager, and can be said to be 'appropriating' them as soon as they are removed from the shelf.

The uncertainty was eventually removed by the House of Lords.

R v *Gomez* (1993)
The defendant was the assistant manager of a shop, and obtained permission from the manager to supply goods to a Mr Ballay, who wanted to pay with two building society cheques. Unknown to the manager, the defendant and Ballay were accomplices and the building society cheques were stolen and therefore worthless. The legal difficulty was that the goods were, on the face of it, handed over to Ballay with the full consent and authority of the manager, but the defendant had been charged with theft of those goods. The House

of Lords ruled that this still amounted to theft, and therefore confirmed the earlier decision in *Lawrence* v *Metropolitan Police Commissioner* (1971), which had been doubted for many years.

2.3 'Property'

The basic definition is set out in the Theft Act 1968, s. 4(1), and includes 'money and all other property, real or personal, including things in action and other intangible property'. However, there are further complex provisions which define exactly what is capable of being stolen for the purposes of the Act. In effect there are four categories. First, all tangible property, including money and any other object that can be touched physically. Secondly, intangible property. Thirdly, land, which although included under tangible property at first sight, is affected by special rules laid down by s. 4(2) which mean that, in effect, it must be regarded as a separate category. Fourthly, wild animals, plants and flowers. These last three categories merit separate discussion.

2.4 Intangible property

The Theft Act 1968 refers specifically to 'choses in action'. These are rights which can only be enforced by taking legal action, as they have no physical existence.

Example

A man owes £500 to a company. This debt is a chose in action. It 'exists' in the sense that the company could actually sell it to somebody else, who would then have the right to collect the money from the man.

Other examples of intangible property are copyrights, trademarks and patents. However, secrets are not property.

Oxford v *Moss* (1978)
A student had borrowed an examination paper, copied the questions and then returned the paper. He had not stolen the paper therefore, and the court ruled that the questions themselves did not amount to property for the purposes of the Act.

Note that electricity is regarded as a special case and accordingly there is a specific offence of dishonestly using electricity under the Theft Act 1968, s. 13.

2.5 Land

Land is included under the basic definition of 'property' in s. 4(1). However s. 4(2) begins by stipulating that land cannot be stolen except in three particular circumstances:

(a)   Where a person is dealing with land in a special capacity, for example as trustee.

(b)   Where a person not in possession of the land severs something from it, for example crops or turf.

(c)   Where a person in possession of the land as tenant appropriates a fixture or structure let with the land, for example by selling an outbuilding. Note that in this situation it does not matter whether the object is actually removed from the land or not.

2.6   *Wild animals, plants and flowers*

There are complicated rules under the Theft Act 1968, s. 4(3) and (4). Simply stated, it is not theft to take mushrooms or flowers, fruit or foliage from a wild plant. It would be theft to take the whole plant, or to take anything for a commercial purpose. Thus it would be theft if mushrooms were picked in order to sell them later. Similarly, it is not theft to take a live or dead wild animal unless it has already been taken into possession by somebody else. Note however that there are other statutes which create specific criminal offences for poachers.

2.7   *'Belonging to another'*

Usually this will cause no difficulties. However, there are three particular situations which are dealt with by the Theft Act 1968, s. 5.

2.7.1   Possession and control.   Property is deemed to belong to any person who has possession or control of it. There is thus no clear distinction between ownership and possession for the purposes of this section.

Example

A woman lends her car to a friend. The car is stolen later that day. There has thus been a theft from both the woman (the owner) and her friend (the person having possession).

2.7.2   Obligation to deal.   The section also provides that it is theft if a person receives property under an obligation to deal with it in a certain way but instead uses it for his own purposes.

Davidge v *Bunnett* (1984)
The defendant shared a flat with several other people who gave her cheques for their share of the common gas bill. Strictly speaking the money now belonged to her, and in fact she cashed the cheques and spent most of the money on Christmas presents. The Divisional Court ruled that this was theft under the special provisions of s. 5.

2.7.3   Mistake.   If a person is given property by mistake it will still be treated as belonging to the person who gave it (subject to some complex civil law rules as to whether there is a civil obligation to return the property or not).

R v *Stalham* (1993)
The defendant's employers by mistake paid the whole of his annual salary increase direct to his bank account, as well as giving him the first month's instalment by cheque. He realised what had happened, but withdrew the money without telling his employers what had happened. When the mistake was discovered he was charged with theft, and the Court of Appeal confirmed his conviction.

2.8   *'Dishonestly'*

This is the first part of the mens rea for theft and no definition is given by the Act. However, there are two situations noted where certain behaviour may be dishonest, and three specific situations where certain conduct is not to be viewed as dishonest. Finally, outside the scope of these special situations, the courts have given some guidance as to the meaning of the term.

2.9   Situations which may be viewed as dishonest.

First, under the Theft Act 1968, s. 1(2), it is immaterial whether an appropriation is made with a view to gain or for the thief's own benefit, or not. Secondly, under the Theft Act 1968, s. 2(2), an appropriation can be dishonest even if the thief intends to pay for the property.

Example

A man takes a book belonging to someone else. He may still be acting dishonestly if he intends to give it to a third person; intends to destroy it; or even if he leaves enough money to cover the cost of its replacement. Note, however, that all the other circumstances of his behaviour must be looked at to determine finally if he was dishonest or not.

2.10   Situations which do not amount to dishonesty

These three situations are set out in s. 2(1) and may be viewed as defences to a charge of theft.

(a)   An appropriation in the belief that there is a legal right to deprive the other person of the property.

(b)   An appropriation in the belief that the person to whom the property belongs would consent to it.

(c)   An appropriation in the belief that the person to whom the property belongs cannot be found by taking reasonable steps.

Example

A man takes a bicycle belonging to someone else. He would have a defence to a charge of theft if he thought that he was entitled in law to take items amounting to the debt owed to him by the owner. He would also have a defence if he thought that the owner would agree if he knew that he needed it to catch his train; and it would be a defence if he thought it had been lost and that the owner could not be found.

Note that these three situations only call for an honest belief on the part of the accused, and so it does not matter if the accused's behaviour would be viewed with disapproval by other people. However a jury may find it difficult to believe a story if it is too wild!

Example

In the first example, the man should obviously take the bicycle to the police station if he thinks it has been lost. Would a jury believe him if he tried to argue that he honestly thought this would not be a good way of tracing the owner?

2.11   Other situations

The basic test for dishonesty is a matter for the jury, by applying the standards of ordinary people. In the case of *R* v *Ghosh* (1982) the Court of Appeal stated a two-part test. First, would the accused's conduct be viewed as dishonest by ordinary, reasonable people? If so, then secondly did the accused realise that his conduct was contrary to those standards? This second part of the test could potentially cause difficulties.

Example

A man regards himself as a modern Robin Hood and gives everything that he steals to the poor. If he merely thinks that he has higher moral standards than other people, then he will be 'dishonest'. If, however, he thinks that ordinary people regard his actions as perfectly honest, then he would not have the mens rea for theft.

Note that in *R* v *Roberts* (1987) the Court of Appeal ruled that this second point should not be mentioned to the jury unless the defendant has raised it as an issue.

2.12   'Intention of permanently depriving the other of it'

'Borrowing' property is not a crime unless it is covered by a specific statutory offence. For example, under the Theft Act 1968, s. 12, it is an offence to take a motor vehicle without the authority of the owner, even if it is only for the purpose of a 'joy-ride'. Therefore it would usually be a defence for the accused to say that the property would have been returned to the owner in due course, and most difficulties in practice revolve around whether the defendant can be believed or not! Unless there are special circumstances (see 2.13 below) even long-term or indefinite borrowing will not amount to theft.

***R* v *Warner* (1970)**
The accused took a tool-box to annoy the owner but panicked and hid it when the police were called. He claimed that he intended to replace it as soon as he could do so undetected, but the judge directed the jury that an intention to keep property indefinitely could amount to theft. The Court of Appeal quashed the conviction.

Presumably in practice a jury simply would not believe such a story, as a person taking goods either intends to borrow them for a short time, or to keep them for ever. Note, however, two particular situations. First, it is not a defence to claim that money that has been taken would have been repaid.

***R* v *Velumyl* (1989)**
The defendant had taken money from his employer's safe and claimed that he intended to pay it back after the weekend. The Court of Appeal ruled that he had not intended to return the exact coins and notes, and that therefore he was properly convicted of theft.

Secondly, the accused will not be guilty unless the owner is to be deprived of the property.

***R* v *(Adrian) Small* (1987)**
The defendant was charged with theft of a car. He claimed that he thought that it had been abandoned by the owner because it had been left for over a week with the keys in it. The

Court of Appeal ruled that he could not be guilty of theft if he had an honest belief to that effect, as if the car had been abandoned, the owner would not be 'deprived' of it.

2.13   Special forms of borrowing

There are other situations which present legal difficulties and which are dealt with under the Theft Act 1968, s. 6.

2.13.1   Intention to use or dispose of the goods.   This is covered in s. 6(1), which stipulates that borrowing may be regarded as an intention to deprive permanently if the borrower has an 'intention to treat the thing as his own to dispose of regardless of the other's rights; and a borrowing or lending of it may amount to so treating it if, but only if, the borrowing or lending is for a period and in circumstances making it equivalent to an outright taking or disposal'. Thus the exact circumstances of the borrowing must be scrutinised, especially the efforts of the borrower to return the property, and the value of the property once the owner has regained it.

Example

Borrowing an item and leaving it in the street, hoping that it will find its way back to the owner, could be regarded as theft. Similarly borrowing a railway ticket and returning it to the owner after it has been used would be theft, as the property would then be worthless to the owner. There is some doubt as to the position where a season ticket is borrowed and returned before the season is fully over, as its value is considerably reduced but not exhausted.

2.13.2   Conditional disposal.   This is dealt with under s. 6(2), which covers the specific situation where a person takes property and then uses it as security for a loan. The intention may be to pay off the loan in due course, but the section states that, where a person parts with property belonging to another 'under a condition as to its return which he may not be able to perform, this . . . amounts to treating the property as his own to dispose of regardless of the other's rights'.

3   Obtaining property by deception

3.1   The definition

Under the Theft Act 1968, s. 15, it is an offence where 'a person by any deception dishonestly obtains property belonging to another, with the intention of permanently depriving the other of it'. As with theft it is necessary to break the definition down into its different parts, although the exact wording has to be adjusted to produce a neat chart showing the actus reus and mens rea (see p. 238).

Many of the words and phrases used for the definition of this offence are identical to those used in the definition of theft. However they do not necessarily have the same legal effect, and so again each must be looked at in turn, starting again with the phrases making up the actus reus of the crime.

Part of definition	Actus reus/mens rea
'Dishonestly'	mens rea
'By deception'	actus reus
'Obtains'	actus reus
'Property'	actus reus
'Belonging to another'	actus reus
'With the intention . . .'	mens rea

3.2 'By any deception'

Deception is the key element in the definition, and is also the main element in other offences covered by this part of the book (see 4 and 5 below). It is further defined in s. 15 (4) to mean 'any deception (whether deliberate or reckless) by words or conduct as to fact or law, including a deception as to the present intentions of the person using the deception or any other person'. Its basic meaning therefore is an untruth which the accused either knew was untrue (i.e., he was 'deliberate') or knew was possibly untrue (i.e., he was 'reckless'). Note also that the deception must be practised on a person. Therefore it is not a criminal deception to insert the wrong information into a car-park machine in order to pay a reduced price at the exit. The extended meaning of the word 'deception' in s. 15 (4) is given in order to avoid doubt in specific situations.

3.2.1 'Words or conduct'.   This ensures that the woman who pays for goods by cheque will be practising a deception if she knows that her bank will not honour it. She knows that the shopkeeper is only selling her the goods because he assumes that the cheque is valid.

It has also been decided that an omission can amount to a deception.

R v *Firth* (1991)

The defendant was a consultant gynaecologist who had arranged for several of his private patients to receive preliminary tests at the hospital where he worked. He knew that the hospital would assume that they were NHS patients, although he did not state specifically what category they were in. As a result none of the patients received a bill for the tests. The Court of Appeal ruled that that amounted to a deception for the purposes of the Theft Act.

3.2.2 'Fact or law'.   This ensures that the solicitor who tells her client that every will must contain a legacy in favour of the solicitor who prepared it, is also covered by the section.

3.2.3 'Present intentions of the person using the deception . . .'.   This covers the man who sits down in a restaurant ostensibly intending to pay for his meal but actually knowing that he has no money on him.

3.3 Statements of opinion

There is one other situation which causes difficulties. It is only in exceptional circumstances that a statement of opinion can amount to a criminal deception and that is when the opinion of the accused has the force of a statement of fact as far as the victim is concerned. This will typically occur where the accused has special knowledge or standing in the eyes of the victim.

Example

A second-hand car salesman says to a customer that one car is 'better' than another. If he is clearly basing this statement on his personal knowledge of the cars or on his expertise as a mechanic, then it will be a deception if it turns out to be false and he knew or was reckless as to its falsity.

This can give rise to difficult decisions.

R v *Silverman* (1987)
The defendant had been employed by a family on many occasions, and was asked by the two elderly sisters of the family to give a quotation for work on their house. The quotation was grossly excessive and the Court of Appeal decided that in the circumstances of this case it amounted to a deception. The atmosphere of mutual trust between the parties gave rise to a special relationship, so that the defendant in effect was stating that the quotation was fair.

3.4 'Obtain'

This is usually straightforward. Under s. 15(2) it is stated that 'a person is to be treated as obtaining property if he obtains ownership, possession or control of it, and "obtain" includes obtaining for another or enabling another to obtain or retain'.

Example

A man who says that he wants to test-drive a car will be obtaining possession of it rather than ownership. He will be guilty of obtaining it by deception however if he intends to drive it away and sell it.

The principal difficulty therefore is that the 'obtaining' must be because of the deception.

R v *Collis-Smith* (1971)
The defendant had his vehicle filled with petrol at a garage. He was then asked if his employer would pay for it, and when he confirmed this the bill was charged to his firm's account. He was acquitted of obtaining the petrol by deception because the deception occurred after he had obtained the petrol, not before.

Note as well that even if the deception occurs before the property is obtained, it must operate on the mind of the victim.

Example

Two women look at clothes on a market stall. The stall-holder states that the clothes are pure silk, although they are not. One woman buys them not believing a word, the other buys them because of the statement. Only one of the women has been deceived therefore.

The problem with this is that too much emphasis can be placed on the statements of victims after the event, as to their attitudes at the time of the transaction. An extreme result was reached by the court in the following case.

R v *Lambie* (1982)
The defendant had paid for goods with a Barclaycard credit card, although she knew that her credit allowance had been exceeded and that Barclaycard were trying to track her down. The House of Lords ruled that she deceived the shop-keeper by impliedly stating that she was still authorised to use the card. However it clearly did not matter to the store as the bill would be paid to them by Barclaycard regardless, and the shop-assistant who performed the transaction confirmed that she was only concerned to ensure that the card was valid for the store's purposes. However the House of Lords decided that the assistant would not have gone through with the transaction (presumably for moral reasons) if she had actually known that the defendant was using her card wrongly.

3.5 'Property'

There is no definition which applies except that in s. 4(1) of the Act (see 2.3 above). Thus it covers money, real property (i.e., land), things in action and intangible property. The additional provisions in s. 4 only apply to theft and therefore the only thing which could not be 'obtained by deception' would be secrets (see 2.4 above).

3.6 'Belonging to another'

The definition under the Theft Act 1968, s. 5, applies here (see 2.7 above).

3.7   The mens rea for the offence

It is almost identical to that for theft (see 2.8 to 2.13 above). First, the issue of whether the accused acted 'dishonestly' was considered in the case of *R* v *Ghosh* (1982) which was in fact concerned with a charge under the Theft Act 1968, s. 15, and is therefore directly applicable (see 2.11 above). Although there is no partial definition of 'dishonestly' as in the 'defences' under s. 2(1), the courts have ruled that a direction which follows the guidelines in *Ghosh* will inevitably involve the jury in considering the same principles.

R v *Woolven* (1983)
The defendant had tried to withdraw money from a bank account by pretending to be the owner of the account. He claimed that he thought that he was entitled to do so, a claim which is specifically mentioned as a defence in s. 2(1)(a). The Court of Appeal ruled that there had been no need for the judge to call the attention of the jury specifically to s. 2(1)(a) and that therefore his conviction should stand.

Secondly, the accused must have had 'the intention of permanently depriving' the owner of the property. Under s. 15(3) the same provisions apply as are set out in s. 6, with appropriate adaptation to 'obtaining by deception' instead of 'appropriation' (see 2.12 to 2.13 above).

Example

A woman borrows a train ticket from a man, saying that she wants to show it to the ticket office so that she can get an identical one. In fact she intends to use it and then return it to him. As the ticket would then be valueless to the man, her intention would be 'to treat it as her own to dispose of regardless of the other's rights' as under s. 6(1). She would thus have obtained property belonging to him (the ticket) by deception with the appropriate intention to deprive him of it permanently.

4   Obtaining services by deception

4.1   The definition

Under the Theft Act 1978, s. 1, it is a criminal offence where a person 'by any deception dishonestly obtains services from another'. Thus a value is placed on the time and labour that a person may be misled into expending to the same extent that property is valued under the Theft Act 1968, s. 15. There is clearly some overlap between this offence and the offence of obtaining property by deception and therefore it seems likely that the crime will tend to be used where it is only services that have been obtained.

Example

A man obtains a camera in a discount warehouse by producing a worthless cheque. He has clearly obtained property by his deception that the cheque is valid, but he has also obtained services in that the goods are packaged and delivered to him. However, if he paid for the camera but induced the shop assistant to assemble and demonstrate it by a false promise to buy another one, that could only come under the Theft Act 1978, s. 1.

4.2   The actus reus of the offence

This is described by the words 'by any deception . . . obtains services from another'.

4.2.1   'Deception'.   This has the same meaning as under the Theft Act 1968, s. 15 (see 3.2 above). It is worth noting again, however, that someone must be deceived. Thus an offence has not been committed by a person who merely avoids the ticket collector at a concert.

4.2.2   'Obtains'.   Again this requires a causal connection between the deception and the actions of the person providing the services. If the gateman lets a girl into the football match, not because of the rather obvious lie that she has lost her ticket, but because he feels sorry for her, then no offence would be committed.

4.2.3   'Services from another'.   This is partially explained in the Theft Act 1978, s. 1(2), and requires closer consideration. Services are obtained under s. 1(2) 'where the other is induced to confer a benefit by doing some act, or causing or permitting some act to be done, on the understanding that the benefit has been or will be paid for'. Thus the deception must 'benefit' the accused or some other person, although this can arise either by the provision of a service or by allowing something to be done.

Example

One youth persuades the cinema usher that he has lost all the tickets for his group of friends, so that his friends are allowed in without paying. The 'services' are provided already by the cinema, but the deception has the effect of 'permitting some act to be done', namely the friends to enter the cinema.

Note, however, that it will only be an offence if it is on the 'understanding that the benefit has been or will be paid for'. Thus there must be some value placed by the parties on the service although it does not need to be that price which is being evaded.

Example

A man pretends to have hurt his back so that his next door neighbour will dig his garden for him. As the neighbour is doing it for nothing, this would not fall under the Act. However, if a price was agreed and paid, it would still be an offence if the neighbour would not otherwise have performed the service.

4.3   The mens rea for the offence

This is simply 'dishonestly', and the same principles apply as under the Theft Act 1968, s. 15 (see 3.7 above).

5   Evading liability by deception

5.1   The definition

This offence is set out in the Theft Act 1978, s. 2, and is meant to cover all situations where the accused has avoided payment of a debt (defined as a 'liability') by deception. It should first be noted that under s. 2(2) a 'liability' first means 'a legally enforceable liability' and secondly 'shall not apply in relation to a liability that has not been accepted or established to pay compensation for a wrongful act or omission'.

Example

The first stipulation would exclude debts that are illegal or not legally enforceable, such as money owed for prostitution or gambling. The second stipulation would exclude damages for an accident unless these had been agreed between the parties or fixed by a court.

There are three separate ways in which it is an offence to evade a 'liability'. First, by securing cancellation of a debt. Secondly, by delaying payment of a debt with the intent to avoid it altogether. Thirdly, by avoiding incurring a debt. Each must be considered in turn as there is a precise definition in each case under s. 2(1).

5.2 Cancellation of a debt

Under s. 2(1)(a) the offence is committed when a person 'dishonestly secures the remission of the whole or part of any existing liability to make a payment, whether his own liability or another's'. Thus first the debt must already exist. Secondly, it need not be the accused's own debt. Thirdly, it must be avoided 'dishonestly'.

Example

A man owes £50 to a shopkeeper for a stereo system. His girlfriend tells the shopkeeper that the stereo was faulty and accordingly manages to agree a reduction in the debt of £10. If she was lying and acting 'dishonestly' she would have committed the offence.

5.3 Delaying payment of a debt

Under s. 2(1)(b) the offence is committed when a person 'with intent to make permanent default in whole or part on any existing liability to make a payment, or with intent to let another do so, dishonestly induces the creditor to wait for payment (whether or not the due date for payment is deferred) or to forgo payment'. Thus there are three requirements:

(a) There must have been an inducement to the creditor to wait. Under s. 2(3) this specifically includes handing the creditor a cheque, on the basis that payment will not occur in reality until the cheque is cleared.

(b) Again, it need not be the accused's own debt.

(c) Not only must it be done 'dishonestly', but also 'with the intent to make permanent default'. This last requirement shows the line that has been drawn between civil and criminal liability for debts.

Example

If in the example in 5.2 above the girlfriend answered the door to the shopkeeper and falsely told him that the man owing the money had moved away, she would be guilty of an offence unless it was only to give him a 'breathing space'. It may be that he genuinely needs time to organise his finances, and therefore the shopkeeper's proper remedy is to sue him in the civil courts. The civil courts can then judge whether it is right to allow him more time to pay or not.

5.4 Avoiding incurring a debt

Under s. 2(1)(c) it is an offence when a person 'dishonestly obtains any exemption from or abatement of liability to make a payment'. Thus first the debt in this situation is avoided before it has arisen. Secondly, again exemption can be 'obtained' for another person. Thirdly, the mens rea is simply 'dishonestly'.

Example

See *R* v *Firth* (1991) (3.2.1 above) where the hospital did not issue bills to the patients because the administrators thought that they were NHS patients.

6   Making off without payment

6.1   Introduction

This offence is similar to evasion of a liability under the Theft Act 1978, s. 2, in that it also imposes criminal liability on the dishonest debtor in certain cirumstances. The circumstances here, however, are limited to a specific type of debtor as well as the manner in which the debt is being avoided. After the Theft Act 1968 came into force it became clear that there was a loophole where people obtained goods without practising an obvious deception, and then refused to pay for them. Normally this would be a matter for the civil courts, but restaurants and petrol stations in particular were vulnerable to people who took advantage of the law. Accordingly a special offence was created by the Theft Act 1978, s. 3.

6.2   The definition

Under the Theft Act 1978, s. 3, it is an offence when a person 'knowing that payment on the spot for any goods supplied or service done is required or expected from him, dishonestly makes off without having paid as required or expected and with intent to avoid payment of the amount due'. There are three issues that need to be considered. First, the actus reus of the crime which is 'making off without having paid as required or expected'. Secondly, the mens rea required is threefold, namely 'knowing that payment on the spot is required or expected from him . . . dishonestly . . . with intent to avoid payment of the amount due'. Thirdly, there is a special provision to enable the supplier to take immediate action by arresting a dishonest customer.

6.3   The actus reus of the offence

This is satisfied by 'making off', without the need for any deception or stealth. However under s. 3(3) the offence cannot be committed unless payment for the goods or services would be legally enforceable.

Troughton v Metropolitan Police (1987)
A taxi driver had taken the defendant to the police station after an argument in the cab about the route he was taking to the defendant's home. The defendant 'made off' but was acquitted by the Divisional Court as the taxi had not taken him to the agreed destination and therefore no fare was legally due.

As soon as payment is due, however, it does not matter how or where the defendant 'makes off'.

R v Aziz (1993)
A taxi driver had driven two men to a club, but when they refused to pay him the proper fare he turned round and tried to drive them to the police station. En route the defendant managed to escape, and subsequently at his trial claimed that he had therefore not made off from the spot where payment had been demanded (i.e., the club). The Court of Appeal upheld his conviction.

6.4 The mens rea for the offence

This requires three elements:

(a) A knowledge that payment on the spot is required. This includes situations where goods are collected after having had work done on them, but usually will be a question of fact based on normal trading practices.

(b) The accused must have acted 'dishonestly'. The general principles apply as discussed in 2.11 above, but it should perhaps be noted that some customers may refuse to pay legitimately because they are dissatisfied with the goods or services!

(c) There must be an intention to avoid payment.

R v *Allen* (1985)

The defendant had left a hotel without paying a bill in excess of £1,000. Two days later he telephoned to explain his financial difficulties, offered to pay by instalments, and eventually returned to the hotel to make arrangements. The House of Lords ruled that the offence requires an intention never to pay, and therefore he was acquitted.

6.5 The special power of arrest

Under s. 3(4) any person may arrest without warrant anyone who is making off, or whom he thinks with reasonable cause is about to make off, without payment. This is a useful weapon for the supplier, as it avoids the often impossible task of tracing an unknown person. However, it should be noted that once the crime has actually been committed (for example once the customer has made a clean getaway) then the general rules as to powers of arrest will apply.

6.6 The relationship with other Theft Act offences

It should be noted in conclusion how this offence overlaps in practice with the other Theft Act offences. If it can be established that the accused had practised a deception in order to obtain the goods or services, then an offence may have been committed under the Theft Act 1968, s. 15, or the Theft Act 1978, s. 1. If the goods or services were obtained and then a deception was practised to avoid payment, then clearly an offence may have been committed under the Theft Act 1978, s. 2. It is only where there was no deception, or more likely where it would be difficult to prove a deception, that the Theft Act 1978, s. 3, need be used.

CRIMINAL DAMAGE

1 The Criminal Damage Act 1971

1.1 Introduction

The statute covers all offences involving destruction of, or damage to, property. There is a basic offence involving simple damage or destruction, and also a provision that such an offence shall be charged as 'arson' if it is committed by the use of fire. Arson is then treated as more serious and has a maximum penalty of life imprisonment, in contrast to a maximum penalty of ten years' imprisonment for the basic offence. Of the other offences, the most serious is the offence of endangering life by damaging or destroying property, which also carries a maximum penalty of life imprisonment. Apart from that offence it is also a crime to threaten to damage property, or to possess an object to be used to damage property. Each of these offences is only a crime if the accused acted 'without lawful excuse'. This is simply a reference to the general defences that are available to any crime. However the Criminal Damage Act 1971, s. 5, also sets out some specific defences. These only apply to the basic offence and to the two other, less serious, offences. These special defences will therefore be considered separately.

1.2   Property

Under the Act 'property' is defined in the same way as for theft (see *Offences under the Theft Acts 1968 and 1978*, 2.3) but excluding intangible goods and land altogether.

Example

Spraying wild flowers with weed-killer would not be criminal damage unless it killed the whole plant. Similarly it would not be an offence to pull the leaves off a non-cultivated tree, but it would be an offence to chop off a branch or cut down the tree altogether.

The property must belong to another unless the serious offence of endangering life has been charged.

Example

A man burns down his own house in order to claim on his insurance policy. This is not the basic crime of criminal damage, but if he knew that there were people in the house who were put in danger, he could be charged with the more serious offence.

Note that 'belonging to another' is defined to include property which is in the possession or control of another person.

2   The basic offence

2.1   The definition

Under s. 1(1) it is an offence when a person 'without lawful excuse destroys or damages any property belonging to another intending to destroy or damage any such property or being reckless as to whether any such property would be damaged or destroyed'. The actus reus is thus causing damage or destroying property belonging to another. The mens rea is intention or recklessness.

2.2   Damaging or destroying property

Neither of these terms is defined and the courts have tended to say that it is purely a matter of common sense.

Roe v *Kingerlee* (1986)

The defendant had smeared mud over the walls of a police cell. It cost £7 to clean it off, but no damage as such was caused to the wall or the paintwork. The Divisional Court ruled that this could still amount to criminal damage, as could graffiti, but that the facts of every case must be looked at.

A similar decision was reached in the following case.

R v *Whiteley* (1991)

A 'hacker' had deleted or altered information held in an institution's computer system. The Court of Appeal ruled that by altering the magnetic particles on the computer discs the defendant had damaged the discs themselves for the purposes of the Criminal Damage Act 1971.

Note that Mr Whiteley's behaviour would now be covered by the Computer Misuse Act 1990, s. 3(6), which states that modification of the contents of a computer only amounts to criminal damage if the actual 'physical condition' of the computer or the disc is impaired. He would, however, be liable instead under s. 3(1) for 'unauthorised modification of the contents of any computer'; and the case remains as authority for the erasure or alteration of audio or video tapes to be regarded as criminal damage.

2.3 The mens rea for the offence

This offence requires either intention or recklessness. Recklessness has the meaning given in *R* v *Caldwell* (1982) (see *Principles of Liability*, 3.6.2). This test has been strictly applied with harsh results.

Elliot v *C (a minor)* (1983)

A 14-year-old girl with a low IQ had been out all night without sleep before entering a garden shed. She set fire to some white spirit with the result that the shed was burned down. The Divisional Court ruled that her age, inexperience, low IQ and exhaustion were all irrelevant to the issue of whether she was reckless under the Criminal Damage Act 1971. The test is whether the risk would have been obvious to the reasonable man, not this particular defendant.

This decision seems particularly unfair, but the girl would perhaps now fall within one of the categories of 'excuses' in *R* v *Reid* (1992) (see *Principles of Liability*, 3.6.3).

3 The defence of 'lawful excuse'

3.1 Introduction

Under s. 5(2) there are two situations where an accused will be treated as having a lawful excuse to damage or destroy property. First, where the accused believed that the owner would consent. Secondly, where the accused did it to protect other property. In both cases it is only necessary that the accused have an honest belief in the relevant circumstances, even if that belief is unreasonable.

Jaggard v *Dickinson* (1981)

The accused was so drunk that she had broken into a stranger's house thinking it was her friend's. The Divisional Court ruled that voluntary intoxication did not invalidate her mistake as the belief was still 'honest'. This is obviously an exception to the usual rules on voluntary intoxication (see *General Defences*, 8.2 and the case of *O'Grady*).

3.2 Belief in the owner's consent

An accused will be treated as having a lawful excuse 'if at the time of the act . . . he believed that the person or persons whom he believed to be entitled to consent to the destruction of or damage to the property in question had so consented, or would have so consented if he or they had known of the destruction or damage and its circumstances'. *Jaggard* v *Dickinson* is a useful illustration of the principle, as the accused was not guilty even though the house did not belong to her friend. It is the accused's belief both as to ownership and as to consent which is the critical issue. That belief may even be completely unreasonable.

R v *Denton* (1981)

The defendant set fire to a factory because he thought that his employer wanted it to be destroyed. This belief was based on a chance remark by his employer that a 'good fire' would improve the company's finances by enabling him to make an insurance claim. The Court of Appeal decided that this could form the basis of a valid defence to a charge of arson under s. 1(1).

3.3 To protect property

An accused will be treated as having a lawful excuse if the damage was caused 'in order to protect property belonging to himself or another or a right or interest in property which was or which he believed to be vested in himself or another'. However, at the time the accused must have believed 'that the property right or interest was in immediate need of protection and that the means of protection adopted . . . were . . . reasonable having regard to all the circumstances'. There are thus three key elements. First, the act was in order to protect property. Secondly, there was a belief that immediate protection was needed. Thirdly, there was a belief that the steps taken were reasonable. The Court of Appeal has ruled that the accused's beliefs should be considered first, followed by an objective assessment of whether the acts actually protected property.

R v *Hill* (1989)

The accused had intended to cut the fencing around a US naval base as part of her campaign against nuclear arms. She was convicted and the Court of Appeal refused her appeal. Clearly she believed that it was reasonable to take this step, and it could be argued that it would protect her home (which was nearby) because it would reduce the necessity for a pre-emptive attack by the Soviet Union if the base's security was so bad that it had to be moved elsewhere. However, the argument never reached that stage because she clearly did not believe that there was an 'immediate need' for protection.

3.4 Other lawful excuses

If neither of the specific defences under s. 5(2) applies, the defendant can still use any of the general defences. These will of course be limited by the appropriate restrictions applying to each defence, in particular the necessity for 'reasonableness' when relevant.

DPP v *Lloyd* (1992)

The defendant's car was clamped while parked on private land, and the landowner demanded £25 to release it. The defendant refused to pay, and instead damaged the clamp in order to remove it. His conviction for criminal damage was upheld by the Divisional Court on the grounds that he should have paid the £25 and then sued for it in the civil courts if he felt that he should not have been obliged to pay it.

There are also strict limits to the availability of general defences, and even a powerful and genuine belief in divine consent and authority for an act will not amount to a lawful excuse.

DPP v *Blake* (1993)

During a protest about the use of military force in the Gulf War the defendant (a vicar) wrote a Biblical quotation on the wall around the Houses of Parliament. The Divisional Court dismissed his appeal against conviction for criminal damage.

4 Damage endangering life

4.1 The definition

Under the Criminal Damage Act 1971, s. 1(2), it is a more serious offence if the basic offence is committed 'intending by the destruction or damage to endanger the life of another or being reckless as to whether the life of another would thereby be endangered'. Thus the actus reus and mens rea of the basic offence must be present, with the additional mental element of intention or recklessness as to endangering life. The principal differences are that the offence will be committed even if it is the accused's own property that is being damaged (see 1.2 above) and the special defences under s. 5 do not apply.

4.2 The actus reus of the offence

This requires that life be endangered 'by the destruction or damage' rather than by the act itself.

R v *Steer* (1987)

The defendant fired a gun through a window to frighten the occupants. As there was no danger to their lives from the damage that he caused to the window, the House of Lords ruled that the charge under s. 1(2) was misconceived.

4.3 The mens rea for the offence

This requires intention or recklessness as to the damage and as to the danger to life.

R v *Sangha* (1988)

The Court of Appeal decided that recklessness in this context means that the ordinary prudent bystander would have recognised the risks. The defendant had set fire to a building, but it was argued that an expert would have recognised that the fire could not have spread to endanger life. However that was irrelevant as ordinary people would have seen it as a danger.

5   Other offences

5.1   Threats to property

Under s. 2 it is an offence to threaten to destroy or damage property belonging to another if it is done with the intention of causing the other person to fear that the threat will be carried out. A clear intention to cause fear is therefore required, rather than mere recklessness.

Example

It would be an offence under this section if a man threatens to poison a shop-keeper's food in order to persuade him to pay him money. However it would not be an offence if the threat was made as a joke, even if the shop-keeper took it seriously. In that situation the man making the threat would only be reckless as to its effects.

5.2   Possession of items to cause damage

Under s. 3 it is an offence to have an item with the intention of using it to cause damage to the property of another person.

Example

A woman is arrested with a box of matches in her possession. She admits that she was going to set fire to her neighbour's house. She is therefore liable to conviction under s. 3.

5.3   Endangering life

Both of these offences have a special provision that it is also an offence if the damage is to be caused to the accused's own property in the knowledge that this is likely to endanger life. In those circumstances the defences under s. 5 are not available.

Example

If the woman in the last example was intending to burn down her own house it would only be an offence if she knew that someone's life would be likely to be endangered. If she was aware of that danger then she would not be able to use any of the defences under s. 5.

QUESTIONS

CRIMINAL LAW

Part A

1. Distinguish between the *actus reus* and *mens rea* of a crime, with examples from offences under the Theft Acts 1968 and 1978.

2. Explain the circumstances in which voluntary intoxication may be a defence to a criminal charge.

3. What is meant by the term 'voluntary manslaughter'? Outline the different situations when it applies.

4. Explain the meaning of 'dishonesty' in the law of theft.

Part B

5. Abigail asks Richard to buy some goods for her from the local shop, and she gives him a five pound note and a list of groceries. Richard takes her bicycle without asking her and goes to the shop. He buys the groceries but spends the change of one pound on sweets for himself. On the way back he lends the bicycle to a friend before handing over the groceries to Abigail.

Advise Richard of any criminal offences that he might have committed.

Outline answer

  (a)   Explain that the question is about the theft of two items (the change of one pound and the bicycle). Give the definition of theft (citing the Theft Act 1968) and explain briefly the separate elements (citing the relevant sections).
  (b)   Discuss the actus reus of theft in relation to the change. 'Appropriation' and 'property' are straightforward. Cite *R v Morris* (1983). 'Belonging to another' depends upon Richard's legal obligation to return the change. Cite *Davidge v Bunnet* (1984).
  (c)   Discuss mens rea in relation to the change. There are no problems with dishonesty (cite *R v Ghosh* (1982) briefly) or intention to permanently deprive.

(d)   Discuss actus reus in relation to the bicycle. All three elements are straightforward.

(e)   Discuss mens rea in relation to the bicycle. Dishonesty depends again on the *Ghosh* test. It is not clear that there is an intention to deprive permanently. Note the special provisions in s. 6(1). Lending the bicycle to another person could be regarded as treating it 'as his own to dispose of regardless of the [owner's] rights'.

(f)   Conclude by summarising your advice to Richard.

6.   Rachel is climbing in the mountains with Dennis and Mary when Dennis slips and falls. Fearful that he might pull Mary with him, Rachel cuts the rope which holds them together. As a result Dennis falls and is severely injured.

Advise Rachel of any defence she may have to a charge of causing Dennis grievous bodily harm. Would your answer be different if Dennis were killed in the fall and Rachel charged with his murder?

7.   Susan drives to a garage and asks the attendant to fill the car with petrol. As soon as this has been done she drives off without paying. Advise her of any crimes that she might have committed.

8.   Robert jumps out in front of Harold in the street and points a toy gun at him, intending to rob him. Unknown to Robert, Harold suffers from a glandular problem which makes him sensitive to shock. Harold collapses and dies. Advise Robert of his criminal liability for the death.

FOUR

LAW OF TORT

INTRODUCTION

The law of tort is both interesting and difficult. It is this combination which provides a challenge for students and practitioners.

The law of tort deals with a wide variety of behaviour from physical assaults to financial loss and consequently it is not easy to define. The word 'tort' means 'wrong', so it is conduct which affects another person in some way and for which they may take legal action. The law of tort sets out the rules governing for which losses a person can sue. Some of the more common torts are negligence, nuisance, occupiers' liability, defamation, trespass, deceit and *Rylands* v *Fletcher*.

This chapter will look at negligence, occupiers' liability, nuisance and *Rylands* v *Fletcher* before dealing with the concept of vicarious liability. It will then briefly cover limits on the right to sue and remedies.

Tort is essentially a case law subject, so knowledge of cases is vital for the student. However, it is not the purpose of this section simply to provide a list of cases. It is far more important to understand the principles on which the cases are based and to be able to apply these principles to new situations. Tort continues to change and expand; see, for example, the tort of nuisance (*Khorasandjian* v *Bush* (1993)), and students are urged to keep up to date by reading the law reports in the newspapers, e.g. *The Times, The Guardian* and *The Independent*.

The main aim of the tort system is to provide money compensation for the person affected by the wrong. The wrong may cause damage to property, personal injury or both. A subsidiary aim is deterrence, i.e., to stop people committing torts. This latter aim probably only has a significant effect in the case of defamation, as usually the person paying the compensation is not the wrongdoer (tortfeasor) but an insurance company. The typical claim which a legal executive will face, is a client seeking damages for personal injuries arising from a road accident or an accident at work. Although providing compensation for personal injuries is the major function of the law of tort, this should be seen in the context of the whole personal injury system, including payments available through social security, criminal injuries compensation and personal insurance.

The law of tort is mainly based on the principle of 'fault', and so the plaintiff may only obtain damages if someone else can be shown to be at fault. The Pearson Report (1978) highlighted the high administrative costs of the tort system and the fact that only seven per cent of the three million people injured every year successfully sue in tort. In recent years, a number of group actions have been taken concerning prescribed drugs to try to establish negligence for side effects or addiction. In *AB & Others* v *John Wyeth & Brother Ltd* (1993) a group claim against doctors who prescribed *Ativan* and *Valium*, which claimed the drugs caused addiction, was struck out on the grounds it would be an injustice to the prescribers and of little benefit to the plaintiffs. However, claims against the manufacturers continue. This raises the question whether the tort system is appropriate for compensating such victims. The idea of a 'no-fault' system, where someone may claim if they suffer loss without having to prove fault, has many advantages over the present system. In 1972 New Zealand introduced an 'Accident Compensation Scheme' under which the victims of accidents could claim compensation from the state, up to certain financial limits, without proving fault. Some steps have been taken towards this in the United Kingdom by the Consumer Protection Act 1987 which established liability for damage caused by defective products, without proof of fault. The Lord Chancellor's Department has also proposed a 'no fault' scheme, funded through insurance premiums, for claims for injuries between £250 and £2,500, arising from road accidents.

SPECIFIC TORTS

1 Introduction

The torts covered in the syllabus are:

(a) *negligence*. A person is liable for damage caused by breach of a legal duty owed to someone else;

(b) *nuisance*. Private nuisance protects a person's interest in the use and enjoyment of land from the activities of neighbours;

(c) *occupiers' liability*. An occupier owes various duties to visitors and others who come onto the occupier's land.

(d) *Rylands* v *Fletcher*. A tort based on the case of that name, which imposes liability on a person if something dangerous escapes from their land and causes damage.

Some of the other torts which are met in practice, though to a lesser extent, are:

(e) *defamation*. The publication of an untrue statement which lowers another person in the eyes of right thinking members of society. This may be written (libel) or spoken (slander);

(f)   *trespass*. This covers direct interference with the land, goods or person of others;

(g)   *deceit (or fraud)*. A false statement, made wilfully or recklessly, which causes loss to another;

An action in tort is typically a claim in negligence. In 1992 in the Queen's Bench Division of the High Court, of the cases set down for trial, two thirds were personal injuries actions. Of these, 39 per cent arose from road accidents and 43 per cent from work accidents. In recent years there have been many important changes in this tort and the courts have restricted its scope. Clients will also seek advice on nuisance, which often involves disputes between next door neighbours. It is pertinent to remember that the parties may still have to live next door to each other after the case! The relationship with other branches of law should be kept in mind, there may also be a contract between the parties. Normally a duty will not be imposed in tort where the plaintiff has a remedy under a contract. There is also an overlap with the criminal law and one act may be both a crime and a tort (see *English legal system, Classification of Law*, 3.3). Changes in the jurisdiction of the civil courts mean that more tort cases are now dealt with in the county courts. In 1992 in the Queen's Bench Division of the High Court, 6,481 cases were set down for trial, which was 4,381 fewer than in 1991.

2   The parties to an action in tort

The general rule is that anyone may sue in tort or be sued in tort.

2.1   Minors

Anyone under 18 years old may sue through their 'next friend', which means an adult and will usually be a parent. A minor may be made liable in tort and there is no minimum age as there is in criminal law. However, it is unlikely that very young children will be made liable.

A child born disabled as a result of a negligent act by someone before its birth, has a right of action in tort. This right is given by the Congenital Disabilities (Civil Liability) Act 1976. The child's action is derived from the defendant's duty to the parents (usually to the mother). The mother is not liable unless the negligence consists of driving a vehicle.

Example

If the mother smokes during pregnancy and this causes injury to the child, the child has no right of action under the 1976 Act.

2.2   The Crown

At common law the Crown could not be sued in tort. The Crown means the Queen and the Government but does not include members of the Queen's family. Under the Crown Proceedings Act 1947, the Crown is now vicariously liable for torts committed by employees or agents. There are some exceptions to this, e.g., the Crown is not liable for torts committed by judges in carrying out their duties.

2.3   The mentally disabled

Mental disability is not a defence in tort, as the aim of the law of tort is to compensate the plaintiff. The criminal law rules concerning this defence therefore do not apply to tort.

2.4   Corporations

A corporation has legal personality and can commit torts or be the victim of torts. Some torts like assault, however, obviously cannot be committed against a corporation.

2.5   Unincorporated associations

These have no legal personality, so the plaintiff has to sue the individual or individuals responsible or a representative. Examples of such associations are sports clubs and social clubs.

Example

In the case of *Bolton* v *Stone* (1951), someone who was hit by a cricket ball sued the committee of the cricket club.

NEGLIGENCE

1   Introduction

Learning about negligence is like doing a jigsaw. It is difficult to get a clear picture and understanding of all the elements involved in a negligence claim, and how they fit together, until all these elements have been studied. The approach taken in this chapter is first to set out the basic elements of a claim, i.e., duty, breach and damage. This will be followed by looking at the more complex matters, such as nervous shock and economic loss. This should enable the student to see how they all fit together and to be able to apply the principles to a practical problem.

2   Elements of negligence

The tort of negligence does *not* impose a general duty to act carefully on everyone. What the law does is to lay down standards for particular circumstances, and if someone fails to reach those standards and damage is caused, that is negligence. In *Lochgelly Iron & Coal Co.* v *McMullan* (1934), Lord Wright said:

> . . . negligence means more than heedless or careless conduct, whether in omission or commission; it properly connotes the complex concept of duty breach and damage thereby suffered by the person to whom the duty was owing.

Someone claiming negligence must prove three things:

(a) the defendant owed the plaintiff a duty of care;
(b) the defendant was in breach of this duty;
(c) the plaintiff suffered damage as a result.

These categories of 'duty', 'breach' and 'damage' are not watertight and problems will not fall neatly in to one of these categories but may overlap all three. Lord Denning has urged a pragmatic approach to consider the particular relationship and decide as a matter of *policy* whether the loss should be recoverable, rather than worrying about which category is the correct one. Lord Scarman has warned, in *McLoughlin* v *O'Brien*, that although the courts have to take some account of policy, their function is to apply legal principles, leaving policy decisions to Parliament.

3 The development of negligence

The starting point for the modern law of negligence is the following famous case.

Donoghue v *Stevenson* (1932)
The plaintiff and a friend went into a cafe in Paisley where the friend bought her a bottle of ginger beer in an opaque bottle. The plaintiff drank some of the ginger beer and when the rest was poured out, the decomposed remains of a snail floated into the glass. The plaintiff suffered shock and became very ill. She sued the manufacturers for negligence. The defendants argued that if they were made liable this would open the floodgates of litigation. The House of Lords held by a majority of 3 to 2 that the manufacturer who sells products which will reach the consumer without the possibility of an intermediate examination, owes a duty to take reasonable care to see that the consumer is not injured. Lord Atkin stated:

> You must take reasonable care to avoid acts or omissions which you can reasonably foresee would be likely to injure your neighbour. Who then in law is my neighbour? The answer seems to be persons who are so closely and directly affected by my act that I ought reasonably to have them in contemplation as being so affected when I am directing my mind to the acts or omissions which are called in question.

This became known as the 'neighbour principle'.

Donoghue v *Stevenson* was important for the following reasons:

(a) establishing a new duty, i.e., that owed by a manufacturer to a consumer;
(b) showing that the tort of negligence could expand;
(c) creating a general principle of liability for negligence, i.e., the 'neighbour principle'.

If the facts of a case are not within the existing duty situations, Lord Macmillan said, in *Donoghue* v *Stevenson*:

> . . . the conception of legal responsibility may develop in adaptation to altering social conditions and standards . . . the categories of negligence are never closed.

So in the years following, the courts gradually recognised new duty 'situations' in negligence in particular cases.

Example

A local authority was made liable for letting children out of school early, when one child
was injured in a traffic accident.

4   Recent developments

In *Home Office* v *Dorset Yacht Co.* (1970), Lord Reid said:

> In later years there has been a steady trend towards regarding the law of negligence as
> depending upon *principle* so that, when a new point emerges, one should ask not whether
> it was covered by *authority* but whether recognised principles apply to it. *Donoghue* v
> *Stevenson* may be regarded as a milestone, and the well known passage in Lord Atkin's
> speech should I think be regarded as a statement of principle . . . I think the time has
> come when we can and should say that it ought to apply unless there is some justification
> or valid explanation for its exclusion. [emphasis added]

So instead of asking in a new case whether it fitted within an existing case, the court would
ask whether it would fit within an existing principle. This would give negligence a much
wider scope. It was further expanded by Lord Wilberforce in *Anns* v *London Borough of
Merton* (1978) where his Lordship put forward a two stage test to decide if a duty was owed
in negligence:

> (1)   Is there a sufficient relationship of proximity between the plaintiff and the defendant,
> that the defendant ought to contemplate that his carelessness may cause damage to the
> plaintiff ? If the answer is 'yes' – then a second question is asked.
> (2)   Are there any considerations which would end or limit this duty? If the answer to
> (2) is 'no', then a duty exists.

Not every judge agreed with this approach and a series of cases criticised it. In *Curran* v
Northern Ireland Co-ownership Housing Association (1987), Lord Bridge said:

> *Anns* . . . may be said to represent the high-water mark of a trend in the development of
> the law of negligence by your Lordships' House towards the elevation of the 'neighbour-
> hood' principle derived from the speech of Lord Atkin in *Donoghue* v *Stevenson* (1932)
> . . . into one of general application from which a duty of care may always be derived
> unless there are clear countervailing considerations to exclude it . . .

In *Murphy* v *Brentwood District Council* (1990) the House of Lords overruled *Anns*.

The courts would seem to be moving away from the development of negligence through
general principles. In *Caparo* v *Dickman* (1990), Lord Bridge quoted Brennan J from
Sutherland Shire Council v *Heyman* (1985) (an Australian case):

> It is preferable in my view, that the law should develop novel categories of negligence
> incrementally and by analogy with established categories, rather than by a massive extension
> of a prima facie duty of care restrained only by indefinable 'considerations which ought to
> negative, or to reduce or limit the scope of the duty or the class of person to whom it is owed'.

Lord Bridge also pointed out that the law takes a different approach to different types of damage depending on whether it was injury, shock or economic loss.

In *Caparo* the House of Lords discussed the requirements for establishing a duty of care in negligence. They identified: (a) foreseeability; (b) proximity; and (c) that it was just and reasonable to impose liability. Lord Oliver made the point that 'to search for any single formula which will serve as a general test of liability is to pursue a will-o'-the-wisp'.

5   Duty of care

In many cases the fact the plaintiff owes the defendant a duty of care will be beyond argument e.g., doctor and patient; manufacturer and consumer; driver and road users. But in less conventional relationships the courts have moved away from using general principles to establish that one party owes a duty to another. It seems that four factors are now relevant to the basis on which they will impose a duty:

(a)   foreseeability;
(b)   proximity;
(c)   just and reasonableness;
(d)   judicial policy.

All four factors will not always be separately identifiable, they may overlap or include others in some cases.

5.1   Foreseeability

'English law does not recognise a duty in the air so to speak, that is, a duty to undertake that no one shall suffer from one's carelessness' (Greer LJ in *Bottomley* v *Bannister* (1931)). The courts developed the test of 'foreseeability', which involved the concept of the 'reasonable man' who is a purely hypothetical person. The idea is to impose an *objective* standard on people, rather than to judge them *subjectively*.

The test in any particular case is: could the reasonable man in the defendant's position have reasonably foreseen that the plaintiff might be injured? The test is *not*: could the defendant have reasonably foreseen that by his actions the plaintiff might be injured? If the reasonable man could not foresee injury or damage, then no duty was owed. If he could, then there may be a duty. The fact that damage is foreseeable does not make the defendant liable.

Example

Fardon v Harcourt-Rivington (1932)
The defendant's car was parked in the street, with a dog inside it. As the plaintiff walked past, the dog jumped up, broke a window and a splinter of glass went into the plaintiff's eye. The eye had to be removed. The test applied was: would the reasonable man have foreseen that, if he left his dog in the car, the plaintiff would be injured? The court held that this was not negligence, there was no duty to guard against 'fantastic possibilities'.

Another example of how the test of foreseeability applies can be seen in the following case.

Bourhill v *Young* (1942)

The defendant was speeding on his motorbike, collided with a car and was killed. The plaintiff, who was eight months pregnant, was 45 feet away behind a tram and could not see the accident but heard screams and later saw blood on the road. She suffered nervous shock and lost the baby. She sued the defendant's estate for negligence. The court held that the defendant owed a duty of care to other road users and those near the road, but it was not reasonably foreseeable that the plaintiff would suffer shock. She was outside the area of risk and the defendant was not liable.

5.2   Proximity

The concept of proximity was set out by Lord Atkin in *Donoghue* v *Stevenson* (1932):

> Who then in law is my neighbour? The answer seems to be persons who are so closely and directly affected by my act that I ought reasonably to have them in contemplation.

What this means is 'proximity of relationship', i.e., that the law requires the parties to have a certain closeness of relationship before one can be made liable to the other. If just the test of foreseeability was used, this would have a very wide application because most things that can happen are foreseeable, even if they are not likely. This point was emphasised in *Yuen Kun Yeu* v *AG of Hong Kong* (1987), by Lord Keith who said that foreseeability in itself is not enough to lead to a duty of care, otherwise:

> there would be liability in negligence on the part of one who sees another about to walk over a cliff with his head in the air, and forbears to shout a warning.

5.2.1   What does 'proximity' cover?   The first point to make is that it means legal proximity and not simply physical proximity.

   (a)   Physical proximity.
This is relevant in deciding if a duty is owed but is not always essential. For example in *Donoghue* v *Stevenson* there was no physical proximity between the manufacturer and the consumer, but there was legal proximity.
   (b)   The relationship between the parties.
The closer the relationship, the more likely it is that it will satisfy the requirement of proximity; for example, the relationship between a legal adviser and a client.

Osman v *Ferguson* (1993)

In May 1987 P, a teacher, began to pester a 15-year-old boy at the school. He damaged the boy's home a number of times and also rammed a car in which the boy was travelling. P told both the police and the education authority that he would do something mad. The police started a prosecution for the motoring offence but this never came to court. In March 1988 P shot the boy and the boy's father, killing the father. The boy sued the police, claiming negligence. The Court of Appeal held that there was a close degree of proximity between the family and the police, as the family had been exposed to a greater risk than the public. It was against public policy, however, to impose a duty to prevent crime on the police, as to do this would mean them diverting resources.

(c)   It may involve public policy.

This is a wider concept than judicial policy. It brings in a consideration of the values held by society at large, which could influence the decision made by a court and could, for example, restrict liability. Examples of this can be seen in the following cases.

Hill v *Chief Constable of West Yorkshire* (1988)

The mother of the 'Yorkshire Ripper's' last murder victim sued the police on behalf of her daughter's estate. She claimed that the police had been negligent in not arresting Sutcliffe earlier. The court accepted that the police owed a duty to the public to prevent crime, but had to consider whether they owed a duty to this particular victim. This involved a consideration of whether there was sufficient proximity. The police had no control over Sutcliffe, he was never in their custody; the victim was just one of a large number of women at risk; there was no close relationship between the police and Sutcliffe or the police and the victim. Public policy was also considered. If the police were made liable, this might have a restricting effect on their investigations; old investigations might have to be re-opened. They would be hampered in their main duties. It was held that in all the circumstances the police were not liable.

Further attempts have been made to make the police liable in negligence.

Alexandrou v *Oxford* (1993)

A burglar alarm went off in the plaintiff's clothes shop in Liverpool and simultaneously warned the police station. The police went to the shop but failed to check the back entrance, which the burglars had used to get in. Later clothes were stolen. At first instance the court held that a duty was owed to owners of that type of alarm and the police had breached this duty. On appeal, the Court of Appeal held that this was just an emergency call and it was not in the public interest to impose a duty on the police, as it would lead to diverting resources from tackling crime.

In *Hughes* v *NUM* (1991) the court held that senior officers owed no duty of care to police officers injured in riots during the miners' strike in 1984.

One aspect of the relationship between foreseeability and proximity was pointed out in *Caparo* v *Dickman* in the Court of Appeal by Bingham LJ who said that, in considering the closeness of the relationship in proximity, foreseeability is relevant. The more likely it is that the defendant's act will cause harm to the plaintiff, the more likely it is that the relationship will satisfy the test of proximity.

5.3   Just and reasonableness

Even if the above tests of 'foreseeability' and 'proximity' are satisfied, a claim may fail on the basis that it would not be 'fair, just and reasonable' to impose liability. This gives the courts scope to limit liability in negligence if they believe that, in a particular situation, it would be unjust to impose liability. For example, in *Hill* v *Chief Constable of West Yorkshire*, it would not be 'just and reasonable' to impose liability on the police, when the class of victims was so large. (Also see *Hemmens* v *Wilson Browne* (1993) and *Negligence – other factors*, 10.4)

5.4   Policy

Here the courts may say that even if the other requirements are satisfied, as a matter of judicial policy it would be wrong to impose liability.

Example

As a matter of policy the courts are reluctant to impose liability in negligence for the acts of third parties. See *Smith* v *Littlewoods* (1987) in *Negligence – other factors,* 6.1.

In bringing policy considerations into its decision, the court is performing a balancing act between not depriving plaintiffs of compensation and not imposing too heavy a liability on defendants.

5.5   Situations where no duty is owed

In some circumstances the courts have established that no duty of care is owed.

Advocates acting in court, whether barristers or solicitors, do not owe a duty of care to their clients.

Rondel v Worsley (1969)
The House of Lords held that a barrister acting in court was not liable in negligence. This was based on public policy, as otherwise barristers could not act independently but would be in fear of claims and the courts would become clogged with retrials.

This protection was later extended to cover preparation for a case, which was intimately connected with the conduct of the case.

Judges do not owe a duty of care in relation to legal proceedings, again on the ground of public policy.

The *police* do not generally owe a duty of care in respect of prevention and investigation of crime: see 5.2.1 above.

There is no duty on people to *rescue* someone in danger.

5.6   Summary

The use of the above four factors (i.e. in 5.1 to 5.4) must be seen in the overall aim of the courts in determining and limiting the liability of defendants. In doing this they are not following some magic formulae worked out from these factors. In *Caparo* v *Dickman* (1990), Lord Oliver stated that foreseeability, proximity and just and reasonableness were merely facets of the same thing and that courts had to take a pragmatic approach to imposing liability.

6   Breach of duty

Once it has been shown that the defendant owes a duty of care to the plaintiff, it then needs to be established whether the defendant has broken this duty.

In deciding this the courts use the concept of the *reasonable man*. A person is regarded as negligent, if he fails to reach the standard of conduct that the reasonable man would reach. This standard is applied even though it is more difficult, or even impossible, for the defendant to reach that standard. As we have seen above, the idea is that the law sets an *objective* standard, so that there is a minimum standard of conduct that people can expect. The reasonable man has been described as 'the man on the Clapham omnibus' (or more likely the man waiting for the Clapham minibus!). In America he has been described as 'the man who brings home the magazines and mows the lawn in his shirt sleeves'.

The test was set out in *Blyth* v *Birmingham Waterworks* (1856) by Baron Alderson:

> Negligence is the omission to do something which a reasonable man would do or doing something which a prudent and reasonable man would not do.

From this it should be noted that it may be an *act* or an *omission* (omissions will be looked at below in *Negligence – other factors*). This was further elaborated in the following case.

Glasgow Corporation v *Muir* (1943)

The manageress of a tea room allowed a private party to use it. Two people from this party were carrying a tea urn, which was about half full, down a narrow passage to the tea room. One of them let go of the handle and hot tea scalded some children in the passage. It was held that the reasonable man could not have foreseen such an event. The law did not require the passage to be closed while the tea urn was being carried. Lord Macmillan stated:

> The standard of foresight of the reasonable man is in one sense an impersonal test. It eliminates the personal equation and is independent of the idiosyncracies of the particular person whose conduct is in question. Some persons are by nature unduly timorous and imagine every path beset with lions; others of more robust temperament, fail to foresee or nonchalantly disregard even the most obvious dangers. The reasonable man is presumed to be free from over-apprehension and from over confidence.

6.1 Qualifications on the standard

Although in theory this is a strictly objective standard, in practice it is the judge in individual cases who decides what this standard is. In determining this the judge may take account of policy considerations. The standard is also qualified in other respects by taking certain subjective factors into account. These include special skills of the defendant, knowledge about the plaintiff and in the case of children, their age.

6.1.1 General knowledge. A person is expected to know what adults learn from experience, for example, that fire burns, rivers are dangerous etc. The law also takes account of advances which improve the standard possible; see *Roe* v *Minister of Health* (1954) at 6.1.3 below.

6.1.2 Intelligence. If the defendant does not reach the standard of the reasonable man, he will be liable. It is no defence that he is of low intelligence. By the same token, a very intelligent person does not have to reach a high standard, as long as he reaches the standard of the reasonable man. These rules do not apply, however, in the case of a particular skill; see 6.1.3 below.

6.1.3   Skill.   Someone who professes to have a particular skill must show the skill of an experienced person doing that task, rather than the standard of the reasonable man. A skilled defendant is judged by the 'Bolam test'.

Bolam v Friern Hospital Management Committee (1957)
The plaintiff was mentally ill and was advised to have electro-convulsive therapy which was administered without relaxant drugs or physical restraints. As a result of the treatment, the plaintiff suffered a fractured jaw. There were different medical opinions on whether to give drugs or tie the patient down or neither. It was held that the defendant was not liable. McNair J said:

> The test is the standard of the ordinary skilled man exercising and professing to have that special skill. A man need not possess the highest expert skill at the risk of being found negligent . . . it is sufficient if he exercises the ordinary skill of an ordinary competent man exercising that particular art.

If the defendant is following an accepted method, it does not mean he is negligent because there is a contrary view.

Hughes v Waltham Forest Health Authority (1990)
A decision of a specialist and experienced surgeon which was mistaken, or criticised by other surgeons, did not prove that the surgeon had failed to reach the standard of care required. The court said that the test was whether the surgeon in making the decision, showed such a lack of clinical judgment that no surgeon exercising proper care could have reached the same decision.

The standard expected may be less, depending whom the plaintiff chooses to carry out the task.

Philips v Whiteley (1938)
The defendant jeweller pierced the plaintiff's ears, which caused an infection. The court had to deal with the question whether a jeweller had to reach the same standard as a surgeon. It was held that washing the hands and putting the instrument in a flame, was sufficient to reach the standard required. A further example can be seen in the standard expected of learner drivers.

Nettleship v Weston (1971)
The plaintiff agreed to teach the defendant to drive. On the third lesson the defendant hit a lamp post and the plaintiff was injured. The defendant was held liable and Megaw LJ stated that 'the standard of care required by the law is the standard of the competent and experienced driver'.

The time for judging the standard is the time of the breach.

Roe v Minister of Health (1954)
The plaintiff went into hospital for a minor operation and was given a spinal anaesthetic. The glass ampoules of the anaesthetic had been kept in a solution, but minute cracks had occurred in the ampoules and because of this the solution entered the ampoules and

contaminated the anaesthetic. As a result the plaintiff was paralysed. It was held that this practice was widely used at the time (1947) and no one realised the risk, therefore the defendants were not negligent. 'We must not look at the 1947 accident with 1954 spectacles' (Denning LJ).

6.1.4 Professional people. The law does not distinguish between professional people and others. The test applied is as above, i.e., whether in all the circumstances the defendant acted with the skill and competence to be expected from a person undertaking that particular task. In *Wilsher* v *Essex Area Health Authority* (1986), the court said that a doctor must be judged by reference to the 'post' in a specialist unit and the skills that post required and not by looking at the experience of the individual doctor.

6.1.5 Children. The test applied for children is: what degree of care can a child of that age reasonably be expected to take?

Mc Hale v *Watson* (1966) (An Australian case)
A 12-year-old threw a metal spike at a post. It glanced off and hit someone standing nearby. The court applied the test of whether the defendant had done anything which a reasonable child of that age would not have done. It was held that expecting the child to consider whether the spike would stick in or glance off was to expect too much. Therefore the defendant was not liable.

In *Staley* v *Suffolk County Council* (1985), however, a 12-year-old was found liable for throwing a tennis ball at another pupil in a classroom and hitting the dinner lady.

As a general rule, parents are not liable for the torts of their children, but parents may be negligent for not supervising children.

6.1.6 Knowledge of the plaintiff. If the defendant has special knowledge about the plaintiff, e.g. that the plaintiff is pregnant, this may increase the standard of care.

6.1.7 General practice. It will normally be a good defence to show that the defendant was following a general practice, as in *Bolam* v *Friern* above. However, this is not an absolute defence, for the courts may declare a general practice to be negligent.

Example

If window cleaners cleaned first floor windows by standing on the window sill.

6.1.8 Emergencies. If someone is acting in an emergency, this will be taken into account in determining the standard of care required.

Marshall v *Osmond* (1983)
It was held that the police, in a car, chasing suspected criminals did owe them a duty, but in the circumstances had fulfilled it.

6.1.9 Disabilities. If an adult has physical or mental disabilities these should be taken into account, if the defendant knows or should know of them. A higher standard, for example, is owed to blind people. An example of the higher duty owed to disabled people can be seen in the next case.

Morrell v Owen (1993)
During a disabled sports event, the discus and archery took place in the same hall, divided only by a net. The plaintiff paraplegic was practising archery, when she was hit by a discus which caused the net to 'billow'. The plaintiff suffered brain damage and sued the organisers. It was held that the defendants were liable, as they had not given any safety instructions or taken any special precautions.

7   Factors relevant to determining the standard of care

We have looked at the objective standard applied by the courts and how this may be altered in particular circumstances. The next matter is to look at the factors which the courts will take into account in deciding whether the defendant is in breach of the duty owed. The following factors are not exhaustive and others may also be taken into account:

    (a)   likelihood of harm;
    (b)   risk of serious injury;
    (c)   social value of the defendant's action;
    (d)   cost of avoiding the harm.

7.1   Likelihood of harm

How likely is the defendant's conduct to cause injury? The more likely it is that harm will occur, the more caution is necessary.

Bolton v Stone (1951)
A batsman struck a cricket ball 100 yards over a 17 foot high fence and hit the plaintiff, Stone, who was standing in the road. Balls had been hit out of the ground about six times in 30 years. It was held that the club did owe a duty to people outside the ground and that the risk of this happening was foreseeable. As the chance of being hit was very small, however, the defendants were not liable. The court also took into account the seriousness of the consequences.

Compare this decision with *Miller* v *Jackson* (1977) in *Nuisance*, 2.7.5, where the risk was so great that the club was liable.

Another illustration of the likelihood of injury is to be found in the following case.

Haley v London Electricity Board (1964)
The defendants had dug a hole along the pavement in a London street and they put a sledgehammer handle diagonally across one end. The plaintiff, who was blind, missed the handle and fell into the hole. The defendants argued that they only owed a duty to ordinary pedestrians. The court held, that as one in 500 people is blind, and blind people walk along pavements, it was reasonably foreseeable that a blind person would be injured.

7.2   Risk of serious injury

In determining whether the defendant has fulfilled the duty owed to the plaintiff, the risk of more serious injury is relevant. This can be clearly seen in the following case.

Paris v Stepney Borough Council (1951)

The plaintiff who worked in the defendants' garage as a mechanic only had one eye. The defendants knew this. The plaintiff was working under a vehicle when a piece of metal went into the good eye. As a result the plaintiff went blind. The court held that although the risk of injury was small, the gravity of the injury to this plaintiff was great and the defendants should have provided goggles, so they were liable.

7.3   Social value of the defendant's action

If a person is doing something which is socially useful this may justify an abnormal risk.

Watt v Herts County Council (1954)

Someone was trapped under a vehicle after a road accident. The fire brigade transported a heavy jack, needed to lift the vehicle, in an unsuitable lorry. The lorry braked suddenly and a fireman was injured as the jack was thrown across the lorry. Waiting for a vehicle suitable to carry the jack would have taken another ten minutes. The fireman sued for negligence. It was held that the defendants did owe a duty of care to the plaintiff, but in the circumstances of trying to save a life they had fulfilled this duty. Denning LJ stated:

> . . . the commercial end to make a profit is very different from the human end to save life or limb. The saving of life or limb justifies taking considerable risk . . .

7.4   Cost of avoiding the harm

The question to be answered is what would the reasonable man do to avoid the harm? Many risks can be avoided by spending more money but at what point will the reasonable man have done enough? This is just one factor to be weighed with the others. If the risk can be reduced drastically for little money, this should be done. If spending a large sum of money would only reduce the risk a little, the reasonable man would not do this.

Latimer v AEC Ltd (1952)

An exceptional rainstorm caused a river to burst its banks and this flooded a factory, where the water, mixing with some oil, made the floor slippery. The defendants put down sawdust, but there was not enough to cover the entire floor. The plaintiff slipped on the uncovered part. The plaintiff argued that the defendants should have closed the factory. It was held that the defendants did owe a duty of care to their employees, but they did not have to close a factory employing 400 people, nor were they expected to have enough sawdust for the entire floor. In the circumstances they had done everything that could reasonably be expected and were not liable.

8   Causation

Even if it has been proved that the defendant owes the plaintiff a duty of care and that the defendant is in breach of that duty, the remaining element to be proved is that the breach caused the loss.

Example

A was doing some welding on his car, when a piece of metal went into A's eye because A was not wearing goggles. It had been snowing and the ambulance rushing A to hospital, which was driven by B, went out of control and collided with a car driven by C. In this accident B suffered a broken arm. D drove past the scene of the accident and carelessly threw a lighted cigarette end out of the window. The petrol tank on C's car had fractured and there was an explosion, in which C was badly burned. Can A be made liable in negligence for *all* the damage which results?

A distinction is made between:

(1)   causation in fact; and
(2)   causation in law.

8.1   Causation in fact

Here the question is, whether as a matter of fact the defendant's negligence caused the plaintiff's loss? To decide this the law applies the 'but for' test; i.e., would the plaintiff have suffered the loss 'but for' the defendant's negligence? If the answer is 'no', then the defendant is liable. Applying this to the above example, would B and C have suffered damage 'but for' A's negligent act? Clearly not.

An example of the application of the 'but for' test is the following unusual case.

Barnett v Chelsea Hospital (1969)
In January 1966 three nightwatchmen called into Chelsea Hospital on their way home from work. They told the nurse at reception that they had vomited after drinking tea. The nurse phoned the duty doctor who replied 'Well, I am vomiting myself and I have not been drinking'. He then said that they should go home and see their own doctors. A few hours later one of the men died. It was discovered that he had taken arsenic and would have died even if he had been admitted. His widow sued the hospital for negligence. The court held that the hospital did owe a duty of care to examine the three men and was in breach of duty by sending them home; but the defendant's negligence did not *cause* the husband's death, because even if he had been admitted he would have died in any event.

In the above case the cause of death was clear but causation is often a difficult hurdle for the plaintiff.

Wilsher v Essex Area Health Authority (1988)
The plaintiff was born three months prematurely and sustained retrolental fibroplasia (RLF) which caused blindness. A catheter used to measure oxygen had been put in a vein instead of an artery and so gave a misleading reading and consequently too much oxygen was given. The plaintiff claimed that the defendants were negligent. Both the High Court and the Court of Appeal found that the hospital had been negligent; but the House of Lords examined the question of causation and said that there were five possible reasons for RLF. The plaintiff had suffered from the other four conditions which can cause it and had not proved that it was solely caused by too much oxygen. A retrial was ordered on the issue of whether it was the negligence of the defendants, in giving too much oxygen, which caused RLF.

8.2   Qualifications on the 'but for' test

The plaintiff has to show that the defendant's negligence caused the damage and this must be done on a balance of probabilities. However, the 'but for' test does not solve all problems and the courts will then use alternatives.

8.2.1   Multiple causes.   If there are two or more causes, the plaintiff does not have to show that the defendant's negligence was the main cause. In *Bonnington Castings* v *Wardlaw* (1956) the House of Lords said that it was enough to show that the defendant's breach made a 'material contribution' to the damage.

McGhee v *NCB* (1972)

The plaintiff worked in a brick kiln. No washing facilities were provided and the plaintiff had to cycle home covered in dust. The plaintiff contracted dermatitis and sued the defendants for negligence. It was accepted that brick dust caused dermatitis, but which brick dust? Was it the dust with which the plaintiff came into contact during working hours (for which the defendants were not negligent)? Or was it the dust with which he was covered on the way home (for which the defendants were negligent in not providing showers)? The application of the 'but for' test posed the question: would the plaintiff have suffered dermatitis 'but for' the dust on the way home? The medical evidence could not prove this, but the House of Lords held that, by not providing showers, the defendants materially increased the risk of dermatitis, so the defendants were liable.

This decision was applied in the following case.

Fitzgerald v *Lane* (1987)

The plaintiff crossed the road at a pelican crossing, which was green for traffic. The plaintiff was struck by a car driven by the first defendant, fell off the bonnet on to the road and was hit by another car driven by the second defendant. The plaintiff suffered tetraplegia, but could not establish which car caused this. The Court of Appeal held that even though the plaintiff could not prove which defendant caused the injury, each of them had 'materially contributed' to the risk of such injury and both were jointly liable. If the plaintiff had not ignored the red light for pedestrians, the accident would not have happened, but both defendants responded negligently to the plaintiff crossing the road.

In the above cases, the plaintiffs were unable to prove causation in the normal way, so the courts took a common sense approach and used policy to decide in their favour.

8.2.2   Consecutive causes.   The problem in this situation can be seen by examining the following case.

Baker v *Willoughby* (1970)

The plaintiff's left leg was damaged as a result of being knocked down by the defendant's car, whilst the plaintiff was crossing the road. Three years later, during a robbery at work the plaintiff was shot in the left leg which had to be amputated. The defendant argued that the second injury obliterated the effect of the first injury, so that any loss after the second injury was the fault of the robbers. The House of Lords held that after the first injury the plaintiff was unable to lead a full life or earn as much as before the accident. The second injury did not lessen these factors and could not be regarded as obliterating them. Therefore the defendant was liable for damages for the remainder of the plaintiff's life and not just for three years.

What happens if the plaintiff develops a disease after the tort?

Jobling v *Associated Dairies* (1982)

The plaintiff worked in the defendants' butchers. In 1973 the plaintiff slipped and suffered injury due to the defendants' negligence. In 1976, before the trial, the plaintiff developed a disease of the spine which was completely unrelated to the accident. The High Court ignored the later condition and awarded damages for life; but the House of Lords held that the disease was one of the 'vicissitudes of life'. The courts regularly took this into account in assessing damages and the plaintiff was only entitled to damages for the period 1973–76.

In *Jobling* the courts are taking judicial policy into account. If the plaintiff was given compensation after 1976 this would put him in a better position than if he had never suffered the injury because he would have got the disease anyway. The aim of compensation in tort is to put the plaintiff in the same position as before the tort.

The present position is that *Baker* v *Willoughby* will apply if the second event is a tort and *Jobling* v *Associated Dairies* will apply if the second event is a naturally occurring disease.

8.3   Causation in law

If the defendant is liable under the 'but for' test, then the next question is, whether the defendant should be liable as a matter of law? To answer this the principle of 'remoteness of damage' needs to be examined. This principle is that a person will not be held liable in law, if the damage caused is too remote from the original negligent act.

9   Remoteness of damage

Even if it is proved that the defendant's act caused the damage, the defendant will not be liable if the damage is too remote. (Note that remoteness of damage is also relevant in establishing whether a duty is owed.) The test for determining if the consequences of a negligent act are too remote, is the test of 'reasonable foreseeability' set out in the following case.

The Wagon Mound (No. 1) (1961)

The defendants negligently spilt furnace oil from their ship into Sydney Harbour. The oil had a flashpoint of 170 degrees Fahrenheit and it was believed that it would not burn on water. The plaintiffs made enquiries if it was safe to continue welding at their wharf 200 yards away and this was confirmed. Two days after the spillage some molten metal from the plaintiffs' welding fell on some cotton rag soaked in the oil. This started a fire and the plaintiffs' wharf was destroyed. It was held by the Privy Council that the defendants were not liable. A reasonable man could not reasonably have foreseen that the wharf would be damaged by fire as a result of the defendants' negligent act.

Does the defendant have to foresee the exact chain of events leading to the damage or the full extent of the damage? The cases have shown that the defendant will be liable, even though he could not foresee the precise set of circumstances. The leading case is:

Hughes v Lord Advocate (1963)

Some Post Office employees were working down a manhole. They put a tent over the hole and red warning lights round it and went for a cup of tea. Two boys aged eight and ten years were playing in the road. One of the boys, the plaintiff, picked up a lamp and accidentally knocked it down the hole. Paraffin from the lamp vaporised, was ignited by the flame and there was an explosion. The boy was badly burned. The defendants argued that it was not foreseeable that the plaintiff would be injured by an explosion, so they were not liable. The court held, however, that even though this precise chain of events was unlikely and unforeseeable, the defendants were liable. The lamp was dangerous and it was foreseeable that someone might be burned. The distinction between burning and explosion was too fine. This can be contrasted with the following case.

Doughty v Turner Ltd (1964)

A cauldron of sodium cyanide at 800 degrees Centigrade had an asbestos cover. This was negligently knocked into the cauldron. Shortly afterwards it reacted with the liquid and there was an explosion. The plaintiff, who was standing nearby, was injured. The High Court held that the type of risk foreseeable was burning by splashing and, as the plaintiff was burned, the defendant was liable. On appeal, however, the Court of Appeal held that as it was not known at the time that the cover would undergo a chemical change, the explosion could not be foreseen. The only foreseeable risk was splashing and there was no evidence of this, as the explosion happened a couple of minutes after the lid was knocked in. Therefore the defendants were not liable. The court distinguished *Hughes* v *Lord Advocate* but it seems a very thin distinction!

The principle from *Hughes*, i.e., that the harm suffered must be of the 'kind, type or class' foreseeable if the defendant is to be made liable, was applied in the following case.

Bradford v Robinson Rentals (1967)

The plaintiff, aged 57 years, worked for the defendants. One cold day in winter, the plaintiff travelled from Exeter to Bedford and back in a van with no heater. As a result the plaintiff suffered frostbite on the hands and feet. The court held that the foreseeable risk was injury from extreme cold; frostbite was the same type of harm, just more severe. Consequently the defendants were liable.

The approach taken in *Bradford*, involving physical injury, is quite a flexible one and rather wider than in the case of damage to property. In *The Wagon Mound (No. 1)* (1961) damage to property was foreseeable in the sense of fouling by oil, but nevertheless the defendants were not liable for damage by fire. The court required foreseeability of a more specific kind of damage. The reasons for this are based on policy. It is more likely that someone will be insured against damage to property than for personal injury (people are more likely to insure their home or car than themselves!); also property damage is likely to be more extensive than physical injury.

9.1   The extent of the damage

If the *type* of harm is foreseeable, the extent of the damage does not need to be. This applies to both personal injuries and property.

Vacwell Engineering v BDH Chemicals Ltd (1971)

The defendants made a chemical which reacted with water. The plaintiffs bought some but were not given a warning. The plaintiffs put some in a sink and there was an explosion which caused extensive damage. It was held that the defendants had been negligent in not giving a warning. Some damage to the plaintiffs' property was foreseeable, it did not matter that the extent of that damage was not foreseeable, so the defendants were liable.

10   The 'eggshell-skull' rule

If some harm is foreseeable, then the *eggshell-skull rule* or *thin skull rule* says, that if the plaintiff has a special sensitivity and suffers more than a normal person would as a result of the defendant's negligent act, the defendant is fully liable for all the damage. The defendant cannot avoid liability by pointing out that the plaintiff has some weakness. The rule is expressed in the maxim: 'you must take your victim as you find him'. The aim of this rule is to protect the plaintiff and the plaintiff's property.

Examples

thin skull;
weak heart;
haemophiliac;
nervous condition.

In such cases if the normal test of foreseeability was applied, then the damage would not be foreseeable.

Smith v Leech Brain Ltd (1961)

The plaintiff's husband worked at the defendants' ironworks. In 1950 due to the negligence of the employers, a little bit of molten metal splashed on to the husband's lip. This was treated. Some time later a latent cancer developed at the site of the burn and the husband died in 1953. The defendants argued that the death of the husband was not reasonably foreseeable, as a result of a small burn. The court said that the question was whether the defendants could reasonably foresee the type of injury the husband suffered, namely a burn. The answer was yes, therefore it was held that the defendants were fully liable for his death. So the damage suffered as a result of the burn depends on the constitution of the victim.

Another example of the rule in operation can be seen in the following case.

Robinson v Post Office (1974)

The plaintiff slipped on an oily ladder at work and cut his shin. He was later given an anti-tetanus injection but was allergic to this and suffered brain damage. Even if the doctor had given him an allergy test, it would not have shown the allergy. The defendants argued they were only liable for the initial injury to the shin. It was held that the defendants must take their victim as they found them; in this case the plaintiff having to have an anti-tetanus injection was reasonably foreseeable if the plaintiff was cut.

The eggshell-skull rule has also been applied to an 'eggshell personality', in the following odd case.

Meah v Mc Creamer (1985)

The plaintiff, a passenger in the defendant's car, knew that the defendant had been drinking. Due to the defendant's negligent driving there was an accident and the plaintiff suffered head injuries. These caused a personality change and some years later the plaintiff started attacking women. He raped one and assaulted another and was sent to prison for life. He sued the defendant for negligence claiming that, *but for* these head injuries, he would not have committed these offences. The court held that although the plaintiff had previously committed some minor offences, he would not have committed serious offences of this nature but for the negligence of the defendant. In awarding £60,000 compensation, the court took into account the fact the plaintiff would get free board and lodgings in prison! This was followed by a claim against the plaintiff in which the women he attacked were jointly awarded compensation of £17,000. The plaintiff then sued the car driver to recover this sum; but this claim was refused on the grounds of policy, that it would impose indeterminate liability on the defendant.

There are no cases on the point, but the eggshell-skull rule could equally apply to property as well as personal injuries.

Example

The defendant picks up a model ship in the plaintiff's shop, wrongly believing it is a robust model. In fact it is very delicate and is damaged by the defendant, who will be fully liable for the damage.

11   A new intervening act

The defendant's negligent act may be just part of a chain of events (the chain of causation) leading to damage to the plaintiff. If after the defendant's original negligent act, a new act happens, which overrides the defendant's negligent act, this is called a new intervening act (*novus actus interveniens*). The effect is that the defendant will not then be liable for negligence.

Examples

In the example in 8 above, could D's act of throwing the lighted cigarette away amount to a new intervening act which overrides A's original negligent act?

The court has to make a decision whether the new act is sufficiently serious to make it the cause of the damage, rather than the defendant's act. A clear example of a later act which overrides the original act can be seen in the following case.

Hogan v Bentinck Collieries (1949)

The plaintiff miner fractured his thumb at work, due to his employers' negligence. Later he had it amputated and then sued the employers. It was held that the defendants were liable for the pain and suffering caused by the original injury, but the amputation was not necessary, as the thumb would have healed up. The amputation amounted to a *new intervening act* and the defendant was *not* liable for this.

The later act (or supervening act) may be:

(a) a human act of either the plaintiff or a third party;
(b) an act of nature.

11.1   Act of the plaintiff

This is an act after the defendant's act, which completely overrides the defendant's act. This situation would be rather unusual and it would be more likely that the plaintiff is only partly to blame (see section 14 on contributory negligence in *Negligence – other factors* below).

Mc Kew v Holland & Hannon & Cubitts Ltd (1969)

The defendants negligently injured the plaintiff's left leg, which resulted in the occasional loss of control of the leg. Some time after the accident the plaintiff was going down a steep flight of stairs, the leg gave way and the plaintiff was badly injured. It was held by the House of Lords that the plaintiff's act of going down the stairs hand in hand with his granddaughter was unreasonable and amounted to a *new intervening act*. Therefore the defendants were not liable for the plaintiff's injuries.

A contrast to this case may be found in the following case.

Wieland v Cyril Lord Carpets (1969)

Through the defendants' negligence, the plaintiff was injured and had to wear a surgical collar which made the plaintiff unable to use her glasses properly. A few days after the original accident she fell down a flight of stairs. It was held that the effect of the collar was that she could not use her glasses, so the defendants' original negligence had made her unable to cope and they were therefore liable for her further injury.

The distinction between the above two cases seems to be that in *Wieland* the plaintiff's later act was regarded as *reasonable*, because she was getting her son to take her home: in *McKew* the plaintiff was acting unreasonably in going down the stairs with his granddaughter.

11.2   Act of a third party

Here the new act is by a *third party* (i.e., not the plaintiff or the defendant). The courts try to balance all the circumstances including whether the third party's act was foreseeable, whether it was reasonable and whether the defendant should owe a duty to the plaintiff. The act by the third party must be of sufficient magnitude to break the *chain of causation*.

Scott v Shepherd (1773)

The defendant threw a squib into the market. It landed near T's stall. T picked it up and threw it away. It landed near the plaintiff and exploded. It was held that T had acted reasonably in the 'agony of the moment'. Throwing the squib away did not amount to a 'new intervening act' and break the chain of causation, therefore the defendant was liable.

A more complex situation arose in the following case.

Knightley v *Johns and Others* **(1982)**

Johns negligently caused an accident in a one-way tunnel. The police arrived under the control of an inspector who forgot to close the tunnel immediately, as provided in regulations. The inspector then sent two police motorcyclists, one of whom was the plaintiff, back down the tunnel against the flow of traffic to close it! The plaintiff collided with X, who was driving into the tunnel. The plaintiff sued Johns, the inspector, X and the Chief Constable for negligence. The court decided that: the Chief Constable was not negligent, as the regulations covered the incident; X could not expect to meet someone coming the wrong way so was not negligent; it was too remote to make Johns liable; but the inspector's negligence in not closing the tunnel *and* in sending the motorcyclists the wrong way, did amount to *a new intervening act* to override Johns' negligence. Only the inspector was liable.

A more recent example is the following case.

Topp v *London Country Bus Ltd* **(1993)**

The defendants followed a common business practice of leaving buses unlocked, with the keys in, during shift changes. Because a driver failed to turn up, a minibus was left at a bus stop for nine hours. It was stolen and a few minutes later hit and killed the plaintiff's wife. The driver was never found. The plaintiff claimed that this event was foreseeable and the defendants were negligent. The Court of Appeal held that there was not sufficient proximity between the defendant and the plaintiff's wife, for a duty of care to exist. Even if a duty did exist, the act of the third party broke the chain of causation. The court regarded a parked minibus as not being inherently dangerous and the defendant was not liable for the act of the third party.

11.3 Act of nature

In this case the damage is caused by an act of nature and is independent of the defendant's negligent act. Although the act would not have happened without the defendant's breach, the defendant is not liable.

Example

D negligently collides with P's car and causes minor damage to a wheel. While P is waiting for the breakdown truck, P's car is struck by lightning and set on fire. This is an act of nature and D is not liable.

NEGLIGENCE — OTHER FACTORS

1 Introduction

Once the basic rules of negligence concerning duty, breach, causation and remoteness, have been examined, other relevant factors fall to be considered. These have not been set out in a particular order, and finish with the defences to a negligence claim. Even though the topics are in self-contained sections, they should be seen as interlocking parts in the overall picture of a negligence claim. Relevant links will be mentioned in the text, but it is important to re-read briefly the earlier section on negligence once the end of this section has been reached.

2 Proof of negligence

As in all civil claims, the plaintiff must prove, on *a balance of probabilities*, that the defendant was negligent; so the plaintiff has the legal burden of proving negligence. The exception to this is the Civil Evidence Act 1968, s. 11 which allows a criminal conviction to be used as evidence of the facts. This is not absolute proof, as evidence may be given to the contrary effect, that the defendant did not commit the crime, but it would be unusual for such an argument to succeed.

Examples

In road accidents a criminal conviction can be used in a later negligence claim.

The plaintiff must have established that the defendant owed a duty, broke it and that the defendant's breach caused the damage. There is a link here with causation, i.e., the plaintiff has to show on a balance of probabilities that the breach *caused* or *materially contributed* to the damage. The plaintiff may fail at this hurdle as in *Wilshire* v *Essex Area Health Authority* (1988), where the negligent administration of oxygen was only one of five possible causes of the baby's blindness.

In complicated matters like medical negligence claims, it is often difficult to produce sufficiently strong evidence to tilt the balance in favour of the plaintiff.

Ashcroft v *Mersey Regional Health Authority* (1983)
The plaintiff underwent an ear operation and during this a facial nerve was cut, causing partial paralysis. Evidence showed that this could happen even if there was no negligence. The court held that as the evidence of causation was equally balanced, the claim failed.

In such cases plaintiffs would benefit from a no fault scheme and a number of the medical associations are in favour of this. Where a defendant is *vicariously liable* for others, then the plaintiff does not have to prove which individual was negligent.

Example

In a claim arising from an operation the plaintiff does not have to prove which member of the operating team was negligent. The hospital authority is vicariously liable for the negligence of its employees.

3 *Res ipsa loquitur*

The phrase *'res ipsa loquitur'* means 'the thing speaks for itself'. In other words, the circumstances point to negligence by the defendant. In *Lloyde* v *West Midlands Gas Board* (1971), Megaw LJ described it in the following terms:

I doubt whether it is right to regard *res ipsa loquitur* as a 'doctrine'. I think that it is no more than an exotic, although convenient, phrase to describe what is in essence no more than a common sense approach, not limited by technical rules, to the assessment of the effect of evidence in certain circumstances.

Scott v London & St Katherine Docks Co. (1865)
The plaintiff customs officer was working in the defendants' warehouse, when six large bags of sugar, being lowered by a hoist, fell on him. The court said that bags of sugar did not normally fall on people if proper care was used and in the absence of an explanation by the defendants, this was evidence of negligence. It was held therefore that the defendants were liable.

For *res ipsa loquitur* to apply three conditions must be met:

(1) there is no explanation for the accident;
(2) the harm does not normally happen if care is taken;
(3) the instrument causing the accident is in the defendant's control.

3.1 No explanation for the accident

If there is evidence of how the accident happened, then *res ipsa loquitur* does not apply. In such a case the plaintiff simply proves negligence in the normal way.

Barkway v South Wales Transport (1950)
The defendants' bus suddenly mounted the pavement and went down an embankment. The plaintiff's husband, who was a passenger, was killed. Although such an event would not normally happen, the evidence showed that a defective tyre had burst. It was held that because of this explanation of the tyre bursting, *res ipsa loquitur* did *not* apply. It was up to the plaintiff to establish negligence in the normal way and this was done by showing that the system of inspection of tyres was negligent.

3.2 The harm does not normally happen if care is taken

A good example of this is to be found in *Scott v London & St Katherine Docks*, i.e., bags of sugar do not normally fall out of the sky! Another example is that trains do not normally collide. A spark from a domestic fire, however, is not enough evidence of negligence for *res ipsa loquitur* to apply.

3.3 The instrument causing the accident must be in the defendant's control

The amount of control needed is illustrated by a comparison of two railway cases.

Gee v Metropolitan Rly Co. (1873)
The plaintiff leaned against the door of a train shortly after it had left the station, fell out and was injured. It was held that because the train had recently been in the station, it was under the defendants' control and *res ipsa loquitur* applied.

A different conclusion was reached in the following, later case.

Easson v LNER **(1944)**

The plaintiff, aged four years, fell out of the door of a corridor train travelling from Edinburgh to London. The train was seven miles from the last station. The court held that the defendants could not be regarded as in control of the doors throughout the journey. Therefore *res ipsa loquitur* did not apply.

The requirement of control may be met through the doctrine of *vicarious liability*, i.e., one person being liable for the actions of others. (See *Vicarious liability*.)

Cassidy v Minister of Health **(1951)**

Denning LJ said:

> If the plaintiff had to prove that some particular doctor or nurse was negligent, he would not be able to do it. But he was not put to that impossible task: he says 'I went into hospital to be cured of two stiff fingers. I have come out with four stiff fingers, and my hand is useless. That should not have happened if due care had been used. Explain it if you can'. I am quite clearly of opinion that that raises a prima facie case against the hospital authorities.

3.4   The effect of res ipsa loquitur

If *res ipsa loquitur* is established, what effect does this have? There are two different views of its effect.

3.4.1   It raises prima facie evidence of negligence. It is then up to the defendant to give an explanation of how the accident could have happened, without any negligence by the defendant. If the defendant can do this, then it is up to the plaintiff to prove the defendant was negligent on a balance of probabilities.

Example

In *Wilshire v Essex Area Health Authority* (1988) the fact of the baby's blindness raised prima facie evidence of negligence by the hospital. The hospital authorities then showed that there were other causes of blindness, apart from their act. It was then up to the plaintiff to prove negligence on a balance of probabilities. In practice the plaintiff will often not be able to do this.

3.4.2   It reverses the burden of proof.   Once the plaintiff establishes *res ipsa loquitur*, it is up to the defendant to prove that the defendant was not negligent.

Henderson v Jenkins **(1970)**

A lorry was going down a hill when its brakes failed and it killed the plaintiff's husband. The defendants produced evidence that the brake pipes were corroded, but that these could not be seen by visual inspection. The defendants also showed that the lorry had been properly maintained and that the manufacturers did not recommend removing the brake pipes to check them. The House of Lords held that the defendants, by claiming a latent defect, had taken on the evidential burden of proving they were not negligent. Showing they were not at fault in inspecting the pipes did not satisfy this burden, therefore they were liable.

This was followed in the next case.

Ward v *Tesco* (1976)

The plaintiff slipped on some pink yoghurt on the floor of one of the defendants' shops in Liverpool. The Court of Appeal held that this could not have happened if the floor had been kept clean. It was up to the defendants to show that they had not been negligent and as they were unable to do this, they were liable. In a *dissenting* judgment, however, Ormrod LJ said that it was important to determine how long the yoghurt had been on the floor. This accident could easily have happened without negligence by the defendants, if, for example, the yoghurt had been knocked on the floor moments before the plaintiff slipped on it.

The view that the effect of *res ipsa loquitur* is to reverse the burden of proof was disapproved of by Lord Bridge in *Wilshire* v *Essex Area Health Authority* (1988). In *Ng Chun Pui* v *Lee Chuen Tat* (1988), Lord Griffiths stated:

> . . . it is misleading to talk of the burden of proof shifting to the defendant in a *res ipsa loquitur* situation. The burden of proving negligence rests throughout the case on the plaintiff.

The courts seem, therefore, to be turning against the reversal of the burden of proof; but *Ng Chun Pui* is a Privy Council case and not binding on English courts. *Henderson* v *Jenkins* remains good law.

4 Omissions

The law distinguishes between:

   (a) a positive act, i.e., doing something (sometimes called *misfeasance*); and
   (b) an omission, i.e., not doing something (sometimes called *non-feasance*).

The general rule in negligence is that a person is *not* liable for an omission. The fact that damage can be foreseen does not impose an obligation to act.

Example

If a person sees someone drowning in a river and walks past, the law does *not* make that person liable in negligence.

Sometimes it is difficult to distinguish between an act and an omission, because the omission is part of a course of conduct by the defendant.

Example

If a person digs a hole in their garden and someone falls in to it, is the negligence a positive act, i.e., digging the hole, or is it an omission, i.e., not putting a fence round it?

The approach of the law to omissions is partly based on the idea of *fault*, i.e., that doing something negligent is worse than simply allowing something to happen. There is also the difficulty of causation, i.e., by not doing anything, a person can hardly be regarded as causing something to happen.

Even if the law imposed liability for omissions, there would be the problem of identifying who is liable for the omissions and the problem of deciding on the extent of the duty to act.

Example

If someone falls off Westminster Bridge into the River Thames during the rush hour, who would be under a duty to act? Everyone who goes past *or* only those who can swim, *or* those with life-saving certificates?

4.1   Duty to act

In some circumstances the law does impose a duty to act.

4.1.1   Earlier actions.   If the defendant's earlier actions create a duty of care, then the defendant will be liable for an omission.

Example

A pilot who omits to brake when a plane is landing will be liable in negligence to the passengers.

4.1.2   Existing relationship.   There may be an existing relationship between the parties which imposes a positive duty to act.

Example

The relationship between a parent and a child or between a local education authority and a child or between an employer and employee or in special circumstances..

Carmarthenshire County Council v Lewis (1955)
A four-year-old child ran out of school through an unlocked gate, and went 100 yards down the road before running in front of a lorry. The driver was killed trying to avoid the child. It was held that the education authority owed a positive duty to the child and they owed a duty to the driver.

Barrett v Ministry of Defence (1993)
The defendants were held liable for failing to look after a naval airman who had drunk himself into a coma on cheap alcohol and then choked on his vomit.

Is a person under a duty to stop someone committing suicide?

Kirkham v Anderton (1990)
The plaintiff's husband was arrested by the police. They knew that he was a suicide risk, but omitted to tell the prison authorities when he was handed over. It was held that this was not simply an omission, because the police had assumed a duty to the husband in taking him into custody to pass on information which would be for his well-being.

5 Statutory duties

As can be seen in Chapter 1 (*Delegated legislation*, 2.4) public authorities may be given power by Act of Parliament to carry out particular tasks. Problems may arise if the public authority either does not do the task or does it badly. There is an overlap here between private law (an action in negligence) and public law (claiming judicial review). (See Chapter 1, *The redress of grievances*, 5.)

Jones v Dept of Employment (1989)

The plaintiff was wrongly refused unemployment benefit but successfully appealed to a Social Security Appeal Tribunal. The plaintiff then claimed that the original decision had been made negligently. It was held that, as there was a right of appeal against such a decision, no claim should be allowed in private law.

5.1 Discretion

If a public authority has been given a discretion as to how to carry out its powers, it could argue that exercising such a discretion cannot make it liable in negligence, because this would limit how it could act. This argument was put forward in the following case.

Home Office v Dorset Yacht Co. (1970)

A group of borstal boys was staying at a camp on Brownsea Island in Poole Harbour. The boys were under the control of three officers who, disregarding their instructions, went to bed one night leaving the boys unsupervised. Seven boys escaped and took a yacht which collided with the plaintiff's yacht. The Home Office put forward a number of arguments: (1) it could not be liable for the acts of third parties (the borstal boys); (2) public policy required that the officers could not be liable; (3) in exercising statutory powers the Home Office could not be liable to members of the public as this would limit its discretion as to how to deal with the boys and stifle initiative. It was held by the House of Lords that it was foreseeable that if the boys escaped they would take a yacht and might damage it. The officers had disobeyed instructions and the Home Office was therefore liable in carrying out its statutory duties negligently.

5.2 Duties and powers

A traditional distinction is made between an authority being under a *duty* to act (it must) and being given a *power* to act (it may). In the latter case it was believed that authorities could not be made liable in negligence because they did not have to do the act in the first place. In *Anns v Merton London Borough Council* (1987) Lord Wilberforce said:

> It is said there is an absolute distinction between statutory duty and statutory power — the former giving rise to possible liability, the latter not. I do not believe any such absolute rule exists.

This suggests that a public authority may be liable in negligence, whether carrying out a duty or exercising a power. Later cases have made the point, however, without actually ruling on it, that public authorities carrying out their duties should not be under a common law duty of care.

5.3   Operational and policy decisions

The courts have also made a distinction between *policy* decisions and *operational* decisions.

5.3.1   Policy decision.   This is a decision by a public authority as to what policy it should follow on a particular matter and what resources are going to be devoted to it. There could not be liability in negligence for such a decision.

5.3.2   Operational decision.   Once a policy has been decided and was being put into effect, this involved making operational decisions. There could be liability in negligence at this stage.

Example

In *Home Office* v *Dorset Yacht Co.* (1970) it was a *policy* decision whether to allow borstal boys out at camps; but it was an *operational* decision as to how this policy was carried out, e.g., the number of officers used, the places where the boys might go etc.

In *Rowling* v *Takaro Properties Ltd* (1988) Lord Keith made the following observations (N.B. these are *obiter dicta* and therefore are not a ruling of the court): (1) the above distinction between policy and operational decisions was not necessarily correct; (2) because a decision was operational it would not automatically lead to liability in negligence; (3) would making public authorities liable in negligence improve standards anyway?

5.4   Summary

A public authority may be made liable in negligence in the carrying out of its statutory duties, but the exact circumstances are clouded in doubt because of the artificial nature of the above distinctions. The courts are also reluctant to impose liability in negligence where there are alternative remedies available and if to do so would open up liability in favour of a large class of potential plaintiffs. If a claim of negligence is made, the normal requirements of duty, breach and damage have to be proved.

6   Third parties

6.1   General rule

The general rule is that the law does *not* impose liability on a person for injury caused to another person, by a third party. Even if such an injury is foreseeable, there is no liability.

Example

If a person sees a neighbour go out leaving the front door wide open and a third party goes into the house and steals the video recorder, the person who saw the door left open by their neighbour is not liable in negligence.

In determining whether a person is liable for the acts of third parties, all the requirements for the existence of a duty of care must be considered.

Perl v *London Borough of Camden* (1984)

The defendant council owned a block of flats, one of which was let to the plaintiff for business use, the others being used for residential purposes. The basement flat became unoccupied. The front door had no lock and it was known that tramps used the basement flat. Thieves entered the basement flat, knocked a hole in the wall adjoining the flat used for the plaintiff's business, and stole 700 jumpers. The plaintiff sued the council for negligence. The court held that even though the risk of burglary was foreseeable, no duty was owed to the plaintiff to guard against burglary. The defendants did not control the third parties, in this case burglars, and could not be made liable for their actions. This decision is partly based on policy, i.e., that the plaintiff could have insured against his loss. (The case can also be seen as an example of an *omission*, i.e., the defendants not stopping the third parties gaining entry.)

The question of liability for the acts of third parties was also considered by the House of Lords in two later cases.

Smith v *Littlewoods* (1987)

The defendants bought an old cinema in Dunfermline which was left empty for a month. Vandals broke in and caused damage and although this was known by the defendants' contractors and the police, no one told the defendants. Later a fire was started which spread to the plaintiff's property next door. The plaintiff claimed that the defendants should have stopped the vandals gaining access. The court held that the law does not impose a duty to mount guards for 24 hours a day on empty premises, as this would impose an intolerable burden on property owners. Here there was nothing dangerous or alluring on the premises and the defendants didn't know about the vandals. Lord Goff stated:

> It is very tempting to try to solve all problems of negligence by reference to an all embracing criterion of foreseeability, thereby effectively reducing all decisions in this field to questions of fact. But this comfortable solution is, alas, not open to us. The law has to accommodate all the untidy complexity of life; and there are circumstances where considerations of practical justice impel us to reject a general imposition of liability for foreseeable damage.

Hill v *Chief Constable of West Yorkshire* (1988)

The plaintiff claimed that the police were negligent, in failing to prevent a third party (Sutcliffe) from causing death and injury. The court refused to make the defendants liable. (See *Negligence*, 5.2.1.)

More recently the Court of Appeal has held that a bus company which left a minibus unlocked, with the keys in it, was not liable for a death caused by a third party who took the minibus (*Topp* v *London Country Bus Ltd* (1993); see *Negligence*, 11.2).

6.2   Exceptions to the general rule

6.2.1   Special relationship between plaintiff and defendant.   This can best be illustrated by the following case.

Stansbie v *Troman* **(1948)**
The defendant was left alone to decorate the plaintiff's house. The defendant went to get some wallpaper and did not lock the front door. A thief went into the house and stole some jewellery. It was held that there was a special relationship between the plaintiff and the defendant, as the latter had agreed to lock the door. Therefore the defendant was liable.

6.2.2   Special relationship between defendant and third party.   This can be seen in *Home Office* v *Dorset Yacht* where the borstal boys (third parties) were under the control of the Home Office (the defendant). It was not established in *Hill* v *Chief Constable of West Yorkshire* that there was a special relationship between the police and Sutcliffe. Establishing such a relationship brings in proximity between the parties.

6.2.3   The defendant creates a danger and it is foreseeable that a third party will become involved.   This is illustrated by *Haynes* v *Harwood* (1935); see 7.1 below.

6.3   Links with other factors

Liability for the actions of third parties is also relevant in considering causation, remoteness of damage and new intervening acts.

Lamb v *Camden London Borough Council* **(1981)**
While replacing a sewer the defendants negligently broke a water main outside the plaintiff's house. The water damaged the foundations and the plaintiff's tenant had to move out (the plaintiff was in America). Squatters moved in and then left. Boards were put up to protect the house. More squatters moved in and caused £30,000 worth of damage. The plaintiff sued the defendants for negligence. It was held that even though there was a foreseeable risk of damage, no duty was owed in respect of the actions of third parties. Lord Denning based his decision on policy. It was the plaintiff's job to keep out squatters; the defendants had no right of entry; the plaintiff had only spent £10 on boards; the loss could be covered by insurance. Watkins LJ based his decision on remoteness, saying that a person could not be held liable for the criminal acts of another.

7   Rescuers

7.1   Plaintiff put in danger

What if the defendant negligently puts a plaintiff in danger and someone tries to rescue the plaintiff and is injured?

Example

Quicklie negligently steers a powerboat close to Slowlie's canoe and Slowlie falls out. Nosie sees this and dives into the river to rescue Slowlie.

A number of questions need to be answered to determine if the defendant is liable to the rescuer:

(a)   does the defendant owe a duty of care to the rescuer?

(b) does the rescuer accept the risk by acting?

(c) is the rescuer's act a new intervening act?

Haynes v *Harwood* (1935)

The defendant left a horse-drawn van unattended in the street. A boy threw a stone at the horses which bolted. The plaintiff, a police officer, seeing that people in the street might be injured, grabbed one of the horses. The plaintiff was injured when a horse fell on him. It was held that the defendant was negligent in leaving the horses unattended in the street. It was foreseeable that someone would try to stop them if they bolted, and the defendant owed a duty to that person. It was also said that the plaintiff had not accepted the risk because there was a legal and moral duty to act in a crowded street. This can be distinguished from the following, earlier case.

Cutler v *United Dairies Ltd* (1933)

The plaintiff saw a horse and cart, without a driver, go down a quiet country lane. The driver was later trying to quieten the horse in a field and was shouting for help. The plaintiff went to help and was injured. The court held that the defendants were not liable, because the plaintiff in these circumstances had accepted the risk.

Applying these cases to the above example, Nosie has not accepted the risk as he is trying to save life in an emergency.

7.2 Defendant put in danger

What if the defendant negligently puts himself in danger and someone tries to rescue him and is injured?

Baker v *Hopkins Ltd* (1959)

The defendants used a petrol engine in cleaning out a well. Two employees were told not to start work until the manager arrived, but they did and were overcome by carbon monoxide fumes. The plaintiff (a doctor) went down to rescue them and all three died. It was held that the defendants were negligent in not warning the employees of the danger. If the employees got into difficulties it was foreseeable that someone would rescue them. The plaintiff was acting to save life and had not been reckless, nor had he voluntarily accepted the risk. Therefore his executors were entitled to compensation.

7.3 Duty to public or emergency services

A duty is owed to rescuers, whether they are members of the public or the emergency services. An example of the former is provided by the following case.

Chadwick v *British Railways Board* (1967)

The defendants were held liable for nervous shock caused to a rescuer at a train crash.

An example of the latter is provided by the following case.

Ogwo v *Taylor* (1987)

The defendant was stripping paint with a blow lamp and negligently set fire to the roof. The plaintiff fireman was burned by steam fighting the blaze, despite wearing protective clothing. The defendant argued that there could only be liability to a fireman if the injury was caused by an exceptional risk and not for ordinary risks. It was held that if the nature of the fire creates a risk, even when the plaintiff is exercising all due skill, the defendant is liable.

A different result has been reached in the following case.

Crossley v *Rawlinson* (1981)

The defendant negligently set fire to a tarpaulin cover on a lorry. The plaintiff, an AA patrolman, ran along a grass verge to help put the fire out. He caught his foot in a hole and was injured. It was held that although it was foreseeable that the plaintiff would come to help, it was not foreseeable that he would suffer this injury. Therefore the defendants were not liable.

7.4　Summary

The approach of the courts can be summed up in the short phrase: 'danger invites rescue' (Cardozo). They take a benign view of rescuers, although liability may be reduced by contributory negligence or stopped from arising by a new intervening act. Saving property, rather than life, is looked on less favourably. The duty to rescuers is *independent* of any duty owed to the victim and may arise even if no duty is owed to the victim. An example of this is *Videan* v *British Transport Commission* (1963) where the defendants were liable to a station-master who was killed rescuing his son, who was trespassing on the line, although no duty was owed to the son.

8　Unborn children

The Congenital Disabilities (Civil Liability) Act 1976 gives a right of action to a child born alive but disabled, if this is caused by something which affected:

(a)　the parents' ability to have a normal child; or
(b)　the mother during pregnancy; or
(c)　the child in the course of its birth.

The defendant is liable to the child, if the defendant would have been liable in tort to the parent, if the parent had been injured.

Example

The defendant gives the mother a drug which has adverse effects.

The mother is not liable to the child under the Act, except as regards causing injury to the child by driving a motor car, when she knows or ought reasonably to know she is pregnant.

Example

If the mother smokes during pregnancy and this damages the child, the mother is not liable.

The nature of the claim under the Act is unusual, because the child's claim is based on a duty owed to the parent by the defendant. The parent, however, does not have to suffer damage. The Act applies to all those born after 22 July 1976. It replaces any action which may have been taken at common law.

9 Nervous shock

9.1 Introduction

'Nervous shock' is not a medical term but a legal one. It means a psychiatric illness or disorder. It is distinguished from the 'normal shock' or grief, that someone might suffer on hearing bad news. No compensation can be given for this normal shock. The courts have long recognised claims for nervous shock which resulted in physical injury (*Wilkinson* v *Downton* (1897)). In *Dulieu* v *White* (1901) they accepted that a plaintiff put in fear of his own safety, could claim for nervous shock. Since then the law has developed to permit a claim for nervous shock caused by fear for the safety of one's spouse or children or those with a close relationship with the victim or persons being rescued.

9.1.1 Reasons for caution. The courts have always been cautious in awarding damages for nervous shock. The reasons for this caution include the following points.

(1) The courts' reluctance to accept the idea of psychiatric injury. In *Hevican* v *Ruane* (1991) the court awarded damages for nervous shock arising from the news of the death of a child in a school minibus accident. The judge dealt with the argument that fraud was always possible in such claims, by saying that the plaintiff would have to undergo 'the close scrutiny of psychiatrists well able to detect humbug'.

(2) The difficulty of assessing the 'injury' in money terms; although the courts have always seemed to cope with assessing physical injuries.

(3) The difficulty of proving that the defendant's negligent act actually *caused* the plaintiff's nervous shock, e.g. in *Bourhill* v *Young* there was doubt as to whether the shock caused the miscarriage.

(4) The worry that if some claims were allowed, there would be a flood of similar claims; i.e., the 'floodgates' argument.

9.2 Requirements for a claim

(a) Injury by shock must be foreseeable.

(b) The event would cause shock in a person of ordinary phlegm or reasonable fortitude.

(c) The plaintiff must suffer a recognised psychiatric illness, not simply ordinary grief.

(d) The illness must have been caused by a sudden shock.

(e) The plaintiff must have a close relationship with the victim.

(f) As regards proximity, there must be a closeness in time and space, which includes the immediate 'aftermath'.

(g) The shock must be caused through sight or hearing of the event or the immediate aftermath.

9.3 Current developments

The House of Lords has examined the law on nervous shock in two important cases.

McLoughlin v *O'Brian* (1982)

The plaintiff's husband and her three children were in a car accident which was caused by the defendant's negligence. One child died and the other members of her family were badly injured. At the time of the accident the plaintiff was at home two miles away. She was told by a friend one hour afterwards. The plaintiff then went to the hospital and saw her family in pain, and covered in oil and blood. She suffered clinical depression. She sued the defendant motorist for negligence. In delivering the judgment of the House, Lord Wilberforce stated that there were three elements to be considered in any such claim: (1) the *class* of person whose claims should be recognised. This covered husband and wife; parent and child but not others; (2) the *proximity* of such persons to the accident. There must be closeness in time and space. This is not limited to the actual event but includes the immediate aftermath; (3) the *means* by which the shock was caused, i.e., through sight or hearing of the event or the aftermath.

In applying these factors to the facts of this case, the court stated that the plaintiff was the mother and wife of the victims, she learnt about the accident soon afterwards and the shock was caused by actually seeing her family in pain. The defendant could have foreseen that the plaintiff would suffer nervous shock and was therefore liable.

Later cases tried to expand the frontier of claims by allowing a parent not present at the scene or aftermath to recover for psychiatric injury (*Hevican* v *Ruane* (1991) and *Ravenscroft* v *Rederiaktiebolaget Transatlantic* (1991)) and allowing a claim for seeing the incident live on television (*Jones* v *Chief Constable of South Yorkshire* (1990)). The House of Lords has now reconsidered these matters.

Alcock v *Chief Constable of South Yorkshire* (1991)

The plaintiffs claimed damages for nervous shock because the defendants had negligently let too many fans into Hillsborough football ground, causing the death of 95 people. The plaintiffs were relatives (but not parents or spouses) and one fiancé. Some were in the ground, others saw it live on television or heard it on the radio, some identified the dead later. It was held that their claims would be dismissed. Lord Oliver said that cases could be put into two categories: (1) plaintiffs who are *participants* in the events which cause the shock; and (2) plaintiffs who are merely *passive witnesses*.

In (1) the involvement of the plaintiff means that a duty is owed to them. One example is *Dooley* v *Cammell Laird* (1951) in which the plaintiff crane driver was lowering material into the hold of a ship when the rope broke. The plaintiff, fearing for the safety of colleagues in the hold, suffered nervous shock. It was held that the plaintiff was entitled to damages, as he had been made a participant by the negligence of the defendant. Similarly in *Chadwick* v *British Railways Board* (1967), a rescuer in a train crash recovered damages for nervous shock.

In (2) there were four factors to take into account.

9.3.1   Relationship between the plaintiff and the victim.   The court said this was not based on particular relationships like parent-child, the crucial factor was the 'love and affection' between the plaintiff and the victim. It had to be foreseeable that such persons would suffer shock. There was a rebuttable presumption that such a close relationship existed between *spouses* and between *parents and children*. In *other cases* the closeness of the relationship had to be proved. Psychiatric injury to a *bystander* is not normally reasonably foreseeable but it was accepted that if the event was particularly horrific, a bystander might be able to claim, if a strong-nerved person would have been affected (this enables 'professional rescuers', among others, to claim).

9.3.2   Proximity of the plaintiff to the accident or aftermath.   The plaintiff must be at the accident or arrive soon afterwards. Plaintiffs who identified bodies of relatives at the mortuary eight hours after the event did not meet this test of proximity.

9.3.3   Means by which the plaintiff saw the events.   The plaintiff must see or hear the event or its aftermath. It is not sufficient to be told about the events by a third party. Seeing the events on television was not sufficiently proximate. The broadcasting code of ethics prevented showing recognisable individuals, so the defendant could not foresee the plaintiffs would suffer shock. The possibility of a duty of care to television viewers was not ruled out, if it was a simultaneous broadcast. (In the Court of Appeal Nolan LJ gave the example of a live television broadcast, showing a balloon carrying children and the balloon bursts into flames. Parents watching the events live on television could recover for nervous shock.)

9.3.4   Sudden shock.   There must be sudden shock. Seeing something on television could not be regarded as causing a sudden shock to the nervous system. For example, seeing a recording of a motorway accident on the news (but see the example on live television at 9.3.3 above).

The House of Lords doubted the correctness of *Hevican v Ruane* (1991) and *Ravenscroft v Rederiaktiebolaget Transatlantic* (1991), as in both cases the means by which the nervous shock was caused was by being given the news of the son's death. In *Ravenscroft v Rederiaktiebolaget Transatlantic* (1992) the Court of Appeal applied *Alcock* and reversed the original decision, as the shock suffered by the plaintiff did not arise from sight or hearing or the aftermath of the accident.

Alcock limits the boundaries for recovery, although the possibility of exceptions makes the law uncertain. Lord Oliver said the law was unsatisfactory and called for legislation on the matter. The House of Lords seems to be worried about a flood of claims if it relaxes the requirements and seems wary of accepting the advances of medical science in identifying genuine cases of nervous shock. It has used policy to limit claims in a situation where an horrendous event, directly witnessed by nearly fifty thousand people, had resulted in only a few hundred claims for nervous shock.

Alcock was also applied in a claim for nervous shock arising from the *Piper Alpha* disaster.

McFarlane v Caledonia Ltd (1993)
The plaintiff worked on the Piper Alpha oil rig and witnessed the explosion from a support ship. The support ship went to the rescue, but never nearer than 100 metres. The plaintiff suffered nervous shock and sued for negligence. The Court of Appeal held that the plaintiff was not actually a rescuer, as he had only helped a couple of people who arrived on the support ship. He was merely a bystander, but although he had friends on the rig, he could not establish a close tie and his claim failed.

The event causing the shock must be an external event.

Taylor v *Somerset Health Authority* (1993)

The defendants were negligent in failing to diagnose serious heart disease in the plaintiff's husband, who died of a heart attack. Within an hour the plaintiff went to the hospital and was told of the death and saw his body. It was held that proximity required an external traumatic event, whereas here it was heart disease. Further, the means by which the shock was caused, i.e., being told by a third party, lacked immediacy. Therefore the plaintiff's claim failed.

10   Economic loss

10.1   Introduction

Economic loss means financial loss which does not involve injury to the person or damage to property. The courts distinguish between a negligent act leading to economic loss and a negligent statement which leads to economic loss. This section deals with negligent acts and section 11 below with negligent statements.

The purpose of the tort of negligence is to compensate someone for personal injury, or damage to property, which arises from a breach of the duty of care. The general rule is it does not provide compensation for economic loss which arises independently of physical damage. This is regarded as pure economic loss. The courts have stressed that claims for economic loss should be made in *contract*.

Example

Keith negligently causes an accident while driving along the motorway. Drew, who is on his way to work, is stuck in the traffic jam caused by the accident and loses half a day's pay.

To make a claim for economic loss the plaintiff must have a possessory or proprietary interest in the property at the time of the damage, i.e., possession or ownership.

A good example of a claim for economic loss is provided by the following case.

Weller v *Foot and Mouth Institute* (1966)

The defendants carelessly allowed cattle to become infected with foot and mouth disease. The disease spread to neighbouring farms and restrictions were introduced on the movement of cattle. As a result, the plaintiff auctioneers could not hold any sales and they sued the defendants for negligence, claiming loss of profits. It was held that even though it was foreseeable that the plaintiffs would suffer loss, no duty was owed to them. A duty was owed to farmers whose cattle had become infected and had to be slaughtered, as they had suffered *physical* damage.

10.2   Economic loss and physical damage

The law accepts that a person can claim for economic loss if they have also suffered physical damage. For example, if someone suffers a physical injury as a result of negligence and this results in having to take time off work, they can claim for loss of· earnings. An example of a claim for both can be seen in the following case.

Spartan Steel v Martin (1973)

The defendants negligently cut the cable taking electricity to the plaintiffs' factory and power was off for 14 hours. Damage was caused to the metal in the furnaces (£368) and the plaintiffs also lost the profit (£400) they would have made on that 'melt'. The plaintiffs also lost profit on the other 'melts' they would have processed during the power cut. It was held that the claims would only be allowed for the physical damage to the metal in the furnace and the loss of profit on that 'melt'. The claim for the other 'melts' was pure economic loss and was not allowed.

The fact that the plaintiff has suffered economic loss *and* physical damage does not mean the plaintiff can claim for economic loss. The economic loss must be *consequential* on the physical loss, i.e. follow from it, and not be merely additional to it. This was emphasised in the following case.

Esso v Hall Russell (1989)

An Esso tanker was berthing in the Shetlands when the engine of one of the assisting tugs blew up. The tanker went out of control, oil was lost, the tanker was damaged and pollution was caused. The plaintiffs sued the defendants, who designed and built the tug for: (a) lost oil and loss of use; (b) money paid to local farmers for damage to sheep; and (c) money paid to clean the foreshore. It was held that the claim in (a) was recoverable, as these losses were foreseeable and were consequential on the negligence. The claims in (b) and (c), however, could not be recovered as they were damage to the property of third parties and not consequential loss.

10.3   Principles on which claims are based

The courts allowed a claim for economic loss in the following case.

Anns v London Borough of Merton (1978)

The plaintiffs occupied flats which were built on inadequate foundations which led to cracking walls. They sued the local authority for negligence in inspecting the foundations. This was a novel claim as it did not involve personal injuries or damage to other property, but damage to the actual building caused by a defect in the building. The court held that the defendants were liable. This was justified on the grounds that there could be no distinction between damages for personal injury and other property *and* work done to prevent such damage; there was physical damage to the building, so it was not just pure economic loss; there was an imminent danger to the health and safety of the occupiers.

The approach in *Anns* based on general principles was used in later cases to expand liability in negligence.

Junior Books v Veitchi Co. Ltd (1983)

The plaintiffs had a new factory built. They told the main contractors to take on the defendants to lay the floor. The defendants did this negligently. The floor had to be relaid. The plaintiffs claimed: (a) the cost of relaying the floor; and (b) the loss of profits from closing while the floor was being relaid. It was held that the defendants were specialists nominated by the plaintiffs; they did the work, knowing that the plaintiffs relied on their skill; and it was foreseeable that if they did the work negligently, the plaintiffs would suffer these losses. This created a very close degree of proximity and therefore the defendants were liable for both claims.

Later cases sought to distinguish *Junior Books* and to restrict liability.

Peabody v *Sir Lindsay Parkinson & Co. Ltd* (1984)

The plaintiffs were developers. The council approved the plans for the drainage system for a site but these were later amended by the plaintiffs' architect. The system was unsuitable and had to be relaid. It was held that the plaintiffs were under a duty themselves to follow the approved plans, and the purpose of the council's statutory powers of inspection was to safeguard people from danger to their health. Therefore the council did not owe a duty of care to the plaintiffs in respect of economic loss.

In another case a claim was made in tort in a situation where there was a series of *contractual* relationships. The courts are reluctant to impose duties in tort which get round contractual agreements.

Simaan v *Pilkington* (1988)

The plaintiffs were main contractors for a building in Abu Dhabi. Their contract with the owner specified green glass made by the defendants. The plaintiffs made a sub-contract with Feal to install the glass. When it was finished the owner refused to pay the full price because the glass was not a uniform colour. The plaintiff sued the defendants in negligence for the economic loss they had suffered, as there was no contract between them. The court said that a claim for pure economic loss would only succeed if the plaintiff could show a special relationship with the defendant, which was such that the plaintiff relied on the defendant. Here the plaintiffs only bought the glass from the defendants because they were bound to by contract, they could not claim they relied on the defendants, nor could it be shown that the defendants had assumed a direct responsibility to the plaintiffs. It was held that in these circumstances the defendants were not liable. The plaintiffs could have sued Feal for breach of contract, who in turn could have sued the defendants for breach of contract. Such an action could be taken via third party proceedings.

D&F Estates v *Church Commissioners* (1988)

The plaintiffs leased a block of flats which had been built by the defendants who had engaged sub-contractors to do the plaster work. A number of years later some of the plaster work fell down and remedial work had to be carried out. The plaintiffs claimed the cost of this remedial work; costs of cleaning the carpets; loss of rent; and damages for disturbance. It was held that the cost of replacing the plaster was pure economic loss. The defendants had selected the sub-contractors carefully and did not owe the plaintiffs any duty in tort. The court said that if a defect in a building caused personal injury or damage to goods, then a remote purchaser would have an action against the builder. If, however, the building merely became less valuable or needed repairs, this was pure economic loss and was not normally recoverable in tort. The plaintiffs, however, could claim for the carpet cleaning!

Lord Bridge said that with a 'complex structure', one element might be regarded as separate from another element. So with damage by one part to a second part, the second part could be treated as 'other property', and this could then be claimed for under the principle in *Donoghue* v *Stevenson*. He gave the example of a central heating boiler exploding and damaging a house.

The above cases all involved buildings, but the principles have also been applied to other circumstances.

Reid v Rush (1989)

The plaintiff was driving his employers' Landrover in Ethiopia, when it was involved in an accident caused by someone else who could not be traced. There was no compulsory insurance in Ethiopia and the plaintiff now claimed that the defendant employers had 'assumed responsibility'. It was held that although an employer owed a common law duty to see that an employee was safe, this did not extend to providing accident insurance, nor advising the employee to obtain it, when working abroad. Such a loss was pure economic loss. This was followed by:

Van Oppen v Bedford Charity Trustees (1990)

The plaintiff suffered spinal injuries in a school rugby match. The school had received a circular 15 months earlier from the association of school medical officers suggesting insurance cover. It was found as a fact that the injury was an accident rather than negligence. The plaintiff claimed that the school had been negligent in not taking out insurance or in not advising pupils to do so. The court held that the school was not under a duty to do either of these things. There was no general duty owed in respect of the economic welfare of pupils.

The House of Lords overruled *Anns* in the following case.

Murphy v Brentwood District Council (1990)

The plaintiff bought a house built on a concrete raft, which had been approved by the defendant council. The walls cracked and the plaintiff had to sell for £35,000 less than it should have been worth. The House of Lords overruled *Anns* and said that the loss in *Anns* was purely economic. It was held that the defendants were not liable. It was said that where there was a *latent* defect in a building and this was discovered before any personal injury was caused or damage to other property, i.e., not the building itself, then any expense in putting right the defects was pure economic loss. This could not be recovered in the tort of negligence. If such a duty was imposed on a local authority to any later owner, then logically this duty would have to be imposed on the builder and indeed on the manufacturers of goods. To do this would be giving purchasers a transferable guarantee of quality, which would open a wide field of claims. Lord Keith rejected the 'complex structure' argument in the case of a small house which had been built by one contractor.

The importance of this decision is to restrict liability in negligence for pure economic loss. It establishes that a local authority is not liable to a building owner or occupier for the cost of remedying a dangerous *latent* defect, if the local authority is negligent in inspecting the building. *Murphy* was applied in a later case, to show that compensation can be claimed for damage to 'other property' caused by the defective property.

Nitrigin Eireann Teoranta v Inco Alloys Ltd (1992)

The defendants supplied steel tubes for the plaintiffs' chemical factory. In 1983 the plaintiffs discovered cracks in the tubes and repaired them but they could not discover the cause of the cracks. In 1984 the tubes cracked again allowing gas to escape and this caused an explosion, which damaged the factory. It was held that the original cracks were damage to the property itself, which was economic loss, but the later damage to the factory was damage to 'other property' and the plaintiff was entitled to damages.

With regard to defects a plaintiff knows about, i.e., *patent* defects, there is generally no liability if someone continues to use the property. The following case, however, shows that there is a qualification to this rule. It also shows that damages can be claimed in negligence for *personal injury* caused by the defect.

Targett v *Torfaen Borough Council* (1992)
The plaintiff lived in a council house, designed and built by the defendant. Access was down steps, with no handrail or lighting. The plaintiff complained about the lighting but nothing was done. One night the plaintiff fell down the steps in the dark and was injured. He sued for negligence. The Court of Appeal held that the defendant was under a duty to take care to see that the house was free of defects likely to cause injury to those whom it ought to have in contemplation. It was not reasonable to expect the plaintiff to move out or fix the defects. The defendant was liable but because the plaintiff knew of the defects, he should have taken more care and was treated as 25% contributorily negligent.

Would the council have been liable to a guest who fell down the stairs?

10.4   Exceptions to the general rule

First, *Junior Books* above, which now seems to be limited to its own special facts of a close relationship of proximity and cannot be seen as creating a general duty of care for economic loss. Although it has not been overruled, it was heavily criticised in *D & F Estates*.

Secondly, if there is a sufficiently proximate professional relationship and a limited class of plaintiffs.

Ross v *Caunters* (1980)
The plaintiff was a beneficiary under a will. The defendant solicitors, in drawing up the will, allowed the plaintiff's spouse to witness it. A witness or the spouse of a witness cannot benefit from a will. This meant that the gift to the plaintiff was invalid. The plaintiff sued the solicitors for negligence. The court identified the important factors as: close proximity between the defendants and the plaintiff, who was a beneficiary and it was foreseeable that the plaintiff would suffer loss if the defendant was negligent; the defendants owed a duty to the testator; the duty owed to the plaintiff was to an individual not an unlimited group. It was held therefore that the defendants were liable for the economic loss to the plaintiff.

This case is also unusual in having a high degree of proximity and it was distinguished in the following case.

Clarke v *Bruce Lance & Co.* (1988)
The plaintiff was to receive an interest in a service station, under a will drawn up by the defendant solicitors. Later the solicitors acted for the testator, in granting an option to the lessee to buy the service station at a fixed price on the testator's death. When the testator died it was worth a lot more than the fixed price. The plaintiff now claimed that the solicitors owed a duty to the plaintiff to advise the testator that the option was not good

sense and that it would affect the plaintiff's interest. It was held that *Ross* could be distinguished because in the present case: the proximity of relationship between the plaintiff and defendant was not close enough; there was an indeterminate class of beneficiaries; there was a remedy available to the testator's estate to sue; therefore the defendants were not liable.

The Court of Appeal has now approved *Ross* v *Caunters* in a case of negligence by omission.

White v *Jones* (1993)

A testator quarrelled with his two daughters (the plaintiffs) and then instructed the defendant (a legal executive!) to draw up a will cutting the daughters out of his estate. Later they made friends again and the testator instructed the defendant, by letter, to change the will and leave £9,000 to each daughter. Although the letter was received on 17 July, the defendant missed three appointments with the testator and did not ask the probate department to draw up a will until 16 August. On 17 August the defendant went on holiday and on return arranged to see the testator on 17 September. However, the testator died on 14 September. The court held that it was foreseeable that the beneficiaries would suffer financial loss; there was sufficient proximity between the defendant and the beneficiaries (one of whom had telephoned to confirm the change); and it was fair, just and reasonable that liability should be imposed on the defendant who was in breach of his professional duty, when there was no effective remedy in contract. Each plaintiff was entitled to damages of £9,000.

The above case was distinguished in a later case, in which the testator did have a remedy in contract.

Hemmens v *Wilson Browne* (1993)

Panter told the defendant solicitors to prepare a document giving the plaintiff (his mistress) the right to claim £110,000 from him. The document failed to give her this right and when Panter refused to give her the money, she sued the defendants. It was held that although it was foreseeable that the plaintiff would suffer damage if the defendants did not act skilfully and there was sufficient proximity between the plaintiff and the defendants, it would not be fair, just and reasonable to impose a duty, because Panter could rectify the situation by instructing another solicitor and could sue the defendants for breach of contract.

10.5   Conclusion

The courts have examined a number of factors as being relevant to deciding whether a party can recover for economic loss. They include 'proximity', 'reliance' and 'assumption of responsibility'. Although distinctions between the cases on this are not always clear, what is clear is that the courts are reluctant to impose liability for economic loss arising from negligent acts. *Murphy* now requires a high degree of proximity to establish a duty of care for economic loss.

11   Negligent statements

11.1   Introduction

In *Hedley Byrne* v *Heller* (1964) Lord Reid said that the law must treat *negligent statements* differently from *negligent acts* for two reasons:

(a)   a statement may be made on a social occasion, but it was unlikely that a casually made product would be put into circulation;

(b)   the effects of words spread easily, particularly via the media as compared with acts, and so liability must be kept within narrower bounds.

Apart from this, negligent statements must be understood within the context of the general principles of negligence. It is important to keep in mind the principles for establishing whether a duty of care exists, for this may limit liability. The decision of *Murphy* v *Brentwood District Council* (see 10.3 above) must also be borne in mind. The spectre of indeterminate liability can be seen in many of the judgments.

Example

If a BBC programme recommended a particular company's shares, one million viewers bought them and shortly afterwards the company went into liquidation, would the BBC be liable?

There is also the consideration of how the parties may insure against risk and whether the plaintiff or defendant is better able to do this.

11.2   Fraudulent advice leading to economic loss

If someone knowingly or recklessly makes a false statement which causes economic loss, then they will be liable in the tort of deceit (*Derry* v *Peek* (1889)).

11.3   Negligent advice leading to physical injury

If a negligent statement leads to physical injury or damage to property, this will result in liability. The following case provides a rather odd example of this.

Sharp v Avery & Kerwood (1938)
The defendant motorcyclists told the plaintiff motorcyclists, 'I know the way, follow me'. They set off in the dark. The defendants went straight ahead at a bend and drove through a hedge, the plaintiffs followed and were injured. It was held that the defendants were liable for their negligent advice, which resulted in injury to the plaintiffs.

11.4   Negligent advice leading to economic loss

When is a duty owed to be careful in making statements? No duty was owed until the following case.

Hedley Byrne v Heller (1964)
The plaintiffs were going to run an advertising programme for E Ltd, which involved giving E Ltd credit. The plaintiffs asked their own bank to find out about the financial position of E Ltd. The plaintiffs' bank asked E Ltd's bank (the defendants) which replied that E Ltd were good for ordinary business. This was negligent advice as E Ltd were heavily overdrawn. This information was given to the plaintiffs who made the contract with E Ltd. E Ltd then went into liquidation and the plaintiffs lost £17,000. The court held that in the

circumstances there was a 'special relationship' between the plaintiffs and the defendants, because the defendants knew that the plaintiffs would rely on the advice and the defendants had assumed responsibility. In such circumstances, therefore, the defendants should have been liable. However, the defendants' letter had stated 'without responsibility' and this meant that in the actual case the defendants were not liable.

For some time after this the courts moved towards treating *Hedley Byrne* as the basis for imposing a *general duty* not to cause economic loss through negligent advice. During the 1980s, however, there was an increasing trend against permitting suing in tort for economic loss, culminating in *Murphy v Brentwood District Council* (see 10.3 above). An example of the restrictions imposed by the courts is provided by the following case.

Yuen Kun Yeu v A G of Hong Kong (1987)

The Commissioner of deposit-taking companies registered a company which later went into liquidation. The plaintiff had deposited money in that company and lost it as a result. The plaintiff claimed that the Commissioner had been negligent, in that he knew or ought to have known that the company was being run fraudulently. It was held that a close relationship of proximity had to be established between the plaintiff and defendant. Foreseeability of harm was not sufficient to create such a duty. The Commissioner had no control over the running of the company and had no special relationship with the company. Further the plaintiff was one of an unascertained class of potential depositors. The Commissioner had not assumed responsibility to investors and it was not reasonable for the public to rely on registration as a guarantee of the financial standing of the company. Also, the Commissioner's duty of supervision was in the public interest and he could not accept responsibility for individual depositors. In all the circumstances the Commissioner was not liable.

Example

Compare the position of the Bank of England with regard to the failed Bank of Credit and Commerce International (BCCI). Is the Bank of England under a duty, in the tort of negligence, to carry out more stringent tests than ordinary company registrations?

Recently a claim for making a negligent statement succeeded, where a claim for negligence failed.

T v Surrey County Council (1994)

T left her child with a registered childminder after checking on the minder with a council adviser. The child suffered brain damage and the mother then discovered the childminder had earlier been suspected of causing brain damage to another child. It was held that the council was not liable in negligence for failing to cancel the registration as this would mean that it was liable for the act of a third party. It was liable, however, for the negligent statement about the childminder. There was a special relationship between the adviser and the child and it was clear the advice would be relied on.

11.5   Requirements for a duty to arise

Lord Bridge in *Caparo v Dickman* (1990) set out the requirements according to which, the defendant, when making a statement, will owe a duty. The defendant must know:

(a)   the type of transaction;
(b)   the information will go to the plaintiff (directly or indirectly);
(c)   it is very likely that the plaintiff will rely on the information.

11.5.1   Defendant knows the type of transaction.   The defendant must know that the advice is to be used in connection with a particular transaction or a particular type of transaction. This point can be seen in two cases decided by the House of Lords at the same time.

Smith v Bush (1989)

The buyers of a house applied to a building society for a mortgage, and the building society instructed valuers to carry out a valuation. The buyers were advised in writing to have their own survey carried out. The buyers were given a copy of the valuers' report and in reliance on it bought the house. The surveyor had failed to check that a chimney had been properly supported and it collapsed causing substantial damage. The report contained an exemption clause.

Harris v Wyre Forest District Council (1989)

The buyers applied to the council for a mortgage and paid a survey fee. The form stated that the valuation was solely for the benefit of the council and advised the buyers to have their own valuation. The house was passed by the council's own valuer (Mr Lee). The buyers were then given a mortgage. When the buyers came to sell three years later, the council inspected the house, Mr Lee again being the valuer, and it was found to need structural repairs costing more than the purchase price! The form contained an exemption clause.

It was held for both cases that a valuer instructed by a building society or other mortgagee to value a house, knowing that the valuation would probably be relied on by the purchaser, owed a duty to the purchaser to carry out the valuation with skill and care. Any disclaimer had to be 'reasonable' under the Unfair Contract Terms Act 1977 and in both of these cases it would be unreasonable to rely on the exemption clause, particularly as they were houses of modest value. It is also an important factor in such cases that the surveyor is only employed because the purchaser wishes to buy the house and the purchaser pays the surveyor's fee. This is not far removed from a direct contract between the surveyor and the purchaser.

11.5.2   Defendant knows information will go to the plaintiff.   It is not enough that the defendant can foresee the plaintiff and foresee that the plaintiff will get the information. A closer proximity is needed. The auditor of accounts can foresee that members of the public may see the accounts, but does the auditor owe a duty to those members of the public?

Caparo v Dickman (1990)

The plaintiff owned shares in F Ltd and after seeing the audited accounts prepared by the defendants, which were given to F Ltd's AGM, the plaintiff bought more shares and took over F Ltd. It was then discovered that the accounts were inaccurate and showed a profit of £1.3m instead of a loss of £465,000. The House of Lords held that the auditors owed no duty to the public at large who rely on the accounts to buy shares. The purpose of the audit was to protect shareholders from mismanagement and if the audit was negligent a claim could be made in the name of the company. No duty was owed to the plaintiff, either as an existing shareholder or potential buyer. The principle in *Hedley Byrne* was confined to situations where the maker of the statement was aware that the advice would be made available and relied on by a particular person or class for a particular transaction or type of transaction.

What happens if the statement is made to one person, but a third party acts on it?

McNaughton v *Hicks Anderson & Co.* (1991)

The plaintiffs began negotiations to take over X, a rival company, when X were in financial difficulties. The chairman of X asked the defendants to prepare draft accounts quickly for use in the negotiations. These were shown to the plaintiffs, who were told that X was breaking even. The plaintiffs completed the take-over and then found out that the accounts were wrong. The court identified the following factors as relevant in this situation:

(a)   the relationship of maker, recipient and third party;
(b)   the size of class to which recipient belonged;
(c)   the knowledge of the maker;
(d)   any reliance likely to be placed on statement by recipient.

It was held that the defendant owed no duty to the plaintiff; the accounts were prepared for X and not the plaintiff; they were draft accounts and the defendant could not have foreseen that they would be treated as final; the defendants did not take part in negotiations; the plaintiffs could have consulted their own accountants.

The above requirements were approved in the following later case.

Morgan Crucible v *Hill Samuel* (1991)

The plaintiffs made a take-over bid for X. The directors of X and their financial advisers (the defendants), made representations to the plaintiffs intending that the plaintiffs would rely on them. The plaintiffs did rely on these profit forecasts, which were wrong, to make an increased bid. It was held that here there was sufficient proximity to create a duty of care to the plaintiffs (the case was sent for trial on the issue of whether there was negligence).

11.5.3   It is very likely the plaintiff will place reliance on the information.   If advice is given in the course of a business or in a professional relationship, which the plaintiff relies on, this will give rise to a duty of care. It is not enough, however, that the defendant knows that the plaintiff might rely on it. The House of Lords in *Smith* v *Bush* and *Harris* v *Wyre Forest District Council* (see 11.5.1 above) said it must be 'likely' or 'highly probable' that the purchaser would rely on the valuer's report. In such cases it is well known that house buyers rely on the report prepared for the building society.

It must also be shown that it was 'reasonable' for the plaintiff to rely on the advice. In determining this, a distinction has been made between (a) merely passing on information, when it would be less reasonable to rely on it; and (b) actually giving advice, when it would be more reasonable to rely on it.

As a general rule it will not be 'reasonable' to rely on advice given on a social occasion; but the line between business and social occasions has been blurred by the following case.

Chaudry v *Prabhakar* (1989)

The plaintiff asked the defendant, a family friend who had some knowledge of cars, to find a car for the plaintiff. Through X, the defendant found a car which the defendant knew had had a new bonnet. The plaintiff asked if the car had been in an accident and the defendant said that it had not. The plaintiff, in reliance on this advice, then bought the car which proved unroadworthy because it had been in an accident. Did the defendant owe a duty of care under *Hedley Byrne* in respect of the advice? The court held that this was not just a social matter, because the plaintiff was relying on the defendant's skill and the defendant knew this. Even though the defendant was not paid, there was a duty to take reasonable care in all the circumstances. The defendant had not done this and was therefore liable. May LJ, *dissenting*, said that it was not right to impose such a duty on a family friend.

11.6   Excluding liability

As to attempting to exclude liability in tort, see section 16 below.

11.7   Conclusion

The courts are aware of the need to limit liability for loss resulting from negligent advice. The importance of the purpose of the advice has been emphasised in recent decisions. If advice is used for a different purpose than the one for which it was given, the courts are reluctant to impose liability. In *Caparo* v *Dickman* Lord Bridge stated that there was no duty 'to all and sundry for any purpose'.

12   The Consumer Protection Act 1987

A claim in negligence for damage caused by defective goods must now be seen in relation to possible strict liability under the Consumer Protection Act 1987. Only a brief summary of the Act will be given here. Originally, if someone using a defective product suffered injury or damage to other property, then if they had bought the product they might have a claim in contract against the seller. If the product was bought by someone else, the user might have a claim in the tort of negligence; but many plaintiffs would fail in proving negligence, if the product was complex or there were difficulties in proving causation.

Example

Motorcars and prescribed drugs.

The Pearson Report 1978 recommended imposing strict liability for defective products but this was not implemented; and it was not until the European Council passed a directive that the British Government acted. The Consumer Protection Act 1987 Part I implements this directive for products supplied after 1 March 1988. It is additional to any common law rights a person may have in contract or tort.

To claim under the Act there is no need to establish either:

  (a)   a contractual relationship or;
  (b)   proof that the producer was negligent.

The person claiming will have to prove that:

(a) the product was defective;
(b) damage was suffered (death, injury or property);
(c) the damage was caused by the defect.

This is set out in the Consumer Protection Act (CPA) 1987, s. 2(1), which states:

. . . where any damage is caused wholly or partly by a defect in a product, every person to whom subsection (2) . . . applies shall be liable for the damage.

Subsection (2) sets out who is classed as the 'producer' and includes the manufacturer, processors, assemblers, importers into the European Union and suppliers. Liability under Part I cannot be excluded (s. 7, CPA).

There are, however, a number of qualifications on liability:

(a) no claim for the actual product;
(b) in the case of damage to property (as opposed to injury), the property must be for private use, and the damage must be over £275;
(c) defences available include the 'developments risk' defence, i.e., that in the current state of knowledge the producer could not have discovered the defect.

The CPA should be regarded as an advantage for plaintiffs claiming for damages caused by defective products and should now be the first line of attack in such cases. How effective the Act is will only be seen in the light of claims, but it would certainly have helped the plaintiff in *Donoghue* v *Stevenson*.

13   Defences

13.1   Introduction

A number of general defences are available against an action in tort, but as some are only available in specific torts, it is proposed to look at the defences which apply in the sections on those specific torts. This section will simply give a brief explanation of the possible defences.

13.2   Contributory negligence

If the defendant can show that the plaintiff was partly to blame, then damages will be reduced (see section 14 below).

13.3   Exclusion of liability

In some torts it is possible to exclude liability but since the Unfair Contract Terms Act 1977 the ability to do this has been restricted.

13.4   Warnings

It is possible to avoid liability by giving a warning, but this again is very limited and only applies in some cases, such as occupiers' liability.

13.5   Consent

Both the courts and Parliament have imposed restrictions on the use of consent, but it still applies in some cases.

13.6   Necessity

This may be a defence to avoid liability if the defendant is acting in an emergency, for example, to save life or to prevent a greater evil.

Example

A doctor who gives treatment to an unconscious patient to save her life, without obtaining the patient's consent.

13.7   Statutory authority

This is of limited application but some statutes do provide a good defence to an action in tort (see *Nuisance*, 2.7.2).

13.8   Mistake

Mistake is not a good defence in tort. For example, if someone trespasses by mistake it is still a trespass.

13.9   Inevitable accident

If it can be shown that the incident could not have been avoided by the reasonable man, this may provide a good defence. Effectively, however, this is saying that someone has not been negligent.

Example

Someone out with a shooting party fired at a pheasant, but the pellet hit a tree and came off at right angles. They would not be liable for damage caused by that pellet.

13.10   Act of God

Here the cause is a natural thing which the defendant could not guard against, for example, a hurricane.

13.11   Limitation

If the plaintiff does not sue within the time limits laid down by the Limitation Acts, the defendant has a good defence.

13.12 Illegal acts

If the parties are engaged in an illegal venture, the courts may decide on the grounds of public policy that the defendant is not liable to the plaintiff.

14 Contributory negligence

14.1 Introduction

Originally at common law if the defendant could show that the plaintiff was partly to blame for the accident, then the defendant had a complete defence and was not liable in negligence.

Example

Nigel is driving his car in a suburban street at 50 mph. Jason steps off the pavement without looking and is knocked down by Nigel. Because it is partly Jason's fault, Nigel is not liable.

This rule produced unjust results, particularly if the plaintiff was only a little at fault. The law was changed by the Law Reform (Contributory Negligence) Act 1945. Section 1(1) provides:

> Where any person suffers damage as a result partly of his own fault and partly of the fault of any other person or persons, a claim in respect of that damage shall not be defeated by reason of the fault of the person suffering the damage, but the damages recoverable in respect thereof shall be reduced to such extent as the court thinks just and equitable having regard to the claimant's share in the responsibility for the damage.

'Damage' covers injury, death and property damage (Law Reform (Contributory Negligence) Act 1945, s. 4).

Section 1(2) also provides that the court should assess the *total damages* and then reduce them accordingly. This means that if the plaintiff is partly to blame, the damages awarded will be reduced according to how much the plaintiff was at fault.

Example

As in the example above, if the court assesses Jason as being 30 per cent to blame and awards him £10,000, this amount will be reduced to £7,000.

The effect of finding that the plaintiff is partly to blame is that the plaintiff's damages are reduced. This means that the plaintiff bears this loss personally, whereas the defendant will usually be insured.

The Law Reform (Contributory Negligence) Act 1945 applies to negligence, nuisance, occupiers' liability and *Rylands* v *Fletcher*, but not to torts involving an intentional act.

14.2   Establishing contributory negligence

The defendant must prove that:

    (a)   the plaintiff acted carelessly;
    (b)   the plaintiff's act caused some of the damage.

14.2.1   The plaintiff acted carelessly.   In the following case Denning LJ set out what was required of the plaintiff.

Jones v Livox Quarries (1952)

The plaintiff was riding on the back of the defendant's dumper truck when another vehicle negligently hit it from behind and the plaintiff was crushed. It was held that the plaintiff ought reasonably to have foreseen that, if he did not act as a reasonable man, he might be injured.

There is no need to show that the plaintiff owed a duty of care to the defendant, but simply that the plaintiff acted *carelessly*. In deciding if the plaintiff has acted carelessly an objective standard is applied, in the same way as judging if the defendant's conduct has been negligent.

Example

The plaintiff does not wear a crash helmet when riding a motorbike, believing it would splinter in a crash and cause worse injuries. This would be regarded as unreasonable behaviour.

There are a number of exceptions to this objective standard:

    (a)   children;
    (b)   infirm people;
    (c)   employees;
    (d)   emergencies.

    (a)   Children.
The standard applied by the law is whether an 'ordinary child' of the plaintiff's age could have realised the danger. Age is therefore taken into account.

Gough v Thorne (1966)

A lorry driver stopped and indicated to a group of children that they could cross the road. As they were doing so, the defendant negligently overtook the lorry and hit the plaintiff, who was $13\frac{1}{2}$ years old. It was held that the plaintiff was not contributorily negligent. Lord Denning MR stated:

> A judge should only find a child guilty of contributory negligence if he or she is of such an age as reasonably to be expected to take precautions for his or her own safety . . .

In theory a child of any age could be guilty of contributory negligence but it is unlikely that the courts would find young children contributorily negligent.

Yachuk v *Oliver Blais Ltd* (1949)

The plaintiff, a nine-year-old boy, falsely told the defendants that his mother needed petrol for her car. They sold him some and whilst playing Red Indians with it, he was burned. It was held that the defendants were negligent in selling petrol to a young child. The plaintiff could not be expected to know of the danger and was not contributorily negligent.

A different decision was reached in the following unreported case.

Gannon v *Rotherham MBC* (1991)

The court found that a 14-year-old boy who had dived into the shallow end of a swimming pool and broke his neck, was contributorily negligent. The court said that he was of such an age and experience that he should not need to be told not to dive into the shallow end at such a steep angle ('Foul Play – Criminal and Civil Liability for Violent Acts on the Playing Field', Edward Grayson 141 NLJ 742).

The Pearson Report recommended that in the case of motor accidents, plaintiffs under 12 years old should not be made liable for contributory negligence.

(b)   Infirm people.

The plaintiff must exercise such care as is reasonable. In determining what is reasonable, the law takes into account the plaintiff's age and physical condition; but the plaintiff's mental condition is judged objectively.

If the defendant knows that the plaintiff has a disability, or if the defendant can foresee that a disabled person could be affected by the defendant's actions, then the defendant must take additional precautions. See *Haley* v *LEB* (1965) (*Negligence*, 7.1).

(c)   Employees.

Under the Factories Act and similar legislation, the employer is under a statutory duty to ensure that employees are safe in carrying out their jobs. The aim of such legislation is to protect employees. If the employee sued the employer for breach of these duties and the employer could claim contributory negligence by the employee, the employer would effectively avoid liability. The courts therefore take a more lenient approach to contributory negligence by employees and will be reluctant to make findings of contributory negligence. The employer must make allowance for employees being careless, bored, tired and even disobeying instructions. It is possible for an employer to establish that an employee has been contributorily negligent if, for example, the sole cause of the accident was the employee's act or omission. Often the employer will be under a duty of supervision.

Example

The employer may not only have to provide goggles but also supervise the wearing of them.

An employee may bring a claim in negligence at common law, rather than for breach of statute. It is not clear from the cases whether the courts would then take a similar approach to contributory negligence.

(d)   Emergencies.

In an emergency, if the plaintiff has acted 'reasonably', the conduct will not be treated as contributory negligence. In deciding what is reasonable, the fact there may be a threat to life or that the plaintiff is acting in the 'heat of the moment' is taken into account by the courts. This is illustrated by the following old case.

Jones v Boyce (1816)

The plaintiff was a passenger on top of the defendant's coach. As the coach was going downhill, a coupling broke. The plaintiff, believing it was going to crash, jumped off and sustained a broken leg. The coach did not crash. It was held that in this situation a reasonable man would have acted in a similar way. Therefore the plaintiff was not contributorily negligent.

The courts faced a novel situation in the next case.

Sayers v Harlow Urban District Council (1958)

Mrs Sayers left her husband at the bus stop and went into the ladies' public toilets run by the defendants. When she tried to leave she found the door lock had jammed. After shouting and banging on the door for 15 minutes to no avail, she tried to climb out. She put one foot on the toilet seat and the other on the toilet roll holder. The toilet roll rotated and she fell down and was injured. It was held that the defendants owed a duty of care to maintain the locks properly. The court then had to deal with the question whether the reasonable man in such a position would have tried to climb out! This was regarded as reasonable, but Mrs Sayers had done it in a negligent manner, and her damages were reduced by 25 per cent.

14.2.2   The plaintiff's act caused some damage.   It must be shown that the plaintiff's act caused some of the damage. Also it must be shown that the harm to the plaintiff was the kind likely to happen. In *Froom v Butcher* an important distinction was made by Lord Denning between the cause of the accident and the cause of the damage.

Froom v Butcher (1976)

The plaintiff was a passenger in the defendant's car. The defendant's negligent driving was the sole cause of an accident and the plaintiff, who was not wearing a seat belt, was injured. At the time seat belts were not compulsory. Lord Denning stated:

> The accident is caused by bad driving. The damage is caused in part by the bad driving of the defendant and in part by the failure of the plaintiff to wear a seat belt.

So the plaintiff had to share the responsibility and damages were reduced by 20 per cent. Lord Denning then went on to lay down guidelines for apportionment of damages.

(a)   If failure to wear a seat belt made no difference to the injuries, then damages should not be reduced.

(b)   If injuries would have been prevented altogether by wearing a seat belt, then damages will be reduced by 25 per cent.

(c)   If wearing a seat belt would have reduced the injuries, then there will be a 15 per cent reduction in damages.

The criminal law made it an offence not to wear a front seat belt from 1982. There are some exceptions, e.g., reversing, taxi drivers or having a doctor's certificate. Recently rear seat belts have been made compulsory for adults travelling in the back of cars fitted with rear seat belts (Motor Vehicles (Wearing of Seat Belts in Rear Seats by Adults) Regulations 1991).

Hogan and Ryan v Smith (1991)
This concerned a passenger in the rear of a car in 1989 who did not wear a seat belt. It was held not to be contributory negligence because the public were not aware of the danger. It remains to be seen how this will change in the light of the new regulations.

The percentage reductions suggested in *Froom* v *Butcher* may be increased in certain circumstances. An example can be found in the following case.

Gregory v Kelly (1978)
The plaintiff would have suffered no injury if a seat belt had been worn. The plaintiff also knew that the car had no footbrake. It was held that the plaintiff's damages should be reduced by 40 per cent.

Similar guidelines have been used in cases where a crash helmet has not been worn.

Capps v Miller (1989)
The plaintiff was a pillion passenger on the defendant's moped and suffered head injuries in an accident caused by the defendant's negligence. The plaintiff was wearing a crash helmet, but had not fastened the strap (which is an offence). It was held by the High Court that, by not fastening the strap, the plaintiff's injuries had been increased by an 'incalculable degree'; but because the plaintiff was not to blame for the accident, the plaintiff was not contributorily negligent. The Court of Appeal ruled that, once it was found as a fact that the plaintiff's failure to fasten the strap had contributed to the injuries, then damages had to be apportioned. It was accepted that Lord Denning's guidelines in
Froom v *Butcher* should normally be applied in cases where a crash helmet was not worn. The court drew a distinction, however, between not wearing a helmet *and* wearing a helmet but not fastening it. Damages in the latter case should be reduced by 10 per cent. It was also said that even if contributory negligence is under 10 per cent, damages should be reduced.

With regard to reducing damages, can someone be 100 per cent contributorily negligent? The courts can reduce the plaintiff's damages on the basis of what they think is 'just and equitable' under the Law Reform (Contributory Negligence) Act 1945, but can they reduce them by 100 per cent?

Pitts v Hunt (1990)
The plaintiff (aged 18 years) and the defendant (aged 16 years) set off home on the defendant's motorbike, after spending the evening drinking. The plaintiff knew that the defendant was under age, had no licence and no insurance. The defendant rode in a reckless manner, weaving across the road to frighten people and was encouraged to do so by the plaintiff. They hit a car and the defendant was killed. It was held by the High Court that no duty of care was owed to the plaintiff and the plaintiff was 100 per cent contributorily

negligent. The Court of Appeal dismissed the plaintiff's appeal, but said that the 1945 Act presupposes that the plaintiff will recover *some* damages, so it was illogical to make the plaintiff 100 per cent contributorily negligent.

Note that if the plaintiff is the sole cause of the accident, this could amount to a new intervening act and the defendant would not be liable.

14.3 Drinking cases

If someone accepts a lift from a drunken driver, does this amount to contributory negligence by the passenger?

Dann v *Hamilton* (1939)
The plaintiff voluntarily accompanied the defendant in the defendant's car to a social event and spent some time drinking. On the way home, due to the defendant's negligence, they crashed and the defendant was killed. The plaintiff was injured and sued the defendant's estate. The court held that, by taking a lift, the plaintiff was not allowing the defendant to drive dangerously. The court was faced with a similar problem in the following case.

Owens v *Brimmell* (1977)
The plaintiff and defendant went out drinking together and had about eight pints each. On the way home the defendant hit a lamp post. It was held that the plaintiff was 20 per cent contributorily negligent by getting in a car with a driver known to be drunk. The court said that a person could be contributorily negligent either by getting into a car with a drunken driver or going out drinking with the defendant knowing that the defendant would drive later.

The point was considered more recently in the following case.

Morris v *Murray* (1990)
The plaintiff and defendant spent most of the afternoon drinking and the defendant had the equivalent of 17 whiskies. The defendant then suggested going flying in the defendant's plane and the plaintiff drove them to the aerodrome. Although there was poor visibility and other flying had been suspended, the defendant took off. Shortly afterwards the plane crashed and the defendant was killed and the plaintiff seriously injured. The High Court said that the plaintiff had been 20 per cent contributorily negligent. The Court of Appeal held, however, that the plaintiff knew that the defendant was extremely drunk and had accepted the risks, so was not entitled to any damages.

15   Consent

15.1   Introduction

The defence of consent is also known as *volenti non fit injuria*, i.e., no wrong is done to one who consents, or *volenti* for short, or voluntary assumption of risk. It means that if someone consents to the risk of injury, they cannot claim compensation. It must be examined alongside the defence of contributory negligence. Consent provides a complete defence to a claim of negligence, whereas contributory negligence is only a partial defence.

Barrett v Ministry of Defence (1993)

The defendants negligently provided cheap alcohol to an airman, who drank himself into a coma and choked to death on his vomit. It was held that although the airman was too drunk to *consent* to fatal injury because he could not appreciate the risk, nonetheless he had been 25 per cent *contributorily negligent*.

Consent to a negligent act must be distinguished from consent to an intentional act. For example, a patient who consents to an operation is consenting to the tort of trespass but is not consenting to the surgeon carrying out the operation negligently.

15.2   When consent operates

For consent to operate as a defence, the following conditions must be met:

(a)   agreement to accept the risk;
(b)   consent must be voluntary;
(c)   full knowledge of the risk.

15.2.1   Agreement to accept the risk.   There must be an agreement that the plaintiff accepts the risk. This agreement may be express or implied.

If the agreement is *express*, the defendant will have the defence of consent; but such an agreement may be subject to the Unfair Contract Terms Act 1977. In the case of business liability under s. 2(1) a person cannot exclude liability for death or personal injury resulting from negligence. Under s. 2(2) as regards damage to property, the exemption must be reasonable. Under s. 2(3) it is provided that a person's agreement to or awareness of such a notice (i.e., consenting to a risk) is not to be taken on its own as a voluntary acceptance of any risk.

The courts are reluctant to accept that the plaintiff can give the defendant permission in advance to commit negligent acts. It is argued that in such a situation the plaintiff cannot have full knowledge.

An agreement may be *implied* from conduct. It is clear, however, that the mere knowledge of a risk does not mean someone consents to it. If the plaintiff acts unreasonably, this may be regarded as consenting.

ICI v Shatwell (1964)

Two brothers, who were shotfirers, were working for the defendants in a quarry. They ignored regulations and tested charges without using the shelter provided. They were both injured and one of them sued the defendants, claiming that they were vicariously liable for the acts of the other brother. It was held that both brothers were aware of the risks and by their actions had impliedly consented to take them. Therefore the defendants were not liable.

15.2.2   Consent must be voluntary.   The plaintiff's consent to the risk must be freely given. This can be illustrated by the following case.

Smith v *Baker* **(1891)**

The plaintiff was employed by the defendant to drill holes in rock. A crane constantly swung crates of rocks overhead and the plaintiff complained about this. Some time later a rock fell from a crate and injured the plaintiff. It was held that although the plaintiff knew of the risk and continued to work, this did not mean that he had consented to the risk. There was no real choice if the plaintiff wanted to keep the job.

As has been discussed earlier, in the case of rescuers their actions cannot normally be regarded as consent to the risks. If it is not an emergency they may be regarded as consenting (see *Cutler* v *United Dairies*).

15.2.3   Full knowledge of the risk.   It must be proved that the plaintiff knew about the nature of the risk and the extent of the risk. A person cannot consent to a risk of which he is ignorant. Knowledge on its own is not consent, a plaintiff must also act unreasonably. The courts are reluctant to accept consent as a defence because its effect is that the plaintiff gets no compensation. In extreme cases a plaintiff will be regarded as consenting to the risk and the classic example is found in the following case.

O'Reilly v *National Rail & Tramway Appliances* **(1966)**

The plaintiff was sorting scrap with a number of others and found a live round of ammunition nine inches long. The plaintiff had a sledgehammer and someone told him to hit the round. Not surprisingly the plaintiff was badly injured! The court held that in these circumstances the plaintiff had acted in a foolhardy way and had consented to the risks.

Also see *Morris* v *Murray*, 14.3 above.

15.3   Drinking cases

This section should be read in conjunction with the drinking cases in *Contributory negligence*, 14.3.

If someone accepts a lift from a drunken driver, have they consented to the risk of injury?

In *Dann* v *Hamilton*, Asquith J said that accepting a lift from a drunken driver does not mean that you consent to the driver driving negligently. He added, however, that if conduct was extremely stupid, e.g., meddling with an unexploded bomb, it may be regarded differently.

Under the Road Traffic Act 1988, s. 149, the defence of consent is not available against road accident victims.

Example

A notice in someone's car states: 'Passengers travel at their own risk'. If a passenger is injured through negligent driving, the driver cannot claim that the passenger consented. Even if there is no such notice, the passenger has not consented to injury.

The defence of consent may be used in the case of negligent flying of an aeroplane: *Morris* v *Murray* (1990), where *Dann* v *Hamilton* was distinguished as, in the latter case, the negligence occurred during a social occasion. In *Morris* the plaintiff had actively helped in getting the 'plane ready and had full knowledge of the risks.

15.4 Sports events

Spectators at sports events are regarded as consenting to the normal risks of that particular sport, but they do not consent to negligent acts by the players. The same applies to competitors. They consent to the normal risks of the game but not to grossly negligent play or deliberate assaults.

Condon v Basi (1985)

The plaintiff, an amateur footballer playing in a local league, was tackled by the defendant during a game. This tackle broke the plaintiff's leg. The defendant was sent off. It was held that the tackle was made in a reckless and dangerous manner and was not a normal risk. By playing football the plaintiff was not consenting to negligent acts.

15.5 Criminal acts

It is a legal principle that a person cannot bring a claim if it is based on, or has involved, an unlawful act. This is expressed in the phrase *ex turpi causa non oritur actio*.

Ashton v Turner (1981)

The plaintiff and defendant committed a burglary and the defendant, in driving away negligently, injured the plaintiff. It was held that no duty of care was owed to the plaintiff under the principle of *ex turpi causa*. Even if a duty of care was owed, the defendant could rely on the defence of consent by the plaintiff.

This principle was also considered in *Kirkham* v *Anderton* (1990) where it was said that the defence of consent was not available. Even though the suicide was the plaintiff's husband's own deliberate act, because he was suffering from clinical depression he could not be regarded as consenting. This was particularly the case here, because the duty owed was to guard against the very thing that happened.

16 Exemption clauses

A person may attempt to exclude liability in tort. Any such exclusion is subject to the Unfair Contract Terms Act (UCTA) 1977 as regards business liability.

16.1 Death or injury

As has been shown above, the clause is invalid so far as death or injury arising from negligence is concerned.

16.2 Damage to property

As regards other liability, (i.e., damage to property), then such a clause is subject to the test of 'reasonableness' under the Act. This was considered in the following cases.

Smith v *Bush* and *Harris* v *Wyre Forest District Council* (1989)

The question arose whether a disclaimer inserted by the valuer in *Harris* (or by the council in *Smith*) was within the UCTA. The Court of Appeal had ruled that the existence of a disclaimer prevented a duty of care from arising. The House of Lords said that if an exemption notice is taken into account in determining whether or not a duty existed, this would remove all cases of liability from the protection of the UCTA. This could not have been Parliament's intention.

The next question, once it had been established that the disclaimer did not prevent a duty arising and was within the UCTA, was whether the disclaimer was 'reasonable'.

It was argued that:

(a)   the disclaimer was clear, unambiguous, and was drawn to the buyer's attention;
(b)   the buyer's solicitor would tell the buyer to get their own survey;
(c)   if disclaimers were not allowed, buying a house would be dearer;
(d)   if disclaimers were not allowed, the cost of professional negligence insurance would increase and so would the cost of valuations.

The House of Lords, however, stated that the valuer was a professional who was paid and who knew that most buyers relied on the valuation survey and could not afford a second survey. Because of the high cost of houses, it would not be fair and reasonable for the defendants to rely on the clause. Lord Griffiths said the following factors were relevant:

(i)   The relative bargaining strength of the parties, i.e., a building society as opposed to an individual.
(ii)   Was it practicable for the buyer to obtain alternative advice? The transactions had taken place at the bottom end of the market and the buyers would be paying twice for a survey.
(iii)   The difficulty of the task. In these cases it was fairly simple to see the defects on examination, so exemption was less reasonable than if the survey had been a difficult one.
(iv)   The practical consequences of allowing the exemption taking into account each party's ability to bear losses. A valuer could insure; but it might well mean ruin for the individual buyer.

Therefore in the circumstances, taking all these factors into account, it would not be reasonable to allow reliance on the disclaimer. The houses were of modest value in both cases and it might be different with expensive houses or blocks of flats or commercial properties.

OCCUPIERS' LIABILITY

1   Introduction

This tort is really a specialised form of negligence, which applies to injuries and damage caused on someone's land. The rules are now contained in statutes, the Occupiers' Liability

Act 1957 which applies to *visitors* and the Occupiers' Liability Act 1984, which applies to *others*. In contrast, if damage is caused off the premises, as a result of something done on them, the claim will normally be in nuisance or *Rylands* v *Fletcher*. However, occupiers' liability will often overlap with a claim in negligence at common law and in practice action may be taken in both.

Example

In *Ward* v *Tesco* the defendants were liable in *negligence* when the plaintiff slipped in some yoghurt on the floor of their shop. They could equally have been liable for breach of the *common duty of care* under the Occupiers' Liability Act 1957.

Liability to visitors will be examined first and then liability to others.

2   Liability to visitors

The Occupiers' Liability Act (OLA) 1957 makes a distinction between lawful *visitors* and *others*. The occupier owes a 'common duty of care' to visitors. It is generally accepted that this 'duty' relates to the *state of the premises* rather than an *activity* on the premises. The latter claim would normally be in negligence.

3   Definitions

3.1   Occupiers

The OLA 1957 does not define who is an occupier, but provides that the common law rules apply (s. 1(2)), i.e., the rules devised by the courts before the OLA 1957 was passed. The most important factor is who is in control of the land. The leading decision in this area is the following case.

Wheat v Lacon (1966)

R was manager of a pub owned by the defendants. One night, the plaintiff (R's lodger), was going down stairs in the private part of the pub, fell and received fatal injuries. Part of the handrail was missing and someone had stolen the bulb shortly before the accident. The question arose as to whether the defendants were 'occupiers' under the OLA 1957.

It was held that both R and the defendant were occupiers of the stairs and owed a common duty of care to the plaintiff; but they were not in breach of this duty because of the act of a stranger in taking the bulb. Lord Denning set out the following four groups of occupiers:

(a)   if a landlord lets premises to a tenant, the tenant is the occupier;

(b)   if a landlord lets part of premises to a tenant, the landlord is still occupier of the part retained;

(c)   if a landlord grants a licence less than a tenancy, then both landlord and licensee are occupiers (*Wheat* v *Lacon*);

(d)   if a landlord engages an independent contractor on premises, the landlord is still the occupier and the contractor could be as well.

It is clear from the cases that more than one person may be an occupier.

Collier v *Anglian Water Authority* (1983)

The plaintiff tripped on a paving slab sticking up on Mablethorpe promenade. The promenade was owned by the local authority who cleaned it and granted leases but the defendants were under a statutory duty to repair it. It was held that both the defendants and the local authority could be 'occupiers'. It is not necessary to be in possession to be regarded as an occupier.

Harris v *Birkenhead Corporation* (1976)

The defendants made a compulsory purchase order on a house. The owner left without telling them and the defendants did not board it up. The plaintiff (aged four years) went into the house and fell out of an upstairs window. The Court of Appeal held that even though the defendants had never had physical possession, because they had the legal right of control they were the 'occupiers' and not the owner.

Example

At an auction on a farm, both the auctioneer and the farmer are occupiers.

3.2 Visitors

The common duty of care is only owed to visitors. A visitor is anyone with permission to be on the premises. This permission may be:

  (a)   express, e.g., asking a milkman to deliver milk or asking a friend to call;
  (b)   implied, e.g., a postman or door to door salesperson.

If the landowner knew that someone had trespassed and did nothing to prevent it, this may be the same as giving permission.

3.2.1 Limits on the visitor.   The occupier may put *limits* on the visitors as regards the area in which they can go, the time they stay and the purpose of their visit.

3.2.2 Area.   The visitor may be restricted to a certain area and outside this area becomes a trespasser.

Example

A guest in an hotel who goes through a door marked 'Private'.

The limits can be seen, however, in the following case.

Pearson v *Coleman Bros* (1948)

The plaintiff was a girl of seven who visited a travelling circus. She wanted to go to the toilet and, as none was provided, went to look for a suitable place. She wandered into the animal enclosure and was mauled by a lion which put its claws through the bars of a cage. The defendants argued that she was a trespasser. It was held that in all the circumstances, including the fact that the area was not marked off, she was not a trespasser and the defendants were liable.

3.2.3   Time.   The permission may be limited as regards the time that the visitor can stay.

Stone v *Taffe* (1974)
A pub manager gave an unauthorised party after closing time. The plaintiff fell down stairs and died. It was held that the plaintiff could not be regarded as a trespasser by the brewery, as the plaintiff did not know that they objected to the party.

3.2.4   Purpose.   If someone acts outside their lawful purpose, they become a trespasser. This can be illustrated by a criminal case.

R v *Smith and Jones* (1976)
The defendants burgled Smith's father's house early one morning and stole two televisions. They were charged with burglary under the Theft Act 1968, s. 9(1)(b), which required entry 'as a trespasser'. Smith's father said that Smith had an unrestricted right of entry at any time. In affirming their conviction, the Court of Appeal held that someone who enters knowing they are acting in excess of their permission could be a trespasser.

3.2.5   Rights given by law.   OLA 1957, s. 2(6) provides that:

> persons who enter premises for any purpose in the exercise of a right conferred by law are to be treated as permitted by the occupier to be there for that purpose, whether they in fact have his permission or not.

Example

Firemen, police officers executing a warrant, health and safety inspectors, anyone using public facilities like a library.

3.3   Rights of way

A person using a public or private right of way is not a trespasser, but s. 2(6) does not apply to them, so they are not a visitor either.

3.3.1   Private right of way.   A private right of way is now covered by the Occupiers' Liability Act 1984.

3.3.2   Public right of way.

Greenhalgh v *British Railways Board* (1969)
The plaintiff, while using a public footpath which went over a railway bridge, tripped in a pothole. It was held that the plaintiff was not a visitor under the OLA 1957 and the claim failed.

Note that someone using a public right of way is not covered by the OLA 1984. Their only protection is at common law, and that is that an occupier is liable for negligent acts but not for failure to repair. There are two exceptions when the occupier will be liable:

(a)   If the danger arises from something done on the land. In *Thomas* v *British Railways Board* (1976) the defendants were held liable when a two-year-old climbed through a fence and was hit by a train.

(b)   If the right of way is maintainable at public expense, for example, under the Highways Acts.

Anyone exercising rights under the National Parks and Access to the Countryside Act 1949 is *not* a visitor under the OLA 1957.

3.4   Premises

There is no complete definition of premises under the OLA 1957 but s. 1(3)(a) states that the Act covers:

the obligations of a person occupying or having control over any fixed or movable structure, including any vessel, vehicle or aircraft.

Wheeler v *Copas* (1981)

The plaintiff was building a house on the defendant's land and borrowed the defendant's ladder. This proved unsuitable and the plaintiff fell off and was injured. It was held that the OLA 1957 could apply to a ladder, but in this case the defendant was not the occupier anymore as the plaintiff had control of it. However, the defendant was liable to the plaintiff in negligence.

4   The common duty of care

The Occupiers' Liability Act 1957, s. 2(1), states that:

An occupier of premises owes the same duty, the 'common duty of care', to all his visitors, except in so far as he is free to and does extend, restrict, modify or exclude his duty to any visitor or visitors by agreement or otherwise.

This 'common duty of care' is defined in s. 2(2) as:

. . . a duty to take such care as in all the circumstances of the case is reasonable to see that the visitor will be reasonably safe in using the premises for the purposes for which he is invited . . .

Three important factors emerge from this:

(1)   The occupier must make the *visitor* safe, not the premises.
(2)   The duty is to take care that is *reasonable* in the circumstances.
(3)   The visitor must only be using the premises for their *lawful purpose*.

In deciding what duty is owed by an occupier to visitors, the court takes into account the same factors as a claim in negligence, for example, the occupier will not be liable for highly unlikely consequences. The duty owed to the visitor, however, will partly depend on who the visitor is. The *qualifications* on this duty are laid down in s. 2(3)(a): children; s. 2(3)(b):

someone doing their job; s. 2(4)(a): warnings; s. 2(4)(b): independent contractors; s. 2(5): consent.

5   Special points

In determining whether the occupier has fulfilled the duty of care, a number of special points may need to be examined. These are set out in the next sections from 6 to 9.

6   Children

The Occupiers' Liability Act 1957, s. 2(3)(a), provides that 'an occupier must be prepared for children to be less careful than adults'.

It is clear that children are not as sensible as adults and have less experience. The OLA 1957 recognises this and demands a higher standard of care towards them. The occupier must realise that children are naturally inquisitive and do not appreciate dangers that are obvious to adults. Children may be attracted to something dangerous, like broken glass or water (this is known as the doctrine of 'allurements') which takes them away from the permitted area. The law may regard this as an 'allurement' and in such a case the child will be treated as a visitor.

Glasgow Corporation v Taylor (1922)
A child aged seven picked some poisonous berries from a belladonna bush in a public park, ate them and died. It was held that the child would have been a trespasser, as he did not have permission to pick the berries, but was attracted to the berries and therefore the defendants were liable.

The court was saying that the child had 'implied' permission to be in the bushes. Since the OLA 1984 trespassers may be owed a duty of care and the concept of implied permission will not then be needed.

6.1   Young children

If the children are *very* young, the occupier can expect parents to look after them. At what age they may be left can only be gleaned from the cases.

Phipps v Rochester Corporation (1955)
A girl of seven and her brother aged five went blackberry picking next to a building site and wandered on to the site. The defendants knew that children played on the site, so the children were regarded as implied visitors. The boy fell into a trench and broke his leg. It was held that the occupier is entitled to assume that very young children will be accompanied by a responsible person and therefore the defendants were not liable.

The court made the point that in the case of a public park or recognised playground, where parents could assume children would be safe even if not accompanied the occupier may then be liable.

In the following case, however, the occupier was found not liable.

Simkiss v *Rhondda Borough Council* (1983)

The plaintiff, a girl of seven, was injured sliding down the defendant's hill on a blanket. Her father had said that he did not consider the hill to be dangerous. The court held that it could be assumed that parents would warn children of dangers and the father did not consider it dangerous, therefore the defendant was not liable.

7 Specialists

The Occupiers' Liability Act 1957, s. 2(3)(b), states that:

> an occupier may expect that a person, in the exercise of his calling, will appreciate and guard against any special risks ordinarily incident to it, so far as the occupier leaves him free to do so.

The occupier can expect a skilled person to guard against the normal risks of their job.

Example

If a plumber fixing a burst pipe drowns, the occupier is not liable.

This does not mean that the occupier does not owe any duty to specialists.

Woollins v *British Celanese* (1966)

A post office engineer fell through some hardboard roofing at the defendants' factory. The court held that the engineer could be expected to guard against live wires, but not defects in the structure of the building. Therefore the defendants were liable.

The courts have enlarged the scope of the duty owed to specialists in a number of recent cases.

Salmon v *Seafarer Restaurants* (1983)

The defendants negligently left the fryer on when they closed their fish and chip shop. This started a fire and when the plaintiff fireman attended, he was injured in a gas explosion. The defendants argued that they only owed a duty to protect the plaintiff from exceptional risks and that they were not liable because an explosion was an ordinary risk of the job. It was held that the occupier owed the same duty to a fireman as to other visitors. In determining, however, whether the occupier had fulfilled this duty, the occupier could expect the fireman to exercise the normal skills of a fireman. The fire was caused by the defendants' negligence, it was reasonably foreseeable that the fireman would attend and an explosion might happen. The defendants were therefore liable. If the plaintiff had taken an unreasonable risk however, for example, not wearing appropriate clothing, this might break the chain of causation.

This decision was *approved* by the House of Lords in the later case of *Ogwo* v *Taylor* (1987), which was decided as a common law claim in negligence. (See *Negligence – other factors*, 7.3.)

8 Independent contractors

The Occupiers' Liability Act 1957, s. 2(4)(b), provides that:

> . . . where damage is caused to a visitor by a danger due to the faulty execution of any work of construction, maintenance or repair by an independent contractor employed by the occupier, the occupier is not to be treated without more as answerable for the danger if in all the circumstances he had acted reasonably in entrusting the work to an independent contractor and had taken such steps (if any) as he reasonably ought in order to satisfy himself that the contractor was competent and that the work had been properly done.

The occupier will not be liable if damage is caused to the visitor by an independent contractor, if the occupier:

(a) acted reasonably in all the circumstances; and
(b) checked that the contractor was competent; and
(c) checked that the work was done properly.

The normal rule is that a person is *not* liable for the negligence of an independent contractor.

8.1 The occupier acted reasonably in all the circumstances

The first issue here is whether the occupier acted reasonably in engaging an independent contractor. If the job is tricky or needs specialist skills then it is reasonable for the occupier to get an independent contractor. If the work is simple, then it is more likely the occupier should do the job. It may also be reasonable if it is normal business practice to engage someone for the task in question.

Example

Office cleaning.

An example of engaging an expert is provided by the following case.

Haseldine v *Daw* (1941)
The plaintiff was injured when a lift in the defendants' block of flats fell to the bottom of the shaft. It had just been serviced by a firm of engineers. The court held that the defendants had no reason to doubt the competence of the contractors, so they were not in breach of duty to the plaintiff and were not liable.

8.2 The occupier checked that the contractor was competent

Taking on a reputable person will normally be sufficient, unless the circumstances suggest that further checks be made. A large company is better able to carry out checks than a private individual.

8.3   The occupier checked that the work was done properly

If the work done by the contractor is complex, then the occupier will be less able to check it in detail. In the example above, it would be sufficient for the occupier to check that the lifts worked.

9   Third parties

This section must be read in conjunction with the section on third parties in *Negligence – other factors,* 6.

An occupier may be liable for acts of third parties which cause injury or damage to visitors on the premises, if the occupier has control over those third parties.

Cunningham v *Reading Football Club Ltd* (1991)

During a football match between Reading and Bristol City at the defendants' ground, the visiting fans rioted. The rioters broke off lumps of concrete from the terraces and threw this at the plaintiff police officers who were on duty at the game. The plaintiffs said that violence was expected and that the defendants were in breach of their common duty of care under the OLA 1957 and were negligent at common law in not maintaining their ground. Although the violence was caused by *third parties*, i.e., the visiting fans, the defendants knew that Bristol City supporters had a 'hooligan' element and they knew from previous incidents that concrete could be broken off. A prudent occupier would have done more to minimise the risk, therefore the defendants were liable both under the OLA 1957 and in negligence.

An important factor in this decision is that similar incidents had happened before at the defendants' ground: but can football grounds, or anywhere else, be made vandal-proof? What if fans brought in crowbars to break off concrete, or had steel-capped boots to kick it and break it up?

10   Defences

The next three sections deal with the main defences to a claim under the OLA 1957 but other defences may arise in all the special cases above (5 to 9). For example, if a child of three is left to wander round a safari park and is injured, the occupier will not be liable.

11   Warnings

The Occupiers' Liability Act 1957, s. 2(4) states that:

> In determining whether the occupier of premises has discharged the common duty of care to a visitor, regard is to be had to all the circumstances, so that (for example) –
>
> (a)   where damage is caused to a visitor by a danger of which he had been warned by the occupier, the warning is not to be treated without more as absolving the occupier from liability, unless in all the circumstances it was enough to enable the visitor to be reasonably safe . . .

The occupier can give the visitor a warning about the danger, but this warning will not avoid liability unless it is enough to make the visitor reasonably safe. So it may be necessary for the warning to say what the danger is and where the danger is. The warning must be given by the occupier or an agent.

Example

'DANGER – DISUSED MINEWORKINGS' would not be sufficient if the mineworkings were hidden. Even if they were not, it might be necessary to fence them off.

12   Exclusion clauses

The Occupiers' Liability Act 1957, s. 2(1), provides that the occupier owes a common duty of care to all his visitors 'except in so far as he is free to and does extend, restrict, modify or exclude his duty to any visitor or visitors by agreement or otherwise'.

The occupier can therefore exclude or alter the duty owed to visitors to the extent that the law allows him to do so. The occupier may either have a contract with the visitor or simply put up a notice to exclude liability in tort.

A distinction is made between:

(a)   an exclusion notice by which the occupier is trying to exclude liability. Such a notice is subject to the UCTA 1977;
(b)   a warning notice by which the occupier is trying to tell the visitor of the danger. Such a notice is subject to the OLA 1957, s. 2(4)(a).

White v *Blackmore* (1972)
The plaintiff was a member of an old bangers racing club. He went to a meeting and as a competitor entered free. A notice stated 'Warning to the Public: Motor Racing is Dangerous' and excluded liability. As the plaintiff was watching a race, a car collided with the safety ropes and he was killed. The court held that the notice was an exclusion under OLA 1957, s. 2(1) and applied to spectators and as the plaintiff was a spectator the defendants were not liable.

Under the Unfair Contract Terms Act 1977 any attempt to exclude liability for death or injury resulting from negligence in the course of a *business* is void ('business liability'; (s. 2(1)); any attempt to exclude liability for other loss or damage, must be reasonable. The UCTA 1977, s. 1, defines negligence as including the common duty of care under the OLA 1957. Note, however, these restrictions do not apply to *private* occupiers who may exclude themselves from the common duty of care.

Example

If a person puts a notice on their garden gate: 'Beware of the Prickly Cacti – No Liability is Accepted for Injuries to Visitors', and an adult visitor is injured, the occupier would not be liable.

It has been argued that the OLA 1984 creates a minimum duty to trespassers, which should not be excluded and if liability to visitors could be excluded under the OLA 1957, they would be in a worse position than trespassers!

The effectiveness of an exclusion clause depends in part on whether the occupier has taken reasonable steps to bring it to the attention of visitors. It should be noted that the race meeting in *White* v *Blackmore* was a meeting for charity, so it may not have been covered by the term 'business liability' under the UCTA, and so liability could be excluded.

The Occupiers' Liability Act 1984, s. 2 has amended UCTA 1977, s. 1, to the effect that visitors for recreational or educational purposes are not to be treated as within 'business liability' unless this is a business purpose of the occupier.

Example

A party of law students go on a farm visit. This would not be regarded as within 'business liability' and the farmer could exclude liability. Would the situation be any different if the farm charged an entrance fee and organised such trips as part of the business?

13   Consent

An occupier is not liable to a visitor for risks which the visitor willingly accepts (OLA 1957, s. 2(5)).

Simms v *Leigh RFC Ltd* (1969)
The plaintiff, a professional rugby league player, was thrown against a concrete wall surrounding the pitch in the course of a game. It was held that the ground met league standards and the plaintiff had accepted the risks.

14   Contributory negligence

The OLA 1957, s. 2(3), provides that in determining the common duty of care 'the degree of care, and want of care, which would ordinarily be looked for in such a visitor' is taken into account. Even if the occupier is in breach of the common duty of care, the visitor may be partly to blame and damages will be reduced accordingly under the Law Reform (Contributory Negligence) Act 1945.

15   Liability to trespassers

15.1   Introduction

The OLA 1957 does *not* apply to trespassers. Originally at common law no duty was owed to trespassers as long as the occupier did not deliberately injure them. Gradually the courts developed the idea of the 'implied' visitor, to give trespassers some protection.

British Railways Board v *Herrington* (1972)
A six-year-old boy climbed through a hole in a fence, trespassed on a railway line and was badly burned by an electrified rail. Many people used this as a short cut and as it was near

a station the station-master knew about it. The House of Lords held that in all the circumstances the defendants were under a duty of common *humanity* to see that trespassers were safe.

This common law duty covers injury to people and damage to their property.

15.2   To whom does the OLA 1984 apply?

The OLA 1984 determines whether any duty is owed to those other than visitors for *injury* 'by reason of any damage due to the state of the premises or to things done or omitted to be done on them' (s. 1(1)(a)). It defines injury as including death, injury, disease or mental condition.

The Act applies to:

(a)   trespassers;
(b)   anyone exercising rights under the National Parks and Access to the Countryside Act 1949;
(c)   anyone exercising a private right of way, for example, through a neighbour's garden.

The OLA 1984 has a wider scope than just trespassers, but they will be the main category of claimants.

The OLA 1984 does not apply to anyone using a public right of way, so the common law rules apply to them.

15.3   When is a duty owed?

The OLA 1984, s. 1(3), provides that the occupier owes a duty if:

(a)   he is aware of the danger or has reasonable grounds to believe that it exists;
(b)   he knows or has reasonable grounds to believe that the other is in the vicinity of the danger concerned or that he may come into the vicinity of the danger;
(c)   the risk is one against which, in all the circumstances of the case, he may reasonably be expected to offer the other some protection.

To owe a duty, the occupier must:

(a)   know of the danger (or ought to know);
(b)   know someone is near (or ought to know);
(c)   know the type or extent of risk which requires protection.

Example

If someone lives next to a school and they know that children climb over their garden fence to steal apples, will they be liable if (a) a child falls out of the apple tree; (b) a child drowns in an ornamental pond?

White v *St Albans City Council* **(1990)**
The plaintiff fell into a 12-foot-deep trench on fenced off council property, while taking a
short cut. The plaintiff argued that because the council had fenced off the area they believed
that someone would be near the danger. The court held that although the fence was flimsy,
there was no evidence that people used this as a short cut, therefore the council was not
liable.

15.4   What does the duty cover?

If it is decided that the occupier does owe a duty, then s. 1(4) provides that 'the duty is to
take such care as is reasonable in all the circumstances of the case to see he does not suffer
injury on the premises by reason of the danger concerned'. The occupier is only liable for
personal injury, not for damage to *property*.

In determining whether or not the occupier has taken reasonable care, a number of factors
will be taken into account, such as the nature of the entry (e.g., accidental or deliberate),
the type of premises, nature of the risk, cost of precautions, age of the person, and the
likelihood of people entering.

15.5   Can the occupier avoid liability with a warning?

The Occupiers' Liability Act 1984, s. 1(5), provides that:

> Any duty owed . . . may in an appropriate case, be discharged by taking such steps as
> are reasonable in all the circumstances . . . of the case to give warning of the danger
> concerned or to discourage persons from incurring the risk.

The occupier can fulfill the duty owed by giving a warning. This may not be enough for
children, however, and the nature of the danger must be taken into account.

Example

Parts of the London to Glasgow railway line run through urban areas. Is it sufficient for
British Rail to put up a rope fence with notices saying: 'Danger – Keep Away'?

15.6   Can someone consent to the risk?

The OLA 1984, s. 1(6), provides that no duty is owed for risks 'willingly accepted'. In
deciding this the normal principles for consent are taken into account, e.g., knowledge of
the risk is not necessarily consent to it.

15.7   Can the occupier exclude liability?

The OLA 1984 does not provide for exclusion of liability. The UCTA 1977 does not apply
to the OLA 1984. It has been argued that the duty imposed by the OLA 1984 is a minimum
duty and as a matter of public policy should not be excluded, but this point has not been
decided.

15.8 What if a trespasser is not within the OLA 1984?

Someone may not be owed a duty under the Act, for example, if the occupier does not know or have reasonable grounds to believe that a danger exists. In such a case the trespasser would have to rely on the common law duty under *British Railways Board* v *Herrington.*

NUISANCE

1 Introduction

There are two types of nuisance, *private nuisance* and *public nuisance. Private nuisance* protects a person's interests in land, both its physical state and the use of it and if someone interferes with these, the owner can sue in tort. *Public nuisance* protects certain public rights which a person has, for example, a right to walk along a public street, which are not connected with ownership of land. If someone commits a public nuisance, they can be prosecuted, as it is a criminal offence. If, as a result of a public nuisance, a person suffers particular damage, which is more than other people would have suffered, they may have a civil claim in tort.

Private nuisance will be looked at first, followed by public nuisance. There is a certain overlap between nuisance and other torts like trespass, negligence and *Rylands* v *Fletcher* and a close relationship with occupiers' liability. In some cases it does not matter if a claim is brought in nuisance or negligence; e.g., *Bolton* v *Stone* (the case concerning a cricket ball). Claims in nuisance will normally be pursued in the county courts.

2 Private nuisance

2.1 Introduction

This may be defined as an unlawful act, indirectly causing physical injury to land, *or* substantially interfering with enjoyment *or* interests in land, and which is unreasonable in all the circumstances.

Examples

Roof tiles pitted by acid fumes from a factory.
Tree branches growing from adjacent property.
Noise from a neighbour's burglar alarm.
Blocking a private right of way over land.

Nuisance is not actionable *per se* (in itself) and *actual damage* must be proved. The exception is interference with easements, profits and natural rights, when damage will be presumed; e.g., right of support, right of way or right to take water.

The law distinguishes between *physical damage* to land and *interference with the enjoyment* of land.

2.2   Physical damage

The plaintiff must prove a sensible material injury.

St Helen's Smelting Company v Tipping (1865)
The plaintiff lived in a manufacturing area. Fumes from the defendants' smelting works damaged shrubs on the plaintiff's land. The court held that as the plaintiff had proved physical damage to the plants, the locality was not relevant and the defendants were liable.

A plaintiff may also recover compensation if the only damage suffered is to *goods* on the premises. Thus, in *Halsey* v *Esso* (1961) the plaintiff recovered for damage to washing on a line.

2.3   Interference with enjoyment

It is fairly straightforward to prove physical damage, but interference with enjoyment is a more elusive right.

2.3.1   Interests protected.   The law only protects certain 'interests'. There are some well established ones like noise (*Leeman* v *Montague* (1936), crowing of a cock), smoke, smells, dust, fumes; and newer interests, such as those in the following cases.

Thompson-Schwab v Costaki (1956)
The plaintiffs lived next door to the defendants who used their house for prostitution. It was held that, taking into account that it was a residential street, it could be a nuisance and an interlocutory injunction was granted to stop this use pending trial.

This was followed in a later case.

Laws v Florinplace (1981)
The defendants wished to open a sex shop in a residential area. It was held that an injunction would be granted because of the danger to local residents of 'perverts'.

New interests will be recognised from time to time. One attempt to establish a novel interest was in the following case.

Bridlington Relay v Yorkshire Electricity Board (1965)
The plaintiff operated a television service and put up a high mast. The defendants' power line interfered with the signal for BBC programmes. It was held that receiving television for recreational purposes, free from interference, was not such an important part of the ordinary enjoyment of property that interference would be a nuisance. The plaintiff's claim was dismissed.

More recently the Canadian courts have accepted that interference with television reception was a nuisance (*Nor Video Services* v *Ontario Hydro* (1978)).

2.3.2   Balance of interests.   Under interference with enjoyment, the law tries to balance two conflicting interests, i.e., the right of the *occupier* to use land as he wishes *and* the right of his *neighbour*, who does not want his own use interfered with. Most activities which cause a nuisance under this head are perfectly lawful in themselves but only become unlawful if done unreasonably.

The interference must be substantial and the standard is measured by an ordinary person, not the plaintiff. In *Walter* v *Selfe* (1851), Knight-Bruce V-C said that such interference must be:

> . . . an inconvenience materially interfering with the ordinary comfort physically of human existence, not merely according to elegant or dainty modes and habits of living, but according to plain and sober and simple notions among the English people.

2.4   Unreasonableness

The test is: what is reasonable according to the ordinary uses of mankind living in society. This applies to both physical damage and interference with enjoyment but physical damage will usually mean that the defendant is liable and the balancing exercise is largely irrelevant apart from sensitivity. In deciding what is reasonable in this context, the courts will examine the following factors.

2.4.1   Locality.   If the claim is based on interference with enjoyment, then locality is taken into account.

Sturges v Bridgman (1879)

The plaintiff was a doctor who lived and practised in an area which had many other doctors. The plaintiff was disturbed by noise from the defendant's biscuit factory. The court held that taking into account that the area was one of medical specialists, this was a nuisance. Thesiger LJ said that 'what would be a nuisance in Belgrave Square would not necessarily be so in Bermondsey'.

This means that someone living in a poor or predominantly industrial area cannot expect the same standards as someone living in a residential area. However, if the disturbance is greater than normal standards they would have a claim. The character of an area can change, however, so where the local authority gave planning permission to change a naval docks to a commercial port, noise from heavy lorries was not a nuisance (*Gillingham Borough Council* v *Medway Dock Co.* (1992)).

As has been noted above, locality is not relevant in the case of physical damage (see 2.2 above).

2.4.2   Abnormal sensitivity.   If a person or their property is abnormally sensitive, they cannot complain about something which would not have affected an ordinary person or ordinary property.

Robinson v Kilvert (1889)

Heat from the defendants' manufacturing damaged sensitive brown paper belonging to the plaintiff on the floor above. The heat would not have damaged ordinary paper. It was held that the defendant was not liable.

The same principle applies to enjoyment of land.

Heath v *Mayor of Brighton* (1908)
The defendant's electricity sub-station was next to a church. The vicar complained about the 'buzzing noise'. The court held that as no one else had complained this did not amount to a nuisance.

If the plaintiff does establish a nuisance or that the defendant's act would have interfered with the ordinary use of land, then the plaintiff can claim for sensitive matters. In *McKinnon Industries* v *Walker* (1951) the plaintiff was able to recover for damage to delicate plants (orchids) after establishing nuisance. In *Bridlington Relay* v *Yorkshire Electricity Board*, above, the court said that the plaintiff could not succeed if an ordinary aerial could not get a picture.

2.4.3 Duration of the interference. This is relevant in deciding whether or not the interference was substantial. If the interference is for a short time, this may be evidence that it is reasonable.

Example

Repair work on a building

Some temporary interference may be a nuisance. An example of this is *Andreae* v *Selfridge* (1938) where it was held that noise and dust from demolition work could have been prevented and loss of one night's sleep was a nuisance.

Midwood v *Manchester Corporation* (1905)
Gas accumulated in the defendant's mains and set fire to the plaintiff's premises. It was held that this was a nuisance because the defendant was responsible for a 'state of affairs', i.e., the gas building up.

Permanent interference will usually be evidence of a nuisance.

Castle v *St Augustine's Golf Club* (1922)
The plaintiff was driving along the road and was blinded when a golf ball struck the windscreen. It was held that the defendants were liable for permitting a 'state of affairs' on their land from which damage was likely. The state of affairs was the positioning of the hole.

2.4.4 Public benefit. This is one factor to be considered in deciding whether or not the defendant's acts are unreasonable: the greater the public benefit, the more likely the acts are to be reasonable.

2.4.5 Malice. If the 'interest' is one which is not protected by nuisance, the fact that the defendant acts maliciously will not make the act a nuisance. The standard example of this is to be found in the following case.

Mayor of Bradford v *Pickles* (1895)
The defendant wanted the plaintiff to buy the defendant's land and to this end the defendant obstructed water percolating through the land, to stop it going into the plaintiff's reservoir.

It was held that as the plaintiff had no right to receive this water, the defendant acting maliciously did not make it a nuisance.

Malice may be relevant in deciding if the defendant has acted reasonably.

Hollywood Silver Fox Farm v *Emmett* (1936)
The defendant deliberately fired a shot gun to frighten the plaintiff's mink next door and stop them breeding. The court held that even though mink are sensitive to noise, the defendant was not acting reasonably and the defendant was liable. Had the defendant merely been shooting rabbits, this would probably not have been a nuisance.

2.4.6 Negligence. The fact that the occupier has not acted negligently does not mean that the use of land was reasonable.

Example

If someone operates stables in a residential area, they may run them without being negligent but this could still be a nuisance.

If the plaintiff can establish negligence, however, this may show that use is unreasonable.

2.4.7 Natural condition of the land. The common law rule was that an occupier was *not* under a duty to abate a nuisance that arose on his land from natural causes. This rule has been modified.

Goldman v *Hargrave* (1967)
A 100 foot high tree on the defendant's land was struck by lightning and caught fire. The defendant had the tree cut down and chopped up but it was left to burn itself out. The fire spread to the plaintiff's land. The court held that, as the defendant knew about the hazard, could foresee the fire might spread and could easily have put it out, then the defendant was liable. This case is really based on negligence.

Leakey v *National Trust* (1980)
The plaintiff owned a house at the bottom of the defendants' steep hill. Natural subsidence caused soil and rock to move and threatened the plaintiff's house. The defendants said that they did not have to do anything about it because it was a natural occurrence. The Court of Appeal held that the defendants' duty, if they knew or ought to have known of the risk, was to do what was reasonable to prevent or minimise that risk. In deciding what is reasonable the courts impose a subjective standard, i.e., what that particular person can do. Factors taken into account include the money needed, physical abilities, resources available and the plaintiff's duty to protect himself. Megaw LJ said that:

> If, as a result of the working of the forces of nature, there is poised above my land, or above my house, a boulder or a rotten tree, which is liable to fall at any moment of the day or night, perhaps destroying my house, and perhaps killing or injuring me or members of my family, am I without remedy?

The courts have therefore imposed a positive duty to act in such circumstances.

2.5   Who can sue?

Private nuisance protects a person's interest in land. Traditionally the plaintiff must have such an interest to be able to sue. An owner in possession can sue; a tenant can sue; and a landlord can sue for permanent damage. Someone who cannot show a right of ownership or possession has no right to sue in nuisance.

Malone v Laskey (1907)
Mr M was the tenant of the defendant's house. Mrs M was injured when a lavatory cistern fell on her as a result of vibrations from the defendant's premises next door. Mrs M sued for nuisance. It was held that her claim failed as she had no interest in the land.

However, the rule that a person must have an *interest* in land has been changed by the following recent decision.

Khorasandjian v Bush (1993)
The plaintiff lived with her parents. When she left her boyfriend (the defendant), he began to pester her by following her, assaulting her and continually telephoning her. The defendant was sent to prison for a short time but continued this behaviour on his release. The plaintiff obtained an injunction to stop the defendant 'harassing, pestering or communicating with' her. The defendant appealed saying there was no such tort. The Court of Appeal said that (a) persistent telephone calls were a private nuisance and (b) the plaintiff could sue, even though she had no proprietary interest in her parents' house. Dillon LJ said:

> To my mind, it is ridiculous if in this present age the law is that the making of deliberately harassing and pestering telephone calls to a person is only actionable in the civil courts if the recipient of the calls happens to have the freehold or a leasehold proprietary interest in the premises.

Peter Gibson J, dissenting, pointed out that this was a major change in the law.

The court in the above case has taken account of changing social conditions since 1907 and the changed nature of property rights to recognise the plaintiff's rights as an occupier.

2.6   Who can be sued?

A person is liable if they bear some degree of responsibility. There are three possible defendants and there may be joint liability:

(a)   the creator of the nuisance;
(b)   the present occupier of the land;
(c)   the landlord.

2.6.1   Creator.   Anyone who creates a nuisance by a positive act is liable. The creator remains liable, even if no longer in occupation.

2.6.2   Occupier.   The occupier is liable for nuisances created by the occupier and for others, namely:

(a) those whom the occupier controls;
(b) independent contractors when the duties are non-delegable;
(c) previous owners;
(d) trespassers;
(e) acts of nature.

(a) *Those whom the occupier controls.* The occupier is liable for acts of employees and visitors.
(b) *Independent contractors.* Normally someone is not liable for acts of independent contractors; but if a duty which should not be delegated is delegated, the person remains liable. So if a nuisance is inevitable by the very act of doing the work, the employer of the contractor remains liable.
(c) *Previous owners.* The new owners will only be liable if they know or ought to know about the nuisance and adopt or continue it.
(d) *Trespassers.* The occupiers are not liable for a nuisance created by a trespasser unless they adopt or continue it.

Sedleigh-Denfield v *O'Callaghan* (1940)
The defendants owned an open ditch which ran along the plaintiff's land. Without the defendants' permission the local authority trespassed and laid a pipe in the ditch, but forgot to put a grid over the end of it. The pipe became blocked and the plaintiff's land was flooded. It was held that the defendants were liable, they knew about the pipe and used it to take water from their own land. The court said that someone *continues* the nuisance if they know about it but do not end it; and *adopt* it if they make use of it.

The occupier will only be liable if it was something that the occupier could stop.

Page Motors v *Epsom Borough Council* (1982)
Gypsies camped without permission on the defendant's land, which was next to the plaintiffs' garage. Because of the behaviour of the gypsies the plaintiffs lost business. It was held that the local authority was liable, as it could have found another site for gypsies.

(e) *Acts of nature.* If the nuisance is hidden (latent), the occupier is not liable. If the occupier knows of the danger then the considerations from *Leakey* v *National Trust* apply; see 2.4.7 above.

2.6.3 *The landlord.* The general rule is that a landlord who has parted with possession of the land is *not* liable for nuisances arising. The landlord will be liable, however, if: (i) he authorised it; (ii) the nuisance started before the land was let; and (iii) the landlord has a duty to repair (*Wringe* v *Cohen* (1940)).

If the tenant is using the premises for the normal purposes for which they were let, and this causes a nuisance, the landlord is liable.

Tetley v *Chitty* (1986)
The local authority let land to be used for go-karting. Neighbours brought an action because of the noise. It was held that as the noise was a necessary consequence of letting the land for go-karting, then the local authority was liable.

2.7 Possible defences

2.7.1 Prescription. If someone carries on a private nuisance for 20 years, this will give them a legal right to commit the nuisance by prescription. The defendant must show that the interference was a *nuisance* for 20 years, not simply that the defendant did the act for 20 years. This can be seen from the following case.

Sturges v Bridgman (1879)
The defendant confectioner had been in business for over 20 years. The plaintiff doctor lived next door and built consulting rooms and then complained about the noise. The defendant claimed a prescriptive right to make noise. The court held that the noise had only been a nuisance from the time the consulting rooms were built, so the defendant failed to establish this right. It is to be noted that to claim a right by prescription, the act must not be done forcibly, secretly or with permission.

2.7.2 Statutory authority. If a statute authorises the defendant's activity, the defendant will not be liable for any nuisance which is an inevitable result. The test is: could the nuisance have been avoided by the exercise of reasonable care?

Allen v Gulf Oil (1981)
An Act of Parliament gave the defendants power to buy land and build a refinery but said nothing about operating it! The plaintiff alleged nuisance through smell, noise, vibrations etc. The court held that the power to buy land for a refinery implied that the refinery could be operated. This meant a change in the environment from countryside to industrial and therefore a change in the standards applied. It was held, therefore, that this was not a nuisance.

2.7.3 Contributory negligence. If a number of people are liable, then damages can be apportioned. It is not a defence that one person's actions would not be a nuisance on their own.

2.7.4 Care and skill. It is not a defence that the defendant exercised all possible care and skill to prevent a nuisance being caused. In *Adams* v *Ursell* (1913) (see 2.7.6 below), the defendants argued unsuccessfully that they had the most modern equipment available.

2.7.5 Consent. It is no defence that the plaintiff knew about the nuisance, but chose to live by it.

Miller v Jackson (1977)
The defendants had played cricket for 70 years on the same site before houses were built nearby. The plaintiffs complained that balls were hit on to their property eight or nine times a year. It was held that it was not an excuse for the defendants that the plaintiffs had come to the nuisance. Also see *Kennaway* v *Thompson* (1980).

2.7.6 Public benefit. The argument that the defendant's activities are useful to the public is not a defence if the activities are unreasonable.

Adams v *Ursell* **(1913)**

The defendants opened a fish and chip shop in a residential street. The defendants owned the house next door and complained about the vapours like 'fog or steam' filling their house. Even though the defendants argued that they were providing a public service, it was held that their activities were a nuisance.

2.8   Remedies

The remedies briefly are damages, injunctions and abatement. They are dealt with in the last section in this chapter, entitled *Remedies*.

3   Public nuisance

Public nuisance is primarily a *crime* and will only be a tort if the plaintiff suffers damage over and above the public generally. It was defined by Romer LJ in *Attorney General* v *PYA Quarries* (1957) as an act or omission 'which materially affects the reasonable comfort and convenience of life of a class of Her Majesty's subjects'. This could cover almost anything.

Example

Obstructing the highway, selling unfit food, being naked in public.

R v *Shorrock* **(1993)**

The defendant farmer let a field to three people for the weekend, after they told him they wanted to hold a disco to raise money for a wheelchair. The defendant was paid £2,000 and then went away for the weekend. In fact the field was used for an 'acid house party', which attracted 3,000 people and lasted 15 hours. Local residents complained about the noise and the organisers and the defendant was charged with public nuisance. The defendant was convicted and appealed, saying he did not know a public nuisance would be committed. It was held by the Court of Appeal that actual knowledge did not have to be proved. The defendant ought to have known that, in these circumstances, this would be the consequence of letting the field and he was therefore responsible for the nuisance.

3.1   Elements

(1)   The activity must affect the *public* or a *class* of the public. This requirement marks it out from private nuisance. It must be such that it is not reasonable to expect one person to take action to stop it. The question of whether a sufficient number of people have been affected to constitute a 'class' is a matter of fact. A Canadian case has held that seven families constituted a class.

(2)   The plaintiff must show that he has suffered *particular damage*, over and above the rest of the public affected. The aim is to stop everyone affected bringing claims.

Two examples of the rights protected by public nuisance are public health rights and rights on the highway.

3.2   Public health

Public health is now largely controlled by statute. The Environmental Protection Act 1990, s. 79 sets out what is needed for a statutory nuisance, e.g., smoke, fumes, dust, smell, noise etc., which is prejudicial or a nuisance. The local authority can serve an abatement notice and failure to comply with this is a criminal offence.

Any individual may make a complaint to a magistrates' court that he is aggrieved by a statutory nuisance but he must give written notice of his intention to do this to the person causing the nuisance.

The Noise and Statutory Nuisance Act 1993 provides that noise which is prejudicial to health, or a nuisance, and which is emitted from or caused by a vehicle, machinery or equipment in the street, is a statutory nuisance. It provides for the same procedure as under the Environmental Protection Act 1990. It also makes provision for the expenses of a local authority in abating the nuisance, to be paid by the owner of premises to which the nuisance relates. The 1993 Act is aimed at such things as burglar and car alarms.

It is, however, still possible to prove a common law nuisance in the area of public health. To establish a common law nuisance it is not necessary to show damage to health.

Halsey v Esso Ltd (1961)
The plaintiff owned a house in Fulham opposite the defendants' depot. The plaintiff complained about:

    (a)   acid smuts damaging washing on the line;
    (b)   smuts damaging the plaintiff's car on the road;
    (c)   the smell of oil;
    (d)   noise from the boilers;
    (e)   noise from lorries in the depot;
    (f)   noise from lorries going into the depot.

It was held that (b) and (f) were public nuisances and that the others were private nuisances. The court said that in an urban area everyone had to put up with some discomfort, but operations at night were particularly significant, as most people were in bed.

3.3   The highway

Obstructing the highway is also a separate criminal offence apart from being a public nuisance. If the obstruction is temporary, it may not be a nuisance if the defendant's use was reasonable.

Trevett v Lee (1955)
The defendant lived on a quiet country road and during droughts put a hose across the road to get water. During the day the plaintiff tripped over the hose. It was held that the defendant's use of the road was reasonable and this was not a public nuisance.

However, in *Lyons v Gulliver* (1914) the defendants' theatre queues obstructed the plaintiffs' coffee shop and this was held to be a nuisance.

Other elements like causation may also be relevant to a claim.

Dymond v Pearce (1972)

The defendant parked his lorry overnight on a dual carriageway. The lorry had lights on and was parked under street lights. The plaintiff was a pillion rider on a motorcycle, which collided with the lorry. It was held that although the lorry was a public nuisance because it had been parked in that position for the defendant's convenience, it was not the cause of the accident. That was the fault of the motorcyclist who was not looking. Therefore the defendant was not liable.

Occupiers who live next to the highway are responsible for the repair of their premises.

Tarry v Ashton (1876)

A loose lamp on the defendant's premises projected over the highway. It fell on the plaintiff. The court held that the defendant was liable, even though the lamp had been put up by an independent contractor.

4   Differences between public and private nuisance

	PUBLIC NUISANCE	PRIVATE NUISANCE
1	a crime and a civil matter	civil matter only
2	affects public (class)	may affect one person
3	personal injury	does not include personal injury
4	no prescription	may acquire right after 20 years
5	'particular damage' must be shown above the public norm	no need to show 'particular damage' if physical damage or interference with enjoyment

RYLANDS v FLETCHER

1   Introduction

Many torts are based on the principle of *fault*, so that a person will only be liable if they are at fault in some way. For example, a motorist who causes an accident by driving too fast will be liable in negligence. Sometimes the law of tort will make a person liable, even though they are not at fault and this is known as *strict liability*. Strict liability may be imposed if the person acting is doing something hazardous or may be imposed for policy reasons, to ensure that someone is made liable. *Rylands* v *Fletcher* is an example of strict liability, for things escaping from land and causing damage. The tort takes its name from the case which first imposed liability for such damage. It overlaps with *nuisance* and an example of this can be seen in *Halsey* v *Esso* (see *Nuisance*, 3.2).

2   The basic principle

This is best explained by examining the case.

Rylands v Fletcher (1866)

The defendants engaged an independent contractor to build a reservoir on the defendants' land. When the reservoir was filled, water seeped through some old mine shafts and flooded the plaintiff's mine. The defendants did not know about the mine shafts and were not negligent themselves. The House of Lords held that, nonetheless, the defendants were liable. At first instance Blackburn J set out the rule:

> the person who for his own purposes brings on his land and collects and keeps there anything likely to do mischief if it escapes, must keep it in at his peril and, if he does not do so, is prima facie answerable for all the damage which is the natural consequence of its escape.

The court also said that the defendant's use of land must be *non-natural*.

3   Requirements

For the rule in *Rylands* v *Fletcher* to apply, the following requirements must be met:

(a)   the thing must cause damage;
(b)   the damage must be reasonably foreseeable;
(c)   the thing must be something dangerous;
(d)   it must be brought on to the defendant's land;
(e)   it must be a non-natural use of land;
(f)   there must be an escape.

3.1   The thing must cause damage

This tort is not actionable *per se* (in itself) and plaintiffs must show that they have suffered damage.

3.2   The damage must be reasonably foreseeable

A defendant will only be strictly liable for the escape of things likely to do mischief, if the defendant knew, or ought to have reasonably foreseen, that damage might be caused if they escaped.

Cambridge Water Company Ltd v Eastern Counties Leather plc (1993)

The defendants used a solvent in their tanning process which spilled on to the concrete floor. This happened before 1971, when working methods were changed. Eventually this solvent seeped through the floor into the ground and reached the plaintiffs' borehole, over a mile away, which was used to take water for domestic use. In 1983 tests revealed that the presence of the solvent meant the water did not meet the quality standards of a European Council directive. The plaintiffs claimed damages in negligence, nuisance and *Rylands* v

Fletcher. The Court of Appeal held that the defendants were strictly liable and awarded the plaintiffs £1 million damages. In reversing this decision, the House of Lords said that for liability to arise under *Rylands* v *Fletcher*, it must be shown that the defendant knew or should have foreseen damage would be caused. Here, when the solvent was brought on the defendants' land, nobody could have foreseen the damage which resulted. Therefore, the plaintiffs' claim in *Rylands* v *Fletcher* failed.

Speaking about the development of *Rylands* v *Fletcher* as a rule of strict liability, Lord Goff stated:

> . . . as a general rule, it is more appropriate for strict liability in respect of operations of high risk to be imposed by Parliament, than by the courts.

The effect of this requirement of foreseeability of damage is to restrict the ambit of the rule to foreseeable damage.

3.3 The thing must be something dangerous

It must be something likely to do mischief if it escapes from the land and does not necessarily have to be something which is inherently dangerous, like a tiger. In *Rylands* v *Fletcher* it was water which, although not necessarily dangerous, was dangerous in such quantities. The thing must also be accumulated on the land. The rule has, for example, been applied to gas, electricity, explosives, trees and even gypsies!

3.4 It must be brought on to the defendant's land

It must be something which the defendant brings on to the land or accumulates there, like water from a river. It does not apply to things naturally on the land, for example, thistles but would apply to something planted on the land.

3.5 It must be non-natural use of land

This means a use which is not an ordinary use of land. If the defendant is using land for a normal or usual purpose, the rule does not apply, for example, the escape of water after a tap was left running.

In deciding if use is *non-natural* the courts will take a number of factors into account, including the harm that might be caused by escape, the social value of the defendant's activity, the precautions taken and the practices of society. This concept of *non-natural use* can be used to restrict or expand liability under *Rylands* v *Fletcher*. For example, electricity used for domestic purposes would be natural use but not if stored in commercial quantities. Making munitions in wartime is a natural use.

3.6 There must be an escape

There must be an escape from the defendant's land, otherwise there will be no liability under *Rylands* v *Fletcher*.

Read v *Lyons* (1947)

The plaintiff munitions inspector was injured by an exploding shell while on the defendant's premises. It was held that the defendants were not liable under *Rylands* v *Fletcher*, as there had been no escape.

The defendant does not need to own the land from which the 'thing' escapes.

4   Type of damage

A plaintiff may recover damages for injury to goods or land. There are conflicting cases as regards claims for *personal injuries* but the Court of Appeal has allowed such a claim.

Hale v *Jennings Brothers* (1938)

The defendant's 'chair-o-plane' escaped at a fairground and injured a stallholder. It was held that she could claim for personal injury under *Rylands* v *Fletcher*.

5   Defences

5.1   Act of God

This is a natural event which the defendant could not be expected to have anticipated and is very limited in its scope.

5.2   Act of a stranger

The defendant will have a good defence if it can be shown that the escape was due to the unlawful act of a third party, over whom there was no control.

Rickards v *Lothian* (1913)

The defendant had the lease of business premises and the plaintiff occupied the second floor. Late one night a stranger turned on a tap in a cloakroom on the fourth floor and blocked the overflow. Water damaged the plaintiff's goods. It was held that the defendant had a good defence to a claim under *Rylands* v *Fletcher*.

However, if the act of the third party is one which the defendant should have foreseen, it will not be a defence. In *Hale* v *Jennings* a passenger had tampered with the 'chair-o-plane' but the owner should have guarded against this.

5.3   Plaintiff's fault

If the escape is due to the plaintiff's actions, the defendant is not liable.

5.4   Consent of the plaintiff

If the plaintiff consents to the 'thing' on the defendant's land, the defendant is not liable. Common benefit is evidence of consent, for example, a sprinkler system in a building shared by several occupiers.

5.5   Statutory authority

Some statutes provide a good defence to a claim under *Rylands* v *Fletcher*. The same principles apply as in nuisance.

VICARIOUS LIABILITY

1   Introduction

The word vicarious means 'on behalf of' and vicarious liability means that one person may be made liable for torts committed by another. Vicarious liability is *not* a tort in itself. As a general rule one person is not liable for torts committed by another, but examples of when this will happen are employers being liable for torts of employees, and a principal being liable for torts of an agent. In fact there is joint liability, as the person committing the tort is also liable.

It may seem curious that one person should be made liable for another's actions but there are a number of reasons why this should be so. First, the employer is in the best position to pay damages through insurance. Secondly it improves standards, because the employer will aim to ensure that employees do not commit any torts. Thirdly, it is the employer who benefits from the work which is causing the damage and so he should pay for losses. Fourthly, the employer is able to pass the cost on to customers, whereas the victim cannot do this. Fifthly, it provides a clearly identifiable person to sue, i.e., the employer, in situations where it could be difficult to identify exactly which employee was responsible. In effect the employer will be made liable, even though the employer is not at fault, so it is an example of strict liability.

This section will look at the differences between employees and independent contractors and the vexed question of when is the employee acting in the course of employment. As more people become self employed this makes them liable for their own torts and they also lose many other rights.

2   Vicarious liability of employers

Three questions must be answered affirmatively to establish that the employer is vicariously liable for an act of someone else.

   (1)   Was it a tort?
   (2)   Was it committed by an employee?
   (3)   Was it in the 'course of employment'?

These three questions will be looked at in the following sections.

2.1   Was it a tort?

An employer may only be vicariously liable if the employee has committed a tort. The usual torts for which the employer will be vicariously liable are negligence, trespass, fraud and deceit.

2.2   Was it committed by an employee?

The distinction between employees and independent contractors is important and needs to be considered because an employer is vicariously liable for the torts of employees but *not* those of independent contractors.

Example

An employer would be liable for the negligent driving of a chauffeur but not a taxi-driver.

An employee is said to work under a *contract of service* and an independent contractor under a *contract for services*. The courts have developed a number of tests to help them decide whether or not someone is an employee or an independent contractor.

2.2.1   The control test.   This test was developed in the nineteenth century and consists of determining whether the employer tells the person *what* to do and *how* to do it. Today many people have a skill and it is less likely that the employer will be able to tell them how to do their job. The test is now probably only useful in relation to unskilled workers. In fact the basis of the control test was about the employer having the *right* to tell a person what to do.

2.2.2   The organisation test.   Here the question is whether a person is an *integral part* of the business. This test was used in *Cassidy v Minister of Health* (1951) to decide that even though the hospital did not tell the surgeon how to do his job, the surgeon was an integral part of the organisation. Therefore the hospital was liable for his negligence.

2.2.3   The multiple test.   In this case the court may take a number of matters into account:

   (a)   method of payment: if a regular wage is received, the recipient is likely to be an employee;
   (b)   deduction of tax: if tax is deducted, the person from whom it is deducted is likely to be an employee;
   (c)   provision of tools: these are likely to be provided to an employee;
   (d)   hours: persons who work set hours are likely to be employees;
   (e)   business risks: someone who assumes them is likely to be independent;
   (f)   place of work: an employee is likely to work in one place only;
   (g)   dismissal: an employee can be dismissed;
   (h)   description by parties: are they customarily described as employee or independent?
   (i)   mutuality of obligation: if this exists, the person in question is likely to be an employee.

The above conclusions are only presumptions and may be changed. No single factor is conclusive, the court has to look at *all the circumstances* to make a decision on balance.

Ready Mixed Concrete v Minister of Pensions and National Insurance (1968)

The Government introduced a payroll tax and the plaintiffs dismissed all their drivers and took them on again as independent contractors. The new terms provided that drivers bought lorries on hire purchase; drivers were responsible for insurance and maintenance; they were paid per delivery (with the consequent risk of no deliveries); lorries were to be in company colours; drivers were to wear uniform; and they had to be available when required. It was held that these factors pointed to the drivers being independent contractors, especially ownership of the lorries and the risk of loss.

A number of cases in recent years have stressed the importance of 'mutuality of obligation'.

Nethermere v *Taverna & Gardiner* (1984)

N took on T and G as homeworkers making trousers. T and G worked when they needed to, took holidays when they wanted, refused work when they wanted, submitted time sheets, were paid at the same rates as full time workers; the machines were provided by N; and T and G worked for over one year. It was held that the regular giving and taking of work over a continuous period established obligations on both parties, i.e., the obligation for N to give and for T and G to take work. Therefore they were employees.

A different result occurred in the following case.

O'Kelly v *Trusthouse Forte* (1984)

Casual waiters worked regularly for THF and could refuse work but did not. It was held that such an arrangement lacked mutuality of obligation and they were not employees.

If an employer 'lends' an employee to someone else, who will be vicariously liable if the employee commits a tort? The presumption is that the first employer remains liable. The burden is on the first employer to show that liability has passed to the new employer.

Mersey Docks and Harbour Board v *Coggins & Griffith (Liverpool) Ltd* (1946)

MDHB hired out a crane and driver to the defendants. While unloading a ship the driver negligently injured someone. Who was liable for the driver's negligence? The agreement provided that the driver was the defendants' employee, the defendants could tell the driver what to do, but the plaintiffs were responsible for pay and could dismiss. The driver's evidence did not help the court as he stated that: 'I take no orders from anybody'. It was held that the driver was still the employee of the plaintiffs.

It will be more difficult to show that liability has shifted if complex machinery is also lent.

It has been argued that the idea of a contract of service is now too rigid and should be replaced by the more flexible concept of the 'employment relationship' (Hepple, 'Restructuring Employment Rights', *Industrial Law Journal*, Vol. 15, 1986, p. 69 (at p. 74)).

2.3   Was it in the course of employment?

The employer is only vicariously liable if the employee commits the tort in the course of employment. Apart from being vicariously liable, the employer may be liable for authorising or ratifying a tort.

The test to decide if the employee is acting in the course of employment is (1) is there a wrongful act which is authorised by the employer or (2) is it a wrongful and unauthorised way of doing an authorised act?

2.3.1 Negligent acts. Just because the employee does the act in a negligent or unauthorised way does not mean that the employer is not liable.

Century Insurance v Northern Ireland Road Transport Board (1942)

The defendant's employee was a petrol tanker driver. While delivering petrol to a garage the driver lit a cigarette and caused an explosion, damaging the plaintiff's property. It was held that, although the driver was not authorised to smoke, this smoking occurred while delivering petrol, which was authorised. So the driver was doing an authorised act, i.e., delivering petrol in a negligent way. Therefore the employer was vicariously liable.

2.3.2 Acts connected with the job. If the employee does something connected with the work, is the employer liable?

Poland v Parr (1926)

H was employed by the defendants. H was going home for lunch and saw a boy about to steal sugar from the defendants' lorry which was passing. H hit the boy who fell under the wheels and had to have a leg amputated. It was held by the court that there is a class of acts which an employee is authorised to do in an emergency. If the employee does more than the emergency requires, that may take the act out of that class. Atkin LJ gave the example that if the employee had shot the boy, that would have been out of the class of allowed acts! The employee was protecting the employer's property and the employer was vicariously liable.

The employee may do something outside the class.

Warren v Henlys Ltd (1948)

The defendant's petrol attendant wrongly accused the plaintiff of trying to avoid paying. The plaintiff paid and threatened to call the police and tell the employer. The attendant then hit the plaintiff. The question was whether this act was a way of doing the job, i.e., collecting money. The court held that it was an act of 'personal vengeance' and had no connection with the discharge of the employee's duties, so the employer was not vicariously liable.

A recent example of acts not connected with the business of the employer is provided by the next case.

Makanjuola v Metropolitan Police Commissioner (1992)

The plaintiff allowed a police officer to have sexual intercourse with her, in return for not reporting her to the immigration authorities. It was held that this was not acting in the course of employment and the defendants were not vicariously liable for the tort of the police officer.

2.3.3 Express prohibition. An employer may prohibit certain conduct by employees. If the employees ignore this, can the employer avoid liability for their acts?

Example

If a notice on the employer's premises stated that: 'Employees Must Not Use the Outside Staircase When Escorting Visitors to Upper Floors', and an employee does this and a visitor slips and is injured, will the employer avoid liability?

If employers *could* avoid liability in such a case, then they could avoid being vicariously liable by providing that employees must not commit torts.

The law allows the employer to limit the *scope* of the employees' work, but a restriction on the *method* of doing it will not be effective. This can best be illustrated by comparing the bus cases.

Limpus v *London General Omnibus Co.* (1862)

The defendants told their drivers not to race or obstruct other buses. One of the defendants' drivers disobeyed this and caused an accident. Were the defendants liable? It was held that the driver was doing an authorised act (driving) in an unauthorised way (racing and obstructing). The prohibition was ineffective and the defendants were vicariously liable.

In contrast to this decision is the following case.

Beard v *London General Omnibus Co.* (1900)

A bus conductor was turning a bus round and negligently injured the plaintiff. The court held that it was not within the scope of a conductor's job to drive, therefore the defendants were not vicariously liable.

2.3.4   Unauthorised lifts.   There are a number of cases dealing with employees giving unauthorised lifts in company vehicles. A prohibition on giving lifts limits the scope of the employment.

Twine v *Beans Express Ltd* (1946)

The defendants' employee was giving the plaintiff's husband (who worked for another company), a lift in the defendants' van. Due to the negligent driving of the employee, the husband was killed. Employees had been told not to give lifts and there was also a notice in the van. It was held that by giving someone a lift, the employee was doing an unauthorised act and so was not acting in the course of employment. Therefore the defendants were not liable.

A different result was reached in the following case.

Rose v *Plenty* (1976)

The defendants told all their milkmen not to give anyone rides on milk floats and a notice was put up in the depot. One milkman paid the plaintiff, aged 13 years, to help with deliveries. The plaintiff was injured while riding on the float, due to the milkman's negligence. It was held that the prohibition did not affect the scope of the job but simply the way of doing it. The defendants were vicariously liable for the milkman's negligence.

These cases are contradictory as in *Twine* the driver was still doing what he was employed to do, i.e., drive the van. The court in *Rose* was influenced by public policy that young people should be protected. One possible distinction is that in *Rose* the boy was helping with the employer's business, whereas in *Twine* the plaintiff's husband was not.

2.3.5   Frolic of one's own.   If a driver leaves the authorised route and negligently causes an accident, is the driver still acting 'in the course of employment' ? The test was originally set out by Parke B in *Joel* v *Morrison* (1834): if the driver goes off route against instructions, but on the employer's business, the employer is liable. If the driver is on a 'frolic of his own', the employer is not liable.

A more recent example is provided by the following case.

General Engineering Services v Kingston Corpn (1988)

Firemen operating a 'go-slow' policy took 17 minutes to reach the plaintiffs' factory, instead of the usual three minutes. The factory was completely burned down. It was held that this was not just an unauthorised method of carrying out an authorised act (going to a fire); it was not doing it at all. The effect was as if they had not gone, they were on a 'frolic of their own'. Therefore the defendants were not liable.

If a driver is giving an unauthorised lift and negligently injures a third party, the employer remains liable to the third party.

2.3.6 Travelling to work. Is travelling to or from work 'in the course of employment'?

Smith v Stages (1989)

M was employed by D Ltd, as a lagger travelling round power stations. M and Stages were sent from Staffordshire to work in Wales for a short time. They were paid a day's wages both for going and returning plus travel expenses. On the way back, Stages crashed into a brick wall and M was killed. M's widow (Smith) claimed compensation against Stages and D Ltd (Stages was uninsured). Lord Goff stated:

> The fundamental principle is that an employee is acting in the course of his employment when he is doing what he is employed to do . . . or anything which is reasonably incidental to his employment.

The court held that all factors must be weighed. Here they were paid for the journey time and D Ltd were vicariously liable.

Lord Lowry made the following points:

(1)   An employee travelling from home to a regular place of work is not acting in the course of employment (unless transport is provided and the employee must use it).

(2)   Travelling in the employer's time between workplaces or in the course of a travelling job is in the course of employment.

(3)   Payment of wages for travelling, and not just travel expenses, points towards being in the course of employment.

(4)   Travelling from home to a non-regular workplace or in a travelling job or emergency, is in the course of employment.

(5)   A deviation or interruption of a journey in the course of employment will change it to being not in the course of employment.

These rules are subject to agreement to the contrary and do not apply to salaried employees.

2.4   Criminal acts

In these cases the courts take a narrower view of what 'course of employment' means.

Heasmans v *Clarity Cleaning Ltd* (1987)

The defendants' employee, an office cleaner, used the plaintiff's phone to make calls costing nearly £1,500. It was held that although cleaning the phones was part of the job, making phone calls was not an authorised way of cleaning them. It was a completely separate act and outside the course of employment. Therefore the defendants were not vicariously liable.

2.4.1 Assault. An assault by an employee will rarely be regarded as within the *course of employment* (see *Warren* v *Henlys* at 2.3.2 above). Even with 'bouncers' the employer will only be vicariously liable if the force used is reasonable.

Daniels v *Whetstone Entertainments Ltd* (1962)

The plaintiff was assaulted by the defendants' bouncer inside the hall and again outside. It was held that the defendants were not vicariously liable for the assault outside.

Can such acts really be regarded as *separate* from the job which the employee is doing?

2.4.2 Theft. If an employee steals property belonging to a third party, this may be regarded as within the course of employment.

Morris v *Martin* (1966)

The plaintiff's coat was sent to the defendants for cleaning. The employee responsible for cleaning it, stole it. It was held that this was an unauthorised way of doing the job, but was within the course of employment.

2.4.3 Fraud. The employer will be vicariously liable if the act is committed within the scope of the employee's actual or apparent authority.

Lloyd v *Grace, Smith & Co.* (1912)

The plaintiff went to the defendant solicitors to carry out a conveyancing transaction. The defendants' managing clerk tricked the plaintiff into conveying property to the clerk, who sold it and disappeared. It was held that although the clerk did not have actual authority to defraud clients, the clerk did have apparent authority to do conveyancing, so it was within the course of employment. The defendants were vicariously liable, even though they did not benefit from the clerk's acts.

2.5   The employer's indemnity

At common law the employer who is made vicariously liable for the tort of an employee, has a *right of indemnity*. This means that the employee must pay back to the employer the amount paid out by the employer. The way this works is illustrated by the following case.

Lister v *Romford Ice* (1957)

The plaintiff was employed as a driver by the defendants. The plaintiff negligently reversed a lorry into another employee (the plaintiff's father). The defendants were vicariously liable for this and paid the father compensation. They then claimed an indemnity from the plaintiff. It was held that the plaintiff owed a duty to the defendant to perform the job with reasonable care. There was an implied term in the contract to indemnify the employer, so the defendants were entitled to this amount.

As the employer and employee are jointly liable for torts, if the employer is made liable, the employer may claim a contribution from the employee under the Civil Liability (Contribution) Act 1978. In practice it is very unlikely that an employer would follow up such a claim, but it could happen if an employee did a deliberate act. Such claims, however, are best met through insurance, not by suing the impoverished employee!

2.6 Liability for independent contractors

The general rule is that an employer is *not* liable for torts committed by an independent contractor. The reason is that the employer does not control the independent contractor in the same way as he controls an employee. However, in some circumstances the employer will be regarded as owing a *primary* duty direct to the plaintiff. This is not vicarious liability but primary liability.

Example

A hospital may be primarily liable for making doctors work long hours leading to negligent mistakes, because the hospital has not taken on sufficient staff.

Exceptions to this rule that an employer is not liable.

(1)   If the employer takes on an independent contractor to commit a tort, the employer is liable.

Ellis v Sheffield Gas Consumers Co. (1853)
The defendants, without authority, employed contractors to dig up the street. The plaintiff tripped on the rubble. It was held that the defendants were liable for engaging the contractors.

(2)   Some statutes impose an absolute duty on employers. One example is the Factories Act. An independent contractor may be taken on to do work, but the employer retains liability, i.e., there is a non-delegable duty.

(3)   If the employer is negligent in choosing the contractor or interferes with the contractor's work or fails to check the work.

(4)   There are a number of common law duties which cannot be delegated;

   (a)   duty to support adjoining land;
   (b)   duty not to commit a public nuisance (see *Rogers* v *Night Riders* (1983));
   (c)   duty to see employees are safe;
   (d)   bailee for reward, that is, someone who has possession of goods for a particular purpose and is paid, for example, a jeweller who takes a watch for repair;
   (e)   very dangerous acts.

Honeywill & Stein v Larkin (1934)
The plaintiffs engaged independent contractors to take photos in a cinema, involving the use of magnesium flares. This started a fire due to the contractors' negligence. It was held that the plaintiffs were liable for the contractors.

2.7 Collateral negligence

Even with a non-delegable duty the employer is not liable for collateral negligence of an independent contractor. This is an act which is not related to carrying out the job.

Padbury v Holliday (1912)

The defendant was building a house and engaged an independent contractor to install the windows. An employee of the independent contractor left a hammer on the window sill. A gust of wind blew the window which knocked the hammer on to the plaintiff. The court held that leaving the hammer on the window sill was incidental to doing the job, so the defendant was not liable.

LIMITATION OF ACTIONS

1 Introduction

The reason for putting a time limit on bringing an action in tort is to stop defendants being made liable for an unlimited period. The effect of a limitation period is to provide a defence if the plaintiff brings a claim outside the period. If there were no time limits, there would be problems over evidence and witnesses, which cause difficulties even with time limits. Time limits, however, have also caused difficulties for plaintiffs. They may not know that they have a claim until years after the incident. They may not realise that there are time limits. This section will briefly examine the normal time limits in tort for personal injury actions and damage to property and then look at cases which have caused problems, such as latent damage.

2 Limitation of actions

2.1 General rule

The law is mainly contained in the Limitation Act 1980, as amended. The general rule is that an action in tort cannot be brought more than six years from the date when the cause of action accrued, i.e., when the right to sue arises.

An exception to this rule is a defamation action where the time limit is three years. If the tort is actionable *per se* (without proof of damage), the right of action arises at the time of the defendant's act. If the tort requires proof of damage, the right of action arises when the damage occurs. This will usually be the date of the defendant's act but may be later.

2.2 Personal injuries

If the plaintiff suffers personal injuries arising from 'negligence, nuisance or breach of duty', the normal limitation period, as set out in the Limitation Act 1980, s. 11 is:

(a)   3 years from when the cause of action accrued; or

(b)   3 years from the date of the plaintiff's knowledge of the right of action, whichever is *later*.

Section 14(1) defines the date of knowledge as when the plaintiff first had (or should have had) knowledge of the following:

(a)   that the injury was significant;
(b)   the injury was attributable wholly or partly to the act;
(c)   the identity of the defendant.

The test applied is what a reasonable man would have known; it is given a subjective element, i.e., what a person of the plaintiff's age, background, intelligence and disabilities would have known.

Examples

1   Alf is knocked down by a car as he is crossing the road at a pelican crossing in August 1994. Alf's leg is broken. Alf has until August 1997 to issue a writ.

2   Bill has been employed in a cement works since 1988. In January 1993 he started coughing up blood, but did not think anything of it. In January 1994 Bill had a medical examination and was told that his lungs were damaged, and probably had been since 1989. The limitation period is three years from January 1993, so he should issue a writ by January 1996.

For intentional acts, the Limitation Act 1980, s. 2 gives a fixed six year period from the time of the act.

Stubbings v Webb (1993)
W issued a writ in 1987, when she was 30 years old, claiming damages against S, her stepfather, for sexually abusing her up to the age of 14 years. W did not realise this abuse had caused her psychiatric problems until she consulted a psychiatrist in 1984. The House of Lords held that the Limitation Act 1980, s. 11 did not apply to intentional acts, like sexual abuse. The relevant section was s. 2, which gave a fixed period of six years, which could not be extended. W had to sue within six years of reaching 18 years old and was therefore outside the limitation period.

Under the Limitation Act 1980, s. 33 the court has a discretion, if the three year period has expired, to allow the case to continue. The court must take into account:

(a)   the reasons for the delay by the plaintiff after the period expired;
(b)   the effect of delay on the evidence;
(c)   the conduct of the defendant after the right of action arose;
(d)   the time period of any disability of the plaintiff after the cause of action accrued;
(e)   Whether the plaintiff acted promptly when he knew he had a cause of action;
(f)   What the plaintiff did to obtain expert advice and the nature of that advice.

2.3 Death

If the victim of a tort dies, there are two possible claims, which can be made independently.

(1)   Law Reform (Miscellaneous Provisions) Act 1934.
This is a claim on behalf of the deceased's estate.
(2)   Fatal Accidents Act 1976.
A claim by the deceased's dependants.

If death happens before the three year period expires, a new three year period starts. If death happens after the three year period expires the court may still extend the period.

3   Latent damage

3.1   Introduction

This means damage which is not obvious, so a person does not know about it. This has caused problems, as in the following case.

Pirelli v *Oscar Faber* (1983)

A 160 foot high chimney was built in 1969. It developed cracks in 1970 near the top, due to negligent design. These cracks were not discovered until 1977. In 1978 the plaintiff issued a writ against the defendants, the designers of the chimney. It was held that the limitation period started to run in 1970 when the cracks first appeared, therefore the writ was too late.

3.2   The Latent Damage Act 1986

The Latent Damage Act 1986 was passed to amend the Limitation Act 1980. It inserts a new s. 14A and s. 14B. These provisions do not apply to personal injuries. The position is now that:

(a)   the normal limitation period is six years from when the cause of action accrued; or
(b)   the period is three years from the starting date if this is later than the period in (a) above.

The 'starting date' is when the plaintiff knew the material facts and they would be considered sufficiently serious by a reasonable man; knew the damage was caused by the defendant's negligence; and knew the identity of the defendant.

Section 14B adds that no action shall be brought after 15 years from the date of the defendant's negligent act, i.e., a long-stop. This period is an absolute bar, so no claim may be brought after this time, even if the plaintiff has not discovered the damage. Compare this with the 10 year period under the Consumer Protection Act 1987. The effect of the Latent Damage Act 1986 was to reverse the decision in *Pirelli* v *Oscar Faber*.

Example

If damage occurs in year 1, but is not discoverable until year 5, the plaintiff has until year 8 to issue a writ.

In *Nitrigin* (1992) the plaintiffs did not discover the cause of the cracking in 1983, despite reasonable investigation, so the limitation period did not run until 1984.

4 Other relevant matters

4.1 Concealment

If the defendant has concealed relevant facts from the plaintiff or has been fraudulent, the limitation period does not start until the plaintiff has discovered the fraud or could with reasonable diligence have discovered it.

4.2 Disabilities

If the plaintiff is under 18 years old at the time that the right of action accrues, time does not run until the plaintiff reaches 18 years or dies, whichever is first.

REMEDIES

1 Introduction

This section will examine the main remedies available through the courts, i.e., damages and injunctions. It will also look very briefly at other non-judicial remedies, which basically involve some form of self help. The main remedy in an action in tort is damages, i.e., compensation in money. An injunction is also useful in particular instances such as nuisance.

2 Damages

2.1 Aim of damages

The aim of damages in tort is to put the plaintiff in the same position as though the tort had not been committed. The qualification on this is 'as far as money can do it', because physical injuries cannot always be made good. The plaintiff should not be put in a better financial position than before the tort was committed. Awards of damages are made in all types of tort action and large amounts are paid in negligence and defamation cases. A record award of damages was made in March 1994, of £3.4 million to Christine Leung, who became tetraplegic after a car accident.

2.2 Types of damages

There are a number of different types of damages.

2.2.1 Nominal damages. Nominal damages are a *small sum* of money. They will be awarded if the defendant has committed a tort but the plaintiff has not suffered loss. They can only be awarded in torts which are actionable *per se*.

Example

A person walks on to the grass in his neighbour's garden. The neighbour may sue in trespass. The damages awarded may be as low as £1.

2.2.2 Contemptuous damages.   These are a *derisory sum* to show that the court thinks that, although a right has been infringed, the claim should *not* have been brought. In such a case the court would probably refuse to award the plaintiff costs.

Example

1p damages in a libel action.

2.2.3 General damages.   The usual meaning for general damages is those damages which cannot be precisely calculated.

Example

In a personal injury action general damages will be awarded for pain.

2.2.4 Special damages.   These are damages which can be precisely calculated.

Example

The cost of medical treatment, up to the trial.
Loss of earnings up to the trial.

2.2.5 Aggravated damages.   If the tort is committed in a malicious or oppressive way or the plaintiff's feelings are particularly hurt, then the court may award aggravated damages. The aim is to give the plaintiff extra compensation to reflect the circumstances.

2.2.6 Exemplary damages.   The aim of exemplary damages is to teach the defendant a lesson. The courts recognise that exemplary damages bring an element of punishment into the law of tort and they have tried to restrict the award of such damages. In *Rookes* v *Barnard* (1964) the House of Lords said they could only be awarded in two circumstances:

(a)   Oppressive, arbitrary or unconstitutional action by servants of the Government, e.g., malicious prosecution.
(b)   Where a defendant has committed a tort deliberately and calculated that it will benefit him. The leading example of this is to be found in the following case.

Cassell & Co. Ltd v Broome (1972)

The defendants were publishing a book which contained libellous statements about the plaintiff. The defendants went ahead with publication despite knowing that another publisher had rejected it as libellous. The plaintiff was awarded £40,000 damages, including £25,000 exemplary damages. The court found that the defendants had published the book in the belief that the profits would be more than any damages awarded against them for libel. A deliberate act done for gain, without consideration of the distress caused, deserved an award of exemplary damages. Exemplary damages will not necessarily be awarded simply because a tort was committed to make a profit. They introduce an element of punishment into the law of tort.

Exemplary damages can only be awarded if they have been given in torts before *Rookes* v *Barnard* and cannot be given in negligence or public nuisance. The Court of Appeal so held in *AB* v *South West Water Services Ltd* (1993), which arose out of the accidental adding of aluminium sulphate to the water supply and the plaintiffs' claim for damages for public nuisance.

2.3   Personal injuries

A plaintiff may suffer financial or pecuniary loss and non-pecuniary loss.

2.3.1   Pecuniary loss.   This includes loss of earnings, medical expenses, travel expenses, special equipment, house-keeper, loss of pension rights.

The plaintiff is entitled to loss of earnings to the date of trial. The amount awarded is the *net* pay. In determining pay the value of other benefits is taken into account, e.g., company car.

So far as the loss of future earnings is concerned, the aim is to provide the income which would have been received by the plaintiff for the period when the plaintiff cannot earn. The court must estimate what would have happened to the plaintiff if the tort had not been committed and what will happen to the plaintiff in the plaintiff's present condition. First, the plaintiff's net annual loss of earnings is calculated, allowing for pay increases and promotion. This is known as the multiplicand. Secondly, the number of years that the loss will continue is to be calculated. This is known as the multiplier. The maximum is usually 18. It will be less than the actual number of years because the money will be invested, and also because of the 'contingencies of life' to take account of illness, redundancy etc. The aim is that at the end of the period, the whole amount of the award will be used up. A major problem is that the courts do not take inflation into account, so many plaintiffs are under compensated.

If the plaintiff's life is shortened, the plaintiff may claim for the earnings which the plaintiff would have had if his life had not been so shortened (the 'lost years'). This is to provide the income his dependents would have had if the plaintiff had stayed alive (*Pickett* v *British Rail Engineering* (1980)).

For torts committed after 1 January 1989, the Social Security Administration Act 1992 provides that certain social security benefits paid to the plaintiff must be repaid to the state directly by the defendant. The defendant must deduct the amount which the plaintiff is likely to receive in the five years after the tort. These provisions do not apply if the compensation is £2,500 or less.

The plaintiff may claim medical expenses incurred as a result of the tort. The Law Reform (Personal Injuries) Act 1948 provides that the plaintiff does not have to have treatment on the National Health Service. Thus the plaintiff is entitled to the cost of private treatment. A plaintiff who cannot look after himself may claim the cost of domestic help. If a relative gives up work to look after the plaintiff, the relative may claim loss of earnings.

2.3.2 Non-pecuniary loss. The plaintiff may suffer in other ways apart from losing money. These matters cannot be measured in terms of money but this is the only way in which the courts can provide compensation. The aim is to give 'fair' compensation. The courts operate a 'tariff' system of payments based on the seriousness of injuries.

The plaintiff may claim for pain, including future pain. Damages may be awarded for nervous shock but not grief. The plaintiff may also claim for suffering, even if no pain is experienced, as it represents the disruption to life caused by the tort. The plaintiff can also claim for loss of amenity which means the loss of the ability to enjoy life to the full.

Example

Loss of an arm is more serious to a tennis player than to a television viewer.

2.4 Property damage

The aim is to put the plaintiff in the same position as before the tort was committed. If the property is completely destroyed, then the value is assessed at that time. If the property is damaged, the plaintiff is entitled to the cost of repair.

2.5 Other relevant matters

2.5.1 Mitigation. The plaintiff who is a victim of a tort is under a duty to mitigate or reduce the damage suffered. The plaintiff need only take 'reasonable steps' to reduce the loss.

Example

Taking a lower paid job, obtaining medical treatment.

2.5.2 One action. The plaintiff may only bring one action for a tort. This may cause problems if the plaintiff is awarded damages and later develops further injuries as no other action can be taken.

2.5.3 Lump sum. The normal damages award is in the form of a lump sum. This can cause problems if the plaintiff's position gets worse. It is possible to have an award of *provisional damages* in cases where the plaintiff may develop a serious condition. When this happens, the plaintiff can apply for an increase in damages. It is also possible to have a *structured settlement*. This is an arrangement under which the plaintiff receives a lump sum of part of the damages, and the balance is invested to provide annual payments. Such an arrangement has to be agreed between the parties.

2.5.4 Taxation. The plaintiff does not have to pay tax on the amount of damages awarded.

2.6   Death

Originally at common law if the plaintiff died so did the right of action. This was changed by statute and there are now two possible claims.

2.6.1   Law Reform (Miscellaneous Provisions) Act 1934.   Under this all rights of action against or by the deceased survive. The exception is defamation. The action may be brought by the dead plaintiff's estate. Damages are assessed on the same basis as for personal injuries. No claim can be made for the 'lost years'.

2.6.2   Fatal Accidents Act 1976.   The dependants of the deceased may bring a claim for the financial loss which they will suffer. The aim is to put them in the same position as though the deceased had lived. The FAA 1976 also provides for an award of damages for 'bereavement'. This may be claimed by:

(a)   a spouse for the loss of a spouse;
(b)   parents for the loss of a child who was under 18 years and unmarried at the time of death.

The amount is fixed at £7,500 from 1 April 1991.

3   Injunctions

3.1   Introduction

An injunction is an *equitable* remedy, which means that it is in the discretion of the court whether or not to grant it. An injunction will not normally be granted where damages are adequate. The court will also take the conduct of the parties into account and whether or not a party has delayed in seeking a remedy.

3.2   Types of injunction

3.2.1   Prohibitory.   This is an order to the defendant to stop a particular tort.

Example

To order the defendant to stop emitting smoke from a factory chimney. Here damages would not be adequate.

3.2.2   Mandatory.   This is an order that the defendant does something. It will not normally be granted unless the plaintiff would suffer serious damage without it.

Example

Ordering the defendant to knock down a wall which the defendant has built on the plaintiff's land.

3.2.3   Quia timet ('because he fears').   If the plaintiff believes that the defendant is likely to commit a tort imminently, a *quia timet* injunction may be obtained to stop the defendant.

Example

If the defendant intends to trespass.

3.2.4 Interlocutory. This is an injunction issued before the trial of the action.

Example

In cases of nuisance it may be used to stop the nuisance continuing. Sometimes there is no need for a trial after it has been granted.

3.3 Use of injunctions in tort

An injunction is useful when damages are not adequate, but they will not always be granted. In *Miller* v *Jackson* (1977) the court refused an injunction against the cricket club, on the ground that the private interest of the plaintiff should be subordinate to the public interest in preserving playing fields and the game of cricket. However, in *Kennaway* v *Thompson* (1980) an injunction was granted, on conditions, restricting powerboat racing. An injunction is also used in trespass, but is of limited use in negligence.

4 Non-judicial remedies

4.1 Introduction

In these instances the plaintiff is attempting to solve the problem without going to the courts. Generally, however, such methods are not encouraged and the plaintiff must only use reasonable force and not cause unnecessary damage. It is not something to be suggested to clients.

4.2 Abatement

This is a right given to the person affected to stop the nuisance. In *Lemmon* v *Webb* (1895) the defendant's trees were overhanging the plaintiff's land, so the plaintiff had a right to stop this nuisance by cutting off the branches. He had to give them back however!

4.3 Ejectment

A person has a right to throw a trespasser off their land, provided that only reasonable force is used.

4.4 Self defence

A person may use reasonable force to protect themselves or their property. This may be used for assaults, or to protect land and goods.

4.5 Escape

If someone has been falsely imprisoned, they may make every effort to escape.

QUESTIONS

LAW OF TORT

Part A

1. What must be established to bring a successful claim for nervous shock, in the tort of negligence?

2. Explain what the 'common duty of care' means, under the Occupiers Liability Act 1957.

3. How do the courts distinguish between employees and independent contractors?

4. Explain when injunctions are used in the law of tort, using examples from cases to illustrate your answer.

Part B

5. Lauren is speeding in her new sportscar, when it goes out of control and crashes through the parapet of a bridge. The car lands on a motor-cruiser being steered along the river below by Dermot, an eccentric inventor. The cruiser is 'homemade' and because of this, disintegrates on impact and Dermot sustains injuries. Chemicals being carried on board pollute the local water supply and Kathleen becomes ill after drinking some contaminated water. Dermot and Kathleen now wish to sue Lauren. Advise them.

Outline answer

(a) Introduce your answer by explaining that the question concerns the tort of negligence. Outline the basic elements necessary for the tort. Explain that Dermot and Kathleen must establish their claims separately.

(b) Consider Dermot's claim. First, does Lauren owe a duty of care to Dermot? This involves a consideration of the factors relevant to establishing a duty. Consider whether the injury and damage were foreseeable. If Lauren drives too fast, then it is foreseeable she may go off the road and cause damage. Is there sufficient proximity? In this case there is physical impact to someone off the road, but probably close enough to it. Policy may also be relevant here, as river users are a limited class of plaintiffs.

(c)   If a duty is established, then the next question is whether Lauren has broken the duty. There are several relevant factors. The likelihood of serious injury if a car lands on a person must be considered briefly (cite *Paris* v *Stepney BC* (1951)). The likelihood of harm is more problematical, as it depends on how busy this river is. The cost of avoiding the harm is straightforward — simply to drive more slowly. Another question to be addressed is whether the type of harm is foreseeable. This requires dealing with both the injury to Dermot and the damage to the boat. If the type of harm is foreseeable, the extent of it does not need to be. Can the 'eggshell-skull' rule apply to the boat?

(d)   Next consider Kathleen's claim. Is injury to Kathleen foreseeable? It is unlikely that negligent driving would lead to this. The question of causation needs to be dealt with — did Lauren's negligent driving cause Kathleen's injury? Apply the 'but for' test — no damage would have occurred but for Lauren's negligence. The principle of remoteness is also relevant — cite *The Wagon Mound (No. 1)* (1961).

(e)   Conclude by summarising your opinion and advising both parties.

6.   David and Madelaine spent the afternoon in a pub drinking. David then suggested going up in his hot-air balloon. Because of David's erratic steering, Madelaine believed the balloon was going to crash into some houses below. She jumped out 20 feet from the ground and broke her leg. Richard was sitting in his conservatory when the balloon suddenly crashed through the roof. Richard was so shocked he was ill for a week. His sister Catherine, who lived nearby was told of the event and she also suffered shock as a result. Madelaine, Richard and Catherine now wish to sue David in negligence. Advise them of the likely success of such claims.

7.   For over 20 years Jo had lived in an isolated cottage. The local authority then granted planning permission for the development of a golf course and club. When this was established, Jo found that golf balls frequently broke her windows and on one occasion she was hit on the head by a ball. Her son Paul was studying for his law exams. The noise from the 24-hour golf driving range interfered with Paul's studies. Further, every year a championship was held for three days and this attracted a crowd of 50,000 people. The noise of cars arriving early each morning disturbed the local residents. Advise Jo and Paul about any claims they may have in private or public nuisance and the remedies which may be available to them.

8.   Danny is employed as a lorry driver at Timmy's furniture factory. Contrary to instructions Danny overloads the lorry, so that he will finish deliveries early. While delivering furniture, Danny decides to visit his mother's house for a cup of tea. On the way there, the lorry skids on a bend because of the extra weight and collides with Sam's car. Rose, another employee, has now been diagnosed as having lung disease caused by dust at work. Advise Timmy as to his liability in both cases.

INDEX